Preface

The aim of this book is to provide a comprehensive yet concise textbook covering all the topics studied for an Advanced Level course in Computing.

The book is divided into 5 sections covering all the material for each paper in a modular scheme such as that offered by the Assessment and Qualifications Alliance (AQA). Within a section, each chapter covers material that can comfortably be taught in one or two lessons, and the chapters are sequenced in such a way that practical sessions can be based around the theory covered in the classroom.

Sections 1 to 3 cover all the requirements of the AQA AS specification, with the remaining sections being studied in the second year.

Each chapter contains exercises and questions from past examination papers, so that the student can gain plenty of experience in 'exam technique'. Answers to all the questions are available, to teachers only, in a separate Teacher's Supplement that can be downloaded from our web site **www.payne-gallway.co.uk**

iii

PAYNE-GALLWAY
PUBLISHERS LTD

Contents

Module 1

Computer Systems, Programming and Network Concepts

In this section:

1

Chapter 1 – Computer Hardware

Introduction

On this course you will be learning about the internal structure of computers, how they operate and how they are used in solving problems. You will also learn the fundamentals of computer programming, and build on your existing knowledge of software packages.

In addition, you will need to develop an awareness of the wider implications for individuals and for society of the increasing use of computers. This is best done by keeping your eyes and ears open, noticing new uses of computers, reading newspapers and magazines which contain computer-related articles, and watching appropriate and relevant television programmes.

This course, with its emphasis on the more technical aspects of computing, including operating systems and programming, is suitable for students who intend to go on to study Computer Science, Computing or Software Engineering at University, or make their career in computing.

Computer systems

A **computer system** consists of **hardware** and **software.**

Hardware: The physical components (electronic circuits) that make up the computer.

Software: The computer programs (sequences of instructions) that tell the computer what to do in response to a command or some event.

In this chapter we'll take an introductory look at hardware.

The components of a computer

All computers, whatever their size or function, have certain basic components. They have input devices for reading data into main memory, a central processing unit (CPU) for processing the data, output devices for printing, displaying or outputting information, and auxiliary storage devices for permanent storage of programs and data.

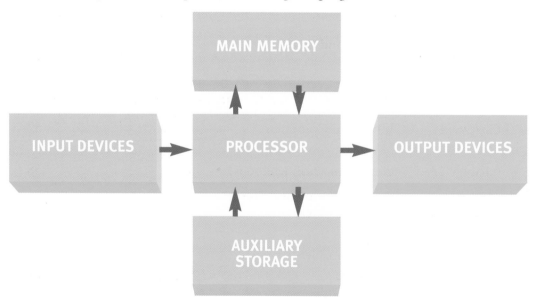

Figure 1.1: Block diagram of a computer system

Types of computer

We are so used to seeing PCs on desktops at home, school, businesses and other organisations that it is easy to forget that there are other types of computer.

Minicomputers are often used as multi-user systems, with hundreds of workstations or terminals attached to a central minicomputer, for example EPOS (Electronic Point of Sale) systems.

Mainframe computers are used by large organisations such as banks, building societies, insurance companies, airlines and government departments. A mainframe may have thousands of terminals attached to it at geographically remote locations, and occupy an entire site with hundreds of disk drives and other hardware units. Frequently, the actual siting of a mainframe computer is kept secret to lessen the danger of a terrorist attack that could cause chaos to an organisation.

Supercomputers are the largest category of computer, costing millions of pounds. They are mostly used by scientific and industrial research departments, government agencies such as NASA, the Weather Centre, Stock Exchanges and by very large commercial organisations.

The processor

The processor has the following functions:
- fetches the next instruction;
- decodes the instruction;
- executes the decoded instruction.

Most computers use integrated circuits, or chips, for their processors and main memory. A chip is about 1cm square and can hold millions of electronic components such as transistors and resistors. The CPU of a microcomputer is called a *microprocessor*. The processor and main memory of a PC are commonly held on a single board called a motherboard.

In 1965 Gordon Moore predicted that the capacity of a computer chip would double every year. He looked at the price/performance ratio of computer chips (the amount of performance available per dollar) over the previous three years and simply projected it forwards. He didn't really believe the rate of improvement would last for long, but in fact to this day chip capacity is still doubling every 18 months or so.

Main memory

The program currently being executed and the data used by this program are held in main memory, which is divided into millions of individually addressable storage units called *bytes*. One byte can hold one character, or it can be used to hold a code representing, for example, a tiny part of a picture, a sound, or part of a computer program instruction. The total number of bytes in main memory is referred to as the computer's memory size. Computer memory sizes are measured as follows:

1 Kilobyte (Kb)	= 1024 bytes		
1 Megabyte (Mb)	= 1024Kb	= 1,048,576 bytes	(about 1 million)
1 Gigabyte (Gb)	= 1024Mb	= 1,073,741,824 bytes	(about 1 billion)
1 Terabyte (Tb)	= 1024Gb	= 1,099,511,627,776 bytes	(about 1 trillion)

1-1

As with processing power, the amount of memory that comes with a standard PC has increased exponentially over the past 20 years. In about 1980, BBC microcomputers with 32K of memory were bought in their thousands for home and school use. In 1981, Bill Gates of Microsoft made his famous remark "640K ought to be enough for anybody". In 2004, a PC with 512Mb of main memory is standard, costing around £1,000 including bundled software.

RAM and ROM

There are basically two kinds of main memory; **Random Access Memory (RAM)** which is the ordinary kind of main memory referred to above, used for storing programs which are currently running and data which is being processed. This type of memory is **volatile** which means that it loses all its contents as soon as the machine is switched off.

Read Only Memory (ROM) is the other type of main memory, and this is non-volatile, with its contents permanently etched into the memory chip at the manufacturing stage. It is used for example to hold the **bootstrap loader**, the program which runs as soon as the computer is switched on and instructs it to load the operating system from disk into main memory (RAM). It may also store fixed data associated with the computer system. In special purpose computers used in video recorders, washing machines and cars, the program instructions are stored in ROM.

Cache memory

Cache memory is a type of very fast memory that is used to improve the speed of a computer, doubling it in some cases. It acts as an intermediate store between the CPU and main memory, and works by storing the most frequently or recently used instructions and data so that it will be very fast to retrieve them again. Thus when an item of data is required, a whole block of data will be read into cache in the expectation that the next piece of data required is likely to be in the same block. The amount of cache memory is generally between 1Kb and 512Kb.

Figure 1.2: How cache memory operates

Disk storage

The most common form of auxiliary storage (also known as *external* or *secondary memory* or *backing store*) is disk. All standalone PCs come equipped with an in-built hard disk, the capacity of which is also measured in bytes. A typical hard disk for a PC stores several gigabytes, and is used for storing software including the operating system, other systems software, application programs and data for long term storage.

Floppy disks consist of a thin sheet of mylar plastic encased in a hard 3½" casing. The standard type of disk in use today has a capacity of 1.44Mb. Flash memory cards or sticks are rapidly replacing floppy disks. These can hold from 32Mb to 1Gb.

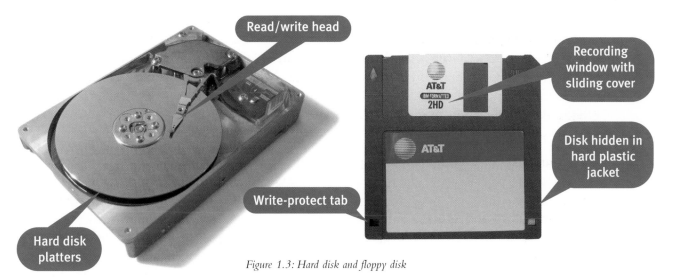

Figure 1.3: Hard disk and floppy disk

Q1: Two advertisements for computers are shown below. What do the various terms and abbreviations mean? Note how the price has fallen and the specification has increased in less than two years. Is Moore's Law still holding?

Pentium 4

- Pentium 4 1.6 GHz Processor
- 128MB DDR RAM
- 20GB HDD
- 17" Colour Monitor
- 20/48x CD-ROM Drive
- 16MB Graphics Card
- On-Board Sound
- Midi Tower case
- Windows XP
- MS Works 6.0

£549

exc VAT

Pentium 4

- Pentium 4 2.66 GHz Processor
- 256Mb DDR RAM
- 80 GB IDE HDD
- 20/48x CD-ROM Drive
- Integrated Intel Extreme Graphics Card
- Integrated Audio
- 17" Flat Panel Monitor
- Integrated Intel Pro 10/100 Ethernet Card
- Tower case
- Windows XP Home Edition
- MS Works 7.0

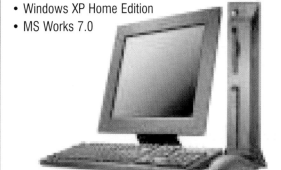

£539

exc VAT

Figure 1.4: A high specification PC advertised in May 2002

Figure 1.5: A high specification PC advertised in March 2004

Input and output devices

Input devices are the means whereby computers can accept data or instructions, and include keyboards, magnetic strip cards, smart cards and magnetic ink character recognition devices for reading the numbers on the bottom of cheques.

Output devices include various types of printer, VDU (Visual Display Unit) and speakers.

Q2: Name some other input and output devices and their uses.

Embedded computers and special-purpose computers

Not all computers are general-purpose computers with a screen, keyboard and disk drive. **Special-purpose** or **dedicated** computers perform a wide variety of tasks from controlling the temperature and humidity in a greenhouse, controlling traffic lights to smooth the flow of traffic or enabling you to use a card at a cash point machine. **Embedded computers** are widely used in household goods, automobiles and in industry. Special purpose computers have the same basic components of input, output, processor and memory, as general purpose computers, but typically the programs that they run are etched permanently into memory (ROM) so that they cannot be altered. These programs are sometimes known as **firmware** – a combination of hardware and software.

1-1

Exercises

1   A computer system is made up of hardware and software. What is meant by
    (a)   hardware;
    (b)   software? (2)
New Question

2   Give an example of
    (a)   an input device;
    (a)   an output device;
    (b)   a storage device. (3)
New Question

3   What is the function of the following components:
    (a)   processor
    (b)   main memory
    (c)   secondary storage? (3)
New Question

4   The table below contains names of several computer system components. For each component, indicate whether it is hardware or software by ticking in the correct column of the table:

1-1

Component	Hardware	Software
Web Browser		
Main memory		
Operating system		
Monitor		
Scanner		

(5)
New Question

Chapter 2 – Classification of Software

Categorising software

Software is the general term used to describe all the programs that run on a computer. There are several categories of software: systems software, general purpose applications (generic) software, special purpose application software, bespoke software. This categorisation is not rigid, however. You will soon discover that very little in computing is black and white; whatever you read, someone will soon come up with an apparently contradictory statement on most topics, leaving you to choose your own truth!

Systems software

Systems software performs tasks needed to run the computer system.

It includes the following types:

1 Operating system. Every computer needs an operating system to act as an interface between the user and the computer hardware. It provides us with a **virtual machine**. An operating system is a set of programs that allows the user to perform tasks without having to know how they are done. For example, a user can give a command to save a file on disk without having to know where the file will be stored or how it will be retrieved again. When a command is given to print a document, the user does not have to be concerned with the details of how the printer works – a program called a device driver takes care of the details.

Application programs are usually written to work with a particular operating system, so that a word processor, which works with Windows, will not work on an Apple Mac, which has a different operating system.

2 Library programs. A library program is available to all users of a multi-user computer system, typically to carry out common tasks required by everyone. For example a routine that searches for lost files or restores corrupted files may be stored in a library. Many of these programs fall into the general category of **utility programs** (see below.)

3 Utility programs. These are programs designed to make life easier for computer users. Utility programs perform common tasks that thousands of computer users need to do at one time or another, such as search for lost files, sort files of data into a particular sequence, copy disk files to magnetic tape for backup purposes and so on.

One common utility is compression software such as PKZip that 'zips' files so that they occupy less space. This is very useful if you want to transmit a graphic or long data file over the Internet, as the transmission time will be much reduced.

> **Q1**: Have you used any utility programs? Where did you get them and what are they used for?

4 Programming language compilers, interpreters and assemblers. Compilers and interpreters are different types of program used to translate the statements in a programming language such as Pascal, Visual Basic or C into a form that the computer can execute. An assembler performs a similar function, translating the statements of a low-level programming language (assembly code) into machine code.

Applications software

Application software: Software designed to carry out some task for the user that is primarily independent of computers, such as writing a letter or processing orders and invoices.

General purpose application software

All common application packages such as word processing, desktop publishing, spreadsheet, database, computer-aided design (CAD) and presentation packages fall into this category. Most general purpose application software is sold as a package, including a CD containing the software and manuals to help you get started and to be used as a reference.

Figure 2.1: General purpose software

The main productivity tools used by organisations include word processing, spreadsheets, databases, presentation graphics and communications software to enable users to communicate with each other either locally or across the world in an international company.

Complete **software suites** such as Microsoft Office or Sun Star Office offer four or more software products packaged together at a much lower price than buying the packages separately. Microsoft Office, for example, includes Word, Excel, Access, Publisher, a multimedia presentation package called PowerPoint and Microsoft Outlook. The advantage of buying such a suite of programs is that the individual applications are completely compatible so that there is no difficulty importing or exporting data from one package to another, if for example you wish to put a spreadsheet in a word processed report. Also, the packages all have the same look and feel, with the same shortcut keys used for various operations (such as F7 for checking spelling) and this makes learning new software an easier task.

General Purpose Application Software: Software that can be made to do many different tasks.

Generic and special purpose software

Note that software such as word processing, spreadsheet and database software is sometimes referred to as **generic** software. This simply implies that any of the dozens of spreadsheet packages, for example, can be made to do many different tasks, and is not designed specifically for one type of application.

Special purpose software

Application software such as a payroll, accounts or stock control system, or software to help fill in an income tax return, for example, is in contrast **special purpose** because it is designed to do one particular task.

Special Purpose Application Software: Software to perform a specific task.

Bespoke software

The software may be designed specifically for one particular organisation, **(bespoke software)** and written especially for them using a programming language or software such as a database management system.

Bespoke Software: Software written to the specification of a particular organisation or customer.

Bespoke or off-the-shelf?

When an organisation decides to computerise an area of its business, a decision has to be made whether to buy an off-the-shelf package or have software specially written. The advantages of buying an off-the-shelf package include the following:

- it is generally a less expensive solution as the cost of developing the software is shared across a wider customer base;
- it may be possible to speak to other users of the package for their evaluation before spending money;
- the software can be bought and installed straight away;
- the software is tried and tested and likely to contain fewer bugs than newly written software;
- the software is usually well documented and additional documentation may be available from other sources;
- training may be available from different providers in common software packages.

Conversely, there are also advantages in buying tailor-made (**'bespoke'**) software:

- it is designed to do exactly what the user wants;
- it has no unwanted features;
- it can be written to run on specified hardware;
- it can be integrated with existing software;
- there may not be a suitable software package on the market.

Exercises

1 (a) Two classifications of software are System Software and Application Software.

What is meant by:

(i) System Software; (1)

(ii) Application Software? (1)

(b) Give an example of:

(i) System Software; (1)

(ii) Application Software. (1)

AQA CPT1 Qu 2 Jan 2001

2 (a) Application software can be subdivided into general purpose and special purpose.

(i) Give a type of general purpose application software package. (1)

(ii) What is meant by a special purpose application software package? (1)

(b) A large organisation is planning to computerise their payroll. The management have the choice of buying a readily available software package or writing bespoke software.

(i) What is meant by bespoke software? (1)

(ii) Give **one** advantage and **two** disadvantages of bespoke software over readily available software. (3)

AQA CPT1 Qu 5 May 2001

3 Parts of a typical computer operating system may be stored in

(a) External (secondary) memory

(b) Read Only Memory (ROM)

(c) Random Access Memory (RAM)

Explain why **each** type of memory is used by the operating system. (6)

New Question

1-2

Chapter 3 – Bits and Bytes

The binary system

All digital computers use the **binary** system for representing data of all types – numbers, characters, sound, pictures and so on. A binary system uses just 2 symbols to represent all information. The symbols could be anything like + and -, or 0 and 1. The great advantage of the binary system is that the digits 1 and 0 can be represented by electrical circuits that can exist in one of two states – current is either flowing or not flowing, and a circuit is either closed or open, on or off, voltage can be high or low.

A closed circuit allowing current to flow represents 1

An open circuit represents 0

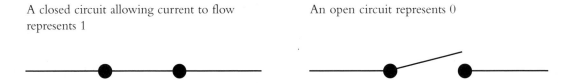

Figure 3.1: Electrical circuits can represent 1 or 0

Bits and bytes

A binary digit (1 or 0) is known as a '**bit**', short for **BI**nary digi**T**. In most computers today, bits are grouped together in 8-bit bytes. A byte can hold 256 different combinations of 0s and 1s, which means that, for example, 256 different characters can be represented.

One byte holds one character.

The ASCII code

Over the years, different computer designers have used different sets of codes for representing characters, which has led to great difficulty in transferring information from one computer to another. Most personal computers (PCs) nowadays use the ASCII code (American Standard Code for Information Interchange), but many mainframe computers use a code called EBCDIC (Extended Binary Coded Decimal Interchange Code – pronounced EB-SUH-DICK or EB-SEE-DICK according to taste). EBCDIC uses 8 bits to encode each character.

ASCII originally used a 7-bit code. The 128 different combinations that can be represented in 7 bits are plenty to allow for all the letters, numbers and special symbols. Later, the eighth bit was also used, which allowed an extra 128 characters to be represented. The extra 128 combinations are used for symbols such as Ç, è, ü, ©, ®, Œ, etc. This is known as extended ASCII.

> **Q1**: About how many different combinations of 0s and 1s are required to represent all the keys on a keyboard? (Remember to include uppercase and lowercase letters).

The first 32 ASCII codes are used for simple communications protocols, not characters. For example ACK stands for 'acknowledge' and would be sent by a device to acknowledge receipt of data or communication signal.

The ASCII codes are shown below.

Character	ASCII	Char	ASCII	Char	ASCII	Char	ASCII
NULL	0000000	space	0100000	@	1000000	`	1100000
SOH	0000001	!	0100001	A	1000001	a	1100001
STX	0000010	"	0100010	B	1000010	b	1100010
ETX	0000011	£	0100011	C	1000011	c	1100011
EOT	0000100	$	0100100	D	1000100	d	1100100
ENQ	0000101	%	0100101	E	1000101	e	1100101
ACK	0000110	&	0100110	F	1000110	f	1100110
BEL	0000111	'	0100111	G	1000111	g	1100111
BS	0001000	(	0101000	H	1001000	h	1101000
HT	0001001	)	0101001	I	1001001	i	1101001
LF	0001010	*	0101010	J	1001010	j	1101010
VT	0001011	+	0101011	K	1001011	k	1101011
SF	0001100	,	0101100	L	1001100	l	1101100
CR	0001101	-	0101101	M	1001101	m	1101101
SO	0001110	.	0101110	N	1001110	n	1101110
SI	0001111	/	0101111	O	1001111	o	1101111
DLE	0010000	0	0110000	P	1010000	p	1110000
DC1	0010001	1	0110001	Q	1010001	q	1110001
DC2	0010010	2	0110010	R	1010010	r	1110010
DC3	0010011	3	0110011	S	1010011	s	1110011
DC4	0010100	4	0110100	T	1010100	t	1110100
NAK	0010101	5	0110101	U	1010101	u	1110101
SYN	0010110	6	0110110	V	1010110	v	1110110
ETB	0010111	7	0110111	W	1010111	w	1110111
CAN	0011000	8	0111000	X	1011000	x	1111000
EM	0011001	9	0111001	Y	1011001	y	1111001
SUB	0011010	:	0111010	Z	1011010	z	1111010
ESC	0011011	;	0111011	[	1011011	{	1111011
FS	0011100	<	0111100	\	1011100	|	1111100
GS	0011101	=	0111101	]	1011101	}	1111101
RS	0011110	>	0111110	^	1011110	~	1111110
US	0011111	?	0111111	_	1011111	del	1111111

Figure 3.2: ASCII codes

Representing numbers

Using ASCII, each character has a corresponding code, so that if for example the 'A' key on the keyboard is pressed, the code '01000001' will be sent to the CPU. If the key '1' is pressed, the code '00110001' will be sent to the CPU. To print the number '123', the codes for 1, 2 and 3 would be sent to the printer.

This is fine for input and output, but useless for arithmetic. There is no easy way of adding two numbers held in this way, and furthermore they occupy a great deal of space. Numbers which are to be used in calculations are therefore held in a different format, as **binary numbers**.

Before we look at the binary system, it is helpful to examine how our ordinary decimal or **denary** number system works. Consider for example the number '134'. These three digits represent one hundred, three tens and four ones.

i.e.

100	10	1	
1	3	4	This represents 100 + 30 + 4 = 134

As we move from right to left each digit is worth ten times as much as the previous one. We probably use a **base 10** number system because we have ten fingers, but essentially there is no reason why some other base such as 8 or 16 could not be used.

In the binary system, as we move from right to left each digit is worth twice as much as the previous one. Thus the binary number 10000110 can be set out under column headings as follows:

128	64	32	16	8	4	2	1	
1	0	0	0	0	1	1	0	This represents 128 + 4 + 2 = 134

Q2: Convert the following binary numbers to decimal:
0011   0110   1010   01000001   01000101

Q3: Convert the following numbers to binary:
5   7   1   26   68   137

Q4: What is the largest binary number that can be held in
(i) 8 bits?   (ii) 16 bits?   (iii) 24 bits?   (iv) 32 bits?

Obviously, using only one byte (8 bits) to hold a number places a severe restriction on the size of number the computer can hold. Therefore four or more consecutive bytes are commonly used to store numbers.

Memory addressing

The main memory of a computer can be thought of as a series of boxes, each containing 8 bits (1 byte), and each with its own unique address, counting from zero upwards. The memory capacity of a computer is measured in 1024-byte units called kilobytes, megabytes or gigabytes.

These measures can be abbreviated to Kb, Mb and Gb. These are all powers of 2; thus although 1Kb is often thought of as being 1,000 bytes, it is actually 1024 bytes.

You will find it useful to memorise certain powers of 2.

2^{10} bytes = 1024 = 1Kb

2^{20} bytes = 1024 x 1024 = 1Mb

2^{30} bytes = 1024 x 1024 x 1024 = 1Gb

Word size

The **word size** of a computer is the number of bits that the CPU can process simultaneously, as opposed to the bus size, which determines how many bits are transmitted together. Processors can have 8-, 16-, 32- or 64-bit word sizes (or even larger), and the word size will be one of the factors that determine the speed of the computer. The standard PCs have 32-bit processors. Recent processor architectures provide for a 64-bit word.

Exercises

1 (a) Show how the denary (decimal) numbers 13 and 32 would be represented
       as 8-bit binary integers.   (2)

   (b) Given that the ASCII code for the character '1' is 00110001, show how
       the text string '1332' would be held in a 4-byte word in a
       computer's memory.   (2)

New Question

2 (a) What will be the highest address in a computer with
       (i) 1K of memory?

       (ii) 16K of memory?

   (b) How many Mb are 2^{24} bytes?

   (c) How many Gb are 2^{32} bytes?   (4)

New Question

3 Some personal computers are referred to as 32-bit machines. This means their
   word length is 32 bits.

   (a) What is a word in this context?   (1)

   (b) State the different values for one bit.   (1)

   (c) Give three different interpretations which can be associated with a pattern
       of bits in a 32-bit word.   (3)

AQA CPT1 Qu 2 Jan 2002

1-3

Chapter 4 – Data Representation (Text and Numbers)

Input-process-output

The main purpose of using computers is to process data as quickly and efficiently as possible to produce useful information.

Computers read incoming data called input, process this data and display or print information called output.

Data: The raw facts and figures that a computer accepts as input and then processes to produce useful information.

A stream of data such as 44, 45, 66, 82, 77, 67 has no meaning until it is processed by the appropriate program and information produced. The numbers could represent the marks of 6 students, the number of computers sold by a manufacturer in the past 6 months (in thousands), the weekly hours of sunshine in the past 6 weeks.

Sources of data

Data can be collected from many sources, either directly or indirectly. Data that is collected for a specific purpose is said to be collected **directly**. For example, the times at which an employee clocks in and out may be collected by punching a time card, and this data is used in the calculation of the weekly pay packet. Similarly, when a library book is borrowed, data about the book and the borrower is collected by scanning the bar codes of the book and the borrower's library card. This data is used directly to produce information on where a particular book is.

On the other hand, information can be derived from data that was originally collected for a completely different purpose – in other words, collected **indirectly**. For example a credit card company collects data about each transaction or purchase made so that the customer can be billed at the end of the month. This is the direct collection of data. At a later date, the data may be used to build a profile of the customer – perhaps how often they use their credit card for holiday travel, for example. The company could sell a list of all well-travelled customers to a travel company who would use it in a direct mail advertising campaign. This is the **indirect** collection of data – use of the data for a purpose other than the one for which it was originally collected.

Q1: Think of several examples of data that is originally collected for one purpose, and then used for additional purposes.

Information: Any form of communication that provides understandable and useful knowledge to the recipient, such as a bar chart of examination grades achieved by a group of students.

Data can be seen as an encoded form of information. For example, an estate agent may collect information about the type of house a client is looking for. This information may be coded before being stored in a computer system: D for detached house, S for Semi-detached house, B for bungalow, LG for large garden, MG medium-sized garden, SG for small garden. The advantage of encoding information in such a way is that less storage space is needed and it is easy to specify search conditions. However, the user needs a list of valid codes and there may be a loss of precision of information. If all the houses the agent has for sale are coded in a similar manner, we may lose the precise size of the garden because the coding only groups the gardens into large, medium or small.

Character coding schemes

In Chapter 3 the ACSII coding scheme was described. This is a 7- or 8-bit code for representing characters and is used by almost all PCs.

Unicode is an international 16-bit coding scheme which can represent 65536 different characters. This is sufficient to represent all the characters in any language or script from ancient Egyptian hieroglyphics to Chinese, Russian, Greek, Japanese or Urdu, to name but a few.

The binary number system

You met binary numbers briefly in Chapter 3, so this is by way of a little recap.

A number such as 1, 25, 378 etc. can be represented in a computer in many different ways. It can be held as a number of characters so that, for example, the number 25 is coded in ASCII as 0011 0010 0011 0101 (refer to Figure 3.2 in Chapter 3). Alternatively, it can be held as a **pure binary integer**.

To translate 25 from decimal to binary, you can draw a table of powers of 2. Then find the largest power of 2 that is less than or equal to 25 (16 in this case). Subtract 16 from 25 and repeat. You end up with

128	64	32	16	8	4	2	1	
0	0	0	1	1	0	0	1	16+8+1 = 25

To translate from binary to decimal, perform the process backwards. Put each binary digit under the correct heading in the table. For example, to translate 01000101 into decimal, arrange the digits in the table as follows:

128	64	32	16	8	4	2	1	
0	1	0	0	0	1	0	1	64+4+1 = 69

The representation of negative numbers, numbers with decimal points and binary arithmetic will be covered in Section 4.

Q2: (i) Translate the number 227 into binary.
(ii) Translate the binary number 1011 0111 into denary (i.e. a decimal number).

Binary Coded Decimal (BCD)

In the BCD system each decimal digit is represented by its own 4-bit binary code.

Decimal	Binary
0	0000
1	0001
2	0010
3	0011
4	0100
5	0101
6	0110
7	0111
8	1000
9	1001

The number 3765 is coded as 0011 0111 0110 0101.

Q3: (i) Write down the BCD representation of 2906.
(ii) Translate the BCD number 0110 0111 1001 0011 into denary (i.e. a decimal number).

Advantages and disadvantages of BCD

The advantage of the BCD representation is the ease of conversion from BCD to decimal and vice versa. For example, when binary numbers have to be electronically decoded for a pocket calculator display, a number held in BCD format simply has to be split into groups of four bits and each group converted directly to the corresponding decimal digit.

When storing fractional numbers, a further advantage of the BCD representation is that since each decimal digit is encoded separately, using as many bits as necessary to represent the complete number exactly, no 'rounding' of numbers occurs. Hence BCD arithmetic is used in business applications where every significant digit has to be retained in a result.

A disadvantage of using BCD is that more bits are required to store a number than when using pure binary. Another disadvantage of BCD is that calculations with such numbers are more complex than with pure binary numbers. For example, try adding the BCD representations of 1 and 19:

We get   0000 0001
            0001 1001

            0001 1010   The first digit, 1, is wrong and 1010 is an invalid code!

The problem arises because only the first ten out of sixteen combinations of four digits are used to encode the decimal symbols '0' to '9'. Therefore, whenever the sum of two binary digits is greater than 9, 6 has to be added to the result in order to skip over the six unused codes. Adding the binary representation for 6 to 1010:

         0001   1010
                   0110

         0010   0000   i.e. 20 in BCD which is the correct answer.

Boolean values

So far we have seen how a given binary pattern could represent an ASCII character, a binary integer, or a number held in BCD. A Boolean variable (named after the English mathematician George Boole) is one that can only have one of two values, **true** or **false**, represented by 1 and 0, or 0 and -1. There are many occasions when it is useful to use one binary digit to show whether something is true or false. For example, a particular bit in memory can be set to show whether a disk drive is connected, another can be set if the 'Break' key is pressed, and yet another set if overflow occurs during an arithmetic operation. Single bits used in this way are called **flags**.

Exercises

1 (a) Data can be stored inside a computer system in several different representations. The number 25 is to be stored in a 16-bit word

What is the bit pattern if the number 25 is to be stored as

(i) a pure binary integer;   (1)

(ii) a BCD (Binary Coded Decimal)?   (1)

(b) The ASCII code for the character '3' is the decimal number 51.

(i) What is the ASCII code for the character '5'?   (1)

(ii) If eight bits are used to store one character, what is the bit pattern when the string '25' is stored in a 16-bit word?   (2)

AQA CPT1 Qu 4 Jan 2002

2 (a) Bit patterns can be interpreted in a number of different ways. A computer word contains the bit pattern 0101 1001. What is its decimal value if it represents:

(i) a pure binary integer;   (1)

(ii) a BCD (Binary Coded Decimal)?   (1)

(b) A binary pattern in a 16-bit word can represent different forms of information, such as pure binary or BCD, as above, or two ASCII characters.

Name **three** different forms of information, excluding those given above.   (3)

AQA CPT1 Qu 9 Jan 2001

3 Members of the public can register with a video club after supplying name and address and proof of identity. Every registered member is issued with a membership card. Each time a member borrows a video, data about the video and the borrower are collected, by scanning the barcodes on the video box and on the membership card.

(a) Sources of data can be *direct* and *indirect*. Complete the table below with the correct type of source.

	Direct / Indirect
(i) The data collected above is used to record where a particular video is.	
(ii) The data collected above is used to build up a profile of the members for targeted advertising.	

(b) What is the difference between data and information?   (2)

AQA CPT1 Qu 8 Jan 2003

1-4

Chapter 5 – Data Representation (Sound and Graphics)

Digital audio

Sound such as music or speech can be input via a microphone, to be processed by a computer. Since sound waves are continuously variable or **analogue** in nature, an **analogue to digital converter** is needed to transform the analogue input to a **digital** form, i.e. a binary pattern, so that it can be stored and processed. Undesirable sounds such as wrong notes or scratches on an old recording can be edited out before a new digital version is produced.

Sound in analogue form may be represented by wave forms. The height of these wave forms can be sampled at regularly spaced time intervals, with the height being represented by, say, a 16-bit code. The more frequently the samples are taken, the more faithfully the sound will be represented. (See Figure 5.1) Each sample represents the intensity of the sound pressure wave at that instant. Digital audio is typically created by taking 16-bit samples over a spectrum of 44.1KHz. Stereo sound doubles the number of samples taken, with 44,100 samples per second taking 32 bits each. This means that CD quality sound requires 1.4 million bits of data per second.

Sampling resolution: The number of bits used to store one sound sample.

The quality of sound produced using a sound sampler depends on the sampling rate and the sampling resolution.

Sampling rate: The frequency at which samples are taken.

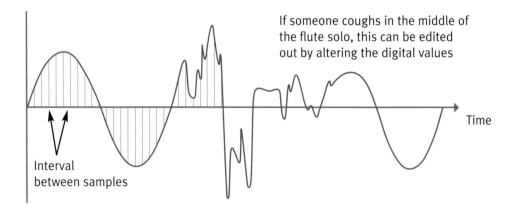

Figure 5.1: Converting sound from analogue to digital form

The sound wave can be recreated from the digital data by a digital-to-analogue (D-A) converter.

Sound Synthesis (Sound generation)

Sounds may be generated using either analogue or digital techniques. Digital sound generation is a recent development in which numbers representing sound waves are manipulated. There are several different methods. One such method uses sampled sounds as well as pure tones and arithmetic operations are carried out on the bit patterns representing the sounds.

Bit-mapped graphics

In a bit-mapped system for displaying text and graphics on a VDU, the screen is divided up into a grid, and each square on the grid is called a **pixel** (picture element). A low resolution screen may have 320 by 240 pixels, and a high resolution screen may have 1280 by 1024 pixels or more. A monochrome screen will need just one bit in memory to represent each pixel; if the bit is 1, the pixel is on, and if it is 0, the pixel is off. On a colour screen, each pixel may correspond to one byte in memory, giving a possible 256 colours for each pixel. Two bytes per pixel gives a possible 64K different colours. The memory used is additional to the RAM used for programs and data; it is supplied on a graphics 'card' specific to the type of screen.

If the screen were magnified you would be able to see the individual pixels. The more pixels to the square inch, the higher the resolution and the smoother the image.

Figure 5.2: An image on the screen is composed of thousands of pixels

Digital images

Pixel: The smallest resolvable rectangular area of an image.

A digital image is composed of pixels arranged in a rectangular array with a certain height and width. A bitmap is characterised by the width and height of the image in pixels and the number of bits per pixel, which determines the number of shades of grey, or colours it can represent. In a colour image, each pixel has its own colour, based on the level of the primary colours red, green and blue required to produce the colour. A 24-bit bitmap will use one byte for each of the red, green and blue intensities.

There are many formats used to store images in files, including BMP, GIF, TIFF and JPEG.

Images are usually taken from the real world via a digital camera or scanner, or they may be generated by computer.

Bit-mapped graphics become ragged when you re-size them. Programs that enable you to manipulate bit-mapped images are called Paint programs.

Bit-mapped images are sometimes called raster graphics.

Vector Graphics

Images are represented as mathematical formulae that define all the shapes in the image such as lines, polygons and text.

For example, a straight line is described by its features: start and end point co-ordinates, length, thickness, colour.

Vector graphics are more flexible than bit-mapped graphics because they look the same even when you scale them to different sizes. It is also easier to render an object. Almost all sophisticated graphics systems, including CAD systems and animation software, use vector graphics. Fonts represented with vector graphics are called scalable fonts or vector fonts. One very well known system is PostScript. Vector graphics often require less memory than bit-mapped images.

Programs that enable you to create and manipulate vector graphics are called Draw programs.

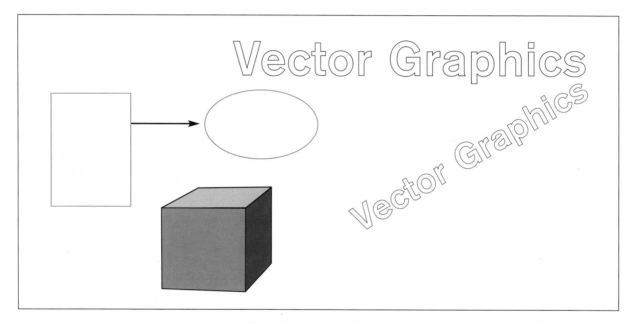

Figure 5.3: A vector graphic image

Note that most output devices such as display monitors and laser printers are raster devices (plotters use vector graphics). This means that all vector graphics must be translated into bitmaps before being output. The difference between vector graphics and raster graphics is that vector graphics are not translated into bitmaps until the last possible moment, after all sizes and resolutions have been specified. This results in a better quality image.

1-5

Exercises

1   State **four** different possible interpretations of a given bit pattern in a computer's memory. (4)

New Question

2   Music is often recorded digitally. Describe briefly **two** advantages of this method of representing sound. (2)

New Question

3   Bit patterns can be interpreted in a number of different ways. A computer word contains the bit pattern 0011 0110.

(a)   What is its decimal value if it represents:

(i)   a pure binary integer (1)

(ii) a BCD (Binary Coded Decimal)? (1)

(b)   Give one advantage of BCD over pure binary. (1)

(c)   (i)   The ASCII value for the character '2' is 50. What is the character stored in the computer word 0011 0100? (2)

(ii) Name **one** other standard coding system for coding information expressed in character or text-based form. (1)

(d)   One method of storing graphics in a computer system is as vector graphics.

(i)   Name **one** other method. (1)

(ii) Describe how a black-and-white image would be stored using your method. (2)

AQA CPT1 Qu 7 May 2002

4   Computer systems store not just information representing numbers and characters, but also sounds and images.

(a)   A microphone converts sound into an electrical signal which may be recorded.

(i)   Explain how the electrical signal from the microphone is converted into a form which can be stored in a computer system (3)

(ii) What piece of hardware is required to convert the digitally recorded sound before it is amplified and played back through speakers? (1)

(b)   Images can be stored as bit-mapped graphics or vector graphics. If vector graphics is used, what information will be stored to describe one straight line? (2)

AQA CPT1 Qu 4 June 2003

5   Video RAM (VRAM) is separate memory on the graphics card, into which the processor writes screen data which are then read to the screen for display. A computer has a colour monitor and 1 Mb (Megabytes) of VRAM, and its screen display has been set to a *resolution of 1024x1024*.

(a)   Exactly how many bytes are 1Mb? (1)

(b)   What is a pixel? (1)

(c)   (i)   What does a resolution of 1024 x 1024 mean? (1)

(ii) How many bytes would be available to represent each pixel in the above computer system? (1)

(iii) How many colours can this computer system display? (1)

AQA CPT1 Qu 5 Jan 2002

Chapter 6 – Programming Concepts

The earliest computers

It is an astonishing fact that as we enter the 21st century, computers have been around for less than 60 years. Many of those who worked on the earliest computers are still alive to tell us of their experiences. If you ever get a chance to visit Bletchley Park, do not miss it – it is the location of the breaking of the Enigma code (used by the Germans to code all their most secret messages), with the aid of the first programmable computer, named Colossus, built for this purpose in 1943. A fascinating exhibition tells the story and Colossus has been reconstructed there.

Generations of programming language
Machine language – the first generation

Programming languages are often characterised by 'generation'. The first generation of computer language, known as machine code, executes directly without translation. Machine code is the actual pattern of 0s and 1s used in a computer's memory. The programming of Colossus and other early computers was laboriously done with toggle switches representing a pattern of binary codes for each instruction.

Machine language, however it is entered into a computer, is time-consuming, laborious and error-prone. Few programmers code in it today. A language suited to the particular application would be used instead.

Assembly code – the second generation

In the 1950s when computers were first used commercially, machine code gave way to **assembly code**, which allowed programmers to use mnemonics (abbreviations that represent the instructions in a more memorable way) and denary numbers (i.e. 0–9) instead of 0s and 1s. Thus ADD or ADX might be an instruction to add two numbers, SUB or SBX an instruction to subtract.

Programs written in assembly languages have to be translated into machine code before they can be executed, using a program called an **assembler**. There is more or less a one-to-one correspondence between each assembly code statement and its equivalent machine code statement, which means that programs can be written in the most efficient way possible, occupying as little space as possible and executing as fast as possible. For this reason assembly code is still used for applications where timing or storage space is critical. Assembly languages are called **low level** languages because they are close to machine code and the detail of the computer architecture.

Since different types of computer have different instruction sets, which depend on how the machine carries out the instructions, both machine code and assembly code are machine-dependent – each type of computer will have its own assembly language.

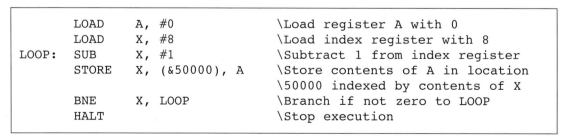

```
            LOAD    A, #0               \Load register A with 0
            LOAD    X, #8               \Load index register with 8
    LOOP:   SUB     X, #1               \Subtract 1 from index register
            STORE   X, (&50000), A      \Store contents of A in location
                                        \50000 indexed by contents of X
            BNE     X, LOOP             \Branch if not zero to LOOP
            HALT                        \Stop execution
```

Figure 6.1: Part of an assembly code program

Imperative high level languages – the third generation

As computer use increased dramatically in the 1950s, the need grew to make it easier and faster to write error-free programs. Computer manufacturers and user groups started to develop so-called **high-level languages** such as Algol (standing for ALGOrithmic Language) and Fortran (standing for FORmula TRANslation). In the 1950s most of the people actually writing programs were scientists, mathematicians and engineers and so both these languages were created to be used in mathematical applications.

COBOL (COmmon Business Oriented Language) was invented by the redoubtable Admiral Grace Hopper in 1960 specifically for writing commercial and business, rather than scientific, programs. Whilst serving in the US Navy in 1947, Grace Hopper was investigating why one of the earliest computers was not working, and discovered a small dead moth in the machine. After removing it (and taping it in her logbook) the machine worked fine, and from then on computer errors were known as 'bugs'.

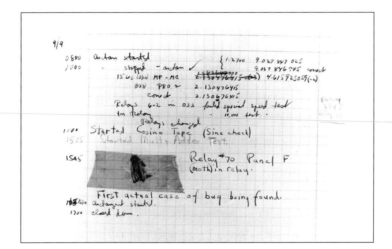

1-6

Figure 6.2: Admiral Grace Hopper and the first computer 'bug'

Other third generation languages followed: **BASIC** was created in the 1960s as a language for students to learn programming. Early versions of the language however did not contain the facilities to write well-structured programs that were easy to maintain and debug, although the language has since developed. In 1971 Nicklaus Wirth designed **Pascal** (named after the seventeenth century French mathematician) to teach structured programming to students.

High level languages are so-called because they are independent of the architecture of any particular computer; one statement written in a high level language is translated into several machine code instructions before it can be executed. The term **imperative** high level language refers to languages such as Pascal, BASIC, COBOL and Fortran – in contrast to **object-oriented** and **declarative** languages, which you will learn about in the second year of this course.

Imperative High Level Languages: The high-level language instructions are executed in a programmer-defined sequence.

Q1: Do you know the names of any other high-level languages? Why do you suppose there are so many of them?

Why use assembly code?

Assembly language, although it is laborious to write and hard to debug, is still used in some circumstances, for example:

• when there is a need for the program to execute as fast as possible;

• when the program must occupy as little space as possible;

Parts of an operating system, and device drivers that control the operation of devices such as a printer, mouse or CD-ROM may be written in assembly code. Programs in embedded systems like satellite decoders, encryption and decryption software, and routines that are called frequently from high-level programs may also be written in assembly code.

Types of program translator

There are three types of program used for translating the code that a programmer writes into a form (i.e. machine code) that the computer can execute. These are:

• assembler;

• compiler;

• interpreter.

Assembler

An assembler is a program that translates an assembly code program into machine code ready for the computer to execute it. Since each type of computer has its own assembly language, it also has its own assembler. The assembler itself could be written in assembly code or in a high level language such as C, which has special facilities useful for this type of programming.

Compiler

A compiler is a program that translates a high level language program into machine code. The Turbo Pascal compiler, for example, translates a program written in Turbo Pascal on a PC into object code, which can be run on a PC. The code written by the programmer is known as the **source code**, and the compiled code is known as the **object code**.

A compiler is a complex program which takes the source code and scans through it several times, each time performing different checks and building up tables of information needed to produce the final object code. When you write a short program, this process appears to happen almost instantaneously, but a long program of several thousand lines can take several minutes to compile.

Compiler: Translates the whole high level language source code into object code, which can then be executed without the presence of a compiler.

Interpreter

An interpreter also translates high-level source code. However the crucial difference between a compiler and an interpreter is **that an interpreter translates one line at a time and then executes it;** no object code is produced, and so the program has to be interpreted each time it is to be run. If the program performs a section of code 10,000 times, then that section of code is translated into machine code 10,000 times as each line is interpreted and then executed.

Interpreter: Analyses the source code statement by statement as execution proceeds, decoding each statement and calling routines to carry out each instruction.

Relative advantages of compilers and interpreters

A compiler has many advantages over an interpreter:

- the object code can be saved on disk and run whenever required without the need to recompile. However, if an error is discovered in the program, the whole program has to be recompiled.
- the object code executes faster than interpreted code.
- the object code produced by a compiler can be distributed or executed without having to have the compiler present.
- the object code is more secure, as it cannot be read without a great deal of 'reverse engineering'.

An interpreter has some advantages over a compiler:

- it is useful for program development as there is no need for lengthy recompilation each time an error is discovered.
- it is easier to partially test and debug programs.

Typically, a programmer might use an interpreter during program development. A program that is tested and ready for distribution would then be compiled and the saved object code would be distributed.

Features of Imperative High Level Languages

If you have chosen to do Computing rather than Information Technology, you will probably find learning to program is one of the most enjoyable parts of the course. The choice of programming language will be a matter for individual schools and colleges, and to some extent it does not matter which imperative high-level language you study. C, Basic and Pascal all have similar statements and structures.

Pascal was invented in the 1970s by Niklaus Wirth to teach structured programming. It is a good language to start with and you will find it easy to learn, say, Delphi (which is based on Pascal) or Visual Basic if you have studied Pascal.

You should have experience of using the following features in your chosen language (the example statements are given in Pascal).

Built-in data types

Integer	`var NoOfSpaces : Integer;`
Real	`var Average : Real;`
String	`var Surname : String;`
Character	`var FirstLetter : Char;`
Boolean	`var Found : Boolean;`

User-defined Types

Records	`type TStudent = record`
	`                FirstName : String [15];`
	`                Surname : String [25];`
	`                DateOfBirth : TDateTime;`
	`        end;`

Symbolic types	`type TSeason = (Spring, Summer, Autumn, Winter);`
Sub-range types	`type TCapitalLetter = 'A' .. 'Z'`

Declarations

Type definitions	`type TSeason = (Spring, Summer, Autumn, Winter);`
Variable declarations	`var NoOfStars : Integer;`
Array declarations	`var Total : array[1..150] of real;` `var Sales : array[1..150, 1..5] of real;`
Constant definitions	`const Pi = 3.14;`

Procedure declarations	`procedure Adjust (var Spaces, Stars : Integer);`
	`begin`
	`    Spaces := Spaces — 1;`
	`    Stars := Stars + 2;`
	`end;`

Function declarations	`function Initial (S: String) : String;`
	`begin`
	`    S := LeftStr (S,1);`
	`    Initial := Uppercase (S);`
	`end;`

Programming statements

Assignment	`Spaces := Spaces — 1;`
Iteration	`for Count := 1 to 10` `    do Writeln(Counter);`

Selection	`if Number = 0`
	`    then Number := Number + 1`
	`    else Number := Number — 1;`

Procedure calls	`Adjust (NoOfSpaces, NoOfStars);`
Function calls	`FirstLetter := Initial (Surname);`

Advantages of using routines

Breaking down code into self-contained routines (for example, a procedure or function) aids understanding of code as statements are grouped together and given a name. This also makes testing easier as a routine can be tested in isolation before being added to a larger program. It helps trouble-shooting as a fault can be narrowed down to a particular routine. It minimises the number of statements as routines can be called from anywhere in the program any number of times. Parameters can be used to pass data within programs.

Procedures vs Functions

A function call must be part of an expression, as a value is associated with its name.
A procedure call is a statement on its own.

Exercises

1   Programming languages are subdivided into generations. An imperative high level
    language is a third generation language.

    (a)   Name the language type for:

          (i)   first generation;   (1)

          (ii)   second generation.   (1)

    (b)   Name **one** specific example of a third generation programming language.   (1)

                                                          AQA CPT1 Qu 3 January 2001

1-6

2   (a)   Give **two** advantages of programming in third generation programming
          languages, rather than in the previous two generations.   (2)

    (b)   Third generation programming languages may be compiled or interpreted.
          Describe the process performed by

          (i)   a compiler   (2)

          (ii)   an interpreter.   (2)

    (c)   When would it be appropriate to use **each** of the following?

          In **each** case give the reason for your choice.

          (i)   a compiler   (2)

          (ii)   an interpreter.   (2)

                                                                     New Question

3   The structured approach when writing programs uses functions and procedures.

    (a)   Give **two** reasons why procedures are used.   (2)

    (b)   What are parameters used for in the context of procedures and functions?   (1)

                                                            AQA CPT1 Qu 6 May 2002

4   The following code is part of a high level language program:

```
CONST Max = 5;
VAR Tptr : INTEGER;
VAR Store : ARRAY[1..Max] OF CHAR;

PROCEDURE add (a: CHAR);
BEGIN
    IF Tptr < Max THEN
    BEGIN
       Tptr := Tptr + 1;
       Store[Tptr] := a;
    END;
END;


FUNCTION Take : CHAR;
VAR Ptr: INTEGER;
BEGIN
    IF Tptr>0 THEN
    BEGIN
       Take := Store[1];
       Tptr := Tptr-1;
       FOR Ptr := 1 TO Tptr DO store[Ptr] := store[Ptr+1]
    END;
END;
```

(a) Identify the following by copying **one** relevant statement from the above code.

(i)   constant definition   (1)

(ii)   variable declaration   (1)

(iii) local variable   (1)

(iv)   global variable   (1)

(v)   parameter   (1)

(vi)   assignment statement   (1)

(vii) selection statement   (1)

(viii) iteration   (1)

(b) Functions and procedures are both subroutines. What is a difference between
a function and a procedure?   (1)

AQA CPT1 Qu 7 January 2002

Chapter 7 – Program Design and Maintenance

Program design aims

Effort put into good program design can often save substantial maintenance and debugging costs later on. The aims of program design may be summarised as:

- reliability - the program must always do what it is supposed to do;
- maintainability - the program must be easy to change or modify if this becomes necessary;
- readability - the program must be easy for another programmer to read and understand;
- performance - the program must do its job fast and efficiently;
- storage saving - the program ideally must occupy as little memory as possible, especially if it is a very large program.

Top-down design

Top-down design is the technique of breaking down a problem into the major tasks to be performed; each of these tasks is then further broken down into separate subtasks, and so on until each subtask is sufficiently simple to be written as a self-contained **module** or procedure. The program then consists of a series of calls to these modules, which may themselves call other modules.

Structure charts

Before writing a program using procedures, it is useful to have some way of representing the **structure** of a program – how the modules all relate to form the whole solution – and a structure chart is one way of doing this. When a program is large and complex, it becomes especially important to plan out the solution before doing any coding, and a structure chart also serves a useful purpose as documentation when the program is complete.

The chart resembles a family tree, with the main program modules written **across** the top line.

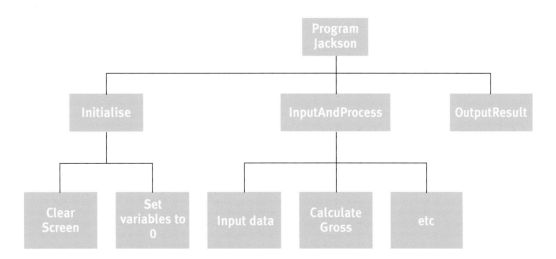

Figure 7.1: A structure chart

The building blocks of a structured program

Only three different 'building blocks' or **program constructs** are needed to write a structured program. These are

- **sequence** – in which one statement follows another and the program executes them in the sequence given
- **selection** – 'if..then..else' is an example of selection, where the next statement to be executed depends on the value of an expression
- **iteration** – a section of the program is repeated many times, as for example in the 'while..do' statement.

Notice the absence of the GO TO statement! Experience has shown that programs which are written without using GO TO statements are easier to follow, easier to debug and easier to maintain.

Programs that are written using **top-down** techniques, and using only the three constructs described, are called **structured programs**.

Representation of a loop

An asterisk in a box, with the condition written outside the box and the statements or modules within the loop written on the next level down, is used to indicate a section of code to be repeated.

```
e.g. while a<b do
        begin
            statement1
            statement2
            statement3
        end   {endwhile}
```

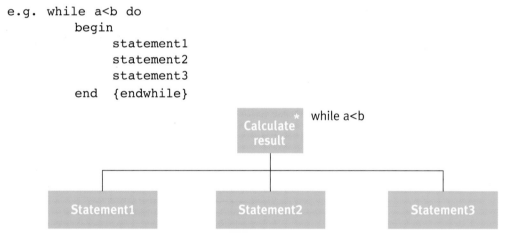

Figure 7.2: Iteration

Representation of selection

Selection is represented by a small circle in each of the boxes representing the alternative paths:

```
if (answer='Y') or (answer='y') then
    statement 1
else
    statement 2
```

Figure 7.3: Selection

The structure chart can also be used to show what parameters will be needed to pass data between procedures. This is the data interface.

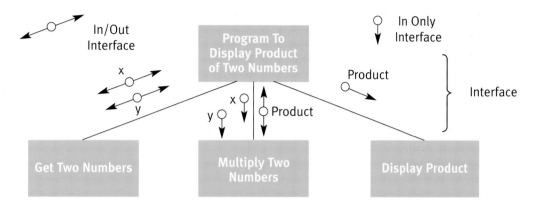

Figure 7.4: Structure Chart showing the data interface

Structure charts, in addition to interfaces may have control information placed on them. (A hierarchy chart is a chart without interface and control information).

Example:

Draw a structure chart and code a program to input a number of sales transaction records each of which contains a salesperson's number (between 1 and 3) and a sales amount in £. Accumulate the total sales for each salesperson and the total overall sales, and output these figures at the end of the program.

The structure chart can be drawn as follows:

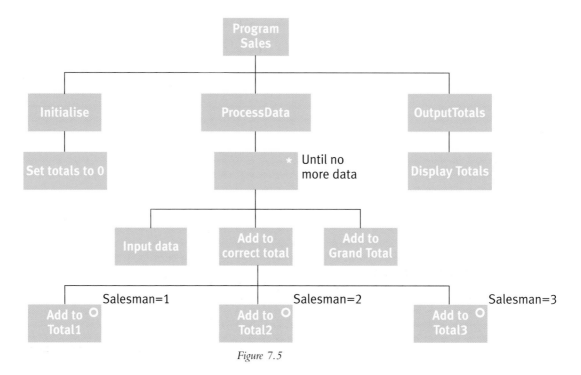

Figure 7.5

A guideline for drawing structure charts is that you should not put boxes representing loops (i.e. boxes containing asterisks) on the same level as other types of boxes. This is why in the diagram above, the box containing the asterisk appears **below** the 'ProcessData' box.

The same guideline applies to boxes containing circles representing selection; **all** the boxes on the same level must be 'selection' boxes if any of them are.

Q1: Compare the structure chart above with the coding on the next page. What details of the procedure **ProcessData** have been omitted from the structure chart? Do you think the omissions matter?

```pascal
program Sales;
{program to accumulate sales totals for three salesmen}

uses crt;   {calls in Turbo Pascal's library routines}

var
    GrandTotal, Total1, Total2, Total3, Amount: real;
    Salesman: Integer;

procedure Initialise;
begin
     Clrscr; {clear screen}
     GrandTotal:=0;
     Total1:=0;
     Total2:=0;
     Total3:=0;
end; {procedure}

procedure ProcessData;
begin
     write('Please enter salesperson''s number (0 to finish): ');
     readln(Salesman);
     while Salesman<>0 do
       begin
          write('Enter sales amount: ');
          readln(Amount);
          if (salesman=1) then Total1:=Total1+amount;
          if (salesman=2) then Total2:=Total2+amount;
          if (salesman=3) then Total3:=Total3+amount;
          GrandTotal:=GrandTotal + Amount;
          write('Please enter next salesperson''s number (0 to finish): ');
          readln(Salesman)
       end
     {endwhile}
end; {procedure}

procedure OutputTotals;
begin
     writeln;
     writeln('Total for salesperson 1: ',Total1:8:2);
     writeln('Total for salesperson 2: ',Total2:8:2);
     writeln('Total for salesperson 3: ',Total3:8:2);
     writeln('Grand Total of all sales: ',GrandTotal:8:2)
end; {procedure}



{***** MAIN PROGRAM ******}

begin
     Initialise;
     ProcessData;
     OutputTotals
end.
```

1-7

Pseudocode

Structure diagrams are one way of developing a solution to a problem, and they are useful in implementing a top-down approach. If, however, we try to write down all the details of every module in a structure diagram, it becomes unwieldy. It is most useful in specifying the structure of a program down to the module level.

Pseudocode provides a means of expressing algorithms without worrying about the syntax of a particular language. (An **algorithm** is a sequence of instructions for solving a problem.)

Typical pseudocode constructs include the following:

```
If .. Then .. Else .. EndIf
Case .. Of .. EndCase
For .. To .. EndFor
Repeat .. Until ..
While .. Do .. EndWhile
Procedure .. EndProc
Function .. EndFun
```

There are no hard and fast rules as to how pseudocode statements should be written; an assignment statement to assign the value 10 to X, for example, could be written in any of the following ways:

```
Assign 10 to X
X ← 10
X:=10;
Put 10 in X
```

1-7

Example:

Write pseudocode for an algorithm to find the maximum, minimum and average of a set of marks.

```
Procedure FindMaxMark
begin
    set max no. of marks and total to zero
    set min to 100
    read the first mark
    while not end of data
      if mark > max then set max = mark
      endif
      if mark < min then set min = mark
      endif
      add mark to total
      add 1 to no. of marks
      read the next mark
    endwhile
    calculate average
    print results
end procedure
```

Note that

- keywords such as **begin**, **end**, **while**, **endwhile**, **if**, and **endif** mark the limits of procedures, loops and conditional statements;
- the actual statements of the algorithm can be written in ordinary English;
- the indentation is important – it gives a visual picture of the extent of loops and conditional statements.

As stated above, there are no absolute rules for writing pseudocode; for example both versions of the **repeat** construct shown below would be quite acceptable:

```
repeat until end of data
     statements
     .....
     .....
     .....
end repeat

repeat
     statements
     .....
     .....
     .....
until end of data
```

Modular programming

Any programs that you write for this course are likely to be relatively short; however, in industry and commerce most problems will require thousands, if not tens of thousands, of lines of code to solve. Windows 2000, at 35 million lines of code, is the biggest program ever written. The importance of splitting up the problem into a series of self-contained modules then becomes obvious. A module should not exceed 100 or so lines, and preferably be short enough to fit on a single page; some modules may be only a few lines.

Advantages of modular programming

1 Some modules will be standard procedures used again and again in different programs or parts of the same program; for example, a routine to display a standard opening screen.

2 A module is small enough to be understandable as a unit of code. It is therefore easier to understand and debug, especially if its purpose is clearly defined and documented.

3 Program **maintenance** becomes easier because the affected modules can be quickly identified and changed.

4 In a very large project, several programmers may be working on a single program. Using a modular approach, each programmer can be given a specific set of modules to work on. This enables the whole program to be finished sooner.

5 More experienced programmers can be given the more complex modules to write, and the junior programmers can work on the simpler modules.

6 Modules can be tested independently, thereby shortening the time taken to get the whole program working.

7 If a programmer leaves part way through a project, it is easier for someone else to take over a set of self-contained modules.

8 A large project becomes easier to monitor and control.

1-7

Exercises

1   (a)   Programmers are encouraged to adopt a structured approach to writing programs. One reason is so that programmers can write code which can be more easily understood by another programmer.

Explain **two** other reasons.   (4)

(b)   Give **three** features of an imperative high level programming language which allow programmers to write "easy-to-understand" code.   (3)

(c)   Distinguish between a compiler and an interpreter.   (2)

AQA CPT1 Qu 4 May 2001

2   The following pseudocode represents a program that reads 5 numbers entered by a user and outputs the sum.

```
Program Add
Table[5] : Array of Real
Sum : Real
Call Procedure Read5Numbers(Table)
Call Procedure CalculateSum(Table, Sum)
Call Procedure Display(Sum)
```

(a)   (i)   Name a parameter used in the above program.   (1)

(ii) Explain how this parameter is used.   (1)

(b)   Draw a structure chart to represent the above program.   (2)

New Question

1-7

Chapter 8 – Dry-run Exercises

Trace tables

When a program is not working correctly (perhaps producing a wrong answer, or getting into an infinite loop), it is useful to trace through the program manually, writing down the values of the variables as they change. The variable names can be written as column headings and their values underneath the headings to form a trace table. Being able to trace manually through the steps of a program is an essential skill in program debugging.

Example:

Use a trace table to show the values of the variables **StudentMark**, **TotalMark**, **NoOfMarks** and **Average** when the program **MarkAvg** is run (see below). You may assume that the user enters the marks 7, 5, 9, -1.

```
Program MarkAvg(input,output);
   {program to calculate average of a set of students' marks}
   var
      StudentMark, TotalMark, NoOfMarks: integer;
      Average:real;

   Procedure Initialise;
   begin
        NoOfMarks := 0;
        TotalMark := 0;
   end; {end of procedure}

Procedure InputAndProcess;
begin
     write('Please enter the first mark, -1 to end: ');
     readln(StudentMark);
     while StudentMark <> -1 do
     begin
        TotalMark := TotalMark+StudentMark;
        NoOfMarks := NoOfMarks + 1;
        write('Please enter the next mark, -1 to end: ');
        readln(StudentMark)
     end; {endwhile}
end;      {end of procedure}

Procedure OutputResult;
begin
     Average := TotalMark / NoOfMarks;
     writeln('Average mark is ',Average:5:2);
     writeln('Total number of students: ',NoOfMarks:3)
end; {end of procedure}

{******   MAIN PROGRAM  - EXECUTION STARTS HERE   *******}
begin
     Initialise;
     InputAndProcess;
     OutputResult
end.
```

Answer:

Take a look at the program and write down the variable names across the page. The order is not particularly important; in the example below, they have been written in the order in which they will first be encountered. Then start at the first instruction in the main program and trace the instructions in the order that the computer will execute them.

NoOfMarks	TotalMark	StudentMark	Average
0	0	7	?
1	7	5	
2	12	9	
3	21	-1	7

Q1: The following extract from a program is intended to calculate the sum of the squares of a series of numbers entered by the user. The end of data entry is signalled by the dummy value -1. Use a trace table to find out why the program is not giving the right answer when the user enters the values 2, 5, 3, 1, -1.

The first couple of lines of the trace table have been filled in for you; Notice that a column has been allocated for the condition n <> -1, and this can only take the values True or False.

What output would you expect the program to produce if it was working correctly?

```
n:=0;
total:=0;
while n<>-1 do
begin
    write ('Please enter a number');
    readln(n);
    total:=total+n*n;
end; {while}
writeln('Total=',n:8:2);
```

n	n*n	total	n<>-1
0	**0**	**0**	**True**
2	**4**	**4**	**True**

Exercises

1 Use a trace table to show the values of var1, n and the condition n < 5 when the following statements are executed:

```
var1 ← 3
n ← 0
while n < 5 do
  begin
    var1 ← var1 + n
    n ← n + 1
  end;
```

var1	n	n < 5

(5)

New Question

2 The operators DIV and MOD perform integer arithmetic.

x DIV y calculates how many times y divides into x, for example 7 DIV 3 = 2.

x MOD y calculates the remainder that results after the division, for example 7 MOD 3 = 1.

(a) The following algorithm uses an array Result. Dry run this algorithm by completing the trace table below.

```
x ← 5
Index ← 0
REPEAT
    y ← x MOD 2
    x ← x DIV 2
    Index ← Index + 1
    Result[Index] ← y
UNTIL x=0
```

y	x	Index	Result		
			[3]	[2]	[1]
-	5	0	-	-	-
1	2	1	-	-	1

(6)

(b) What is the purpose of this algorithm? (1)

AQA CPT1 Qu 8 May 2002

3 (a) A unique numerical code, occupying a single byte, is generated for each key pressed on a computer's keyboard. What is meant by a byte? (1)

   (b) In one coding system, the character digits 0 to 9 are assigned the decimal number codes 48 to 57 and the letters A to Z the decimal number codes 65 to 90.

   Which keys produce the following codes?

   (i) 0100 0001 (1)

   (ii) 0011 1001 (1)

   (c) A number is entered at the keyboard as a sequence of character digits. This sequence is processed to convert the code representation into its decimal integer value using the following algorithm:

   Number ← 0
   While more character digits Do
       get next character digit
       and store its ASCII code in the variable Code
       Number ← Number * 10 + Code − 48
   EndWhile

1-8

Complete the trace table for the sequence 7321.

Code	Number
-	0
55	7

(6)

AQA CPT1 Qu 3 May 2001

4   The algorithm below re-arranges numbers stored in a one-dimensional array called **List**.

Ptr is an integer variable used as an index (subscript) which identifies elements within **List**.

Temp is a variable, which is used as a temporary store for numbers from **List**.

```
Ptr ← 1
While Ptr < 10 Do
    If List [Ptr] > List [Ptr+1] Then
        Temp ← List [Ptr]
        List [Ptr] ← List [Ptr+1]
        List [Ptr+1] ← Temp
    Endif
    Ptr ← Ptr+1
Endwhile
```

(a)   Dry-run the algorithm by completing the table below.

It is only necessary to show those numbers which change at a particular step.

Ptr	Temp	List									
		[1]	[2]	[3]	[4]	[5]	[6]	[7]	[8]	[9]	[10]
		43	25	37	81	18	70	64	96	52	4

(7)

(b)   What will happen when **Ptr**=10?   (1)

(c)   If the whole algorithm is now applied to this rearranged list, what will be the values of:

(i)   List[1]

(ii)   List[9]

(iii) List[10] ?   (3)

AQA CPT1 Qu 10 Jan 2003

1-8

Chapter 9 – Queues and Stacks

Introduction to data structures

All data processing on a computer involves the manipulation of data. This data can be organised in the computer's memory in different ways according to how it is to be processed, and the different methods of organising data are known as **data structures**.

Computer languages such as Pascal have built-in **elementary data types** (such as *integer*, *real*, *Boolean* and *char*) and some built-in **structured** or **composite** data types (data structures) such as *record*, *array* and *string*. These composite data types are made up of a number of elements of a specified type such as *integer* or *real*.

Some data structures such as queues, stacks and binary trees are not built into the language and have to be constructed by the programmer. These are known as Abstract Data Types (ADT). In this module it is only necessary to recognize the different data structures and use them in simple ways. In the second year of the course you will learn how to implement them.

Queues

A queue is a First In First Out (FIFO) data structure. New elements may only be added to the end of a queue, and elements may only be retrieved from the front of a queue. The sequence of data items in a queue is determined, therefore, by the order in which they are inserted. The size of the queue depends on the number of items in it, just like a queue at the cinema or supermarket checkout.

Queues are used in a variety of applications.

• Output waiting to be printed is commonly stored in a queue on disk. In a room full of networked computers, several people may send work to be printed at more or less the same time. By putting the output into a queue on disk, the output is printed on a first come, first served basis as soon as the printer is free.

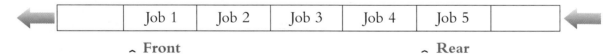

	Job 1	Job 2	Job 3	Job 4	Job 5	

⌃ **Front**　　　　　　　　　　　　　　　　⌃ **Rear**

Pointers mark the front and rear of the queue.

> **Q1:** What will the queue look like when 4 jobs have been printed and 2 new jobs, Job 6 and Job 7, have joined the queue? Remember to mark in the pointers Front and Rear.

• Characters typed at a keyboard are held in a queue in a keyboard buffer.
• Jobs waiting to be run by the computer may be held in a queue.
• Queues are also useful in simulation problems. A simulation program is one, which attempts to model a real-life situation so as to learn something about it. An example is a program that simulates customers arriving at random times at the check-outs in a supermarket store, and taking random times to pass through the checkout. With the aid of a simulation program, the optimum number of check-out counters can be established.

Stacks

A stack is a particular kind of sequence that may only be accessed at one end, known as the top of the stack (like plates on a pile in a cafeteria).

Only two operations can be carried out on a stack. **Adding** a new item involves placing it on top of the stack (**pushing** or stacking the item). **Removing** an item involves the removal of the item that was most recently added (**popping** the stack). The stack is a **LIFO** structure – **L**ast **I**n, **F**irst **O**ut.

Note that items do not move up and down as the stack is pushed and popped. Instead, the position of the top of the stack changes. A pointer called a stack pointer indicates the position of the top of the stack:

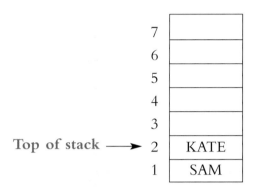

Q2: Show the state of the stack and stack pointer after each of the following operations:

(i)   Initialise the stack

(ii) Add ELAINE

(iii) Add HOWARD

(iv) Remove one item

(v)   Add MICHAEL

(vi) Add TAMARA

Implementation of a stack

A stack can be represented in memory by an array and two additional integer variables, one holding the size of the array (i.e. the maximum size of the stack) and one holding the pointer to the top of the stack (**Top**). **Top** will initially be set to 0, representing an empty stack.

Applications of stacks

Stacks are very important data structures in computing. They are used in calculations, translating from one computer language to another, and transferring control from one part of a program to another.

Using a stack to reverse the elements of a queue

The elements of a queue can be reversed by pushing them one by one on to the stack, and then popping them one by one and replacing them in the queue. For example:

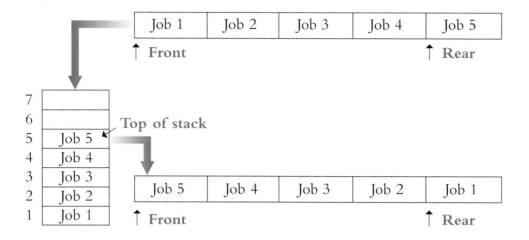

Overflow and Underflow

A queue or a stack may have a maximum size. An attempt to add a new element to a queue or stack which is already full will result in an **overflow** error. An attempt to remove an item from an empty queue or stack will result in an **underflow** error.

Exercises

1   With the aid of a clearly labelled diagram which includes a stack pointer, describe how a previously empty stack would hold these names arriving in the given sequence:

       Shane, Eithne, Greta, Petroc, Abdul

Show what the stack would then contain if three of these names were popped (retrieved) from it, and two more names (**Simon** and **Jasmine**) were pushed (added).(4)

New Question

2   With the aid of a clearly labelled diagram which includes front and rear pointers, describe how a previously empty queue would hold these names arriving in the given sequence:

       Phil, Trevor, Anna, Laura, Gary

Show what the queue would then contain if two of these names were retrieved from it, and one more name (**Sue**) was added.(4)

New Question

3 (a) An example of an iteration in Pascal is:

FOR x := 1 TO 10 DO writeln ('Hello');

In a high level programming language you are familiar with, using the correct syntax, give an example of:

(i) declaration;   (2)

(ii) assignment;   (1)

(iii) selection.   (2)

(b) A one-dimensional array q contains the following characters:

q

D	[5]
K	[4]
C	[3]
T	[2]
M	[1]

(i) Dry run the following algorithm, recording your results in the diagram.

FOR pointer ← 1 to 5
    s[pointer]← q[pointer]
END FOR
pointer1 ← 1
pointer2 ← 5
REPEAT
    q[pointer1]← s[pointer2]
    pointer1 ← pointer1 + 1
    pointer2 ← pointer2 − 1
UNTIL pointer2 = 0

q

D	[5]
K	[4]
C	[3]
T	[2]
M	[1]

s

	[5]
	[4]
	[3]
	[2]
	[1]

q

	[5]
	[4]
	[3]
	[2]
	[1]

(10)

(ii) What is the purpose of the above algorithm?   (1)

AQA CPT1 Qu 10 January 2001

4 A stack is an abstract data type that is often known as a LIFO data type. A stack with a single element 7 may be drawn as follows:

(a) What is meant by LIFO?   (1)

(b) A stack has two operations, **Push** and **Pop**. **Push x** adds item **x** to the stack. **Pop** removes one item from the stack. A number of operations are performed, **in sequence**, on the stack drawn above. Using the stack diagrams below show the effect of this sequence of operations.

    (i) Push 8   (1)

    (ii) Push 3   (1)

    (iii) Pop   (1)

    (iv) Push 4   (1)

(c) Give **one** example of the use of a stack.   (1)

New Question

Chapter 10 – Binary Trees

Introduction

A binary tree is a data structure consisting of a root node and zero, one or two subtrees as shown in the diagram below.

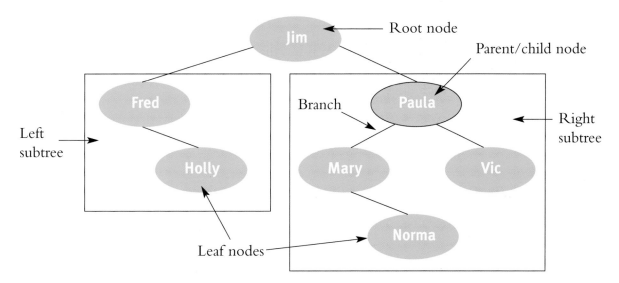

Figure 10.1: A binary tree

Note that:
- Lines connecting the nodes are called **branches** and every node except the root is joined to just one node at the higher level (its parent).
- Nodes that have no children are called **leaf nodes**.
- Some nodes may be both **parent** and **child** nodes. For example **Paula** is the child of Jim and the parent of **Mary** and **Vic**.

An ordered binary tree

A **search tree** is a particular application of a binary tree, such that a list of items held in the tree can be searched easily and quickly, new items easily added, and the whole tree printed out in sequence (alphabetic or numeric).

Constructing a binary tree

We could, for example, store a list of names (and, say, telephone numbers or other data as required) in a binary tree. Take the following list of names:

Long, Charlesworth, Illman, Hawthorne, Todd, Youngman, Jones, Ravage.

In order to create a binary tree that can be quickly searched for a given name, we follow the rules:

• Place the first item in the root.
• Take each subsequent item in turn.
• Start at the root each time. If the item is less than the root, branch to the left and if it is greater than the root, branch to the right.
• Apply the rule at each node encountered.

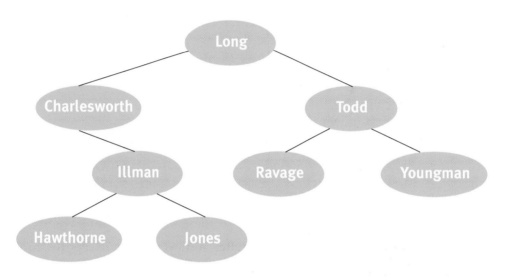

Figure 10.2: Items in an ordered binary tree

Exercises

1 A binary search tree is a data structure where items of data are held such that they can be searched for quickly and easily.

   The following data items are to be entered into a binary search tree in the order given:

   London, Paris, Rome, Berlin, Amsterdam, Lisbon, Madrid.

   (a) Draw a diagram to show how these values will be stored.   (4)

   (b) Circle the root node in your diagram.   (1)

   (c) If Madrid is being searched for in this binary tree, list the data items which have to be accessed.   (1)

   AQA CPT1 Qu 8 May 2001

2 (a) The series of characters J, F, H, U, S, X, T are to be entered into a binary search tree in the order given. Draw a diagram to show how these values will be stored. (4)

(b) The following data are held in arrays Data, L and R:

Data	'J'	'F'	'H'	'U'	'S'	'X'	'T'
	[1]	[2]	[3]	[4]	[5]	[6]	[7]

L	2	0	0	5	0	0	0
	[1]	[2]	[3]	[4]	[5]	[6]	[7]

R	4	3	0	6	7	0	0
	[1]	[2]	[3]	[4]	[5]	[6]	[7]

Using the arrays above, dry-run the following pseudo-code by completing the trace table:

```
Item  ←  'T'
Ptr  ←  1
WHILE Data[Ptr] < > Item DO
    PRINT Data[Ptr]
    IF Data[Ptr] > Item
        THEN Ptr  ←  L[Ptr]
        ELSE Ptr  ←  R[Ptr]
    ENDIF
ENDWHILE
PRINT Data[Ptr]
```

Trace Table:

Item	Ptr	Printed Output
'T'	1	'J'

(6)

AQA CPT1 Qu 10 Jan 2002

Chapter 11 – Inside the Computer

Introduction

A computer system is composed of both internal and external components. In this chapter we'll look in more detail at the computer's **internal components** and how programs and data are stored.

The internal components are contained in the **Central Processing Unit** (CPU). The terminology here is vague and often ambiguous: the term CPU is sometimes used to mean the actual processor unit which carries out the fetching, decoding and executing of instructions. Other times it is used in a broader sense as the unit which houses the components shown in Figure 11.1:

- The processor;
- Main memory;
- I/O controllers, some of which may be input only, some output only, some both input and output;
- Buses.

The **external components** are also known as **peripherals** and include input, output and storage devices such as keyboard, mouse, printer and disk drives. The processor commands the I/O controllers to read and write data from/to devices.

The components of a simple computer system are shown in the diagram below:

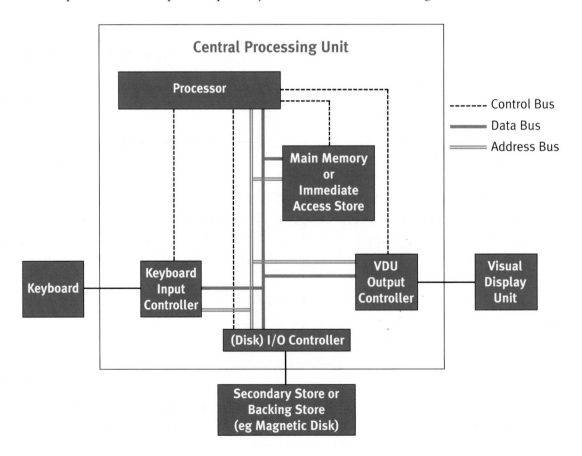

Figure 11.1: The internal and external components of a computer

Memory and the stored program concept

Computers as we know them were first built in the 1940s, and two of the early pioneers were Alan Turing and John von Neumann. Each of them separately came up with the concept of a machine that would hold in a single store (main memory) both the instructions (program) and the data on which the instructions were to be carried out. Virtually all computers today are built on this principle, and so the general structure as shown in Figure 11.2 is sometimes referred to as the **von Neumann machine**.

Memory

0	
1	
2	Instruction
3	Instruction
	•
	•
	•
	•
	Data
	Data

Figure 11.2: The stored program concept

The Processor

The processor contains the **control unit**, the **arithmetic/logic unit (ALU) and registers**.

The control unit coordinates and controls all the operations carried out by the computer. It operates by repeating three operations:

- **Fetch** – cause the next instruction to be fetched from main memory;
- **Decode** – produces signals which control the other parts of the computer such as the ALU;
- **Execute** – cause the instruction to be executed;

The ALU can perform two sorts of operations on data. **Arithmetic** operations include addition, subtraction, multiplication and division. **Logical** operations consist of comparing one data item with another to determine whether the first data item is smaller than, equal to or greater than the second data item.

Registers are special memory cells that operate at very high speed.

Buses

A bus is a set of parallel wires connecting two or more components of the computer.

The CPU is connected to main memory by three separate **buses**. When the CPU wishes to access a particular main memory location, it sends this address to memory on the **address bus**. The data in that location is then returned to the CPU on the **data bus**. Control signals are sent along the **control bus**.

In Figure 11.3, you can see that data, address and control buses connect the processor, memory and I/O controllers. These are all **system buses**. Each bus is a shared transmission medium, so that only one device can transmit along a bus at any one time.

Data and control signals travel in both directions between the processor, memory and I/O controllers. Addresses, on the other hand, travel only one way along the address bus: the processor sends the address of an instruction, or of data to be stored or retrieved, **to** memory or **to** an I/O controller (see figure below.)

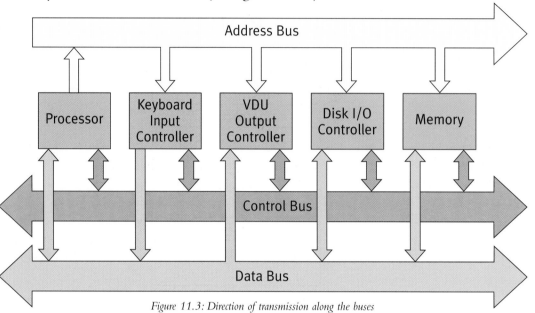

Figure 11.3: Direction of transmission along the buses

Control bus

The control bus is a bi-directional bus meaning that signals can be carried in both directions. The data and address buses are **shared** by all components of the system. Control lines must therefore be provided to ensure that **access to and use of the data and address buses** by the different components of the system does not lead to conflict. The purpose of the control bus is to transmit command, timing and specific status information between system components. Timing signals indicate the validity of data and address information. Command signals specify operations to be performed. Specific status signals indicate the state of a data transfer request, or the status of a request by a component to gain control of the system bus.

Typical control lines include:

- Memory Write: causes data on the data bus to be written into the addressed location.
- Memory Read: causes data from the addressed location to be placed on the data bus.
- I/O Write: causes data on the data bus to be output to the addressed I/O port.
- I/O Read: causes data from the addressed I/O port to be placed on the data bus.
- Transfer ACK: indicates that data have been accepted from or placed on the data bus.
- Bus Request: indicates that a component needs to gain control of the system bus.
- Bus Grant: indicates that a requesting component has been granted control of the system bus.
- Interrupt request: indicates that an interrupt is pending.
- Interrupt ACK: acknowledges that the pending interrupt has been recognised.
- Clock: used to synchronise operations.
- Reset: initialises all components.

Data bus

The data bus, typically consisting of 8, 16, 32 or 64 separate lines provides a bi-directional path for moving data and instructions between system components. **The width of the data bus is a key factor in determining overall system performance**. For example, if the data bus is 8 bits wide, and each instruction is 16 bits long, then the processor must access the main memory twice just to fetch the instruction.

Address bus

When the processor wishes to read a word (say 8, 16 or 32 bits) of data from memory, it first puts the address of the desired word on the address bus. **The width of the address bus determines the maximum possible memory capacity of the system**. For example, if the address bus consisted of only 8 lines, then the maximum address it could transmit would be (in binary) 11111111 or 255 - giving a maximum memory capacity of 256 (including address 0). A more realistic minimum bus width would be 20 lines, giving a memory capacity of 220, i.e. 1Mb.

The address bus is also used to address I/O ports during input/output operations.

No of address lines, m	Maximum no of addressable cells	Maximum no of addressable cells expressed as a power of two, 2^m
1	2	2^1
2	4	2^2
3	8	2^3
4	16	2^4
8	256	2^8
16	65536	2^{16}
20	1048576	2^{20}
24	16777216	2^{24}

*Table 11.4: Relationship between number of address lines **m** and maximum number of addressable memory cells*

I/O Controllers

Peripheral devices cannot be connected directly to the processor. Each peripheral operates in a different way and it would not be sensible to design processors to directly control every possible peripheral. Otherwise, the invention of a new type of peripheral would require the processor to be redesigned. Instead, the processor controls and communicates with a peripheral device through an **I/O or device controller**. I/O controllers are available which can operate both input and output transfers of bits, e.g. floppy disk controller. Other controllers operate in one direction only, either as an input controller, e.g. keyboard controller or as output controller, e.g. VDU controller.

The controller is an electronic circuit board consisting of three parts:
• an interface that allows connection of the controller to the system or I/O bus;
• a set of data, command and status registers;
• an interface that enables connection of the controller to the cable connecting the device to the computer.

An interface is a standardised form of connection defining such things as signals, number of connecting pins/sockets and voltage levels that appear at the interface. An example is an RS232 interface, which enables serial transmission of data between a computer and a serially connected printer. The printer also contains an RS232 interface so that both ends of the connection are compatible with each other.

Exercises

1   Some of the internal components of a computer system are processor, main memory, control bus, address bus, data bus, keyboard controller, VDU controller, disk controller.

The diagram below shows how these are connected.

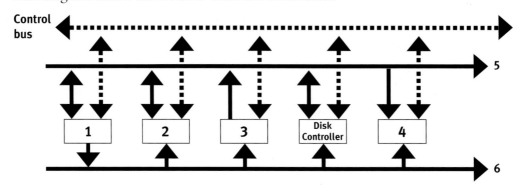

(a)   Give the correct name for each of the components as labelled in the diagram above.   (6)

(b)   If the data bus consists of 8 lines what is the largest denary value which could be transferred in one go?   (1)

(c)   Computer systems built using the von Neumann architecture use the stored program concept.

(i)   Where is a program stored while it is being executed?   (1)

(ii) Where is the data stored?   (1)

AQA CPT1 Qu 4 May 2002

2   Some of the components of a computer system are processor, main memory, address bus, data bus, control bus, I/O port and secondary storage.

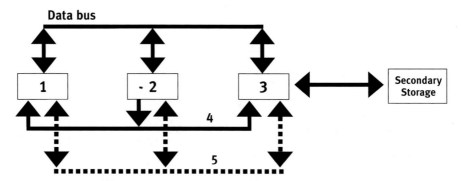

The diagram above shows how these components are connected.

(a)   Name each of the following components 1 to 5   (5)

(b)   (i)   What is the function of the following components:

processor;

main memory;

secondary storage?   (3)

(ii) Give **two** examples of a signal carried by the control bus.   (2)

(iii) Apart from data, what else is carried on the data bus?   (1)

AQA CPT1 Qu 4 Jan 2003

3   Some of the components of a computer system are:

Peripherals:

keyboard   1

monitor   2

I/O Ports:

VDU controller   3

keyboard controller   4

Memory

main memory   5

secondary storage   6

System Bus:

Data Bus   7

Address Bus   8

(a)   In the diagram below, identify each component by writing its number, given in the list above, in the appropriate circle.

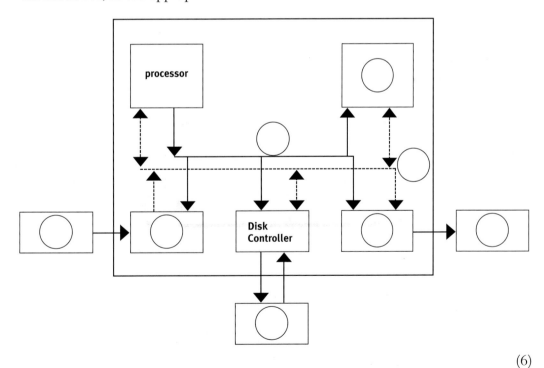

(6)

(b)   The above computer system uses the *stored program concept*.
Explain this term.   (2)

AQA CPT1 Qu 3 June 2003

Chapter 12 – Communication Methods

Principle of electronic data communication

Data communication involves sending and receiving data from one computer or data processing device to another. Applications using e-mail, supermarket EPOS (electronic point of sale) terminals, cash dispensers, facsimile, and video conferencing are all examples of this.

Data communication also takes place between the CPU and its peripheral devices; for example, data to be printed has to be sent to the printer, or in the case of a computer controlling a robot, signals have to be sent to tell the robot what to do.

Serial and parallel data communication

Data can be sent in one of two ways: serial or parallel.

Serial data transmission: Bits are sent via an interface one bit at a time over a single wire from the source to the destination.

Very high data transfer rates can be achieved – for example using fibre-optic cable data transfer rates of 64 Gbits per second can be achieved, which is much faster than parallel transmission in some systems.

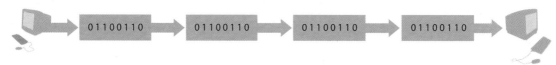

Figure 12.1: Serial transmission

Parallel data transmission: Several bits are sent simultaneously over a number of parallel wires.

This method is used inside the computer (using the various computer **buses**) and for very short distances of up to a few metres. A parallel port, for example, can send 8, 16 or 32 bits simultaneously down separate lines. A printer is often connected to a PC via a parallel port if the printer is sitting right next to the computer.

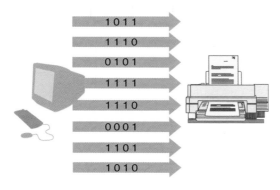

Figure 12.2: Parallel transmission

Parallel transmission will transmit data more quickly than serial transmission. However, because each individual wire has slightly different properties, there is a possibility that bits could travel at slightly different speeds over each of the wires. This produces a problem known as **skew**. So parallel transmission is really only reliable over short distances.

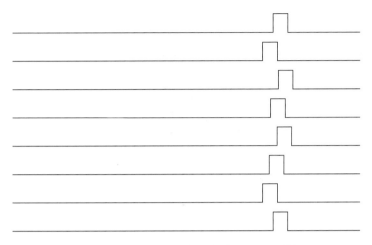

Figure 12.3: Skew developing in parallel wires

Transmission rate

The speed at which data is transmitted serially is measured in bits per second **(bit rate)**.

Baud rate: The rate at which the signal changes.

In baseband mode of operation bit rate is equivalent to **baud rate**. However with higher bandwidths more than one bit can be coded into a signal and the bit rate will be higher than the baud rate (also called symbol rate).

bit rate of channel = (baud rate) x (number of bits per signal)

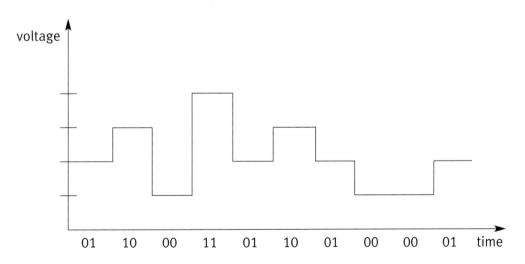

Figure 12.4: One Signal encoding 2 bits: Bit rate is twice the baud rate

Signalling Methods

The principal signalling methods are baseband, broadband and carrierband. In baseband signalling the voltage levels representing 0 and 1 occupy the full bandwidth of the medium. The data in the broadband and carrierband methods are placed onto the medium using a modulated carrier. In carrierband transmission the signal transmitted occupies the whole bandwidth. In broadband transmission multiple channels exist, with each channel having its own frequency range. Each channel can transmit a separate data stream. The greater the bandwidth, the more data can be transmitted per unit time.

Bandwidth: The range of frequencies that a medium can correctly transmit.

Parity

Computers use either even or odd parity. In an even parity machine, the total number of 'on' bits in every byte (including the parity bit) must be an even number. When data is transmitted, the parity bit is set at the transmitting end and parity is checked at the receiving end, and if the wrong number of bits are 'on', an error has occurred. In the diagram below the parity bit is the most significant bit (MSB).

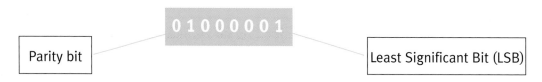

Figure 12.5: Parity bit in even parity system

Q1: The ASCII codes for P and Q are 1010000 and 1010001 respectively. In an even parity transmission system, what will be the value of the parity bit for the characters P and Q?

Asynchronous data transmission

Asynchronous transmission: one character at a time is sent, with each character being preceded by a start bit and followed by one or two stop bits.

The start bit alerts the receiving device and synchronises the clock inside the receiver ready to receive the character. The baud rate at the receiving end has to be set up to be the same as the sender's baud rate or the signal will not be received correctly.

A parity bit is also usually included as a check against incorrect transmission. Thus for each character being sent, a total of 10 bits is transmitted, including the parity bit, a start bit and a stop bit. The start bit may be a 0 or a 1, the stop bit is then a 1 or a 0 (always different). A series of electrical pulses is sent down the line as illustrated in Figure 12.6:

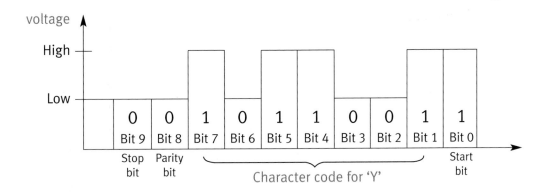

Figure 12.6: Asynchronous transmission

This type of transmission is usually used by PCs, and is fast and economical for relatively small amounts of data.

Handshaking

Handshaking is the exchange of signals between devices to establish their readiness to send or receive data, for example between a computer and printer. It is one method of ensuring that both the sender and receiver are ready before transmission begins. The 'conversation' between two devices is along the lines of the following:

Device 1:   "Are you ready to receive some data?"

Device 2:   "Yes, go ahead."

Device 1:   *(sends data)*

Device 2:   "Message received."

Protocol

Protocol: a set of rules relating to communication between devices.

In order to allow equipment from different suppliers to be networked, a standardised set of rules **(protocols)** has been devised covering standards for physical connections, cabling, mode of transmission, speed, data format, error detection and correction. Any equipment which uses the same communication protocol can be linked together.

Exercises

1 One method of sending data to a printer is by using parallel transmission.

   (a) What is meant by parallel transmission? (1)

   (b) Parallel transmission should **not** be used over long distances.

     (i) Why not? (1)

     (ii) How should data be transmitted over long distances? (1)

                   AQA CPT1Qu 9 May 2002

2 Bit patterns can be interpreted in a number of different ways.

   (a) A computer word contains the bit pattern 0001 0111.

     What is its decimal value if it represents

     (i) a pure binary integer; (1)

     (ii) a BCD (Binary Coded Decimal)? (1)

   (b) A computer system uses **odd** parity. The most significant bit (MSB) is used as a parity bit. The ASCII value for the character "!" is decimal number 33.

     (i) What would be the 8-bit binary pattern to represent the character "!"? (2)

     (ii) Asynchronous data transmission is used if one character is sent at a time. One start bit marks the beginning of a character and one stop bit marks the end of a character.

       What would be the bit pattern if the character "!" above is sent using asynchronous data transmission? (1)

                   AQA CPT1 Qu 2 Jan 2003

3 Baud rate and bit rate tell us about the speed of data transmission.

   (a) What exactly do bit rate and baud rate measure? (2)

   (b) What is the relationship between bit rate and bandwidth? (1)

                   New Question

4 A stand-alone computer and printer use *handshaking* as they communicate with each other. Explain the term *handshaking* in this context. (2)

                   New Question

5 (a) What is serial transmission?

   (b) Explain the difference between serial and parallel data transmission.

   (c) Under what circumstances would it be appropriate to use parallel transmission? (3)

                   New Question

1-12

Chapter 13 – Local Area Networks

Communications networks

A Local Area Network (LAN) is a method of connecting computers together in a small geographical area, for example confined to one building or site.

Computers and peripheral devices are linked via a direct physical connection (cable) or a wireless connection. A LAN can be connected to other LANs, or to a Wide Area Network (WAN).

Network Adapter

To communicate on a network a computer needs a network adapter or network interface card. The network adapter converts data from the computer into a form that can be transmitted over the network and converts data received from the network into a form that can be stored in the computer.

Advantages of networks

A network has several **advantages** over a collection of stand-alone microcomputers:

- It allows the sharing of resources such as disk storage, printers, image scanners, modems and central servers;
- It allows sharing of information held on disk drives accessible by all users;
- It is easier to back up data held on a file server than on many individual machines;
- It is easier to store application programs on one computer and make them available to all users rather than having copies individually installed on each computer;
- It allows electronic mail to be sent between users;
- It is easier to set up new users and equipment;
- It allows the connection of different types of computer, which can communicate with each other.

Disadvantages of networks

The main **disadvantages** of networks are:

- Users become dependent on them; if for example the network file server develops a fault, then many users will be unable to run application programs. (On many sites, a back-up file server can be switched into action if the main server fails).
- If the network stops operating then it may not be possible to access various hardware and software resources.
- The efficiency of a network is very dependent on the skill of the system manager. A badly managed network may operate less efficiently than stand-alone machines.
- It is difficult to make the system secure from hackers.
- As traffic increases on the network the performance degrades unless it is properly designed.

1-13

Network topologies

The **topology** of a network is its physical layout – the way in which the computers and other units (commonly referred to as **nodes**) are connected. Common topologies include **star**, **bus** and **ring**, discussed below.

Star network

Each node in a star network is connected to a central **host computer** that controls the network. This is a common topology for a wide area network in large companies, which have a mainframe computer at the Head Office, and computer facilities (perhaps linked together in a LAN) at each branch. It has the advantage that each node is independent of the others so a fault at one branch will not affect the other branches. On the other hand if the main computer goes down, all users are affected.

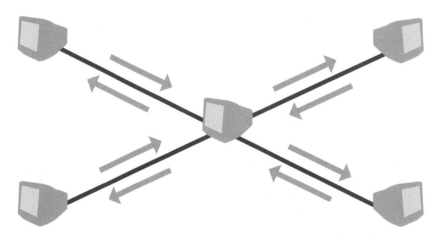

Figure 13.1: A star network

Advantages of a star network

- If one cable fails, only one station is affected.
- Therefore, it is simple to isolate faults.
- Consistent performance even when the network is being heavily used.
- No problems with 'collisions' of data since each station has its own cable to the server.
- The system is more secure as messages are sent directly to the central computer and cannot be intercepted by other stations.
- Easy to add new stations without disrupting the network.
- Different stations can transmit at different speeds.

Disadvantage of star network

- May be costly to install because of the length of cable required. The cabling can be a substantial part of the overall cost of installing a network.

A variation of the star topology is the **distributed star** topology. A number of stations are linked to connection boxes which are then linked together to form a 'string of stars'.

Bus network

This is a common topology for a LAN, with all the devices on the network sharing a single cable. Data is transmitted in all directions from any PC to any other. This system works well if the channels are not too heavily loaded. On the other hand if sixteen students sit down at sixteen computers all at once and all try to load software from the network's hard disk, the whole system may grind to a halt!

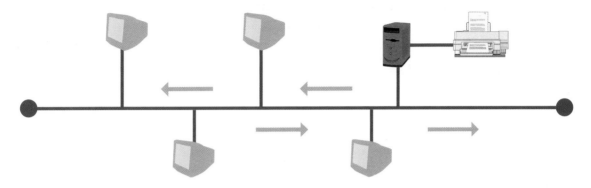

Figure 13.2: A bus network

Advantages of a bus network

• Easy and inexpensive to install as it requires the least amount of cable.

• Easy to add more stations without disrupting the network.

Disadvantage of bus network

• The whole network goes down if the main cable fails at any point.
• Cable failure is difficult to isolate.
• Network performance degrades under a heavy load.

Example of a bus network: Ethernet.

Ring network

In a ring network, computers are connected together and there is no central controlling computer. Each computer may communicate with any other computer in the ring, with messages being specificallyaddressed to the destination computer. Messages are passed around the ring in one direction only.

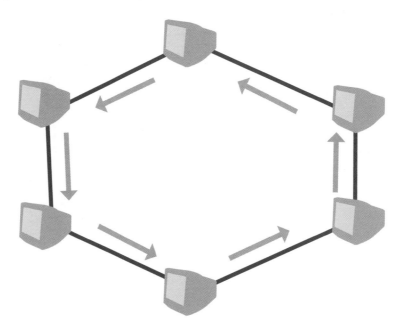

Figure 13.3: A ring network

Advantages of a ring network

- There is no dependence on a central computer or file server, and each node controls transmission to and from itself.
- Transmission of messages around the ring is relatively simple, with messages travelling in one direction only.
- Very high transmission rates are possible.

Disadvantages of a ring network

- If one node in the ring breaks down, transmission between any of the devices in the ring is disrupted.
- If any node fails the whole network may fail.

Example of a ring network: Token Ring.

Exercises

1   Acme Design, a small graphic design firm, has several stand-alone computers which
    staff use for their design work. They would like to use a LAN (Local Area Network)
    to share printers, scanners and plotters.

    (a)   What extra hardware is needed for each stand-alone computer to be connected
          to a LAN via cables?   (1)

    (b)   Computers could be connected in one of the topologies shown below.

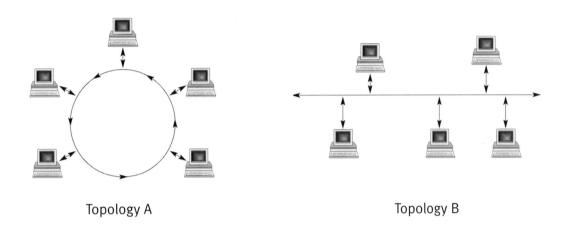

Topology A   Topology B

          (i)   Name these network topologies.   (2)
          (ii) Give **one** advantage of topology A over topology B.   (1)
          (iii) Give **one** advantage of topology B over topology A.   (1)

    (c)   (i)   What is a protocol?   (1)
          (ii) Why is a protocol needed?   (1)

                                                            AQA CPT1 Qu 3 Jan 2003

2   A school has several stand-alone computers which pupils use for word-processing
    coursework and accessing the library catalogue, stored in a database. A copy of the
    database is stored on each computer.

    (a)   The teacher in charge of these computers thinks it would be beneficial to
          network these computers.

          (i)   State **two** advantages for the pupils of a Local Area Network (LAN). (2)

          (ii) What extra hardware is needed on each stand-alone computer to connect
                it to a LAN via cables?   (1)

    (b)   The computers could be connected in a topology such as a bus or a star network.

          State **one** advantage of a bus network over a star network and one advantage
          of a star network over a bus network.   (2)

                                                            New Question

Chapter 14 – Wide Area Networks

Wide Area Network (WAN)

A WAN connects geographically remote computers or networks; for example computers in different sites, towns or continents.

The connection between computers in a WAN may be any of several alternatives, described below.

Communications links

Communication may take place over a combination of connections:

- The public telephone network;

- Dedicated leased lines;

- Radio waves;

- Fibre optic cable through which pulses of light, rather than electricity, are sent in digital form;

- Microwave - similar to radio waves. Microwave stations cannot be much more than 30 miles apart because of the earth's curvature as microwaves travel in straight lines. Mobile telephones use microwave radio links.

- Communications satellite, using one of the hundreds of satellites now in geosynchronous orbit about 22,000 miles above the earth. (Geosynchronous orbit means that they are rotating at the same speed as the Earth, and are therefore stationary relative to Earth.)

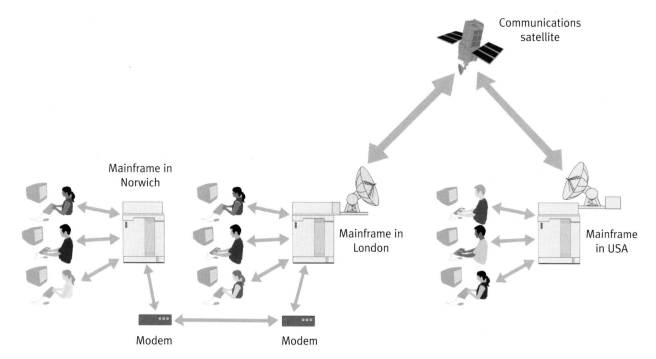

Figure 14.1: Satellite transmission

Modems

When data is sent over long distances, a cable no longer suffices and data must be transmitted by some other means such as a telephone line. Telephone lines were originally designed for speech, which is transmitted in analogue or waveform. In order for digital data to be sent over a telephone line, it must first be converted to analogue form and then converted back to digital at the other end. This is achieved by means of a modem (MOdulator DEModulator) at either end of the line.

digital   analogue   digital

modem   modem

Figure 14.2: A modem converts digital signals to analogue and vice versa.

ISDN lines

The amount of data that can be sent over a line depends on the bandwidth, which is the range of frequencies that the line can carry. The greater the **bandwidth**, the greater the rate at which data can be sent, as several messages can be transmitted simultaneously.

A network that is capable of sending voice, video and computer data is called an **Integrated Services Digital Network (ISDN)**, and this requires a high bandwidth.

Data compression

Data compression is frequently used when transmitting large quantities of data, thereby reducing the number of blocks transmitted and hence the cost. One method works by replacing repeated bytes by one copy of the byte plus a count of the repetitions.

Factors affecting rate of data transmission

- The speed of the modem. Different modems provide different data transmission rates, varying typically between 9K bps (bits per second) to 56K bps.
- The nature of the transmission line. A digital line such as an ISDN line has a much higher transmission speed than an analogue line.
- The type of cable used. Twisted pair cable has a transfer rate of about 1000 Mbps, whereas fibre optic cable is about 100 times as fast.
- The type of transmission, synchronous or asynchronous.

The Internet

The Internet is a world-wide collection of computers using the same protocol (TCP/IP).

The Internet is the largest wide area network in the world. In fact it is not a single network, but a collection of thousands of computer networks throughout the world. These linked networks are of two types:

- LAN (Local Area Network), covering, for example, an office block or University campus;
- WAN (Wide Area Network), connecting computers over a wide geographical area, even over several countries.

All LANs and some WANs are owned by individual organisations. Some WANs act as **service providers**, and members of the public or businesses can join these networks in return for a monthly charge.

There is no central authority or governing body running the Internet: it started with an initial 4 computers in 1969 and grew over the next ten years to connect 200 computers in military and research establishments in the US. Today there are more than 4 million host computers, any of which could be holding the information you are looking for, and as many as 50 million people connected, any of whom could be future customers, friends or problem-solvers.

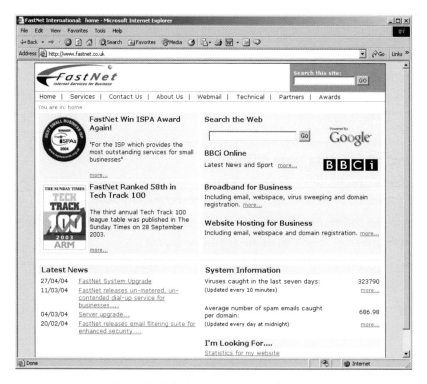

Figure 14.3: An Internet Service Provider

Dial-up Networking

In dial-up networking the connection to a WAN is made using the existing telephone network and a modem or ISDN adaptor. Whenever data transmission is required, the computer dials the number to set up a connection. The connection is dropped when no longer in use.

Dial-up networking: using a telephone line to connect to a network as required.

Leased Line Networking

With leased line networking the local nodes are permanently connected to the WAN. No time is wasted making a connection when data transmission is required. These lines usually have a higher bandwidth than dial-up lines and therefore can transmit more data per unit time. Data transmission is more reliable because no switches are being operated. The line is more secure as it is not shared with other organisations. Leased lines are more expensive than dial-up lines, however, the cost per bit may be lower than for dial-up networking if the data volumes transmitted are high.

Leased-line networking: A dedicated line connecting geographically remote computer systems is permanently on.

Uniform Resource Locator (URL)

A URL is the standard address used to find a page, Web server or other device on the Web or the Internet.

A typical address or URL is

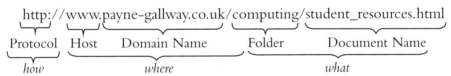

The first part of the address specifies the protocol used for connection to the server. http stands for Hypertext Transfer Protocol, which is used for Web sites. Other kinds of addresses include:

https://   'Hypertext Transfer Protocol, secure' or a Web site with security features. Credit card numbers should be safer here.

ftp://   'File Transfer Protocol' – an FTP site.

Localhost://   Information from a local Web server – typically on a user's own computer.

Domain names

The next part of the URL specifies the name of the server on which the Web resource is held. This name, called the domain name, is a string of identifiers separated by full-stops (called 'dot' when you are reading out an address).

Domain names provide a system of easy-to-remember Internet addresses, which can be translated by the Domain Name System (DNS) into the numeric addresses (Internet Protocol (IP) addresses) used by the network.

DNS is a distributed database of information that is used to translate domain names, which are easy for humans to remember and use, into IP addresses, which are what computers need to find each other on the Internet. The domain name system defines how domain names are structured. Domain names are allocated and registered in this format. The domain name system is based on a tree structure called the domain name space. The top-level domains were assigned by organisation and by country and are shown by the suffix attached to Internet domain names. There are a limited number of predefined suffixes, and each one represents a top-level domain. Current top-level domains include:

.com - commercial businesses; this is the most common top level domain

.gov – U.S. government agencies

.edu – U.S. Educational institutions such as universities

.mil – U.S. Military

.net - Network organisations

UK-specific codes include

.ac an academic institution

.co a company that trades in a single country

.gov a government department or other related facility

.org Organisations (mostly non-profit)

.tm a trade-marked business name

.ltd a UK Limited company

.sch a school

A 2-character country code may follow (the country where the host computer is located) – there are hundreds of these including

au Australia

es Spain

sg Singapore

uk UK

Q1: Suppose you wanted to log on to the IBM Web site but did not know the address. What would you try first?

Q2: What address would you try for the AQA (Assessment and Qualifications Alliance?)

1-14

IP addresses

Every Web site has a unique address known as its IP address. Currently IP addresses are 32-bit (4-byte) binary numbers (IPv4). These addresses are written as a set of four numbers, each in the range 0-255, separated by full-stops, like 177.234.143.186 for example. However, as nobody can remember or work out addresses like these, the domain name system (DNS) server maps the domain names onto the IP addresses.

IP address: Numerical address stored in 4 bytes, used to identify an individual computer.

IPv6 is just beginning to come into use to solve the problem of the shortage of IP addresses (16 byte addresses instead of 4 bytes).

Intranets

An Intranet is an organisation-wide network using the same protocol as the internet, making it possible to share documents, databases and applications. Information on intranets is accessed through browsers. Many schools have Intranets, and selected information is downloaded from the Internet for students to access. This saves wasting time browsing aimlessly through thousands of files and also enables unsuitable material to be screened out.

Intranet: local area network providing Internet facilities within an organisation using Internet protocol.

1-14

Exercises

1 What type of application software is required to access a web site?   (1)

New Question

2 What is an Intranet? Give **two** advantages to a company of setting up an Intranet.   (3)

New Question

3 An example of a Uniform Resource Locator (URL)
   is **http://www.bbc.co.uk/history**.
   (a) What part of the above URL constitutes the domain name?   (1)
   (b) Using the URL, explain what each part can tell us.
       (i)   http
       (ii) www
       (iii) bbc
       (iv) co
       (v)   uk
       (vi) history   (6)
   (c) The IP address of the above site is 212.58.224.32.
       (i)   What is the relationship between the IP address and the domain name?   (1)
       (ii) If each group of digits is stored in one byte, what is the range of
             possible IP addresses?   (2)

AQA CPT1 Qu 6 June 2000

4 (a) A college uses a LAN (Local Area Network) to share software and printers between its students. Describe a LAN. (2)

   (b) The diagram below shows the current topology.

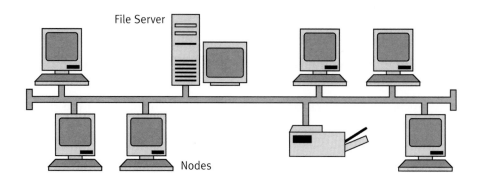

File Server

Nodes

      (i)   Name this topology (1)
      (ii) Give **one** advantage of this topology. (1)
      (iii) Give **one** disadvantage of this topology. (1)

   (c) The college decides to link to a WAN (Wide Area Network). When accessing a website, the connection can be made through either leased line networking or dial-up networking. What is meant by:

      (i)   leased line networking; (1)
      (ii) dial-up networking? (1)

   (d) Give **one** reason for the college selecting leased line networking. (1)
   (e) Give **one** reason for the college selecting dial-up networking. (1)

AQA CPT1 Qu 8 Jan 2001

1-14

Module 2

Principles of Hardware, Software and Applications

In this section:

2

Chapter 15 – General Purpose Packages

Introduction

In your exam or assessment, you may be asked to write about the 'features' of various common software packages. There is no substitute for practical experience, so if at all possible you should use each of these packages yourself and make notes on their capabilities. You are expected to have basic skills in using a spreadsheet and a database, and these packages are discussed in Chapters 16 and 22-23 respectively.

General purpose packages can be used for a variety of tasks. They can usually be customized or tailored to perform specific tasks by creating templates, macros and customised menus and toolbars. They have features such as help systems and wizards that guide the user through the steps of a complex task.

Word processing software

Word processing software is used to write letters, reports, books and articles, and any other document that in the past would have been typed on a typewriter. As the user keys in the text, it appears on the screen and is held in the computer's memory. The user can easily edit the text, correct spelling mistakes, change margins and so on before printing out the final version. The document can also be saved on disk for future amendment or use. Until the instruction is given to save, however, the document held in main memory will be lost if for example there is a power cut. Main memory is a **volatile** storage medium, and users are well advised to save their work frequently.

Below is a summary of some of the things you can do in a word processing package such as MS Word.

- type, correct, delete and move text; copy and paste, cut and paste;
- change font size, set italics, bold and underline, subscripts and superscripts;
- align text (left, right, centre or fully justified), set tabs and margins;
- find and replace text;
- insert graphics and diagrams, import graphics or charts from other packages such as a spreadsheet;
- check spelling and grammar;
- set up templates with type styles for different types of document;
- work in tables or columns;
- add headers and footers to each page, with or without page numbers;
- create indexes and tables of contents;
- type equations with mathematical symbols;
- perform a mail merge to send personalised letters to people selected from a list held in a database.

Desktop publishing

Desktop publishing is an extension of word processing. Desktop publishing packages such as Adobe PageMaker or QuarkXPress allow easier control over page layout for many types of document such as flyers, newspapers, magazines and books. Graphics, scanned photographic images and text can be easily combined and laid out exactly as required.

Using templates and wizards you can select a style suitable for a newsletter, poster, web page, advertisement, theatre programme, business card, invitation, calendar or any of hundreds of types of publication. To create a web site, for example, Microsoft Publisher has a Web Site Wizard which enables you to easily add graphics, animation and hyperlinks to other pages or Internet sites. any of hundreds of types of publication. To create a web site, for example, Microsoft Publisher has a Web Site Wizard which enables you to easily add graphics, animation and hyperlinks to other pages or Internet sites.

A typical desktop publishing system includes a desktop computer, a laser printer and software.

Figure 15.1: Documents produced using a Desktop publishing package

Electronic mail (e-mail)

E-mail systems allow you to send memos, letters and files containing data of all types from your computer to any other computer with an e-mail address and a modem, simply by typing the recipient's name and pressing the 'Send' button.

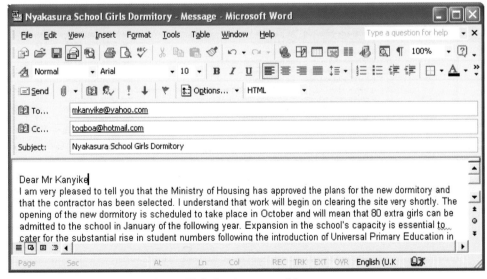

Figure 15.2: Creating an e-mail letter

Advantages of e-mail

E-mail has many advantages over ordinary mail. For example:

• a message can be sent anywhere in the world for the price of a local call;

• it is quicker to type and send because it is less formal - you do not need to type the recipient's address, find and address an envelope, affix the correct postage and go out to post the letter;

• the same message can be sent simultaneously to a group of people;

• the message will arrive in at most a few hours, and can be picked up the next time the recipient looks at their e-mail;

• it is very easy to send a reply to an e-mail as soon as it is received, using a 'reply' button, or forward it to someone else with your comments;

• files, such as graphics, video or software, can be sent as attachments.

Q1: What are some advantages of e-mail over using the telephone?

Disadvantages of e-mail

Viruses and spam e-mails are two of the biggest disadvantages of using e-mail. In 2004 the 'MyDoom' virus became the fastest-spreading virus of all time, replicating itself exponentially to spread millions of copies of itself worldwide. It sends more and more infected messages to every single address found on the hard drive, and although the virus is easy to spot, and a virus checker will disable it automatically, it is infuriating for users to have to sift through dozens or even hundreds of spurious e-mails every day.

A massive 62% of all the e-mail in the world is now spam. Some experts think that spam will bring e-mail to an end by overloading the entire e-mail system by sending out millions of generic, unfilterable messages in a loop, round the clock, for ever. Then we would all have to stop using e-mail.

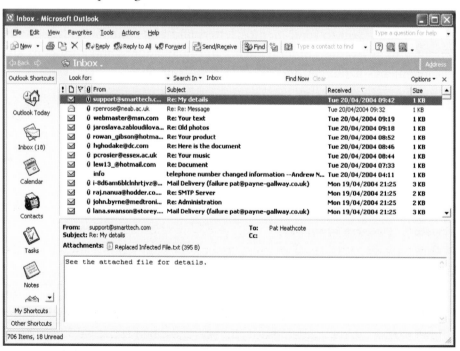

Figure 15.3: Only one of these e-mails does not contain a virus!

Presentation software

Using presentation software such as PowerPoint, professional-looking presentations can quickly and easily be designed. As well as showing text, clip art or scanned pictures and various types of chart, transition effects, sound and animation can easily be added. A transition effect determines how each new screen will appear – it could open like a curtain or blind, come in from left or right, etc. The presentation can then be delivered on a large screen attached to a computer, or by making sheets to be shown using an overhead projector. (Of course in this type of presentation, you can't use sound, animation or transition effects.) Alternatively, the presentation can be automated so that it moves continuously through the slides at a preset rate. This type of presentation is often used in shopping malls and tourist information centres.

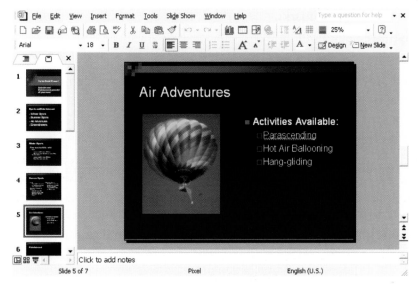

Figure 15.4: Creating a PowerPoint presentation

Exercises

1   A Mathematics teacher using a word-processing package to write a text book needs different features from a school librarian writing reminder letters to pupils who have overdue library books.

State **three** features needed by the Mathematics teacher.

State **three** features needed by the librarian.   (6)

New Question

2   Name the most suitable type of application package to help produce a school magazine.   (1)

State three features that make this package useful for the task.   (3)

New Question

3   Some teachers now communicate with pupils' parents using e-mail.
State **three** reasons why teachers may prefer e-mail to writing a letter or making a telephone call.   (3)

New Question

4   The student union representative in a college wishes to use a presentation package for a presentation she is giving about the year's planned activities. Describe **three** design features she should bear in mind when writing the presentation.   (3)

New Question

Chapter 16 – Spreadsheets

Spreadsheet software is used by people who work with numbers: accountants, bank and building society employees, engineers and financial planners. The user enters the data and the formulae to be used in manipulating the data, and the program calculates the results. If any numbers are changed, the software automatically recalculates the results. One of the most useful features of a spreadsheet is its ability to perform **'What If'** calculations: "What if we produce 30% more widgets and wages increase by 10% – how much will we have to charge in order to show a profit?" Spreadsheets are therefore often used in **planning and budgeting,** but are also widely used by anyone working with figures – for example, keeping a set of students' marks.

Spreadsheet features

Using spreadsheet facilities a user can:

- format cells, rows and columns, specifying for example, the alignment of text, number of decimal places, height and width of cell;

- merge cells;

- enter formulae referencing other cells;

- copy cell contents to other locations, with automatic adjustment of formulae from say B9 to C9, D9 etc.

- insert, move or delete rows and columns;

- use functions such as sum, average, round, trunc, max, min in formulae;

- use a lookup table;

- determine the effect of several different hypothetical changes of data – this facility is termed a 'what-if' calculation;

- create scenarios to examine the effects of changing a number of variables;

- create a simple database and sort or query the data to produce a report of, say, all females earning over £20,000 for a list of employees;

- write macros to automate common procedures;

- create templates – spreadsheets with formats and formulae already entered, into which new figures may be inserted;

- create 'multi-dimensional' spreadsheets using several sheets, and copy data from one sheet to another;

- create many different types of charts and graphs (see Figure 16.6).

Worked Example (using MS Excel)

Set up a spreadsheet as follows:

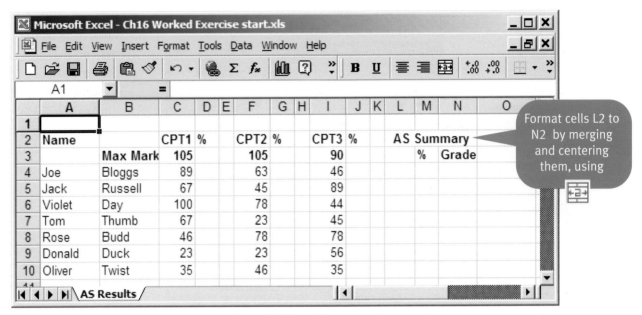

Figure 16.1: Worked Example part 1

Now insert formulae as follows:

Column L: Add the marks gained for each of the three modules.

Type **=C3+F3+I3** into cell L3 and copy it into cells L4 to L10 by filling down.

In cell L10 you should have the formula **=C10+F10+I10**.

Column D: Calculate the marks gained as a percentage of the maximum marks (the number in cell C3). If you precede a column or a row name with $ that makes the reference absolute. This means it will always refer to that specific row/column when you copy the formula into another cell. For example, $C$3 is an **absolute cell reference** of cell C3 and when used in a formula will not change when filled down or across.

In cell D4 enter **=TRUNC(C4/$C$3*100)**

Then fill down to the last row.

In D10 you should have **=TRUNC(C10/$C$3*100)**

Note that the absolute cell reference $C$3 does not change as the formula is copied down. However, the **relative cell reference** C4 changes with each row, and becomes C10 in row 10. TRUNC is a function that returns an integer value as a result, as we are not interested in fractional percentages here. You could have formatted the cells to display zero decimal places instead.

Columns G, J and M: Now complete the formulae in a similar manner to column D.

Columns E, H, K and N will display the grade, which will be looked up from a lookup table.

Set up the grade table as shown below:

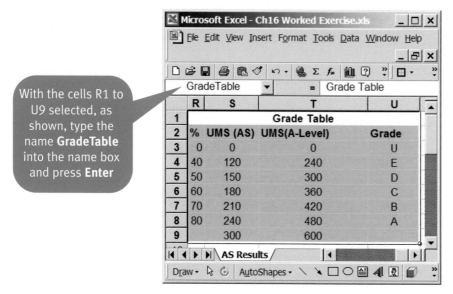

Figure 16.2: Grade Look up Table

2-16

In cell E4 type **=VLOOKUP(D4,GradeTable,4)**

You can fill this formula down to row 10.

Complete equivalent formulae for columns H, K and N.

Explanation of function VLOOKUP(LookupValue, TableArray, ColIndexNum, RangeLookup):

LookupValue is the value to be found in the first column of the array.

TableArray is the table in which data is looked up. (Note the values in the first column must be in ascending order). Use a reference to a range or a range name.

ColIndexNum is the column number in *TableArray* from which the matching value must be returned.

RangeLookup is a logical value that specifies whether you want VLOOKUP to find an exact match or an approximate match. If TRUE is omitted, an approximate match is returned. In other words, if an exact match is not found, the next largest value that is less than **lookup_value** is returned. If FALSE is omitted, VLOOKUP will find an exact match. If one is not found, the error value **#N/A** is returned.

Column O will display the message **Retake** if the AS grade was **U**.

In cell O4 enter the formula **=IF(N4="U","Retake","")**.

Fill this formula down to cell O10.

Use of the Formula Palette to help in the use of a new function:

When you create a formula that contains a function, the Formula Palette helps you enter worksheet functions. As you enter a function into the formula, the Formula Palette displays the name of the function, each of its arguments, a description of the function and each argument, the current result of the function, and the current result of the entire formula.

To display the Formula Palette, click **Edit Formula** in the formula bar.

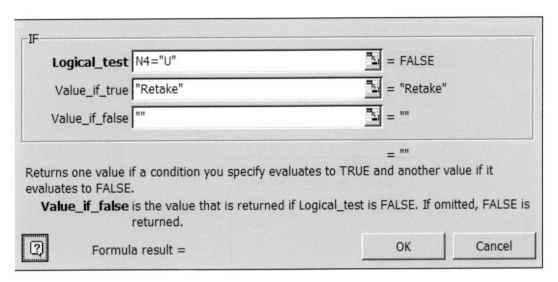

Figure 16.3: Formula Palette

Your spreadsheet should now look like this:

	A	B	C	D	E	F	G	H	I	J	K	L	M	N	O
1															
2	Name		CPT1	%		CPT2	%		CPT3	%		AS Summary			
3		Max Mark	105			105			90			300	%	Grade	
4	Joe	Bloggs	89	84	A	63	60	C	46	51	D	198	66	C	
5	Jack	Russell	67	63	C	45	42	E	89	98	A	201	67	C	
6	Violet	Day	100	95	A	78	74	B	44	48	E	222	74	B	
7	Tom	Thumb	67	63	C	23	21	U	45	50	D	135	45	E	
8	Rose	Budd	46	43	E	78	74	B	78	86	A	202	67	C	
9	Donald	Duck	23	21	U	23	21	U	56	62	C	102	34	U	Retake
10	Oliver	Twist	35	33	U	46	43	E	35	38	U	116	38	U	Retake

Figure 16.4: Worked Example part 2

Set up a Grade Distribution table (Figure 16.5 below), which counts the number of each AS grade and displays the summary.

Use the COUNTIF function as shown in the formula bar for cell T13. Enter similar formulae into cells T14 to T18. COUNTIF will return the number of occurrences of the second argument found in the range given in the first argument.

Cell T19 adds up the number of students at each grade in that column. Use the formula **=SUM(T13:T18)**.

Note we refer to T13:T18 as a range.

2-16

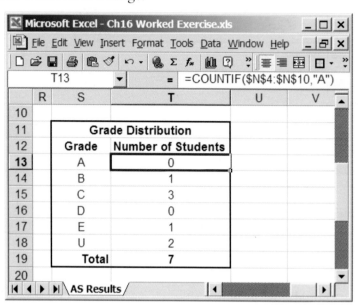

Figure 16.5: Grade Distribution table

Now use the Chart Wizard to make a simple bar chart. Select the chart type *Column*. Use the data range S11:T18 and fill in the appropriate labels for heading, x-axis and y-axis to achieve the following:

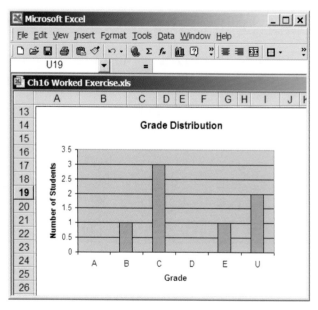

Figure 16.6: A chart created from the Grade Distribution table

You can record macros and assign them to buttons, so frequently performed actions can be executed at the click of a button. Record two macros *SortBySurname* and *SortByGrade* using the following technique:

Use the **Tools, Macro, Record New Macro** menu option. Give your macro a name. As soon as the Record Macro window closes, all your actions are recorded.

When you finish recording press the **Stop** button

Make sure the **Relative Reference** button is deselected

Select the range A4:O10 and choose the menu option **Tools, Sort...**

Choose the relevant columns to order by and then stop the recorder.

From the Forms toolbar you can use the button tool to place two buttons on your form and assign one of your macros to each button.

Test that your buttons work as expected.

2-16

You should practise your spreadsheet skills. You could implement the spreadsheets given in the Exercises on the next few pages.

Exercises

1 The following is an extract from a spreadsheet that shows how many supermarket loyalty points a customer would earn by spending different amounts of money on supermarket goods. The supermarket is currently operating a bonus scheme which adds a fixed percentage of points to the points earned. The fixed percentage used is 10%.

	B	C	D	E	F	G
1	Bonus %	10		Pounds Spent	Points Earned Without Bonus	Points Earned With Bonus
2	Points earned per pound if £10.00 or less spent	2				
3	Points earned per pound when more than £10 but not more than £30.00 spent	3				
4	Points earned per pound if more than £30.00 spent	4				
5				5	10	11
6				15	45	50
7				30	90	99
8				60	240	264
9				90	360	396
				:	:	:
				:	:	:
20				240	960	1056
21				270	1080	1188
22				300	1200	1320

(a) The formula in G5 is F5*(1 + $C$1/100) where $ denotes absolute cell referencing. What is the formula in cell G8? (3)

(b) The value in cell G6 is calculated from 45 x (1 + 10/100) which equals 49.5. However, the value displayed in cell G6 is 50. How might this happen? (1)

(c) Write the formula that was entered in F5 and copied to cells F6 to F22. Your formula should perform an automatic recalculation if the value in C2, or the value in C3, or the value in C4, is changed. (6)

AQA CPT2 Qu 8 May 2002

2 (a) The following is an extract from a spreadsheet which calculates Value Added Tax (VAT) on goods sold by mail-order catalogue. In column E the digit 1 means that VAT is charged at the rate stored in cell I2; the digit 0 means VAT is zero.

	C	D	E	F	G	H	I
1	Catalogue No	Price excluding VAT	VAT rating	VAT	Price including VAT	Postage	VAT rate %
2						£10.00	17.5
3							
4	30	53	1	9.28	62.28	£4.00	
5	45		1				
6	61		0				
:	:		:				
:	:		:				
520	746		1				
521	768		0				
522	777		1				

   (i) When this spreadsheet was being developed the formula I2 x D4 x E4/100 was placed in F4. Why will this formula not work as desired without further editing when copied down into any of the cells in column F below F4? How should it be changed?   (2)

   (ii) The value in cell F4 is calculated from 17.5 x 53 x 1/100 which equals 9.275 to three decimal places. However, the value displayed in cell F4 is 9.28. Why might this happen?   (1)

   (b) Postage is in one of two bands: £2 if the price excluding VAT is less than £10.00, £4 otherwise. Write the formula for cell H4. The postage band boundary price is held in cell H2. Your formula should perform an automatic recalculation if the value in H2 is changed.   (3)

AQA CPT2 Qu 7 January 2002

3 (a) One common business application package is the spreadsheet.
Give two different reasons why a spreadsheet package is particularly useful as a decision making tool. (2)

A spreadsheet is used to record examination scores and grades as follows:

	A Surname	B Percentage	C Grade	D
1	**Surname**	**Percentage**	**Grade**	
2				
3	Bloggs	65	P	
4	Boon	39		
5	Deedes	70		
6				
7				40
8				70

(b) The formula in C3, IF($B3<$D$7, "F", IF($B3<$D$8, "P", "M")) is copied to cells C4 to C5. The symbol $ indicates absolute addressing.
(i) Write the format of the formula in Cell C4. (1)
(ii) After the formula is copied, what is displayed in the cells C4 and C5? (2)

(c) The value in cell D7 is changed to 30. What effect, if any, will this change have on any other cell? (1)

AQA CPT2 Qu 7 June 2003

4 The part of a spreadsheet given below holds a table of product details.

	A	B	C	D
1			Mark up	1.2
2				
3	Product	Part Number	Cost Price	Selling Price
4	Bar Code Reader 1000	BCR123	105	
5	CD ROM Drive 12 speed	CD1286	210	
6	Colour Scanner 24/600	CS24600	450	
7	Hard Disk 1.2 Gb external	HD12	300	
8	Ink Jet printer 100	IP100	120	
9	Keyboard II	KB185	43	
10	LaserWriter 4040	LW4040	675	
11	Monitor 15" Colour	M1536	185	
12	Midi Interface	M1267	56	
13	Mouse plus	MP34	20	
14	Performance Computer 456	PC456	645	
15				

The formula in cell D4 is: =C4 * $D$1 (where the d1 is an absolute reference to cell D1). This formula is to be replicated down the column.

(a) (i) Briefly describe how to replicate the formula in D4 down the column to row 14. (2)
(ii) Why is it necessary to have the cell D1 as an absolute reference? (1)

(b) A different part of the spreadsheet obtains the selling price for any given part number from this table using a lookup function. State the parameters needed by such a lookup function. (3)

NEAB CP04 Qu 8 1998

Chapter 17 – Records and Files

Hierarchy of data

An effective information system provides users with timely, accurate and relevant information. This information is stored in computer files, which need to be suitably organised and properly maintained so that users can easily access the information they need.

We'll look at the way that data is represented and structured in a computer, starting with the very lowest level.

BIT All data is stored in a computer's memory or storage devices in the form of binary digits or **bits**. A bit can be either 'ON' or 'OFF' representing 1 or 0.

BYTE Bits are grouped together, with a group of 8 bits forming a **byte**. One byte can represent one character or, in different contexts, other data such as a sound, part of a picture, etc.

There are different codes used for representing characters, one of the most common being ASCII (American Standard Code for Information Interchange). Using 8 bits it is possible to represent 256 (2^8) different characters.

FIELD Characters are grouped together to form **fields**. Data held about a person, for example, may be split into many fields including ID Number, Surname, Initials, Title, Street, Village, Town, County, Postcode, Date of Birth, Credit Limit and so on.

RECORD All the information about one person or item is held in a **record**.

ID Number:	432768
Surname:	King
Initials:	DF
Title:	Mr
Street:	2 Burghley Crescent
Town:	Ipswich
County:	Suffolk
Post code:	IP3 5WT
Date of Birth:	14/8/78
Credit Limit:	£250

FILE A **file** is defined as a collection of records. A stock file will contain a record for each item of stock, a payroll file a record for each employee and so on.

DATABASE A **database** may consist of many different files, linked in such a way that information can be retrieved from several files simultaneously. There are many different ways of organising data in a database, and many different database software products for use on all types of computer from micros to mainframes.

Text and non-text files

The term **file** can be used in a broader sense to mean a data structure which could hold, for example:

- a source code program written in a high-level language;
- a binary file containing executable code;
- a bitmapped graphics file;
- a word processed letter;
- an ASCII text file.

Text file: a file containing characters organised on a line-by-line basis.
Examples of text files: HTML document, program source code, or a basic text editor file such as a MS Notepad file.

Non-text file: content of file cannot be displayed sensibly in a text editor because it contains binary codes of nonprintable characters.
Examples: pictures, executable files.

For the rest of this chapter, the word **file** will be used in the sense of a **collection of records** such as a file of employees containing one record for each employee.

Record: a set of related data fields.

File: a collection of records.

Primary key

Each individual record in a file needs to be given a unique identifier, and this is termed the **primary key**. It needs to be carefully chosen so that there is no possibility of two people or items having the same primary key; **Surname**, for example, is no use as an identifier. The primary key sometimes consists of more than one field: for example several stores in a national chain may each have a store number, and each store may have Departments 1, 2, 3 etc. To identify a particular department in a particular store, the primary key would be composed of both **Store number** and **Department number**.

Primary key: a unique field of a record used to identify the record.

Q1: What would be a suitable primary key for:
a book in a bookshop?
a book in a library?
a hospital patient?
a car owned by a car-hire firm?

Secondary (alternate) key

Other fields in a record may be defined as **secondary keys**, also known as **alternate** keys. These fields are not unique to each record, but may be used to quickly locate a group of records. For example, the field **Department** may be defined as a secondary key on an Employee file.

Secondary (alternate) key: a field that may not be unique, but may be used to locate a group of records.

Fixed and variable length records

In some circumstances records in a file may not all be the same length. **Variable length records** may be used when either:

- the number of characters in any field varies between records;
- records have a varying number of fields.

A variable length record has to have some way of showing where each field ends, and where the record ends, in order that it can be processed. There are two ways of doing this:

- use a special end-of-field character at the end of each field, and an end-of-record marker at the end of the record, as shown below. (* is used as the end-of-field marker, and # is used as the end-of-record marker in this example.)

```
SH12345*laser printer*HP laserjet2100*750.00*999.99*7#
MH452*colour flatbed scanner*Microtek Scanmaker II*150.00*289.00*3#
```

- use a character count at the beginning of each field, and an end-of-record marker. In the implementation shown below, the byte holding the count is included in the number of characters for the field, and a real number is assumed to occupy 4 bytes, an integer 2 bytes. (You could also have a character count for the entire record instead of the end-of-record marker.)

```
8SH1234514laser printer15HP Laserjet21005270.005399.9937#
6MH45223colour flatbed scanner22Microtek Scanmaker II5150.005289.0033#
```

Advantages and disadvantages of variable length records

The advantages of variable length records are:

- less space is wasted on the storage medium;
- it enables as many fields as necessary to be held on a particular record, for example a field for each subject taken by an A Level student;
- no truncation of data occurs;
- it may reduce the time taken to read a file because the records are more tightly packed.

The disadvantages are:

- the processing required to separate out the fields is more complex;
- records cannot be updated in situ;
- it is harder to estimate file sizes accurately when a new system is being designed.

Estimating file size

In a file of fixed length records, you can estimate the file size by multiplying the number of bytes in each record by the number of records. You need to know how many bytes are in each field, and you need to add a few extra bytes for each **block** of records. Data is physically held on disk or tape in blocks of say 512 bytes. If the record length is 80 bytes, there will be a maximum of 6 records per block. Therefore 1000 records would occupy 1000/6 blocks, each of $^1/2$Kb. Therefore the file will occupy 167/2 Kb, i.e. approximately 84Kb.

If the records are 102 bytes long, 5 records would probably not fit into a block of 512 bytes because a few bytes are required in each block for information about record size etc. However if you were asked to estimate file size in an exam question, this would be made very clear.

2-17

Q2: Estimate the number of bytes used by a file of 800 records each of 120 bytes. You can assume that 4 records fit into each block of 512 bytes.

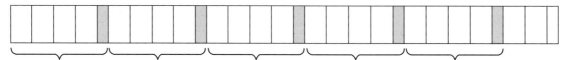

Each block contains 4 records of 120 bytes with some space left over

Exercises

1 A file of 80 records has the following record structure.

ProductID, ProductDescription, QuantityInStock

ProductID is a four-byte integer, ProductDescription is a fifty-six byte fixed length string,

QuantityInStock is a four-byte integer.

(a) What is the size of this file in bytes? Show your working. (2)

(b) Suggest a suitable primary key for this file. Justify your choice. (2)

(c) On closer examination, it is found that 30% of the file storage space is wasted.

   (i) Explain why this may occur with the current record structure. (1)

   (ii) How could the record structure be changed whilst retaining three-fields per record so that this problem is overcome? (1)

   (iii) Give **one** disadvantage of the restructured solution. (1)

AQA CPT2 Qu 2 May 2002

2 Distinguish between the terms **primary key** and **secondary key** as applied to files and give an example of each from within an employee master file. (4)

New Question

3 In a Pascal program the record structure of a file is declared in the following way:

```
type
  TStudent = record
    FirstName: String[15];
    Surname: String[25];
    DepositPaid: Currency;
    DateOfBirth: TDateTime;
  end; {of TStudent}
var StudentFile : File of TStudent;
```

Pascal uses 8 bytes to store the data types **Currency** and **TdateTime**.

If **StudentFile** is to hold 300 records, how many bytes will the file take up? (3)

New Question

Chapter 18 – Serial and Sequential Files

Master and transaction files

In the last chapter a **file** was defined as a collection of **records**. Most large companies have hundreds or even thousands of files that store data pertaining to the business. Some of the files will be **transaction files** and some will be **master files.**

Transaction files contain details of all transactions that have occurred in the last period. A period may be the time that has elapsed since business started that day, or it may be a day, a week, a month or more. For example a sales transaction file may contain details of all sales made that day. Once the data has been processed it can be discarded (although the files may be kept as backup copies for a while).

Transaction file: a collection of records used in batch processing to update a master file.

Master files are permanent files kept up-to-date by applying the transactions that occur during the operation of the business. They contain generally two basic types of data:

- Data of a more or less permanent nature such as, on a payroll file, name, address, rate of pay etc.
- Data which will change every time transactions are applied to the file – for example, gross pay to date, tax paid to date, etc.

Master file: permanent file of data, which is a principal source of information for a job.

> **Q1:** A file of student records is to be kept holding student number, personal details such as name and address, course number and course grade (A–F).
>
> Design a record structure for the file, under the following headings:
>
> **Field description**   **Field length**   **Field type (character or numeric)**

File organisation

Files stored on magnetic media can be organised in a number of ways, just as in a manual system. There are advantages and disadvantages to each type of file organisation, and the method chosen will depend on several factors such as:

- how the file is to be used;
- how many records are processed each time the file is updated;
- whether individual records need to be quickly accessible.

Types of file organisation

- serial;
- sequential;
- indexed sequential; *(Note: not required for the AQA syllabus)*
- direct access (random).

2-18

Serial file organisation

The records on a serial file are not in any particular sequence, and so this type of organisation would not be used for a master file as there would be no way to find a particular record except by reading through the whole file, starting at the beginning, until the right record was located. Serial files are used as temporary files to store transaction data. Records are stored in the order in which they are received, with new records added to the end of the file.

Serial file: a collection of records stored one after another, in no particular sequence.

Figure 18.1: A serial file

Sequential file organisation

As with serial organisation, records are stored one after the other, but in a sequential file the records are sorted into **key sequence**. Files that are stored on tape are **always** either serial or sequential, as it is impossible to write records to a tape in any way except one after the other. From the computer's point of view there is essentially no difference between a serial and a sequential file. In both cases, in order to find a particular record, each record must be read, starting from the beginning of the file, until the required record is located. However, when the whole file has to be processed (for example a payroll file prior to payday) sequential processing is fast and efficient.

Sequential file: collection of records stored one after another, in key sequence.

Figure 18.2: A sequential file

2-18

Adding and deleting records on a serial file

Deleting a record is more complex. It is easy to understand the problem if you imagine the file is held on magnetic tape, and understand that in any particular program run you can **either** read from the tape **or** write to the tape. To find the record to be deleted, the computer has to read the tape from the beginning; but once it has found it, it cannot back up and 'wipe' just that portion of the tape occupied by the record, leaving a blank space. The technique therefore is to create a brand new tape, copying over all the records up to the one to be deleted, leaving that one off the new tape, and then copying over all the rest of the records.

Adding and deleting records on a sequential file

With a **sequential** file, all the records on the tape (or disk) are in order, perhaps of employee number, so just adding a new record on the end is no good at all. Of course the records could then be sorted but sorting is a very time-consuming process. The best and 'correct' way is to make a new copy of the file, copying over all records until the new one can be written in its proper place, and then copying over the rest of the records. It's exactly as if you had just made a list on a nice clean sheet of paper of all the students in the class in order of surname, and then discovered you had left out Carter, A.N. The only way to end up with a perfect list is to copy it out again, remembering to include Carter this time.

Deleting a record is exactly the same as for serial organisation. The file is copied to a new disk or tape, leaving out the record to be deleted.

Algorithms to add a new record to:

Serial File	Sequential File
Open file	Open old file for reading
Append record to	Open new file for writing
end of file	Starting from beginning of old file
	Repeat
	Read next record (call it current record)
	If current record key > new record key
	then write new record to new file
	EndIf
	Write current record to new file
	Until new record inserted or End Of File (old)
	If new record not yet inserted,
	Then write new record to new file
	EndIf
	If not End Of File (old) then
	Repeat
	Read next record (call it current record)
	Write current record to new file
	Until End Of File (old)
	Endif

Algorithm to delete a record from a Serial or Sequential File:

```
Open old file for reading
Open new file for writing
Starting from beginning of old file
Repeat
        Read next record (call it current record)
        If current record key <> key of record to be deleted
                then write record to the new file
        EndIf
Until End Of File
```

The role of various files in a computer system

All data processing systems except the most trivial will need to store data in files. These files can be categorised as:

- master files,
- transaction files (sometimes called **movement** files) **or**
- reference files.

Master and transaction files were defined at the beginning of this chapter. A **reference file** is a file that contains data used by a program during processing. For example, in a payroll system:

- the **master file** contains details on each employee
- the **transaction file** contains details of the hours worked, holiday and sick days etc. last period
- the **reference file** contains data on tax bands, union rates, etc.

> **Q2:** In an electricity billing system, briefly outline the contents of the customer master file, the transaction file and a reference file.

> **Q3:** Why not hold the data in the reference file either on the customer master file or within the program which calculates the customers' bills?

Operations on files

The following operations are commonly carried out on files:

- Interrogating/referencing
- Updating.

Interrogating or referencing files

When a file is interrogated or referenced it is first searched to find a record with a particular **key**, and that record is then displayed on a screen, printed out or used in further processing, without itself being altered in any way.

How the record is located will depend entirely on how the file is organised.

Algorithms to search for a record with a particular key:

Serial File	Sequential File
Open file	Open file
Start from beginning of file	Start from beginning of file
Repeat	Repeat
Read next record	Read next record
Test for a match	Test for match
Until End Of File OR match made	Until record matches wanted record OR key of this record > key of wanted record (i.e. record does not exist)

Note the difference between the two algorithms. Which one will take longer to find out that the record searched for does not exist?

Q4: A bicycle shop selling bicycles and spare parts has a computerised stock control system so that the salespersons can see whether any item is in stock via a terminal in the shop. What file organisation would you recommend for the master file of all stock items? Justify your answer.

2-18

Updating files

A master file is **updated** when one or more records are altered, by applying a transaction, or a file of transactions, to it. First of all the correct record has to be located and read into memory, then updated in memory, and written back to the master file.

Once again, the method of doing this will depend on the file organisation.

If the master file is sequentially organised, it is impossible to read a record into memory, update it and then write it back to the same location.

The method used to update a sequential file was developed when virtually all master files were stored on magnetic tape (or even on punched cards or paper tape!). Although disks are often used nowadays to store sequential files, the same method is still used because it is very efficient under certain circumstances.

The method is called **'updating by copying'** and it requires the transaction file to be sorted in the same order as the master file, so that the updating can be done in one pass.

The steps are as follows:

1 A record is read from the master file into main memory

2 A record is read from the transaction file into main memory

3 The record keys from each file are compared. If no updating is required to the master file record currently in main memory (the master key is less than the transaction key) the master record is copied from main memory to a **new master file** on a different tape or area of disk, and another master file record is read into main memory, overwriting the previous one. This step is then repeated.

4 If there **is** a transaction for the master record currently in main memory, the record is updated. It will be retained in main memory in case there are any more transactions that apply to it. Steps 2–4 are then repeated.

Algorithm to update a sequential master file:

```
Open master file for reading
Open transaction file for reading
Open new master file for writing
Repeat
      Read next transaction record
      While master record key < transaction record key
          Write master record to new master file
              Read next master record
      EndWhile
      Update record
Until End Of File (transaction)
While Not End Of File (master)
      Read next master record
      Write master record to new master file
EndWhile
```

After a sequential file has been updated, two versions or **generations** of the master file exist; the **old master file**, still in the same state it was in prior to the update, and the **new master file** just created. The next time the file is updated, a third version of the master file will be created, and so on.

It is obviously not necessary to keep dozens of out-of-date master files, and the general practice is to keep three generations, called **grandfather**, **father** and **son** for obvious reasons, and then reuse the tapes or disk space for the next update that takes place.

The following diagram illustrates the process.

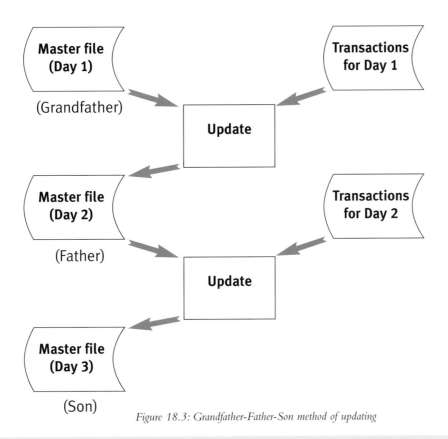

Figure 18.3: Grandfather-Father-Son method of updating

Q5: How would you **change** a record on a sequential file held on magnetic tape? (e.g. if you had got Carter's initials wrong?)

Exercises

1   A stock master file is updated by a transaction file using sequential file access. A purpose of the stock master file is to ensure that the levels of stock will meet demand.

   (a)   (i) Give **four** essential fields for the stock master file.   (4)

        (ii) Give **three** essential fields for the transaction file.   (3)

   (b)   Why should the transaction file be sorted, and in what order, prior to updating the master file?   (2)

   AQA CPT2 Qu 8 January 2001

2   A new copy of a sequentially organised master file is made whenever records are added.

   (a)   A program is written to add a single record to this master file. List the processing steps for this program that generate an amended copy of the master file.   (5)

   (b)   When many records need to be inserted, these records are stored in a transaction file. The program is modified so that it reads the transaction records from the transaction file.

        (i) What file organisation should be used for this transaction file?   (1)

        (ii) In what order should the transaction records be stored in the transaction file? Justify your answer.   (2)

   AQA CPT2 Qu 9 May 2002

2-18

Chapter 19 – Direct Access Files

Direct access files

A direct access file (also called a **hash**, **random** or **relative** file) has records that are stored and retrieved according to either their disk address or their relative position within the file. This means that the program which stores and retrieves the records has first to specify the address of the record in the file.

This is done by means of an **algorithm** or formula, which transforms the record key into an address at which the record is stored. In the simplest case, record number 1 will be stored in block 1, record number 2 in block 2 and so on. This is called **relative** file addressing, because each record is stored at a location given by its key, relative to the start of the file.

More often, however, record keys do not lend themselves to such simple treatment. If for example we have about 1000 records to store, and each record key is 5 digits long, it would be a waste of space to allow 99999 blocks in which to store records. Therefore, a **hashing algorithm** is used to translate the key into an address.

Direct access file: a collection of records, where each record is stored at a disk address, calculated from the record's primary key.

One hashing method is the division/remainder method. Using this method, the key of the record is divided by the total number of addresses on the file, and the remainder is taken as the address of the record.

For example, the address of record number 75481 would be calculated as follows:

$75481/1000 = 75$ remainder 481.   Address = 481.

> **Q1:** Using this hashing algorithm, calculate the addresses of records with keys 00067, 00500, 35648.

Synonyms

This method of file organization presents a problem: however cunning the hashing algorithm, synonyms are bound to occur, when two record keys generate the same address. This is also known as a collision. One method of resolving synonyms is to place the record that caused the collision into the next available free space. When the highest address is reached, the next record can be stored at address 0 (known as wrap round). Another technique is to have a separate overflow area and leave a tag in the original location to indicate where to look next.

Properties of a good hashing algorithm

A hashing algorithm needs to be chosen so that it gives a good spread of records. This will partly depend on the properties of the record keys. Sometimes, to obtain a better spread of record addresses, a prime number close to the number of records to be stored on the file is chosen and the key of the record is divided by this number to obtain the remainder. For example, on the file of 1000 records discussed above, you could try dividing the keys by the prime number 997 instead of 1000 before taking the remainder. Hashing algorithms are also known as randomizing functions.

The algorithm should be chosen so that:

- It can generate any of the available addresses on the file;
- It is fast to calculate;
- It minimises 'collisions' (synonyms).

2-19

Adding new records to a direct access file

To add a new record to a direct access file, its address first has to be calculated by applying the hashing algorithm. If that address is already full, the record can be put in the next available free space.

Example:

Assume we have a file of 1000 records and use wrap round with the hashing algorithm described earlier: **(address = key MOD 1000)**. Records with the following keys, added in the given order, will be stored as follows:

12345	→	stored at address 345
17998	→	stored at address 998
56998	→	stored at address 999 because 998 is already full
35345	→	stored at address 346 because 345 is already full
88000	→	stored at address 000
54999	→	stored at address 001 because 999 and 000 are already full

When searching for a record, the search has to continue until either the record is found or a blank space is encountered.

Adding new records to a direct access file

This poses a problem for deleting records. If the record 17998 in the example above, were subsequently deleted, 56998 would not be found as its proper address 998 would be empty. The way round this problem is to leave the deleted record in place, and to set a flag labelling it as deleted. In other words, although *logically* deleted, the record is still *physically* present. A **'flag'** is simply an extra variable, e.g. a Boolean variable, stored with each record as an extra field. When the file is initialised and contains no records, the flag in each address can be set to 0, meaning that the record position is empty. When a record is written to an address, the flag is set to 1. When the record is deleted, the only change made to the record is to set the flag back to 0. When looking for a particular record, if the record key is found but it has a flag of 0, it is considered to be logically 'not there'. It's as though it's been crossed out, so it is to be ignored, but we can still see that there was a record there at one time. This means the space can be reused if a new record with a key hashing to this address is to be added to the file but, because the space is not actually empty, the search for a record that may have overflowed to the next address will still continue until either the record is found or an empty space is encountered.

Updating by overlay

If the file to be updated is indexed sequential or random, it is possible to access a record directly, read it into memory, update it, and write it back to its original location. This is called **updating by overlay**, **updating in place** or **updating in situ** if you are a Latin speaker. It is possible to do this because, unlike in sequential file processing, the record is accessed by means of its address on the file and so can be written back to the same address.

File maintenance

File maintenance is similar to file updating, but refers to the updating of the more permanent fields on each record such as in a stock file, for example, the description of the item, price, location in warehouse, etc. It also involves adding new records to the file and deleting records for items that are no longer held.

Once again, depending on the file organisation, either the grandfather-father-son technique will be used, or, if the file is direct access, **updating by overlay** may be used.

2-19

File access methods

How a file is **organised** determines how it can be **accessed**:

- a sequential file can only be accessed sequentially;

- a direct access file would normally only be accessed directly (it *could* be accessed serially but the records would not be in any particular sequence so this would be unusual);

Criteria for use of sequential and direct access files

The choice of file organization (or more likely today, database design) is one of the most important decisions made by the system designer. A number of questions needs to be answered, including:

- Must the user have immediate access to the data, with a response time of no more than a few seconds?

- Must the information be completely up to date, or will last night's or last week's information be sufficient?

- Can requests for information be batched, sequenced and processed all together?

- Are reports needed in a particular sequence?

- What is the most suitable storage medium for the volume of data involved?

- What will happen if the information on the files is lost or destroyed?

In addition two further factors need to be considered; **hit rate** and **volatility**.

2-19

Hit rate

Hit rate measures the proportion of records being accessed on any one run. It is calculated by dividing the number of records accessed by the total number of records on the file, and expressed as a percentage.

For example, on a payroll run if 190 out of 200 employees were to be paid, the hit rate would be 95%. In a system for processing car insurance renewals in weekly batches, the hit rate would be about 2% if renewals were spread more or less evenly through the year.

Sequential updating is inefficient with a low hit rate; direct access would be better.

Use of serial files

Serial files are normally only used as transaction files, recording data in the order in which events take place; for example, sales in a shop, customers taking cash from a cash machine, orders arriving at a mail order company. The transactions may be batched and the master files updated at a later time, or alternatively in a real-time system, the files may be updated straight away but the transaction file is kept for record-keeping purposes. It will also be used in the event of a disaster like a disk head crash, to restore the master file from the previous night's backup.

Use of sequential files

Sequential files are used as master files for high hit rate applications such as payroll. The main bulk of processing time is taken up with the weekly or monthly payroll, when every employee's record needs to be accessed and the year-to-date fields brought up to date, and sequential organisation is fast and efficient. It is not efficient when only a few records need to be accessed; for example if an employee changes address and the record needs to be updated, since the entire file has to be read and copied over to a new master file. However as this happens relatively infrequently it still makes sense to use a sequential file organisation.

Use of direct access files

Direct access files are used in situations where extremely fast access to individual records is required. To find a record, the hashing algorithm is applied to the record key and the record address immediately found, so no time is wasted looking up various levels of index. In a network system, user ids and passwords could be stored on a direct access file; the user id would be the key field from which the address is calculated, and the record would hold the password (encrypted for security reasons) and other information on access rights. Direct access file organisation might also be used in an airline booking system, where thousands of bookings are made every day for each airline from terminals all over the country. A fast response time to the desired record is crucial here. Note that direct access file organisation is not suitable if reports are going to be needed in key sequence, as the records are scattered 'at random' around the file.

Generating a direct access file from a sequential file

If the records in a sequential file need to be accessed quickly, it may be necessary to convert the file into a direct access file. A new file is generated using the following algorithm:

Algorithm

Generate new file with sufficient empty records

Work from beginning of sequential file

Repeat

      Read next record

      Hash the primary key to generate address

      Insert record at this position in new file

Until End Of File

2-19

Exercises

1 A *text file* of words is read by a program which creates a *non-text serial file*.

  (a) What is meant by:

    (i) a text file; (1)

    (ii) a non-text file; (1)

    (iii) a serial file? (1)

  (b) The serial file is processed by a program which removes duplicate words and writes the results to a *sequential file* with a *variable length record structure*.

    What is meant by:

    (i) a sequential file; (1)

    (ii) a variable length record structure? (1)

  (c) State **one** advantage and **one** disadvantage of variable length records over fixed length records. (2)

  (d) A program is written which searches the sequential file for a match with a given word that might be recorded in the file. List the steps for this process. (3)

(e) For a very large sequential file looking up words can be quite slow. It is suggested that look up time can be reduced by searching a different file in which the words have been stored according to a hashing algorithm.

List the steps to generate this new file from the sequential file (do not describe the details of any particular hashing algorithm). (4)

AQA CPT2 Qu 8 May 2001

2 The construction of an electronic English–French dictionary is trialled by creating a simpler version using one hundred English–French word pairs stored line-by-line in a text file, file A.

(a) (i) What is a text file? (1)

(ii) Name the most suitable type of software for a typist to use to create the contents of file A. (1)

(iii) What hardware could have been used to enter the word pairs, printed on paper, **directly** into the computer system? (1)

(b) A computer program reads word pairs, one line at a time, from file A.

It stores each word pair in a sequentially organised file of records, file B, by English word.

(i) State **two** characteristics of a sequentially organised file. (2)

(ii) Give the field names for **two** essential fields of file B. (2)

(c) File B is read sequentially and its records are stored in file C, on a direct access medium, by applying the following hashing function to each English word in file B.

(Sum of ASCII codes of all letters in the English word) Mod 150

For example, applying the hashing function to the word BAD using ASCII codes

A = 65, B = 66, D = 68 produces

(66 + 65 + 68) Mod 150 = 49

(Mod gives the remainder after integer division)

File C consists of one hundred and fifty initially empty records.

(i) What use is made of the number produced by the hashing function when storing each word-pair record in file C? (1)

(ii) Why is Mod 150 used? (1)

(iii) Give **two** properties that this hashing function should have. (2)

(d) Using only file C, list the main steps that a computer program must follow to display on a VDU the French equivalent of an English word entered at the keyboard. Your solution must take account of the case when the English–French word pair is **not** present in file C. (5)

AQA CPT2 Qu 8 January 2003

2-19

Chapter 20 – File Security Methods

Threats to information systems

Computer-based information systems are vulnerable to crime and abuse, natural disaster and human error. In this chapter we'll look at some of the ways that an organisation can protect the **security** of data from theft or destruction.

Data security

Maintaining data security means keeping data safe from the various hazards to which it may be subjected. These include:

- natural hazards such as fire, floods, hurricanes or earthquakes;

- deliberate corruption or destruction of data by malicious or terrorist acts;

- illegal access to data by 'hackers';

- accidental destruction of data by hardware failure or program or operator error.

Data Security: Protection against loss, corruption of, or unauthorised access to data.

Q1: Suggest measures to minimize the danger of loss of data from natural hazards.

Keeping data secure from fraudulent use or malicious damage

Data may be at risk not only from outside 'hackers' but from employees within the company. Organisations are often exposed to the possibility of fraud, deliberate corruption of data by disgruntled employees or theft of software or data which may fall into the hands of competitors. Measures to counteract these risks include the following:

- careful vetting of prospective employees;

- immediate removal of employees who have been sacked or who hand in their resignation, and cancellation of all passwords and authorisations;

- 'separation of duties'; i.e. trying to ensure that it would take the collusion of two or more employees to be able to defraud the company. The functions of data preparation, computer operations and other jobs should be separate, with no overlap of responsibility;

- prevention of unauthorised access by employees and others to secure areas such as computer operations rooms, by means of machine-readable cards or badges or other types of locks;

- the use of passwords to gain access to the computer system from terminals;

- educating staff to be aware of possible breaches of security, and to be alert in preventing them or reporting them. This can include politely challenging strangers with a "May I help you?" approach, not leaving output lying around, machines logged on, or doors unlocked;

- appointing a security manager and using special software which can monitor all terminal activity. Such software can enable the security manager to see, either with or without users' knowledge, everything being typed on any screen in a network. It will also record statistics such as number of logins at each terminal, hours of login time, number of times particular programs or databases were accessed and so on. It will even log the security manager's activities!

Password protection

Most password schemes use tables to store the current password for each authorised user. These tables will be stored on disk and will be backed up along with other vital system files, and in addition may be printed out in a dump of system files. For this reason password lists should not be stored in plain form but should be **encrypted**, and held in an irreversibly transformed state.

User IDs and passwords

Each user in an organisation who is permitted to access a company computer system is issued with a user id and a password, which will normally give them a certain level of access rights set by the systems manager. Common rules issued by companies regarding passwords include the following:

- Passwords must be at least 6 characters;
- Password display must be automatically suppressed on screen or printed output;
- Files containing passwords must be encrypted;
- All users must ensure that their password is kept confidential, not written down, not made up of easily-guessed words and is changed regularly, at least every 3 months.

Q2: Describe several ways by which a password may become known to an unauthorised person.

Q3: If the encrypted passwords cannot be decoded, how will the system be able to compare a password entered by the user with the coded password held in the password table?

Q4: What happens if the user forgets his password?

When a user types a password at a keyboard, the password is usually concealed in some way, for example by not echoing it on the screen. However, it can still be observed by wire-tapping. Passwords can be protected during transmission by encrypting them, but this is costly.

Communications security

Telecommunications systems are vulnerable to hackers who discover a user id and password and can gain entry to a networked computer system from their own computer. One way of preventing this is to use a call-back procedure so that when a remote user logs in, the computer automatically calls them back at a pre-arranged telephone number to verify their access request before allowing them to log on.

Data encryption can also be used to 'scramble' highly sensitive or confidential data before transmission.

Data encryption

Data on a network is vulnerable to wire-tapping when it is being transmitted over a network, and one method of preventing confidential data from being read by unauthorised hackers is to **encrypt** it, making it incomprehensible to anyone who does not hold the 'key' to decode it.

Figure 20.1: Data encryption

There are many ways of encrypting data, often based on either **transposition** (where characters are switched around) or substitution (where characters are replaced by other characters).

In a **transposition** cipher, the message could be written in a grid row by row and transmitted column by column. The sentence 'Here is the exam paper' could be written in a 5 x 5 grid:

```
H E R E *
I S * T H
E * E X A
M * P A P
E R * * *
```

And transmitted as HIEMEES★★RR★EP★ETHXA★★HAP★

Q5: Using the same grid, decode the message ITT★O★E★HRWDNIYA★OS★NITT★

Using a substitution cipher, a 'key' that is known to both sender and receiver is used to code the message. A very simple example is to substitute each letter with the next one in the alphabet.

In practice, since the key must be difficult to break, a much more sophisticated algorithm must be used, with frequent changes of key. (See also discussion of strong and weak encryption in Chapter 27.)

Cryptography serves three purposes:

• it helps to identify authentic users;

• it prevents alteration of the message;

• it prevents unauthorised users from reading the message.

Access rights

Even authorised users do not normally have the right to see all the data held on a company computer system – they can see only the data that they need to do their job. In a hospital, for example, receptionists may have the right to view and change some patient details such as name, address and appointments but may not access the patient's medical records. In a stock control system, salesmen may be permitted to view the price, description and quantity in stock of a particular item, but not to change any of the details held.

Access rights to a particular set of data could typically be set to Read-Only, Read/Write, or No Access. This ensures that users within a company can only gain access to data which they are permitted to see, and can only change or delete data on the database if they are authorised to do so.

Likewise, the computer can also be programmed to allow access to particular data only from certain terminals, and only at certain times of day. The terminal in the database administrator's office may be the only terminal from which changes to the structure of a database may be made. An 'access directory' specifying each user's access rights is shown in Figure 20.2.

Access Profile: User ID 26885

Data	Access right	Terminal number	Permitted time	Security level
Customer Number	Read only	04,05	0830-1800	7
Credit Limit	Read/Write	04	0830-1800	10
Payment	Read/Write	04,05	0830-1700	7
Credit Rating	No Access			12

Figure 20.2: A security access table as part of a database

Biometric security measures

Passwords are only effective if people use them properly: if obvious passwords are used, or people tell them to their friends or write them down on a piece of paper blue-tacked to the computer, they are useless. *Biometric* methods of identifying an authorised user include fingerprint recognition techniques, voice recognition and face recognition. One such system uses an infra-red scanner to capture the unique pattern of blood vessels under the skin, and can even differentiate between identical twins by comparing the scan with the one on disk stored for each person.

Case study: National Identity cards

In April 2004 the Government conducted its first trial of a national Identity card using 10,000 volunteers. It has been claimed that a national ID card will help to fight financial services fraud, such as the rising problem of identity theft, credit card fraud and money laundering, all of which have been linked to the funding of terrorism.

The ID cards need to be fraud-proof, and that is likely to mean using some kind of "biometric" form of identification, such as a fingerprint or iris scanning. There is, however, some doubt about the quality of biometric identification – it has been rejected for the new generation of chip and pin credit and debit cards because no system was found to be reliable enough. But, even if a reliable biometric system is developed, it raises a question about how the card will be verified. For example, if iris scanning were adopted as an identifier, then a bank or shop would need some kind of iris scanning device to check that the card details matched the customer's eye. Are customers really going to queue to get their eyes scanned?

Disaster planning

No matter what precautions are taken against fire, flood, power surges, and deliberate or accidental destruction of data, the possibility always exists that data will be destroyed. A simple disk head crash can destroy a disk pack in a fraction of a second. System designers must provide a reasonable backup facility that does not degrade the performance of the system and does not cost too much.

The cost of lack of planning for computer failure can be ruinous. IBM estimates that 70% of organisations that experience a failure (caused by fire, flood, power failure, malice etc) cease operating within 18 months. The main consequence of a computer failure is loss of business, but other problems include loss of credibility, cashflow interruptions, poorer service to customers and loss of production.

Periodic backups

The most common technique used to ensure that data is not lost is to make **periodic backups**, by copying files regularly and keeping them in a safe place. This scheme has several weaknesses:

- All updates to a file since the last backup may be lost;
- The system may need to be shut down during backup operations;
- Backups of large files can be extremely time-consuming;
- When a failure occurs, recovery from the backup can be even more time-consuming.

A **benefit** of periodic backups is that files which may have become fragmented by additions and deletions can be reorganised to occupy contiguous space, usually resulting in much faster access time.

An important feature of all backup systems is the safe storage of the backup copies: it is usually necessary to store one backup copy in a fire-proof safe in the building, and another copy off-site.

Recovery procedures

A contingency plan needs to be developed to allow rapid recovery from major disruptions. In addition to file back-up procedures, it is necessary to:

- identify alternative compatible equipment and security facilities, or implement a service agreement which provides replacement equipment when needed. This may also include putting up temporary office space;

- have provision for alternative communication links.

Exercises

1. (a) What is meant by data security? (1)

   (b) Name one technique for ensuring the security of data. (1)

   New Question

2. A school stores confidential pupil data in an on-line information retrieval system to which teachers, office staff and management have authorised access.

   (a) (i) Name **two** precautions that should be taken to minimise unauthorised access by pupils.

   (ii) Describe how unauthorised access could be detected. (1)

   (b) Why might teachers have different access privileges to office staff? (1)

   (c) Explain how the data should be protected from corruption. (1)

   (d) Every authorised user of the on-line system is given a user ID and a password. Describe **three** ways in which the use of passwords can be made as secure as possible. (3)

   (e) What safeguards should the school use to protect from threats to its data from

   (i) Power failure of the on-line system; (1)

   (ii) Fire; (1)

   (iii) Viruses; (1)

   (iv) Theft. (1)

   New Question

Chapter 21 – Data Processing Integrity Methods

Data integrity

This refers to the **accuracy** of the data. The data held in a computer system may become incorrect or corrupted in many different ways and at many stages during data processing.

- **Errors on input**. Data that is keyed in may be wrongly transcribed. A batch of transaction data could go astray, or be keyed in twice by mistake.

- **Errors in operating procedure**. An update program could for example be run twice in error and quantities on a master file would then be updated twice.

- **Program errors**. These could lead to corruption of files; a new system may have errors in it that will not surface for some time, or errors may be introduced during program maintenance.

- **Viruses**. Files can be corrupted or deleted if a disk becomes infected with a virus.

- **Transmission errors**. Interference or noise in a communications link may cause bits to be wrongly received.

Data integrity: the accuracy or validity of data.

Standard clerical procedures

2-21

To protect against input and operating procedure errors, standard procedures may be documented and followed for both input and output.

Input

- Data entry must be limited to authorised personnel only.

- In large volume data entry, data may be verified (keyed in twice by different operators) to guard against keying errors.

- Data control totals must be used wherever possible to verify the completeness and accuracy of the data, and to guard against duplicate or illegal entry.

Output

- All output should be inspected for reasonableness and any inconsistencies investigated.

- Printed output containing sensitive information should be shredded after use.

Data entry methods

Methods of 'direct data capture' which cut out the need to key in data from input documents are likely to have advantages in terms of speed, accuracy and cost, and so are becoming more and more common. However, we are a long way off from escaping the chore of filling in forms of one sort or another, a large number of which will then have to be keyed into a computer system.

> **Q1:** Name (a) some applications which use direct data entry, eliminating the need for keying in data and
>
> (b) applications which require data to be keyed in.

Types of input error

Figure 21.1 shows an example of an order form filled in by customers of a mail order company.

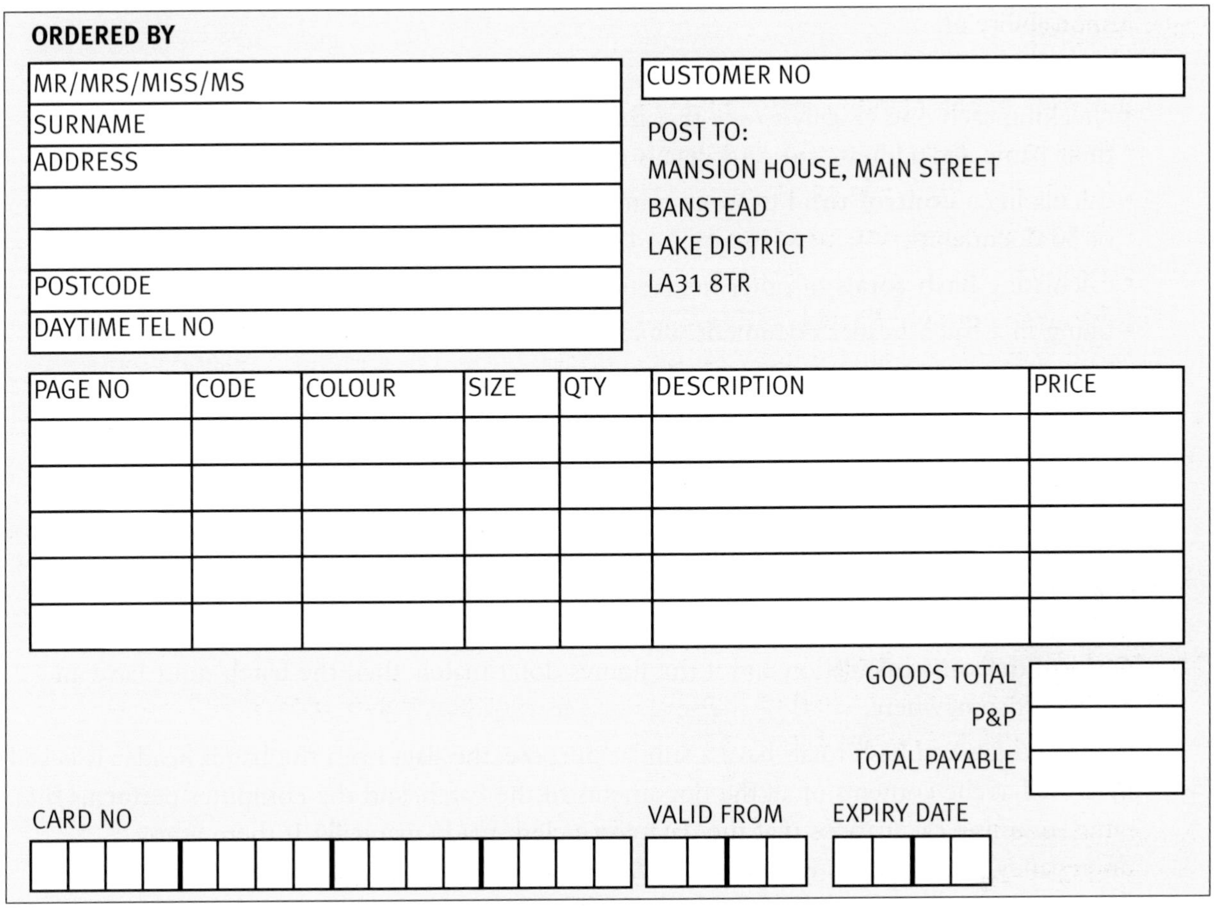

ORDERED BY	
MR/MRS/MISS/MS	CUSTOMER NO
SURNAME	POST TO:
ADDRESS	MANSION HOUSE, MAIN STREET
	BANSTEAD
	LAKE DISTRICT
POSTCODE	LA31 8TR
DAYTIME TEL NO	

PAGE NO	CODE	COLOUR	SIZE	QTY	DESCRIPTION	PRICE

GOODS TOTAL

P&P

TOTAL PAYABLE

CARD NO   VALID FROM   EXPIRY DATE

Figure 21.1: A Mail Order form

The information from this form will be keyed in to the computer and then processed to produce a set of documents including a delivery note and invoice for the customer, as well as updating stock and sales records. There are several possible sources of error before the data is processed:

- the customer could make a mistake, entering the wrong product codes, adding up the total cost wrongly, forgetting to enter their address or card expiry date, etc.

- the person keying in the data could make a **transcription** error, keying in the wrong product code or quantity, misreading the customer's name, adding an extra couple of 0's to the total price by keeping a finger down too long, and so on;

- a form could be blown into the bin by a sudden draught as a fan starts up or someone flounces out, slamming the door – or the operator might decide the writing was so bad it simply wasn't worth the effort of struggling with it, and bin it;

- a bored keypunch operator, chatting to a colleague, could enter the same form twice without realising it;

- a faulty connection between hardware components such as the processor and the disk drive could mean that some characters are wrongly transmitted.

Now clearly a mail order company would not stay in business very long if this was how the operation worked! So what can be done to minimise the possibility of error?

Batch processing

In a batch processing system, documents such as the sales orders described above are collected into batches of typically 50 documents. A **data control clerk** has the responsibility of:

- counting the documents;
- checking each one visually to see that the customer has entered essential details such as their name and address, and card details if that is the payment method;
- calculating a **control total** of some crucial field such as Total Payable, for the entire batch of 50 documents;
- calculating **hash totals** of other fields such as size or quantity (see below):
- filling in a batch header document which will show, for example:

batch number	number of documents in batch
date received	control total
hash total	

- logging the batch in a book kept for this purpose.

A **hash total** is a sum of values calculated purely for validation purposes. For example, if the sizes of all garments ordered on a batch of forms (12, 10, 12, 34, 36, etc.) are added together and the total entered on the batch header and keyed in, the computer will be able to perform the same calculation and if the figures don't match, then the batch must have an error in it somewhere.

Control totals and hash totals have a similar purpose; the data from the batch header is keyed in as well as the contents of all the documents in the batch, and the computer performs the same summing calculations that the data entry clerk made manually. If there is any discrepancy, then an error is reported and the batch is rechecked. The difference between the two types of total is only that a hash total has no meaning, whereas a control total (e.g. number of documents in the batch) does.

Validation checks

As the data is being keyed in, a computer program controlling the input can perform various validation checks on the data. For example:

1 **Presence check**. Certain fields such as customer number, item code, quantity etc. must be present. The data control clerk may have visually checked this but the program can perform a second check. Also, if this is a new customer, a number could be automatically assigned.

2 **Format check** (also called **picture check**). For example the code perhaps has a pattern of 2 letters followed by 4 numbers. The quantity and price must be numeric. In a MS Access database this is set up using an **Input Mask**.

3 **Range check**. The expiry date of a card must have a month number between 1 and 12, and the date must be later than today's date.

4 **Uniqueness check**. If the field is used as an identifier, it must be unique.

5 **Type check**. Only entries of a certain data type are accepted, such as only digits in a number field.

6 **File lookup check**. If the customer has filled in their customer number, the computer can look this up on the customer file and display the name and address. The data entry operator can check that it tallies.

2-21

7 **Check digit check**. (see below).

8 **Batch header checks**. The total number of records in the batch should be calculated by the computer and compared with the figure on the batch header. The control totals and hash totals are also calculated and compared.

Check digits

Code numbers such as a customer number, employee number or product number are often lengthy and prone to error when being keyed in. One way of preventing these errors occurring is to add an extra digit to the end of a code number, which has been calculated from the digits of the code number. In this way the code number with its extra check digit is self-checking.

Check digit: an extra digit added to the end of a code number, which has been calculated from the digits of the code number.

The best-known method of calculating check digits is the modulus-11 system, which traps over 99% of all errors. The most common errors are a single incorrect digit being entered or a transposition error (two digits swapped). The calculation of a check digit is shown below.

1 Each digit of the code number is assigned a 'weight'. The right hand (least significant) digit is given a weight of 2, the next digit to the left 3 and so on.

2 Each digit is multiplied by its weight and the products added together.

3 The sum of the products is divided by 11 and the remainder obtained.

4 The remainder is subtracted from 11.

5 The result is divided again by 11 and the remainder is the check digit. The only exception is:

• If the remainder is 10, we 'borrow' the Roman numeral 'X' and use this as a check digit.

Example:

To calculate the check digit for the number 1587:

Original code number	1	5	8	7
Weights		5	4	3	2
Multiply digit by its weight	5	20	24	14
Add products together		5 + 20 +24 +14 = 63
Divide by 11		5 remainder 8
Subtract remainder from 11	11 – 8 = 3
Divide by 11 again		0 remainder 3

Check digit = 3. The complete code number is 15873.

To check that a code number is valid, it is not necessary to recalculate the check digit completely. If the check digit itself is assigned a weight of 1, and the products of the digits (including the check digit) and their respective weights are calculated, their sum will be divisible by 11 if the check digit is correct.

Q2: All books have an ISBN number which has a modulus-11 check digit. Try checking whether the ISBN number 1-85805-170-3 is valid. (Ignore the hyphens).

Check whether the ISBN 0-582-27544-X is valid.

Verification

Verification is the process of entering data twice, with the second entry being compared with the first to ensure that it is accurate. It is common in batch processing for a second data entry operator to key in a batch of data to verify it. You have probably come across another example of verification when setting a password; you are asked to key the password in a second time to ensure that you didn't make a keying error the first time, as it is not echoed on the screen.

Detecting transmission errors

In order to guard against the possibility of data being wrongly transmitted between the various hardware components of a computer, a **parity bit** is added to each character. In an even parity machine, the total number of 'On' bits in every byte (including the parity bit) must be an even number. When data is moved from one location to another, the parity bits are checked at both the sending and receiving end and, if the wrong number of bits are 'On', an error message is displayed.

Thus a character code of 1101010 will have a parity bit of 0 appended to it, and a character code of 1101110 will have a parity bit of 1 appended.

(See Chapter 12, Figure 12.5.)

Data is transmitted over a transmission line between computers in **blocks** of say 256 bytes. A **checksum** may be calculated by adding together the numeric value of all the bytes in a block, and this sum is transmitted with the data, to be checked again at the receiving end.

Protection against viruses

Steps can be taken which minimise the risk of suffering damage from viruses. These include:

- making sure that all purchased software comes in sealed, tamper-proof packaging;
- not permitting floppy disks containing software or data to be removed from or brought into the office. (This is a sackable offence in some companies.)
- using anti-virus software to check all floppy disks before use.

Accuracy vs validity of data

Validation can only check that data is sensible. To be accurate, data must also be correct when entered and up-to-date. Validation cannot ensure that data entered represents the correct values, so it is possible for data to be valid but not accurate.

Exercises

1 Data integrity is paramount when processing data using computer systems.

    (a) What is meant by data integrity?   (1)

    (b) Outline two ways in which data integrity may be compromised.   (2)

    (c) Name two methods for ensuring the integrity of data.   (2)

New Question

2 When data is first entered into the system it is validated and verified.

    (a) What is validation?   (1)

    (b) What is verification?   (1)

New Question

3 The last digit of an ISBN (International Standard Book Number) is a check digit.
For example, the check digit of the ISBN 1-904467-29-6 is 6.

    (a) How is the check digit arrived at?   (1)

    (b) What is its purpose?   (1)

New Question

4 The following data records are going to be entered as batch number 127 by
keyboard operator 1 (initials AK) and again by keyboard operator 2 (initials BL).

EmployeeID	WeekNo	HoursWorked
003	5	35
005	5	30
007	5	25
011	5	35
023	5	20
030	4	35
101	4	23
205	5	17

2-21

    (a) Complete the batch header document for the above records:

Batch Number		Date received	11/02/2004
Number of documents in batch		Control Total	
Operator Initials		Hash Total	
Verifier Initials		Date completed	

(6)

    (b) What is the purpose of the batch header?   (1)

    (c) How is the information on the batch header used by the system?   (2)

New Question

Chapter 22 – Entity-Relationship Modelling

The conceptual data model

When a systems analyst sits down to design a new system, one crucial task is to identify and state what **data** needs to be held. From the statement of data requirements a **conceptual data model** is produced. This describes how the data elements in the system are to be grouped. Three terms are used in building a picture of the data requirements: entity, attribute and relationship.

An entity is an object, person, event or thing of interest to an organisation about which data is to be recorded.

Example: Customer, Employee, Stock Item, Supplier.

An attribute is a property or characteristic of an entity.

Example: Attributes associated with a Customer include Customer ID, Surname, Initials, Title, Address.

A relationship is a link or association between two entities.

Example: Dentist and Patient; one dentist has many patients, but each patient only has one dentist.

Types of relationship

There are only three different 'degrees' of relationship between two attributes. A relationship may be:

- **One-to-one**   Examples of such a relationship include the relationship between Husband and Wife, or between Householder and Main Residence.

- **One-to-many**   Examples include the relationship between Mother and Children, between Customer and Order, between Borrower and Library Book.

- **Many-to-many** Examples include the relationship between Student and Course, between Stock Item and Supplier, between Film and Film Star.

Entity-relationship diagrams

An entity-relationship diagram is a diagrammatic way of representing the relationships between the entities in a database. To show the relationship between two entities, both the **degree** and the **name** of the relationship need to be specified. E.g. In the first relationship shown below, the **degree** is *One-to-one*, the **name** of the relationship is *Drives*:

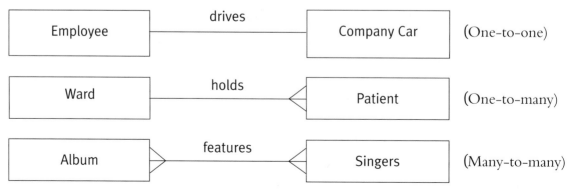

Figure 22.1: Entity-relationships

Sometimes it can be tricky to establish the degree of the relationship. For example, several employees may use the same company car at different times. A single employee may change the company car that he uses. The relationship will depend upon whether the data held refers to the current situation, or is a historical record. The assumption has been made above that the database is to record the current car driven by an employee.

Example:

The data requirements for a hospital in-patient system are defined as follows:
A hospital is organised into a number of wards. Each ward has a ward number and a name recorded, along with a number of beds in that ward. Each ward is staffed by nurses. Nurses have their staff number and name recorded, and are assigned to a single ward.

Each patient in the hospital has a patient identification number, and their name, address and date of birth are recorded. Each patient is under the care of a single consultant and is assigned to a single ward. Each consultant is responsible for a number of patients. Consultants have their staff number, name and specialism recorded.

State four entities for the hospital in-patient system and suggest an identifier for each of these entities.

Draw an entity-relationship diagram to show the relationship between the entities.

Answer:

Entity	Identifier
Ward	WardID
Nurse	StaffID
Patient	PatientID
Consultant	StaffID

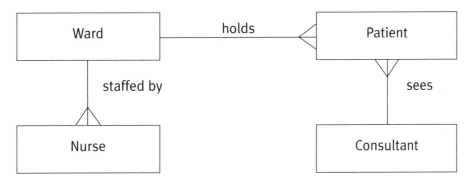

Note that a one-to-many relationship does not necessarily imply that **every** ward, for example, has many patients, merely that is possible that at least one ward has more than one patient. It is possible that some wards have no patients at all.

Q1: Draw entity-relationship diagrams to illustrate the relationships between
(a) Product and Component
(b) Home-owner and Main Residence
(c) Pet-owner and Pet
(d) Racehorse-owner and Racehorse

Once again there may be some argument about these relationships. Can a pet have more than one owner? For the purposes of a vet's database, probably not. A racehorse, on the other hand, is such a valuable animal that it is quite common for several people to have 'shares' in the horse.

When you are designing a database, it can often be quite hard to decide what is an entity and what is an attribute. Is **pet** an attribute of **owner**, or is **owner** an attribute of **pet**? Or is neither the case, since both are entities in their own right? The latter statement is probably the correct interpretation of the real world situation.

> **Q2:** In a database system used by a car dealer, Car is one entity, and it has a primary key RegistrationNumber. Is Manufacturer an attribute of car, or is it an entity?

Exercises

1 A library plans to set up a database to keep track of its members, stock and loans. For members, the fields MemberID, Surname and Address are to be stored. For stock, the fields ISBN, AcquisitionNo, Title and Author are to be stored. For loans the MemberID of the member borrowing the book, and the AcquisitionNo of the book are stored together with the date the book is due to be returned. When the book is returned the loan record is deleted.

   (a) State an identifier (primary key) for each of the entities Member, Stock and Loan.   (3)

   (b) Draw an entity-relationship diagram showing the relationships between the entities. (3)

   New Question

2 A college wants to set up a database for its student, course and course enrolment data. The data to be stored for the student are StudentID, FirstName, Surname, DateOfBirth, Address. The fields required for the course are CourseID, CourseDescription. When a student enrols on a course the StudentID and the CourseID are to be stored.

   (a) State an identifier for each of the entities Student, Course and CourseEnrolment.   (3)

   (b) Draw an entity-relationship diagram showing the relationships between the entities.   (3)

   New Question

3 An exam board wants to set up a database for all its exam modules, candidates and results. For the purpose of this exercise, assume that each candidate can enter each module once only. The data to be stored for the candidate are CandidateNumber, FirstName, Surname, DateOfBirth. The data to be stored for the exams are ModuleCode, Subject. When a candidate takes an exam, the following details are recorded: CandidateNumber, ModuleCode, UMS (Unified Mark Scheme).

   (a) State an identifier for each of the entities Candidate, ExamModule and Result.   (3)

   (b) Draw an entity-relationship diagram showing the relationships between the entities.   (3)

   New Question

4 A company selling office furniture wants to set up a database to keep track of its customers, stock and orders. The data recorded for customers are CustomerID, Name, Address. The data to be stored for the stock are StockID, Description, UnitPrice. For each order the CustomerID, OrderID and OrderDate are recorded. For each item ordered, the StockID and NumberOf ItemsOrdered are recorded. One order form may include several order lines for different items, but the same item would not appear more than once on the same order form.

   (a) State an identifier for each of the entities Customer, Order, OrderLine, StockItem   (4)

   (b) Draw an entity-relationship diagram showing the relationships between the entities. (4)

   New Question

Chapter 23 – Database Concepts

Information is vital to organizations. Often one of the most valuable resources in a business is its accumulated information. The problem is the storage, retrieval and manipulation of all this information.

Traditional file approach

In the early days of computerised data processing, an organisation's data was duplicated in separate files for the use of individual departments. For example the Personnel Department would hold details on name, address, qualifications etc. of each employee, while the Payroll Department would hold details of name, address and salary of each employee. Each department had its own set of application programs to process the data in these files. This led to:

• **duplicated data**, meaning wasted space;

• **inconsistency problems**, where for example an address was updated on one file but not on another; e.g. Mr Johnstone moves house and passes his new address to Personnel who update their file. Unfortunately no-one tells the Payroll Department and his next payslip is sent to the old address.

• **the data was not shareable**; if one department needed data that was held by another, it was awkward to obtain it.

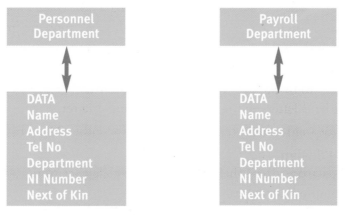

Figure 23.1 Traditional File Processing System

The database approach

In an attempt to solve the above problems, the data from the various departments was centralised in a common pool so that **all applications had access to the same set of data**. For example all the details about stock held by a garden centre would be held in a database which was accessible by all applications using the data. The Sales department would update quantities in stock, the Marketing department would use the data to produce a catalogue, the Reorder system would use it to decide what stock to reorder.

Although this solved problems of duplication and inconsistency, it introduced two major new problems:

• **Unproductive maintenance**; if one department needed some change to the number or length of fields in a record on one of the common files, every department had to change its application programs to take this change into account, even if the field was not one used by that department. In other words, the programs were still dependent on the record structure, and all departments were affected by even minor changes in another department.

- **Problems of security**; even confidential or commercially sensitive data was accessible by every application, because the data was centrally held.

A **database**, therefore, is defined as a collection of non-redundant data sharable between different application systems. The software used to control access to the data is known as a Data Base Management System (DBMS).

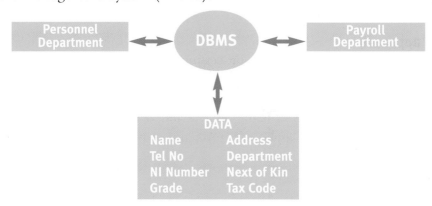

Figure 23.2 Database approach

Validation of input data

Almost every field in a database can be put through some type of **validation** to ensure that data entry is valid (see Chapter 21). There are several types of validation check that may be specified, for example:

- Presence check – must data be entered in this field?

- Range check – is there a low/high limit? (e.g. the date must be greater than or equal to today's date in a theatre booking file, the price of a new car from a particular manufacturer must be between £6,000 and £30,000 in a car sales database.)

- Format check – must the data be in a particular format? (e.g. a National Insurance number must be 2 letters followed by 6 digits and a letter.)

- Is there a list of valid values? (e.g. Gender must be either M or F.)

Relational database design

In a relational database, data is held in tables (also called relations) and the tables are linked by means of common attributes.

Relational database: a collection of tables in which relationships are modelled by shared attributes.

Conceptually then, one row of a table holds one record. Each column in the table represents one attribute.

e.g. A table holding data about an entity *Book* may have the following rows and columns:

Accession Number	DeweyCode	Title	Author	DatePublished
88	121.9	Let's Cook!	Chan, C	1992
123	345.440	Electricity	Glendenning, V	1995
300	345.440	Riders	Cooper, J	1995
657	200.00	Greek in 3 weeks	Stavros, G	1990
777	001.602	I.T. in Society	Laudon, K	1995
etc				

Figure 23.3: A table in a relational database

Standard Notation

There is a standard notation for describing a table in a relational database. For example, to describe the table shown above, you would write

Book (**AccessionNumber**, DeweyCode, Title, Author, DatePublished)

Note that:

The entity name is shown outside the brackets;

The primary key (unique identifier) is underlined;

The attributes are shown in brackets, separated by commas, names written in 'camel caps' and without spaces.

Primary and secondary (alternate) keys

Each entity in a database must have a unique key known as the **primary key**. The primary key in the above table is AccessionNumber. In a database holding data about students, the primary key in a table about students could be a unique student number.

Primary key: An attribute that will identify a particular instance of an entity uniquely.

In order that a record with a particular primary key can be quickly located in a database, an **index** of primary keys will be automatically maintained by the database software, giving the position of each record according to its primary key.

If a database table often needs to be searched on a different attribute, for example, title or author, these can be defined as **secondary keys** (also known as **alternate** keys) so that the table will also be indexed on these attributes.

Secondary or alternate key: An attribute that will identify a particular instance of an entity, but not necessarily uniquely.

Indexing

A database table can have indexes on as many attributes as you choose. An index is, in effect, a list of numerical values, which gives the order of the records when they are sorted on a particular attribute. An index on the Title attribute in the table shown in Figure 23.3, assuming it had only 5 records, would have entries 2, 4, 5, 1, 3. The DBMS constructs and maintains all the indexes automatically. Indexing imposes a logical order on the rows in a table without changing the physical order. There are advantages and disadvantages to having multiple indexes:

• in large tables they speed up queries considerably;

• when a report is required in the sequence of the indexed attribute, they avoid having to sort the database;

• on the negative side, they slow down data entry and editing, because the indexes have to be updated each time a record is added or deleted.

Primary index: an ordered list of primary key values.

A table has only one primary index but may have many secondary indexes.

Secondary index: an ordered list of secondary key values.

Linking database tables

Tables may be linked through the use of a common attribute. This attribute must be a primary key of one of the tables, and is known as a foreign key in the second table.

Foreign key: an attribute in one table, which is the primary key in another table.

Linking tables in one-to-many relationships

In a library database, two entities named **Borrower** and **Book** have been identified. There is a one-to-many relationship between these two entities, because one borrower may borrow several books, but the same book cannot be taken out by many borrowers simultaneously. The relationship can be represented by the following E-R diagram:

Figure 23.4: E-R Diagram

The Borrower and Book tables can be described using standard notation as follows:

Borrower (**BorrowerID**, Name, Address)

Book (**AccessionNumber**, DeweyCode, Title, Author, DatePublished)

The relationship is made through shared attributes. In order to link the two entities, the primary key BorrowerID needs to be added to the Book table as a *foreign key*. So the tables can now be described as

Borrower (**BorrowerID**, Name, Address)

Book (**AccessionNumber**, DeweyCode, Title, Author, DatePublished, *BorrowerID*)

Note that a foreign key is shown in italics.

Note that the foreign key is always the primary key of the table at the 'one' end of the E-R diagram and is added to the table at the 'many' end of the E-R diagram.

Linking tables in a many-to-many relationship

Tables that make up a relational database cannot represent many-to-many relationships. A many-to-many relationship can be removed by creating a link entity. The link entity's identifier (primary key) will often be made up of the original entities' identifiers.

Figure 23.5: Many-to-many relationship

To resolve this many-to-many relationship, a link entity, Enrolment, can be introduced:

Figure 23.6: Link entity introduced

Using the standard table notation, the tables can be described as follows:

Student (**StudentID**, Surname, DateOfBirth)

Course (**CourseID**, CourseName, Level)

Enrolment (**StudentID**, CourseID)

Querying a database

Information can be obtained from a database using **Query by Example (QBE)**.

Using this method the user may:

• combine, into one table, information from two or more related tables;

• select which attributes are to be shown in the 'Answer' table;

• specify search criteria;

• save the query so that it can be executed whenever required;

• save the results of the query (the 'Answer' table).

The figure below shows a **query by example** window in the MS Access database.

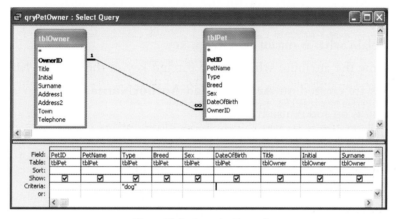

Figure 23.7: Query by Example

The above query is applied to the following tables:

Customer ID	Title	Initials	Surname	KnownAs
1234	Mr	F	Bloggs	Mr Bloggs
45673	Dr	K	Smith	Mr Smith
67821	Mrs	D	French	Mrs French

Figure 23.8: Customer Table

Order ID	Date	Customer ID	Paid	Order Total
4012	10/3/2004	1234	No	£45.60
4034	11/3/2004	45673	Yes	£38.90
4067	12/3/2004	67821	No	£74.35

Figure 23.9: Order Table

The query writes to an answer table the Customer ID, Surname and Order ID of unpaid orders. (The answer table is a new table created automatically when the query is run for the first time.)

Customer ID	Surname	Order ID
12345	Bloggs	4012
67821	French	4067

Figure 23.10: Answer Table

2-23

Exercises

1 A publisher uses a relational database to record details of articles it publishes in a monthly magazine.

Two relations (tables) **MagazineEdition** and **MagazineArticle** are used for this database.

MagazineEdition (MagazineEditionId, Month, Year)

MagazineArticle (ArticleId, ArticleType, ArticleTitle, Content, AuthorName, MagazineEditionId)

Each Article is assigned a unique ArticleId.

(a) What is a relational database? (1)

(b) State a suitable primary key for the MagazineEdition relation.
Justify your choice. (2)

(c) (i) Explain what is meant by foreign key. (2)

(ii) Name the attribute which is the foreign key in the relation MagazineArticle. (1)

(d) Indexes are created on **ArticleId** and **AuthorName** attributes.

(i) Why is an index used? (1)

(ii) Which of the two attribute indexes is a secondary index? (1)

(e) The following shows a sample of the MagazineEdition table and a sample of the MagazineArticle table.

MagazineEdition table

MagazineEditionId	Month	Year
:	:	:
240	December	1999
241	January	2000
242	February	2000
243	March	2000
:	:	:

MagazineArticle table

ArticleId	ArticleType	ArticleTitle	Content	AuthorName	MagazineEditionId
1	Business	....	....	Bloggs	89
2	Management	....	....	Smith	89
3	Business	....	....	Bloggs	89
4	Quality Control	....	....	Jones	89
5	Investments	....	....	Bloggs	90
:	:	:	:	:	:
1201	Recruitment	....	....	Jones	253
1202	Accounting	....	....	Smith	254
:	:	:	:	:	:

The following shows a Query By Example (QBE) applied to the MagazineEdition and MagazineArticle tables.

QBE

MagazineEditionId	AuthorName	ArticleType
	Bloggs	Business

(i) What will be the minimum number of records returned by this QBE? (1)

(ii) Complete the following QBE to extract the author names and article titles of all articles of the article type "Management" appearing in magazines published in the year 1999 or before.

(4)

AQA CPT2 Qu 10 May 2002

2 A charity uses a relational database to keep track of donors and their donations. Donations are given weekly, monthly and annually (donation type).

Two relations (tables) are used for this database.

Donors and **Donations**

Donor (DonorId, Name, Address, DonationType)

Donation (DonationId, AmountGiven, DateDonationGiven, DonorId)

Each donation is assigned a unique DonationId.

(a) What is a relational database? (1)

(b) Select a suitable primary key for the Donor relation. Justify your choice. (2)

(c) (i) Explain what is meant by the term foreign key. (2)

(ii) Name the attribute which is the foreign key in the relation Donation. (1)

(iii) Select a suitable primary key for the relation Donation. (1)

(d) Indexes are created on **DonorId** and **DonationType** attributes.

(i) Why is an index used? (1)

(ii) Which of the two attribute indexes is a secondary index? (1)

(e) The following are samples of the Donor table and the Donation table.

Donor table

DonorId	Name	Address	DonationType
:	:	:	:
:	:	:	:
567	Jones	....	Weekly
868	Smith	....	Monthly
919	Adams	....	Weekly
920	Gregory	....	Annually
:	:	:	:
:	:	:	:

Donation table

DonationId	Amount Given	DateDonation Given	DonorId
1	5	10/7/2000	567
2	7	10/7/2000	919
3	200	17/7/2000	920
4	7	17/7/2000	919
5	5	17/7/2000	567
:	:	:	:
:	:	:	:
12021	20	10/7/2000	868
12022	200	17/7/2000	920

2-23

The following shows a Query By Example (QBE) applied to the Donor and Donation tables.

QBE

DonorId	Name	Amount Given	Donation Type	Date Donation Given
			Weekly	10/7/2000

(i) How many records will be returned by this QBE? (1)

(ii) Using the result of the QBE, calculate the total amount given (1)

AQA CPT2 Qu January 2001

3 A newspaper publisher uses a relational database to record details of advertisements placed by businesses and members of the general public.

Two relations (tables) **Customer** and **Advertisement** are used for this database.

Customer (CustomerId, Name, Address, CustomerType)

Advertisement (AdvertId, Content, DateAdvertPlaced, NoOfNights, Classification, CustomerId)

Each advertisement is assigned a unique AdvertId.

(a) What is a relational database? (1)

(b) State a suitable primary key for the Customer relation. Justify your choice. (2)

(c) (i) Explain what is meant by foreign key. (2)

(ii) Name the attribute which is the foreign key in the relation Advertisement. (1)

(iii) State a suitable primary key for the relation Advertisement. (1)

(d) Indexes are created on **CustomerId** and **Name** attributes.

(i) Why is an index used? (1)

(ii) Which of the two attribute indexes is a secondary index? (1)

(e) The following shows a sample of the Customer table and of the Advertisement table.

Customer table

CustomerId	Name	Address	Customer Type
:	:	:	:
:	:	:	:
920	Jones	......	Business
868	Smith	.....	Non-Business
919	Adams	.....	Non-Business
655	Gregory	.....	Business
:	:	:	:
:	:	:	:

Advertisement table

AdvertId	Content	DateAdvertPlaced	NoOfNights	Classification	CustomerId
1	Lawn Mower for Sale	10/7/2000	3	General Sales	567
2	Child's bicycle...	10/7/2000	2	General Sales	868
3	Ford Mondeo, T reg	11/7/2000	5	Cars for Sale	920
4	Ford Fiesta, T reg	12/7/2000	5	Cars for Sale	655
5	Electrician, no job too small	12/7/2000	10	Electricians	800
: :	: :	: :	: :	: :	: :
12021	Fiat Uno, P reg....	1/12/2000	3	Cars for Sale	868
12022	Study desk for sale	11/12/2000	2	General Sales	919

The following shows a Query By Example **(QBE)** applied to the Customer and Advertisement tables.

QBE

CustomeId	Name	CustomerType	Classification	DateAdvertPlaced
		Business	Cars for Sale	

(i) What will be the minimum number of records returned by this QBE? (1)

(ii) Complete the following **QBE** to extract the names and addresses of all non-business customers placing an advert after 12/7/2000.

(4)

AQA CPT2 Qu 9 May 2001

Chapter 24 – Operating Systems

What is an operating system?

Computers require two types of software: **applications software** such as word processing, spreadsheet or graphics packages, and **systems software** to perform tasks needed to run the computer system. The operating system is systems software to control and monitor the running of application programs, and to allow users to communicate with the computer.

The operating system consists of a number of programs that are typically 'bundled' with the hardware; in other words, when you buy a new PC, for example, you will also be supplied with a CD containing the latest version of the Windows operating system. This then has to be installed by running a special installation program supplied on the CD, which will copy the operating system to your hard disk and customise it to your particular hardware configuration.

Each time you switch on your PC, the operating system kernel (the part you need in memory at all times) will be copied from the hard disk into memory, which takes a few minutes.

Operating system: software that handles the interface to the hardware and manages resources.

2-23

Functions of an operating system

Obviously the operating system (OS) for a standalone microcomputer system will be very much simpler than that of a supercomputer which is controlling hundreds of terminals and running many different kinds of job simultaneously. Nevertheless, all operating systems perform certain basic functions, including:

- **Memory management**. Most computers nowadays are capable of holding several programs in memory simultaneously so that a user can switch from one application to another. The operating system has to allocate memory to each application – as well as to itself!

- **Resource allocation and scheduling**. In larger computer systems, which are capable of running several programs at once (**multiprogramming**), the OS is responsible for allocating processing time, memory and input-output resources to each one. While one program is executing, the operating system is scheduling the use of input and output devices for other jobs. Not all jobs are performed in the order they are submitted; the operating system schedules them in order to make the best possible use of the computer's resources.

- **Backing store management**. The OS controls the transfer of data from secondary storage (e.g. disk) to main memory and back again. It also has to maintain a directory of the disk so that files and free space can be quickly located.

- **Interrupt handling**. The OS detects many different kinds of interrupt such as for example a user pressing the Enter key on the keyboard, a printer sending a message that it is out of paper, the real-time clock interrupting to indicate that the processor should be allocated to the next user in a multi-user system, a hardware or software malfunction.

- **Allowing a user to communicate with the computer**. The user gives instructions to the computer to start a program, copy a file, send a message to another user, and so on by typing in commands recognised by the operating system or by using a mouse to point and click in a graphical user interface such as Windows XP or 2000.

Provision of a virtual machine

The operating system functions in such a way as to hide from the user all the complexities of the hardware. The average user is completely unaware of the operating system working away behind the scenes, and sees only a machine which (with luck) simply does what it is instructed no matter how complex the tasks involved. Switching from one window to another, from one printer to another, creating a new folder or making a backup is simply a matter of a few mouse clicks, as far as the user is concerned. This easy-to-use machine is sometimes referred to as the 'virtual machine'.

Operating System Classification

Operating systems can be classified into different types, some of which are described below.

Batch

The most important operating system capability for sharing computer resources is multi-programming. This permits multiple programs to be active at the same time, with the operating system allowing each one a small 'time-slice' of processor time in turn. This technique was developed when computers were operated in batch-processing mode.

Batch-processing: processing is carried out from beginning to end without user interaction.

Jobs prepared in this way have all their processing requirements defined in advance. By using multiprogramming, a batch of several jobs can be loaded so that, when executed over the same time period, the processor is kept as busy as possible by switching between the jobs as and when necessary. This increases throughput, i.e. the total number of jobs completed per unit time, and reduces the turnaround time, i.e. time between job submission and job completion. There is a significant delay of, say, several hours between submitting a job and receiving the output.

Example:

Payroll system, processing payroll data supplied as data files and printing out payslips.

Interactive

With this type of processing the user interacts directly with the system to supply commands and data as the application program undergoes execution and receives the results of processing immediately. An operating system which allows such interaction is said to support interactive processing.

Interactive processing: user and computer are in direct two-way communication.

Example:

Travel agent booking and confirming a place on a package holiday for a client waiting in the shop.

Real-Time

Real time operating systems are characterised by four requirements:

• they have to support application programs which are non-sequential in nature, i.e. programs which do not have a START - PROCESS - END structure;

• they have to deal with a number of events which happen in parallel and at unpredictable moments in time (for example, a user clicking a mouse button);

• they have to carry out processing and produce a response within a specified interval of time;

• some systems are safety-critical, meaning they must be fail-safe and guarantee a response within a specified time interval.

Example:

Process control in a chemical plant or nuclear power station – up to 1000 signals per second can arrive from sensors attached to the system being controlled. The response time must be less than one thousandth of a second.

2-24

Real-time operating system: response within a certain maximum time, suitable for control of hardware in time-critical applications.

Network

A network operating system is required when a number of computers are connected together in a network. The operating system controls who logs on to the network by means of user names and passwords, in order to protect the data and programs stored on the network. It also makes the network transparent to the user, allowing any user with the appropriate access rights to use software stored on the network's file server, and to store data either on the file server or on a local hard or floppy disk.

Network operating system: includes software to communicate with other computers via a network and allows resources such as files and printers to be shared between computers.

File Management

An important part of a computer's operating system is the **file manager** or **file management system**. A file may be a document created in a wordprocessor or spreadsheet or other software, or it may be an executable file, i.e. a program that can be executed. When the user gives an instruction to save a file, giving it a name and specifying where it is to be saved, it is the job of the file manager to find a space on disk.

The file manager will typically hold the following information about each file or folder:

- file type – e.g., folder file, system file, hidden file, batch, executable, text;
- information indicating the location of the file on secondary storage – e.g., disk address of the first block in the file;
- file size in bytes;
- access rights – who can access the file and how it can be accessed: e.g., read only, read-write, write-only, delete permission;
- date information – e.g. data of creation, date of last access, date of last amendment, purge date;

Using the access rights the file manager is able to control who can share a particular file, and protect that file against unauthorised alteration.

Drives, folders and files

A drive is the hardware that seeks, reads and writes information from and to a disk. A hard disk and its drive are one inseparable unit, unlike a floppy disk which can be removed from its drive. Drives are given letter names like A, B, C etc. Frequently a large hard disk is 'partitioned' by the user or computer technician when the drive is initially formatted so that although there is only one physical drive, there are several 'logical drives' called, for example, F, G, X, Y, Z. This is done for convenience so that different types of work can be held on separate logical drives.

A hard disk is divided into a number of **folders** (called directories in early versions of Windows). Folders can be added and deleted by the user whenever necessary, and they are used to help keep all the thousands of files held on a disk organised so that they can be quickly located when needed. Folders can contain both files and subfolders.

Folder and file names in Windows 2000 and later versions can be up to 255 characters in length. In addition, they usually have an extension, which is added automatically by the particular software package in which they were created, and which identifies them as being, for example, a Word document, an Excel spreadsheet or a Pascal program.

e.g. **BensProject.doc** (The extension .doc identifies this as a Word document.)

ProgSquares.exe (The extension .exe identifies this as an executable file.)

2-24

Pathnames

Folders (or so-called directories) are organised in a tree structure, with the folder at the top of the tree being known as the root. To refer to a particular file in a particular folder, you have to give it its full pathname, which shows exactly which folder it is in.

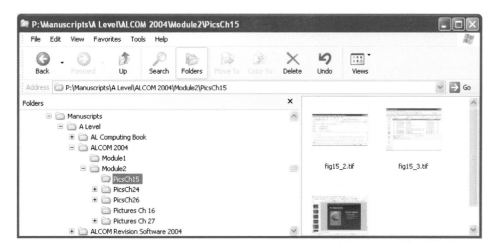

Figure 24.1: Directory structure

In the screenshot above taken from a Windows Explorer screen, the folder **A Level** is a subfolder of the **Manuscripts** folder on the **P:** drive. Within **A Level** there are subfolders named **AL Computing Book, ALCOM2004**, etc. The folder **ALCOM2004** has subfolders **Module1**, **Module2** etc and Module2 has subfolders **PicsCh15**, **PicsCh24** etc.

The full name of the file **fig15_2.tif** is

P:\A Level\ALCOM2004\Module2\PicsCh15\fig15_2.tif

Access rights and other attributes

The file manager enables access rights to be set for particular files or folders. Depending on a user's ID and password, they may for example be given any of the following access rights to a file or folder:

Read	Allows the user to view the contents of the data file
Read & Execute	Allows the user to run a program file
Write	Allows the user to change the contents of the file
Modify	Allows the user to read, change or delete the file

Backing up and archiving

Backing up: a copy of a file is made to guard against data loss from accidents or deliberate action.

A backup is a spare copy of a file for use in the event of loss of the original. Ideally backup copies should be kept at a different site, so that data can be restored if a disaster occurs. Archiving means removing a file from the hard disk and copying it onto another medium, say on a writeable CD, which will not be changed again. For example, old invoices or purchase orders might be archived in order to make a permanent record of such documents.

Archiving: a file is removed from on-line storage and kept for longterm reference, for example on tape.

Exercises

1 (a) Distinguish file backing-up from archiving.   (2)

   (b) The directory structure shown in **Figure 1** contains a **root** directory (\) and
        four sub-directories, named **User1**, **User2**, **Project** and **Homework**.

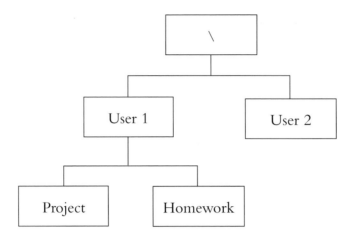

Figure 1

A file with the filename Project1.Pas is stored in the system with the directory
structure shown in Figure 1. What is the pathname for Project1.Pas if it is stored
in the:

(i)   root directory;   (1)

(ii) sub-directory Project?   (1)

(c)

Field 1	Field 2	Field 3	Field 4	Field 5
Project1.Pas	rw	14286	12/12/2001	13:32
Project2.Pas	r	2560	01/01/2002	09:12

Figure 2

Figure 2 displays in five fields a directory listing of the **Project** directory.
The first field is used to display a filename. What might the other **four** fields
display?   (4)

(d)

Field 1	Field 2	Field 3	Field 4	Field 5
	rwx	512	11/12/2001	13:32
	rwx	512	31/12/2001	09:12

Figure 3

Figure 3 shows the directory listing for the directory **User1** with the two
entries for Field 1 removed. What should have appeared in Field 1 for these
two entries?   (2)

AQA CPT2 Qu 5 January 2002

2　A desktop PC has access to a *local disk drive*, C: and a *networked disk drive*, N:

(a)　What is meant by:

　　(i)　local disk drive? (1)

　　(ii) networked disk drive? (1)

(b)　The command "Type" lists the contents of a specified file on the desktop PC's VDU screen as shown in **Figure 1**.

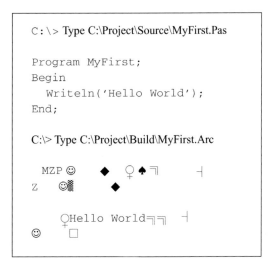

Figure 1

Using **only** the information contained in **Figure 1**, give **one** example of each of the following:

　　(i)　a logical drive (1)

　　(ii) a file pathname (1)

　　(iii) a sub-directory (1)

　　(iv) the filename of a text file (1)

　　(v) the filename of a non-text file (1)

(c)　Using the information contained within **Figure 1** complete the directory structure diagram shown in **Figure 2** for the desktop PC's local drive, C:

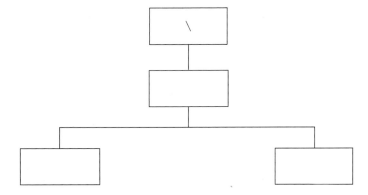

Figure 2

(1)

AQA CPT2 Qu 2 June 2003

3   For each of the following name a suitable type of operating system. Give one reason for your choice.

(a)   A computer system consisting of several desktop PCs sharing each other's files.   (2)

(b)   A computer system dedicated to controlling the flow of chemicals in a chemical processing plant.   (2)

(c)   A computer system dedicated to processing, at the end of each day, a bank's transactions stored on magnetic disk.   (2)

AQA CPT2 Qu 3 May 2002

4   (a)   In the context of file management what is a file?   (1)

The directory structure shown in the diagram contains a root directory (\ ) and three sub-directories, named **Work, Old** and **BackUp**.

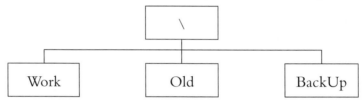

(b)   The sub-directory names **Work, Old** and **BackUp** will be stored in the directory structure. In which part of the directory structure will these names be stored?   (1)

(c)   Two files each with the filename **MyFirst.Pas** are stored in the system with the directory structure shown in the diagram. The sub-directory **BackUp** contains one entry for MyFirst.Pas and the **root** directory contains another.

What is the pathname for:

(i)   the root directory's entry for **MyFirst.Pas**;   (1)

(ii) the sub-directory BackUp's entry for **MyFirst.Pas**?   (1)

(d)   State **three** file access rights that may be applied to files such as **MyFirst.Pas**.   (3)

AQA CPT2 Qu 5 May 2001

5   For each of the following name a suitable type of operating system. Give one reason for your choice.

(a)   A computer system consisting of several desktop PCs and a printer shared on-line.   (2)

(b)   A computer system dedicated to controlling the temperature and humidity level in a pottery kiln.   (2)

(c)   A computer system dedicated to processing OMR forms returned at the end of each day.   (2)

AQA CPT2 Qu 4 May 2001

6   The role of an operating system is often said to be twofold:

1   To provide a virtual machine.

2   To manage the resources of the computer.

(a)   What is meant by "to provide a virtual machine"?   (1)

(b)   Name **three** types of resource managed by the operating system.   (3)

AQA CPT2 Qu 5 January 2003

Chapter 25 – Hardware Devices

In this chapter we will look at some of the common input, output and storage devices.

Keyboard data entry

The keyboard is the most common input device, suitable for a wide range of applications from entering programs to typing all kinds of documents using a word processor, or entering personal details of customers or patients at a hospital, etc. Data entered at a keyboard is commonly copied from a source document, and as such has disadvantages:

- It is easy to make **transcription** errors – that is, copy the data wrongly from the document.

- It is time-consuming.

- Data entry operators who enter data all day every day are prone to **repetitive strain injury** (RSI), a condition which renders them unable to do any further data entry or even perform everyday tasks such as pouring a cup of tea.

Microphone for voice data entry

The user speaks the text into a microphone and the text is displayed on the screen. The accuracy of the voice recognition system is improved by 'training' it to a particular user's voice – an embarrassing process of speaking a given set of a few hundred short sentences to your computer, repeating any that are not accurately interpreted.

2-25

About speech recognition

This feature is available in the Simplified Chinese, English (U.S.), and Japanese language versions of Microsoft Office.

You can use speech recognition to dictate text into any Office program. You can also select menu, toolbar, dialog box (U.S. English only), and task pane (U.S. English only) items by using your voice.

Speech recognition is not designed for completely hands-free operation; you'll get the best results if you use a combination of your voice and the mouse or keyboard.

To use speech recognition for the first time, install it by clicking **Speech** on the **Tools** menu in Microsoft Word, or by doing a custom installation. After speech recognition is installed, it is available on the **Tools** menu in any Office program.

▷ Speech recognition requirements

▽ Training speech recognition

After speech recognition is installed, you can increase speech recognition accuracy by taking a few minutes to train the computer to recognize how you speak.

When you read aloud the prepared training text, the training wizard can look for patterns in the way you speak, and gather voice data that helps interpret the words that you'll dictate into Office programs. The training session includes help with adjusting your microphone, and it should take less than 15 minutes to complete.

Figure 25.1: 'Help' on speech recognition in MS Office XP

Scanners and OCR

An optical scanner can be used to scan graphical images and photographs, and software can then be used to edit or touch up the images. Scanners can also be used to read typed or even hand-written documents and OCR (Optical Character Recognition) software can then be used to interpret the text and export it to a word processor or data file. Scanners are also used to input large volumes of data on preprinted forms such as credit card payments, where the customer's account number and amount paid are printed at the bottom of the payment slip.

Key-to-disk systems

In organisations where large amounts of data is collected on forms which then have to be keyed in for later processing (a **batch processing** system) an entire computer system consisting of a processor, dozens of terminals and central disk storage may be dedicated entirely to data entry. One terminal is nominated as the supervisor's terminal, from whose screen the supervisor can see exactly what every data entry operator is working on and how many keystrokes per hour and how many errors everyone is making. Completed batches of data are stored on disk from where they are either downloaded to the main computer over a communications link, or transferred to magnetic tape which is physically removed and taken to the main computer room.

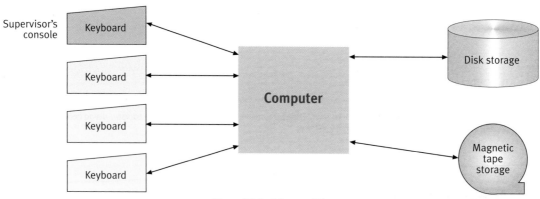

Figure 25.2: A key-to-disk system

Using a key-to-disk system, each data entry operator calls up the data entry program for their particular batch of data (e.g. payroll data entry, Council Tax payments, student grant applications) and keys in the data, which is automatically validated by the computer program.

When the batch of data has been entered and stored on disk, the source documents are passed to a second data entry operator who switches their machine to **verify** mode and keys in the data a second time. The keystrokes are compared with the data already stored on disk and any discrepancy causes the machine to beep so that the error can be corrected.

Mouse, joystick, light pen, touch screen

The mouse and its variants such as a trackball is well known to all users of PCs. A light pen is a device which incorporates a light sensor so that when it is held close to the screen over a character or part of a graphic, the object is detected and can be moved to create or modify graphics.

A touch screen allows the user to touch an area of the screen rather than having to type the data on a keyboard. They are widely used in tourist centres, where tourists can look up various local facilities and entertainments, in fast food stores such as McDonald's for entering customer orders, in manufacturing and many other environments.

Magnetic Ink Character Reader (MICR)

All banks use MICR for processing cheques. Along the bottom of a cheque the bank's sort code, customer account number and cheque number are encoded in special characters in magnetic ink. The amount of the cheque is encoded in magnetic ink when it is handed in at a bank. The cheques can then be processed extremely fast by high-speed MICR devices that read, sort and store the data on disk. MICR has several advantages for processing cheques:

• it is hard to forge the characters;

• the characters can be read even if the cheque is crumpled, dirty or smudged;

• the characters are readable by humans, unlike bar codes.

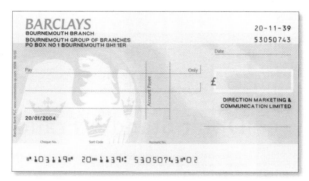

Figure 25.3: MICR characters along the bottom of a cheque

Magnetic stripe reader

Cards with magnetic stripes are used as credit cards, debit cards, railway tickets, phone cards and many other applications. The magnetic strip can be encoded with up to 220 characters of data, and there are over 2.4 billion plastic card transactions every year in Britain, with 83% of adults owning at least one card. Nevertheless, three factors threaten to destroy the lucrative business that high street banks have made out of plastic: crime, the cost of cash and competition. In 1996 card fraud cost the banks £97.1 million, with £13.3 million of it from fake magnetic stripe cards.

Figure 25.4: Magnetic stripe card

Case Study: Tracking your every move

With its reward scheme, Sainsbury's records every purchase made using the reward card, including the store name, the date and time and the price paid. Over a period of time this helps them to monitor trends in purchasing, which helps the store to predict the level of stockholding required in future, and ensures that they send customers information that they will be interested in. Sainsbury's will draw conclusions from your address; are you in an area classified as "rising", "prosperous and metropolitan professional", or "gentrified multi-ethnic"?

Customers are also classified by frequency of visits, average spend per visit and the type of goods they buy. For example, you might fall into the category of customer that "buys products which suggest they enjoy trying new and different ingredients in their cooking".

Under the Data Protection Act, you are entitled to see exactly what information is held about you. For a maximum charge of £10, a company from whom you request your personal information must send it to you within 40 days.

Smart cards

The 220 characters on magnetic stripe cards are simply too easy to copy, which is why the stripes are being replaced by a chip, which is almost impossible to fake. Smart cards look similar to plastic cards with a magnetic stripe, but instead of (or as well as) the magnetic stripe, they contain a 1-millimetre square microprocessor embedded in the middle, behind a small gold electrical contact. Instead of swiping the card, you plug it into a reader.

Chip cards cost only about £1 to produce, and can hold millions of characters of data. Banks are gradually replacing magnetic stripe cards with 'chip and pin' cards which they hope will cut credit and debit card fraud. Instead of signing the credit card slip, customers type in their secret PIN.

Figure 25.5: The www.cardwatch.org.uk site gives advice on combating fraud

Q1: It has been suggested that other information such as kidney donor record and driving licence could be held on the same chip card that allows you to withdraw cash and pay for goods.

What would be the benefits of doing this?

What other information would it be useful to hold on a card of this sort?

Optical Mark Reader (OMR)

An optical mark reader can detect marks made in preset positions on a form. It is widely used for marking multiple-choice exams and market research questionnaires.

Bar code reader or scanner

Bar codes appear on almost everything we buy. The pattern of thick and thin represents the 13-digit number underneath the bar code. There are four main pieces of information on a bar code.

The first two (or sometimes three) digits indicate in which country the product has been registered. The code for the UK and Ireland is 50.

Figure 25.6: A product bar code

The next five digits represent the manufacturer's code – Cadbury's, for example, is 00183.

The second group of five numbers represents the product and package size, but not the price. The last digit is a check digit, which is calculated from the other digits in the code and ensures that the barcode is keyed in or read correctly

Q2: A supermarket has a file of all stock items, which is on-line to the point-of-sale terminals at each check-out. What data is held on the stock file? What processing takes place when an item is scanned by the barcode reader? What is the output from the process?

Hand-held input devices

Portable keying devices are commonly used in such applications as reading gas or electricity meters, where the meter reader displays the next customer name, address and location of meter on a small screen, then reads the meter and keys in the reading. At the end of the day all the readings can be downloaded via a communications link to the main computer for processing.

Digitiser (Graphics tablet)

Professional quality illustrations can be drawn on a digitiser, which is a flat rectangular slab of material onto which a stylus is placed. The position of the stylus can be detected by the computer. As well as, or instead of a stylus, a 'puck' may be used to click on a special template which covers part of the tablet.

Graphics tablets come in a wide range of resolutions and types, from those used by primary school children to create drawings, to those used by engineers and architects in conjunction with computer-aided design (CAD) software. The graphics tablet shown in Figure 25.7 is a high-resolution tablet that translates x-y dimensional data into readable format and transfers it to a computer.

Figure 25.7: A graphics tablet

Digital Camera

Digital cameras convert the captured photograph directly into a digital image. It can be stored in flash memory in the camera and downloaded later to a computer.

Output devices

The most common output device for producing hard copy is the **printer**. Printers come in all shapes and sizes, and the type of printer chosen will depend on several factors such as:

- **volume of output** – for high volumes, a fast, heavy-duty printer is required;
- **quality of print required** – business letters and reports to clients, for example, will require a high quality print, probably on special headed stationery;
- **location of the printer** – if the printer is going to be situated in a busy office, the noise that it makes is an important consideration;
- **requirement for multiple copies** – some printers cannot produce multiple copies;
- **requirements for colour** – does the output need to be in colour?

Dot matrix printer

A dot matrix printer is an **impact printer**, producing its image by striking the paper through a ribbon. Its print head consists of a number of small pins, varying between 9 and 24 depending on the manufacturer. A 24 pin print head will produce a better quality of print than a 9 pin print head because the dots are closer together.

As the print head moves across the page, one or more pins strike the ribbon and make a dot on the paper. The figure below shows how the letter F is produced.

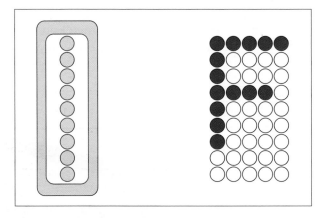

Figure 25.8: Dot matrix print head

In order to produce 'near letter quality' (**NLQ**) print, a line is printed twice, with the print head being shifted along very slightly in the second printing so that the spaces between the dots are filled in. The disadvantage of this technique is that the document then takes approximately twice as long to print. Many dot matrix printers are 'bidirectional', meaning that they can print in either direction, thus eliminating the need to start printing each line from the left hand side of the page.

Dot matrix printers are extremely versatile, with most of them able to print in condensed, standard and enlarged mode, in 'bold' or normal print. They are useful in situations where several copies of a document need to be routinely produced on 2-, 3- or 4-part stationery.

Many dot matrix printers have a graphics mode that enables them to print pictures and graphs by activating individual print head pins separately or in combination to produce any shape or line. With appropriate software any typeface can be produced, and using a special 4-colour ribbon (red, yellow, blue and black), colour output for, say, a graphical presentation can be produced. However the quality of colour is not as good as that produced by other types of colour printer.

One of the main drawbacks of a dot matrix printer is its noise; in an office environment it can be an irritating distraction. Covers can be obtained to cut down the noise, but it is still audible.

Figure 25.9: A dot matrix printer

Ink jet printers

Ink jet printers are a popular type of non-impact printer, with prices ranging between £50 and £500; a popular colour inkjet printer such as Hewlett Packard's Photosmart 7660 costs around £150. They are compact and quiet, and offer resolution almost as good as a laser printer. However, they are slow in operation; on average 3 pages per minute are printed, but a complex combination of text and colour can take several minutes for a single sheet.

Inkjet printers such as the HP Deskjet fire a droplet of ink at the page by boiling it in a microscopic tube and letting steam eject the droplet. Heating the ink can damage the colour pigments and matching the ink chemistry to the broad range of papers used in the office is a technical challenge. Large areas of colour can get wet, buckle, and the ink may smear. Printing an ink jet colour page can cost as much as 75p if all colour inks are supplied in a single cartridge; more thrifty printers will use separate red, blue, yellow and black cartridges which can be individually replaced. Although ordinary photocopy paper can be used, special smooth-coated paper may produce a more satisfactory result.

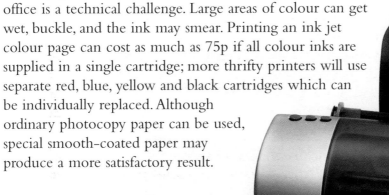

Figure 25.10: An Epson inkjet printer

Laser printers

Laser printers are becoming increasingly popular, with prices dropping rapidly to under £300 for a PostScript printer suitable for desktop publishing applications. Laser printers use a process similar to a photocopying machine, with toner (powdered ink) being transferred to the page and then fused onto it by heat and pressure. A laser printer produces output of very high quality at a typical speed in the region of ten pages per minute, and is virtually silent in operation. The main running expenses are the toner, which costs about £75 for a cartridge lasting for around 5,000 copies, and a maintenance contract which is typically up to £300 per annum.

Colour laser printers range between £600 and £5,000.

Figure 25.11: Colour laser printer

Plotters

2-25

A plotter is an output device used to produce high quality line drawings such as building plans or electronic circuits. They are generally classified as pen (vector plotters) or penless (raster plotters). The former use pens to draw images using point-to-point data, moving the pen over the paper. Pen plotters are low in price and hold a large share of the plotter market.

Penless plotters include electrostatic plotters, thermal plotters and laser plotters. They are generally used where drawings of high densities are required, for example drawings of machines, printed circuit boards or maps. Colour electrostatic plotters are increasingly being used in, for example, assembly drawings of machines and building plans, making them easier to read and understand.

Figure 25.12: Plotter

Monitor, also called Visual Display Unit (VDU)

A VDU has three basic attributes: size, colour and resolution. It has its own fixed amount of RAM associated with it to store the image being displayed on the screen, and the amount of RAM it has will determine the resolution and the maximum number of colours that can be displayed. Note that:

• the resolution is determined by the number of pixels (addressable picture elements) used to represent a full-screen image;

• the number of colours that can be displayed is determined by how many bits are used to represent each pixel. If only one bit is used to represent each pixel, then only two colours can be represented. To display 256 colours, 8 bits per pixel are required, and to display 65,536 (i.e. 2^{16}) colours, 16 bits (2 bytes) per pixel are needed. It is usually possible to adjust both the resolution and the number of colours - *if a high resolution is selected you won't be able to have as many colours because of the memory limitations of the video card.*

For example, if a resolution of 800x600 pixels is selected together with 65,536 colours, the amount of video RAM required will be 800x600x2 bytes = 960,000 bytes, i.e. almost 1Mb. If 1Mb is all the video RAM supplied by the manufacturer, the resolution cannot be increased to say, 1000x800 unless the number of bytes used to represent each pixel is reduced, thus limiting the number of colours which can be displayed.

On a PC, the number of colours and the resolution of the screen can be adjusted on the Display option of the Control Panel.

2-25

Figure 25.13: Adjusting the number of colours and resolution of a PC

Primary and secondary storage

A computer's main memory (RAM) is known as **primary storage**. In order to execute a program, the program instructions and the data on which it is to operate have to be loaded into main memory. Primary storage, however, is **volatile**; when the computer is switched off, all the contents of memory are lost. This is one good reason to perform frequent saves to disk when working on, for example, a word processed document.

A more permanent, **non-volatile** form of storage is required by all computer systems to save software and data files. Magnetic tape, magnetic disks, CD-ROM (Compact Disk Read Only Memory), and microfilm are all examples of what is known as **secondary storage**.

Magnetic Disk storage

A magnetic disk consists of two surfaces, each of which contains concentric circles called tracks. Each track is divided into sectors. If you reformat a disk that already has data on it, all the data will be erased (although you can also do a 'quick format' which erases only the file directory).

2-25

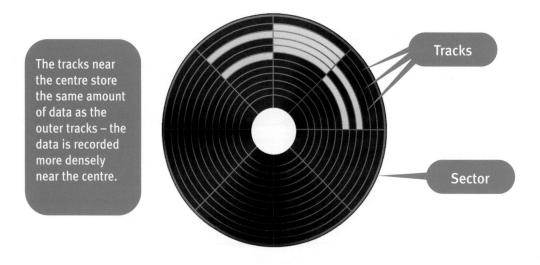

The tracks near the centre store the same amount of data as the outer tracks – the data is recorded more densely near the centre.

Tracks

Sector

Figure 25.14: Tracks and sectors on a magnetic disk

Floppy disks

The standard 3½" floppy disk is a thin, flexible plastic disk coated in metal oxide, enclosed in a rigid plastic casing. A standard high density disk has a storage capacity of 1.44 Megabytes. The disk can be removed from the drive unit and is highly portable. Floppy disks are inexpensive but easily damaged.

Hard disks for microcomputers

The hard disk used with PCs consist of one or more disk platters permanently sealed inside a casing. Hard disks typically have a capacity of between 40Gb and 160Gb.

Each surface has its own read-write head. The heads are mounted on a single spindle so they all move in and out together

Figure 25.15: A microcomputer hard disk drive

External hard drives, which can be plugged into a microcomputer, are available as extra storage.

Hard disks for minis and mainframes

For large-scale applications storing huge amounts of data, several hard disk units will be required. The disks may be either fixed (sealed inside the unit) or removable. Fixed disks are faster, more reliable, and have a greater storage capacity.

As with other types of disk, data is stored on concentric tracks, with tracks being divided into sectors. All the tracks that are accessible from one position of the read-write heads form a **cylinder**; data is recorded cylinder by cylinder to minimise movement of the read-write heads, thereby minimising access time.

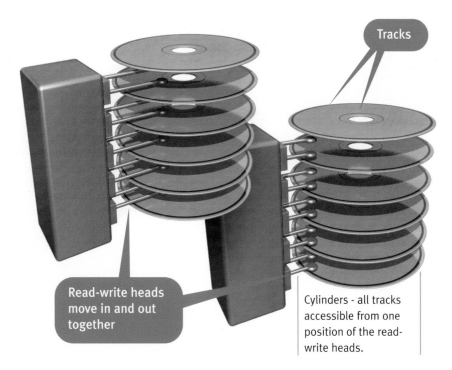

Tracks

Read-write heads move in and out together

Cylinders - all tracks accessible from one position of the read-write heads.

Figure 25.16: A disk drive

2-25

Magnetic tape

Data is recorded in 'frames' across the tape, with one frame representing one byte. The frames form tracks along the length of the tape, with 9 tracks being common, giving 8 data tracks and one parity track.

1	0	1	_Track 1_
1	1	1	
0	1	1	
0	0	0	
1	1	0	
1	1	0	
0	0	1	
0	0	1	
0	0	1	_Parity track_

Figure 25.17: Tracks on a magnetic tape

Magnetic tape is a serial medium, meaning that an individual record can only be accessed by starting at the beginning of the tape and reading through every record until the required one is found. Likewise, it is impossible to read a record, amend it in memory, then backspace to the beginning of the block and overwrite the old record. Therefore, updating a magnetic tape file always involves copying the file to a new tape with the amendments made.

Uses of magnetic tape

Tape is a cheap and convenient medium for backup, and is also used for **archiving** past transactions or other data that may be needed again, such as for example, weather records collected over a number of years.

Cartridge tape drives are in common use for backing up the hard disk of personal computers, being much more convenient than using dozens of floppy disks. A cartridge tape can store several gigabytes of data.

Figure 25.18: Cartridge tape

Q3: Discuss the relative advantages of hard disks, floppy disks and magnetic tape.

Optical Disks

Random access time is longer than that of a hard disk, but some optical storage is writeable or even re-writeable. CD-ROM, DVD-ROM (Read-only), CD-R, DVD-R (Writeable), CD-RW, DVD-RW (Re-Writeable)

CD-ROM

CD-ROMs can store around 680Mb of data, equivalent to hundreds of floppy disks. The data may be in text form, or may be in the form of graphics, photographic images, video clips or sound files. Although they do not transfer data as fast as a hard disk drive, their speed is increasing every year and is acceptable for most applications.

As the name suggests, the disks are read-only. When the master disk is created, a laser beam burns tiny pits in the surface of the disk, which (unlike a magnetic disk) has a single spiral track divided into sectors. To read data from the disk, a laser beam is reflected off the surface of the disk, detecting the presence or absence of pits which represent binary digits.

CD-ROMs are widely used for distribution of software, multimedia files, catalogues and technical manuals.

CD-R disks

Write Once, Read Many optical laser disks (WORM disks) look similar to CD-ROM disks, but they are often gold rather than silver in colour. An end-user company can use these disks to write their own material, typically for archiving or storing, say, graphic or photographic images which will not be changed.

These disks are also widely used for pirated software; whereas silver CDs are pressed in factories, gold CDs are usually written one at a time on PCs in garages and back bedrooms. A £2 blank disk can hold £20,000 worth of software and sell for £50 to £80, and they are sometimes used by less reputable PC manufacturers who install the software on their PCs to make a more attractive deal for the unsuspecting customer. However, because there is a lot of competition among pirates, these CDs sometimes carry viruses which can cause havoc on a hard drive.

CD-RW disks

These are re-writeable disks and are more expensive than CD-R. A CD writer drive costs in the region of £60 to £100. These can be used for backing up where they may need to be overwritten.

DVD-ROM

Digital Versatile Disk Read-Only Memory. These disks are the same size as CD-ROMs and are made using similar materials and manufacturing teachniques. They store about seven times as much data as a CD-ROM, because the track spacing and pit dimensions are smaller.

Figure 25.19: DVD ROM

2-25

> **Q4:** What are some of the applications of CD-ROM? Why is CD-ROM particularly suitable for these applications?

Flash memory

Flash is electrically erasable programmable read-only memory (EEPROM). It is used in memory cards for peripheral devices such as digital cameras, mobile telephones, PDAs and MP3 players. It is also available as USB memory sticks and, when plugged into a computer's USB port, behaves like an external disk drive. Flash memory is inexpensive, high-capacity storage and is rapidly replacing floppy disks as portable secondary storage. A memory stick with 1Gb capacity costs around £180.

Figure 25.20: Flash memory stick plugs into USB port on keyboard or processor box.

Exercises

1 Name the most suitable storage medium for each of the following.

    (a) Backing up a 20Kb file.   (1)

    (b) Backing up 1Gb of data.   (1)

    (c) Distributing a software package requiring 400Mb of storage space.   (1)

    (d) Transferring a 30Kb file from one stand-alone computer to another.   (1)

    (e) A database generated and used in the course of a police investigation of a major crime.   (1)

    (f) Distributing an electronic copy of an encyclopaedia.   (1)

                                               New Question

2 A book lending library lends books to borrowers. Each borrower is assigned a unique borrower code. This code is encoded magnetically onto an identity card issued to each borrower when they join the library. The code is read from the identity card by swiping it through a machine connected to the library's computer system. The code is also printed on the card in human-readable form.

    (a) Name the type of machine used to read the borrower code from the card   (1)

    (b) State **one** reason for having the human-readable form of the borrower code printed on the card.   (1)

                                               New Question

3 (a) **Figure 1** shows a label removed from an item sold at a supermarket.

Figure 1

What input device would have been used in the supermarket to read this label? (1)

    (b) **Figure 2** shows a response form that customers of the supermarket have been asked to complete. The forms are processed using a computer system running a *batch operating system*.

Customer Survey				
Q1	– A –	– B –	– C –	– D –	– E –
Q2	– A –	– B –	– C –	– D –	– E –
Q3	– A –	– B –	– C –	– D –	– E –
Q4	– A –	– B –	– C –	– D –	– E –
Q5	– A –	– B –	– C –	– D –	– E –

Using an HB pencil place a mark through one of
the five letters for questions one to five

Figure 2

Name the most suitable input device to transfer the data on each survey form into a computer system.   (1)

                                               New Question

2-25

Chapter 26 – Computer Crime and the Law

Computer crime and abuse

New technologies generally create new opportunities for crime; as soon as one avenue is blocked to the criminal, another one is discovered. As information technology has spread, so too have computer crime and abuse. The Internet, for example, is used not only by innocent members of the public but also by fraudulent traders, paedophiles, software pirates, hackers and terrorists. Their activities include planting computer viruses, software bootlegging, storing pornographic images and perpetrating all sorts of criminal activities from credit card fraud to the most complex multinational money laundering schemes.

Computer abuse refers to acts that are legal but unethical.

Hacking

Hacking is defined as unauthorised access to data held on a computer system. The extent of hacking is extremely difficult to establish as it is usually only discovered by accident, with only about two percent of security breaches discovered as a result of positive action on the part of security staff. (*Digital Crime* by Neil Barrett, page 40.)

Hacking is often perpetrated by employees of a company who have acquired inside knowledge of particular user Ids and passwords. The ability of such hackers to carry out illegal actions without being detected is often hampered by the audit and monitoring software that all computer operating systems supply.

The motive behind hacking can often be mischievous rather than anything more sinister: computing students who are learning about operating systems may take delight in penetrating a university's security system to prove that it can be done, or to gain access to exam questions and answers. However, international fraudsters are constantly finding new ways of acquiring funds illegally, targeting both banks and individuals.

Case study: 'Trojan' programs

High Street banks have admitted that they are losing money to criminals who record passwords and identities using remotely operated key-logging programs. Most banks have switched their logging-in procedures for online customers to avoid the threat from Trojan programs which have been surreptitiously placed on users' computers to record keystrokes.

Instead of, or as well as, requiring customers to type in their user IDs and passwords, they are asked to select letters from a dropdown menu by clicking on them with a mouse to identify just part of their 'memorable information'.

> To complete log on please enter the requested numbers and/or letters from your Memorable Information using the 3 drop down lists provided. Please click on 'Help' if you require further assistance.
>
> Please enter characters 2, 3 and 7 from your Memorable Information
>
> 2   3   7
>
> [▾]   [▾]   [▾]
>
> ◯ Continue
> ◯ Cancel

Viruses

Viruses are generally developed with a definite intention to cause damage to computer files or, at the very least, cause inconvenience and annoyance to computer users. The first virus appeared at the University of Delaware in 1987, and the number of viruses escalated to over 9000 different variations in 1997. The virus usually occupies the first few instructions of a particular program on an 'infected' disk and relies on a user choosing to execute that program. When an infected program is executed, the virus is the first series of instructions to be performed. In most cases the virus's first action is to copy itself from the diskette onto the PC and 'hide' within obscure files, the operating system code or within unused disk blocks which are then marked as being 'bad' and unavailable for reuse. The virus can then proceed to perform any of a number of tasks ranging from the irritating to the catastrophic such as reformatting the hard disk.

Some viruses lie dormant, waiting to be triggered by a particular event or date – the 'Friday 13th' virus being a well-known one. The virus then infects other diskettes, perhaps by modifying operating system programs responsible for copying programs. From there, the next PC to use the diskette will be infected.

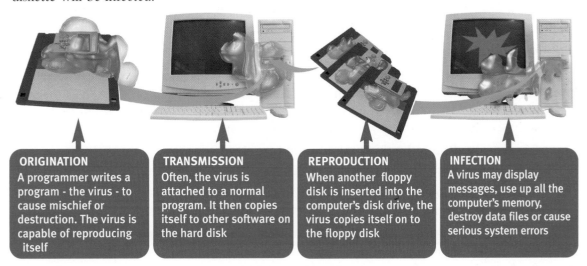

ORIGINATION
A programmer writes a program - the virus - to cause mischief or destruction. The virus is capable of reproducing itself

TRANSMISSION
Often, the virus is attached to a normal program. It then copies itself to other software on the hard disk

REPRODUCTION
When another floppy disk is inserted into the computer's disk drive, the virus copies itself on to the floppy disk

INFECTION
A virus may display messages, use up all the computer's memory, destroy data files or cause serious system errors

Figure 26.1: How a virus works

'Logic bombs' and Macro Viruses

A 'logic bomb' is similar to a virus and is sometimes delivered by means of a virus. The 'bomb' can be written to destroy or, worse, subtly change the contents of an organisation's computer systems. However, it does not begin this activity until signalled to do so by the hacker or extortionist, or it may be activated if a cancelling signal fails to arrive.

Case study: MyDoom

In January 2004 an innocuous attachment in an e-mail sent from Russia triggered a minor alarm at a leading e-mail security firm. Initially the number of copies of the new virus – christened 'MyDoom' after a misspelling of 'My domain' in its code – was small, just a few hundred. Within a few hours, numbers started to rise – to 40,000, 80,000, 200,000.

After 8 hours, millions of copies of MyDoom were circulating across the Internet. In an act of apparent terrorism, a variant of MyDoom and all its copies were programmed to attack a software company at **www.sco.com** simultaneously at 16.09 GMT on February 1st. Right on time, more than a million computers tried to load the homepage three times a second and the site had to be closed down.

MyDoom loops forever, sending more and more infected messages to every single address found on the hard drive endlessly.

Digital crime and the law

The rapid progress of computer technology has led to the need for new laws to be introduced so that all perpetrators of computer crime can be prosecuted. Laws in the US impact on computer users in this country, since the majority of systems and Internet content is American. A general approach to a common standard for Internet-related laws throughout the European Union formed part of a proposed European Commission directive discussed by member states in October 1996.

The Computer Misuse Act of 1990

In the early 1980s in the UK, hacking was not illegal. Some universities stipulated that hacking, especially where damage was done to data files, was a disciplinary offence, but there was no legislative framework within which a criminal prosecution could be brought. This situation was rectified by the Computer Misuse Act of 1990 which defined three specific criminal offences to deal with the problems of hacking, viruses and other nuisances. The offences are:

• unauthorised access to computer programs or data;

• unauthorised access with a further criminal intent;

• unauthorised modification of computer material (i.e. programs or data).

To date there have been relatively few prosecutions under this law – probably because most organisations are reluctant to admit that their system security procedures have been breached, which might lead to a loss of confidence on the part of their clients.

2-26

Case study: Online banking customers targetted

Online banking customers are being targeted by criminals who attempt to find out their passwords in a 'phishing' scam designed to persuade unsuspecting users to type in their security details into a bogus form purporting to come from the bank.

The screenshot shows the scam e-mail, which does not, of course, come from Lloyds Bank. The link takes you to a bogus website asking you to enter your security details. *Don't do it!*

Copyright, Design and Patents Act of 1988

Computer software is now covered by the Copyright Designs and Patents Act of 1988, which covers a wide range of intellectual property such as music, literature and software. Provisions of the Act make it illegal to:

• copy software;

• run pirated software;

• transmit software over a telecommunications line, thereby creating a copy.

Software can easily be copied and bootlegged (sold illegally). It is illegal to buy such software!

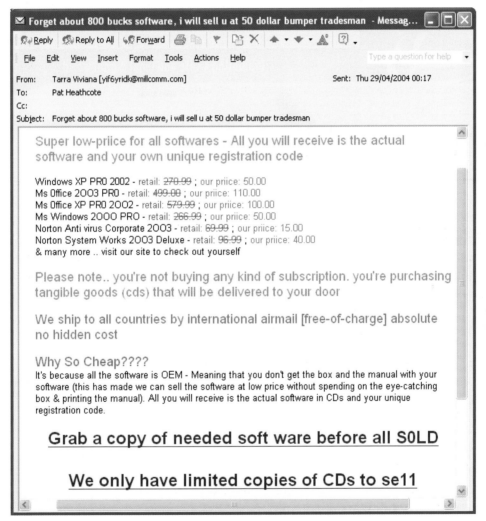

Figure 26.2: An e-mail advertising pirated software

In addition, the programming *ideas* and *methods* can be stolen by a competitor. Microsoft was sued (unsuccessfully) many years ago by Apple Computers for copying the 'look and feel' of their graphical user interface. It is possible for an expert programmer to 'reverse engineer' machine code to establish the specific algorithms used, so that they can be copied. Some software manufacturers put 'fingerprints' into the code – little oddities which do not affect the way the program runs – so that if the same code is found in a competitor's program, they can prove that it was illegally copied.

The Business Software Alliance helps companies to ensure that all software being used is correctly licensed. Offences include using 'pirate' copies of software and using software on more machines than is permitted under the terms of the licence.

Figure 26.3: The BSA website

Exercises

1   A student on work experience in the payroll department of Widgets plc, when left alone, successfully logged into the company's computer system by guessing the administrator's user id and password. The student changed the hourly rate of several employees by accessing the company's payroll file.

   (a)   The Company Misuse Act defines three types of offence. What **two** offences did the student commit according to this Act? (2)

   (b)   Given that the student was left alone in the computer room, the company could have prevented or detected what happened. Describe briefly **three** methods of security that the company could have used. (3)

AQA CPT2 Qu 5 January 2001

2   Name the legislation that applies in the following cases.

   (a)   An Examination Board allows a software reseller access to its database of centre names and addresses so that the reseller can market its products directly to centres that teach AS Computing. (1)

   (b)   A company using an encryption algorithm in one of its software products receives a demand for royalties from another software company that claims that it invented the encryption algorithm. (1)

   (c)   A user sends an attachment to an e-mail which when opened infects the recipient's computer with a virus. (1)

   (d)   A company has its computing equipment seized by the police for using unlicensed commercial software. (1)

AQA CPT2 Qu 5 June 2003

Chapter 27 – Data Protection & Health and Safety

Personal privacy

The right to privacy is a fundamental human right and one that we take for granted. Most of us, for instance, would not want our medical records freely circulated, and many people are sensitive about revealing their age, religious beliefs, family circumstances or academic qualifications. In the UK even the use of name and address files for mail shots is often felt to be an invasion of privacy.

With the advent of large computerised databases it became quite feasible for sensitive personal information to be stored without the individual's knowledge and accessed by, say, a prospective employer, credit card company or insurance company to assess somebody's suitability for employment, credit or insurance.

Case study: James Wiggins – a true story

In the US, James Russell Wiggins applied for and got a $70,000 post with a company in Washington. A routine pre-employment background check, however, revealed that he had been convicted of possessing cocaine, and he was fired the next day, not only because he had a criminal record but because he had concealed this fact when applying for the job. Wiggins was shocked – he had never had a criminal record, and it turned out that the credit bureau hired to make the investigation had retrieved the record for a James Ray Wiggins by mistake, even though they had different birthdates, addresses, middle names and social security numbers. Even after this was discovered, however, Wiggins didn't get his job back.

If the pre-employment check had been made *before* Wiggins was offered the job, he would not have been offered it and no reason would have been given. The information would have remained on his file, virtually ensuring that he would never get a decent job – without ever knowing the reason why.

The Data Protection Acts of 1984 and 1998

The Data Protection Act 1984 grew out of public concern about personal privacy in the face of rapidly developing computer technology. It provides rights for individuals and demands good information handling practice.

The Act covers 'personal data' which are 'automatically processed'. It works in two ways, giving individuals certain rights whilst requiring those who record and use personal information on computer to be open about that use and to follow proper practices.

The Data Protection Act 1998 was passed in order to implement a European Data Protection Directive. This Directive sets a standard for data protection throughout all the countries in the European Union, and the new Act was brought into force in March 2000. Some manual records fall within the scope of the Act and there are also extended rights for data subjects.

2-27

The Data Protection Principles

The Data Protection Act became law on 12th July 1984 and was updated in 1998.

Once registered, data users must comply with the eight Data Protection principles of good information handling practice contained in the Act. Broadly these state that personal data must be:

1 fairly and lawfully obtained and processed;

2 processed for specified purposes;

3 adequate, relevant and not excessive;

4 accurate and kept up to date;

5 not kept longer than necessary;

6 processed in accordance with the data subject's rights;

7 kept securely against unauthorised access and accidental loss or damage;

8 not transferred to countries without adequate protection for the rights and freedom of data subjects.

Useful definitions from the 1984 Act

'Personal Data'   information about living, identifiable individuals. Personal data do not have to be particularly sensitive information, and can be as little as a name and address.

'Data Controllers (users)'   those who control the contents and use of a collection of personal data. They can be any type of company or organisation, large or small, within the public or private sector. A data user can also be a sole trader, partnership, or an individual. A data user need not necessarily own a computer.

'Data Subjects'   the individuals to whom the personal data relate.

Data Subjects

We are all 'data subjects'. All types of companies and organisations ('data users') have details about us on their computers. This growth of computerised information has many benefits but also potential dangers. If the information is entered wrongly, is out of date or is confused with someone else's, it can cause problems. You could be unfairly refused jobs, housing, benefits, credit or a place at college. You could be overcharged for goods or services. You could even find yourself arrested in error, just because there is a mistake in the computerised information.

The Information Commissioner

The Commissioner is an independent supervisory authority and has an international role as well as a national one.

In the UK the Commissioner has a range of duties including the promotion of good information handling and the encouragement of codes of practice for data controllers, that is, anyone who decides how and why personal data, (information about identifiable, living individuals) is processed.

The site **www.informationcommissioner.gov.uk** contains a lot of information on the Data Protection Act and the rights of individuals.

Figure 27.1: The Information Commissioner's Home Page

A data user's Register entry

With few exceptions, all data users have to register, giving their name and address together with broad descriptions of:

- those about whom personal data are held;

- the items of data held;

- the purposes for which the data are used;

- the sources from which the information may be obtained;

- the types of organisations to whom the information may be disclosed i.e. shown or passed on to;

- any overseas countries or territories to which the data may be transferred.

Some exemptions from the Act

- The Act does not apply to payroll, pensions and accounts data, nor to names and addresses held for distribution purposes.

- Registration may not be necessary when data is for personal, family, household or recreational use.

- Subjects do not have a right to access data if the sole aim of collecting it is for statistical or research purposes, or where it is simply for backup.

- Data can be disclosed to the data subject's agent (e.g. lawyer or accountant), to persons working for the data user, and in response to urgent need to prevent injury or damage to health.

Additionally, there are exemptions for special categories, including data held:

- in connection with national security;

- for prevention of crime;

- for the collection of tax or duty.

The rights of data subjects

The Data Protection Act allows individuals to have access to information held about themselves on computer and, where appropriate, to have it corrected or deleted.

As an individual you are entitled, on making a written request to a data user, to be supplied with a copy of any personal data held about yourself. The data user may charge a fee of up to £10 for each register entry for supplying this information but in some cases it is supplied free.

Usually the request must be responded to within 40 days. If not, you are entitled to complain to the Registrar or apply to the courts for correction or deletion of the data.

Apart from the right to complain to the Registrar, data subjects also have a range of rights which they may exercise in the civil courts. These are:

- right to compensation for unauthorised disclosure of data;
- right to compensation for inaccurate data;
- right of access to data and to apply for rectification or erasure where data is inaccurate;
- right to compensation for unauthorised access, loss or destruction of data.

Encryption technology

How secure are e-mails? When you order goods over the Internet and give your credit card number, it is obviously vital that this information cannot be intercepted by anyone. This can be achieved by **encrypting** the data. A common encryption system depends on being able to find the prime factors of two very large numbers, say 155 digits long. It is possible to devise an encryption key, which is virtually impossible to break, and this is termed **'strong encryption'**. However, there are issues here: governments are wary of allowing strongly encrypted data to circulate, fearing that terrorists, criminals and spies could transmit messages that can never be decoded. So far, for example, it has proved impossible to factor 200-digit numbers. **'Weak encryption'** using fewer digits means the code is not breakable except by organisations with massive processing power and the will to do so – organised crime presumably included. In 1999 researchers proved that they could crack a code used by the majority of major international and financial institutions, which used 155-digit numbers. *Yesterday's strong encryption is today's weak encryption.*

E-mails and privacy issues

Standard e-mail is not private. It sits around on various computers on its way to you, and even after you delete an e-mail it will still be accessible to someone with a good utility program. The only way to ensure e-mail privacy is to use an encryption program.

Many employees have their own e-mail addresses at their places of work. How private is e-mail sent to and from these addresses? Commonly, e-mails sent out from these addresses go out with the company footer, which makes it look as if they have been sanctioned by the firm.

In December 1999, twenty-three office staff from the New York Times were fired after managers discovered they had been e-mailing smutty jokes, pornographic pictures and jokes about bosses. The New York Times has a policy specifying that 'communications must be consistent with conventional standards of ethical and proper conduct, behaviour and manners'.

In 1997, Norwich Union paid £450,000 in an out-of-court settlement and had to make a public apology when an e-mail on the Intranet disparaging a competitor got out.

For information on privacy, try Privacy International **www.privacyinternational.org**.

2-27

Health and Safety (Display Screen Equipment) Regulations 1992

Occupational health and safety legislation in Britain is researched, guided and structured by the Health and Safety Executive (HSE), a government body. An EEC Directive on work with display screen equipment was completed in the early 1990s, with member states required to adapt it to become part of their own legislation. As a consequence, the Health and Safety at Work Act of 1974 incorporated legislation pertaining to the use of VDUs, and the relevant section is now referred to as The Health and Safety (Display Screen Equipment) Regulations 1992.

This legislation is intended to protect the health of employees within the working environment. Employers, employees and manufacturers all have some responsibility for conforming to the law.

Employers are required to:

• perform an analysis of workstations in order to evaluate the safety and health conditions to which they give rise;

• provide training to employees in the use of workstation components;

• ensure employees take regular breaks or changes in activity;

• provide regular eye tests for workstation users and pay for glasses.

Employees have a responsibility to:

• use workstations and equipment correctly, in accordance with training provided by employers;

• bring problems to the attention of their employer immediately and co-operate in the correction of these problems.

Manufacturers are required to ensure that their products comply with the Directive. For example, screens must tilt and swivel, keyboards must be separate and moveable. Notebook PCs are not suitable for entering large amounts of data.

The ergonomic environment

Ergonomics refers to the design and functionality of the environment, and encompasses the entire range of environmental factors. Employers must give consideration to:

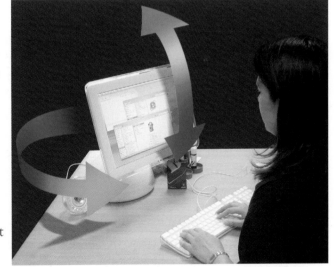

Figure 27.2: Workstations must be ergonomically designed

• **lighting**. The office should be well lit. Computers should neither face windows nor back onto a window so that the users have to sit with the sun in their eyes. Adjustable blinds should be provided.

• **furniture**. Chairs should be of adjustable height, with a backrest which tilts to support the user at work and at rest, and should swivel on a five-point base. It should be at the correct height relative to a keyboard on the desk.

• **work space.** The combination of chair, desk, computer, accessories (such as document holders, mouse and mouse mats, paper trays and so on), lighting, heating and ventilation all contribute to the worker's overall well-being.

2-27

- **noise.** Noisy printers, for example, should be given covers to reduce the noise or positioned in a different room.
- **hardware.** The screen must tilt, swivel, be flicker-free and the keyboard separately attached.
- **software.** Software is often overlooked in the quest for ergonomic perfection. The EEC Directive made a clear statement about the characteristics of acceptable software, requiring employers to analyse the tasks which their employers performed and to provide software which makes the tasks easier. It is also expected to be easy to use and adaptable to the user's experience.

Exercises

1   In some countries government agencies routinely monitor the content of e-mail routed over the Internet.

   (a)   Give **two** reasons why some governments may allow this to happen.   (2)

   (b)   Suggest **one** way in which an individual may make it difficult for any such agency to read the content of a particular e-mail sent over the Internet.   (1)

AQA CPT2 Qu 3 January 2002

2   (a)   The growing level of public concern over data stored in computer systems led the government to pass The Data Protection Act 1984. The Act was introduced to protect the right of individuals to privacy.

Give **three** reasons relating to the nature of computing systems that give rise to this concern.   (3)

   (b)   Name **two** other Acts that relate to computer systems.   (2)

AQA CPT2 Qu 3 January 2003

3   A well-known software company has constructed a media player to query an on-line database at the company's headquarters. It retrieves the titles of tracks on audio CDs for display in the media player's window. In the process it assigns a unique identifying digital fingerprint to the computer playing the audio track.

In a separate transaction, the company can then link this digital fingerprint to an e-mail sent from the same computer. This links the user's e-mail address to the music interests of the user for marketing purposes.

   (a)   Explain one benefit to

   (i)   the user   (1)

   (ii)   the software company.   (1)

   (b)   Why might the use of the link be considered unethical?   (1)

AQA CPT2 Qu 3 June 2003

2-27

Chapter 28 – Information Processing Applications

Computing – a look backwards

Within half a century, computers and information technology have changed the world and affected millions of lives in ways that no one could have foreseen. Here are some of the things that people have said about computers:

"I think there's a world market for maybe five computers."
(Thomas Watson, the chairman of IBM, in 1940)

"I have travelled the length and breadth of this country and talked with the best people, and I can assure you that data processing is a fad that won't last out the year."
(The editor in charge of business books for Prentice Hall, in 1957)

"There is no reason why anyone would want to have a computer in their home."
(President of Digital Equipment Corporation, in 1977)

Consequences of computer failure

Individuals, organisations and society in general are totally dependent on computer systems for everything from withdrawing £10 at the local cashpoint to transferring millions of pounds' worth of shares every day of the week on the Stock Exchange. Computers play a crucial role in thousands of everyday tasks such as figuring out how many pineapples need to be imported from Kenya to meet demand in Waitrose next week, or recording £10 million worth of lottery ticket sales every week.

The consequences of computer failure, however, can be anything from inconvenient to catastrophic. When the bank's computer goes down you may be unable to withdraw cash or pay your bills. When a hospital computer monitoring a patient's vital signs fails, it may be life-threatening.

Study of one major information processing application

The AQA specification requires you to study one major information processing application. You should consider the purpose of the application and its role as an information system. You are required to examine specific user-interface needs and communication requirements of the application. You should be able to discuss the economic, social, legal and ethical consequences of the application.

To help you in this task this chapter discusses, as a case study, one of Waitrose's IT systems.

2-28

Case Study: Waitrose Quick Check System

Wallace Waite, Arthur Rose and David Taylor opened their first small grocery shop in London in 1904. One hundred years later there are over 140 Waitrose supermarkets in England and Wales. Unlike other major supermarkets, Waitrose is not owned by shareholders and the City. Instead, as part of the John Lewis partnership, it is owned by everyone who works for the Partnership.

Behind the scenes, Waitrose uses IT in its buying and distribution centres. The company web site uses e-commerce for online shopping and for dedicated services such as ordering gifts and flowers through Waitrose Direct. In their shops, Waitrose uses EPOS terminals at the checkouts and at the Quick Check till.

Quick Check is Waitrose's "Scan as you shop" service. This service is available only to account-card holders and is currently implemented in around 70 branches. As part of the service, customers are also provided with special bags, so they can pack as they scan.

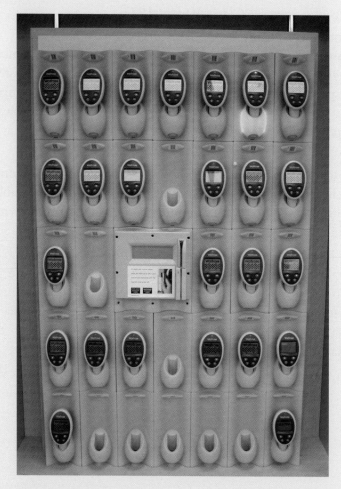

Figure 28.1: Waitrose's Quick Check rack

At the entrance, the customer (we'll call her Mrs Smith) swipes her account card through the card reader (Figure 28.1 middle of picture) on the Quick Check rack, which then releases a scanner to her. You can see Mrs Smith's scanner lit up in the top row of the photograph (Figure 28.1).

Using the hand-held scanner, Mrs Smith scans each item as she places it into her shopping bag.

The price of the last item scanned is shown on the display. The controls on the scanner allow the customer to check the list of items scanned and the current subtotal.

If she changes her mind about a particular item and puts it back on the shelf, the item can be scanned again pressing the 'minus' button to delete the entry.

The scanner beeps if an item scanned is part of a multi-buy special offer, so a customer can take full advantage of these offers.

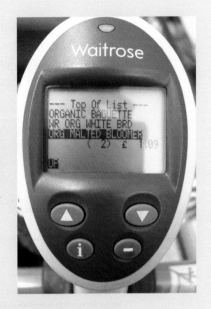

Figure 28.2: A hand-held scanner

Some items, such as freshly baked bread, do not have packaging with barcodes. The customer scans the relevant shelf edge label.

For example, if she selects 6 rolls 'Petit Pain' then the barcode shown in Figure 28.3 is scanned 6 times.

Figure 28.3: Shelf edge bar code

When Mrs Smith has finished shopping, she swipes a special barcode at the checkout.

Figure 28.4: The end-of-shopping bar code

All that is left to do is pay at the Quick Check till, without having to unpack and re-pack the shopping. If paying by debit, credit or account card the customer can save even more time by using Quick Pay. Mrs Smith simply inserts her account card to recall her bill, which is printed at the Quick Pay till.

Figure 28.5: The Quick Pay till

Purpose of the Quick Check

Waitrose introduced Quick Check as a means of gaining customer loyalty. At a time when other stores were offering loyalty cards with money-off vouchers, Waitrose was offering quality of service. The Quick Check system was introduced as a pilot scheme in one store in 1997, and it was soon evident that customers liked the convenience of scanning their own shopping and avoiding queues at the checkouts. Waitrose observed an increase in 'basket value' – that is, customers were spending more money each time they went shopping. Waitrose's original objectives were satisfied at the pilot branch, and slowly the new system was introduced at other branches. It is now a distinguishing feature of a Waitrose store.

Quick Check as an information system

This system provides excellent information to both the customer and the store.

- The customer can easily find out the accurate price of an item, even if it is misplaced on the shelf or the shelf labelling not clear.
- The customer is informed of multi-buy offers and receives an itemised bill at the end.
- Waitrose collect accurate data for stock levels.

The data for the customer's bill and for stock control are supplied by means of a barcode read by the hand-held scanner.

Each product must have a unique identifying number. Manufacturers, wholesalers and retailers need to communicate, so there is a need for a common numbering system. ANA (the Article Numbering Association) allocates numbers used in a wide range of goods. Barcoding was chosen as the best labelling system for products because barcodes are reliable. They are also cheap as they can be produced by the normal printing process used for the product labels. Note that barcodes incorporated into printed labels do not store the price of the product. Different shops, all using the same barcode, are likely to be selling the same product at different prices.

For unwrapped items Waitrose displays barcodes at the shelf edge (Figure 28.3). For produce sold by weight, Waitrose produces barcodes in the store (Figure 28.6). Networked scales with a printer produce barcodes for items weighed and wrapped at service counters, such as cheese, sliced meats, vegetables and fruit.

Figure 28.6 Barcode for weighed produce *Figure 28.7 Barcode for reduced produce*

Reduced items are also labelled with a special barcode (Figure 28.7), which provides Waitrose with detailed information of what item was reduced and by how much. This is important management information.

Waitrose is planning to provide more information to customers via the scanner in the future.

Q1: What other useful information could be provided to customers?

User Interface needs

Quick Scan must be easy to use as it has a large user base and training overheads must be kept to a minimum. The scanner must be easy to operate and information on the scanner's screen must be easy to read and understand.

Communication requirements of Quick Check

The hand-held scanners need to be linked by wireless network to the Quick Check server, so that the price of an item being scanned can be downloaded from the database immediately. When the customer has finished shopping, and performs the end-of-shopping scan, the bill can be recalled by a simple swipe of the customer's account card at the Quick Pay till.

Stock levels need to be adjusted. This is done as soon as a customer ends their shopping, and at the end of the trading day the ordering system is updated. Any required price changes are also made at the end of the trading day when the product database is updated.

At random intervals shopping may be re-scanned to ensure customers do not abuse the trust. The system picks a customer completely randomly. The branch manager also has the right to request the system recalls a specified customer for re-checks.

Records of individual customers' purchases are held at branch levels, but are only used if there is a dispute with a customer. Waitrose does not collect customer profiles (customers' shopping habits).

Waitrose's and customers' needs

Waitrose needs accurate collection of data for billing and stock control.

Costs must be kept to a minimum, but the IT systems must be reliable and secure as the organisation's reputation is at stake.

Customers want to save time shopping and avoid queuing. Customers also want accurate information of the cost of items and the cost of their shopping.

Economic consequences

- The hardware required for Quick Check is expensive and Waitrose estimates that it will take 2-5 years to get a return on their investment.
- Quick Check accounts for 20% of sales. If fewer customers require EPOS checkouts, this can release floor space and increase selling space. Waitrose can save on labour costs as not as many checkout operators will be required.
- Decreasing turnaround time per customer allows more customers to be served per hour. This also makes better use of car parks.
- Waitrose needs to ensure customers are honest and scan each item as it is packed into the bags.

Social consequences

Does Quick Check result in a reduced labour force or just fewer boring jobs? Do customers find a visit to the supermarket less personal, and does this bother them? The shopping trip involves less contact with Waitrose staff because a customer can shop and pay without any human intervention at the checkout.

Legal and ethical consequences

Account card details are not held at the supermarket. The Accounts Department holds customer account details and must register the purpose of holding the names and addresses. Waitrose does not hold any personal data as a consequence of Quick Check, as there is no link made between address and account card, so there is no need to register further with the Information Registrar (Data Protection Act).

Discussion: Waitrose has a policy of not storing the Quick Check data in conjunction with account card holders' addresses, so there is no danger of breaching customers' privacy. However, other shops using similar systems might be less ethical. It would not take a lot of extra information to build up a picture of what individual customers buy, where they buy and when they buy. If the customer pays by credit or debit card the shop could also find out what bank this customer uses. The shop could build up profiles of their customers' shopping habits. How could this information be used by the shop? Would this be ethical?

The future

There is a lot of discussion in the media currently about the future development of RF ID tags (radio frequency identification tags) or 'smart tags'. Such tags are an improvement on old-fashioned barcodes because they can be read from a distance of up to 7 metres, speeding up the process of checking goods.

Currently many shops use these tags as anti-theft devices. However, some retailers, such as Tesco's, are proposing that goods will have RF tags with unique ID numbers. If these tags are not disabled at the point of sale, anyone with suitable equipment could track the movements of the item purchased. For example, if you buy a pair of shoes from Tesco's with an RF tag, your movements could be tracked whenever you enter or leave a Tesco store.

Q2: Would you consider this as an invasion of privacy? Why?

Q3: Might the retailer be in breach of any current legislation?

Q4: What are the advantages to the retailer of RF tagging?

Q5: What steps should the retailer take to avoid any invasion of privacy and yet retain the advantages of RF tagging?

Exercises

1   Players, in a national lottery, show their selection of different numbers by placing marks on an entry form similar to the one shown in Figure 1. The entry form is then inserted into a machine at the point of sale and the numbers are read.

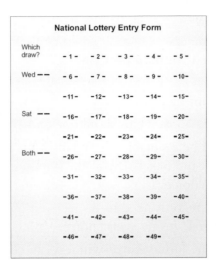

Figure 1

2-28

  (a)   Name the method being used to read the data.   (1)

The data are transmitted to a central computer which allocates a unique transaction code. This code is relayed back to the point of sale where a machine prints the chosen numbers and a transaction code onto the ticket similar to the one shown in **Figure 2**.

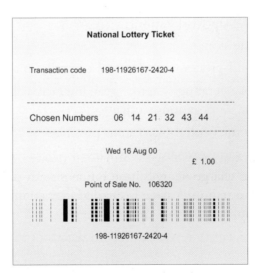

Figure 2

  (b)   Each transaction code includes a check digit. What is a check digit and why is it used?   (2)

(c) Each transaction is recorded in a separate record. All transaction records for a particular lottery draw are stored in a single transaction file.

The transaction record includes the following fields:

> Date of Purchase
> Transaction Code
> Date of Draw
> Chosen Numbers
> Point of Sale Identification Code

(i) What is meant by primary key? (1)

(ii) Which of the above fields should be chosen as the primary key? (1)

(iii) What would be a suitable file organisation for the transaction file if it is required that the ticket(s) with the winning numbers is to be found? Justify your choice. (2)

(iv) If individual records need to be accessed quickly what file organisation should be used? Justify your choice. (2)

(d) After a draw, some lottery prize-winners can check their tickets at any lottery point of sale machine. State the processing steps required by the lottery's computer system to check if the ticket is a winning ticket. (4)

AQA CPT2 Qu 6 January 2001

2 A publisher of a daily newspaper uses a computer system consisting of:

- Reporters' workstations.
- An image processing workstation.
- Sub-editors' workstations.
- A page make-up workstation.
- A central file store.

Each article is word-processed and stored centrally in a separate file.

(a) What type of operating system – real, interactive, batch or network – must be run at each of the workstations so that

(i) access to the central file store is possible? (1)

(ii) reporters can word-process articles? (1)

(b) The editor in charge of an edition enters the layouts of each page at the page make-up workstation. A page is divided into a number of blocks. There is one article per block.

A relational database is used to record details of the page layouts for each edition of the newspaper.

Two relations (tables) **NewspaperEdition** and **PageLayout** are used for this database:

NewspaperEdition (EditionId, Date, NoOfPages, EditorInChargeOfEdition)

PageLayout (EditionId, PageNo, BlockNo, PositionOfBlockOnPage, WidthOfBlock, LengthOfBlock, FilePathName)

Each newspaper edition is assigned a unique EditionId. There is only one edition per day. FilePathName is used to locate the word-processed article assigned to a block.

2-28

State a suitable primary key for the NewspaperEdition relation. (1)

State a suitable secondary key for the NewspaperEdition relation. (1)

Name the attribute which is the foreign key in the relation PageLayout. (1)

State a suitable primary key for the relation PageLayout. Justify your choice. (3)

(c) Word-processed articles are stored on the N: drive of the file server. Each reporter is allocated their own directory in which to store their files on the N: drive. **Figure 4** shows part of the root directory on the N: drive.

Reporter1	dir
Reporter2	dir
Reporter3	dir
:	:
:	:
:	:
Reporter25	dir

Figure 4

What is the pathname for a file Cricket1.Doc that Reporter1 has written? (1)

(ii) At the end of each month all the files written by the reporters are archived. Explain what this means. (1)

(iii) Suggest a suitable cost effective medium that could be used to hold one month's archive of approximately 4GB (4 Gigabytes) of information. (1)

(d) Sub-editors use a split screen workstation with one half of the screen displaying an article for a specific page and the other half showing the corresponding page layout supplied by the editor. The sub-editor adjusts the length of the article so that it fits exactly into a block. A sub-editor's workstation can access any of the word-processed files produced by reporters as well as any of the page layouts produced by the editor.

Sketch and label carefully a possible split screen user interface for the sub-editor's workstation. Consider how this interface can:

• show the page layout and if an article is too long or too short for a block

• select a file

• indicate which article file is being processed

• indicate which page, block and edition of the newspaper is currently selected

• select editing tools/functions

• select different formats for the article

• select on-line help. (5)

(e) A block of space on a page may also contain an image.

State **two** image processing operations that an image processing workstation might apply to images. (2)

AQA CPT2 Qu 7 January 2003

3 A small film production company makes training videos for sale to schools and colleges. It uses a computer to add background music, downloaded from a particular site on the Internet, to its training videos. The editing software that it uses was found on another site on the Internet.

(a) Name the legislation that this company might be breaking and describe one possible way in which this might be happening. (2)

(b) The company wishes to distribute its training videos in digital form so that they can be played directly through a computer system.

   (i) State the most suitable medium for this purpose. (1)

   (ii) Name **two** peripherals excluding video monitor, mouse and keyboard that the computer system must use to play back a training video. (2)

(c) The company also offers a microfilming service to companies dealing in personal information. The personal information is transferred to microfilm. The recording, processing and use of personal information is governed by legislation. Name this legislation and state **one** principle of this legislation that relates to the integrity of the personal data and **one** that relates to its security. (3)

AQA CPT2 Qu 6 January 2002

2-28

Module 3

System Development

In this section:

3

Chapter 29 – The Classical Systems Life-Cycle

Overview of the systems life cycle

Large systems development projects may involve dozens of people working over several months or even years, so they cannot be allowed to proceed in a haphazard fashion. The goals of an information system must be thoroughly understood, and formal procedures and methods applied to ensure that the project is delivered on time and to the required specification.

The systems life cycle methodology approaches the development of information systems in a very methodical and sequential manner. Each stage is composed of certain well–defined activities and responsibilities, and is completed before the next stage begins.

There are several versions of the systems life cycle diagram; the stages include problem definition, problem investigation, feasibility study, analysis, design, construction/implementation (including programming, testing and installation), maintenance and evaluation. Most diagrams like the one below show only 5 or 6 main steps.

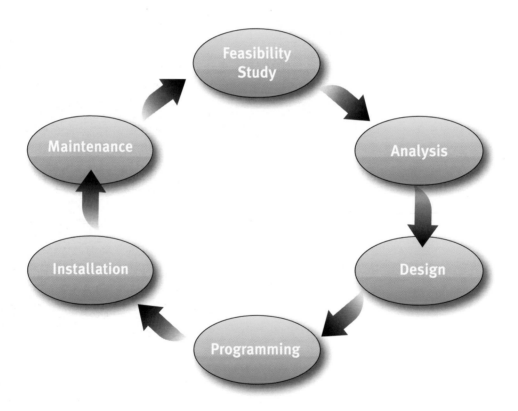

Figure 29.1: The systems life cycle

The waterfall model

The systems life cycle approach to development is also known as the 'waterfall model', and a variation on the basic diagram of 29.1 is shown in Figure 29.2.

Note that the arrows go up and down the 'waterfall', reflecting the fact that developers often have to re-work earlier stages in the light of experience gained as development progresses.

A project milestone terminates each stage of a life-cycle-oriented approach. At this stage, the 'deliverable' resulting from that stage – such as the documentation for the analysis or the design, or the program code or finished database application, is *signed off* by all concerned parties and approval is given to proceed to the next stage. The 'concerned parties' usually include the end-users, management and developers, as well as other experts such as database administration personnel. This sequence continues until the evaluation stage has been completed and the finished system is delivered to the end-users.

In this model, the end-user has very little say in the development process, which is carried out by technical specialists such as systems analysts and programmers. He or she is presented with the finished system at the end of the development cycle and if it is not quite what was wanted, it is generally too late to make changes. Therefore, it is extremely important that the system requirements are very clearly specified and understood by all parties before being signed off.

Such levels of certainty are difficult to achieve and this is one of the major drawbacks of the 'waterfall model'.

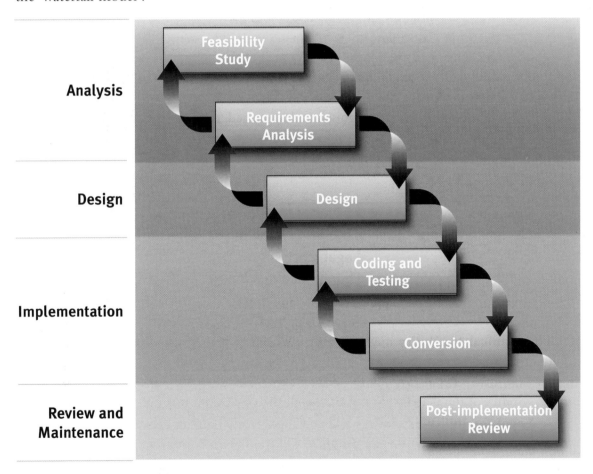

Figure 29.2: Systems development life cycle (the 'Waterfall model')

What prompts a new system?

The development of a new information system is a major undertaking and not one to be undertaken lightly. Wal–Mart, the American discount store which has recently taken over Asda, spent $700m on its computerised distribution system in the 1980s. Tesco, Sainsbury's and Marks and Spencer have spent massive sums of money on their computer systems in the past decade. Businesses must adapt to remain competitive. Some of the reasons for introducing a new system may be:

1 **The current system may be no longer suitable for its purpose**. Changes in work processes, expansion of the business, changes in business requirements or the environment in which the organisation operates may all lead to a reassessment of information system requirements.

2 **Technological developments may have made the current system redundant or outdated**. Advances in hardware, software and telecommunications bring new opportunities, which an organisation cannot ignore if it is to keep ahead of its rivals.

3 **The current system may be too inflexible or expensive to maintain**, or may reduce the organisation's ability to respond quickly enough to customer's demands.

At the end of the millennium, many businesses with old systems that were susceptible to the 'millennium bug' took the opportunity to install new systems, which would provide better information, rather than spend money on having external consultants patch up their old system.

Feasibility study

Once a problem has been recognised and identified, the **feasibility study** is the first stage of the systems life cycle. The **scope** and **objectives** of the proposed system must be written down. The aim of the feasibility study is to understand the problem and to determine whether it is worth proceeding. There are five main factors to be considered:

Technical feasibility
Economic feasibility
Legal feasibility
Operational feasibility
Schedule feasibility

- **Technical feasibility** means investigating whether the technology exists to implement the proposed system, or whether this is a practical proposition.

- **Economic feasibility** has to do with establishing the cost-effectiveness of the proposed system – if the benefits do not outweigh the costs, then it is not worth going ahead.

- **Legal feasibility** determines whether there is any conflict between the proposed system and legal requirements – for example, will the system contravene the Data Protection Act?

- **Operational feasibility** is concerned with whether the current work practices and procedures are adequate to support the new system. It is also concerned with social factors – how the organisational change will affect the working lives of those affected by the system.

- **Schedule feasibility** looks at how long the system will take to develop, or whether it can be done in a desired time-frame.

The completion of this stage is marked by the production of a feasibility report produced by the systems analyst. If the report concludes that the project should go ahead, and this is agreed by senior managers, detailed requirements analysis will proceed.

3-29

Analysis/Requirements analysis

The second phase of systems analysis is a more detailed investigation into the current system and the requirements of the new system.

It is the job of the systems analyst to find out what the user's requirements are, to find out about current methods and to assess the feasibility of the new proposed system. Gathering details about the current system may involve:

- interviewing staff at different levels of the organisation from the end-users to senior management.

- examining current business and systems documents and output. These may include current order documents, computer systems procedures and reports used by operations and senior management.

- sending out questionnaires and analysing responses. The questions have to be carefully constructed to elicit unambiguous answers.

- observation of current procedures, by spending time in various departments. A time and motion study can be carried out to see where procedures could be made more efficient, or to detect where bottlenecks occur.

The systems analyst's report will examine how data and information flow around the organisation, and may use **data flow diagrams** to document the flow. It will also establish precisely, and in considerable detail, exactly what the proposed system will do (as opposed to how it will do it). It will include an in-depth analysis of the costs and benefits, and outline the process of system implementation, including the organisational change required. It must establish who the end-users are, what information they should get and in what form and how it will be obtained.

Alternative options for the implementation of the project will be suggested. These could include suggestions for:

- whether development should be done in-house or using consultants;

- what hardware configurations could be considered;

- what the software options are.

Data flow diagram (DFD)

A data flow diagram shows how data moves through a system and what data stores are used. It does not specify what type of data storage is used or how the data is stored.

The following four symbols are used in data flow diagrams:

External entity – data source or data destination, for example people who generate data such as a customer order, or receive information such as an invoice.

Process – an operation performed on the data. The two lines are optional; the top section of the box can be used to label the process, the middle to give a brief explanation, the bottom to say where the process takes place. An alternative convention is to use a circle for a Process.

Make the first word an active verb – e.g. **validate** data, **adjust** stock level.

Data store – such as a file held on disk or a batch of documents

Data flow – the arrow represents movement between entities, processes or data stores. The arrow should be labelled to describe what data is involved

Example:

A theatre uses a computerised booking system to keep records of customers, plays and bookings. A customer may make a booking in person, by telephone or by preprinted form. The booking clerk first has to check whether there are any seats free for the performance. If there are, the clerk reserves the seats, then checks whether the customer's details are already on file, and if not, types them in. The tickets are then printed out and handed or sent to the customer. Payment is made either in cash or by credit card.

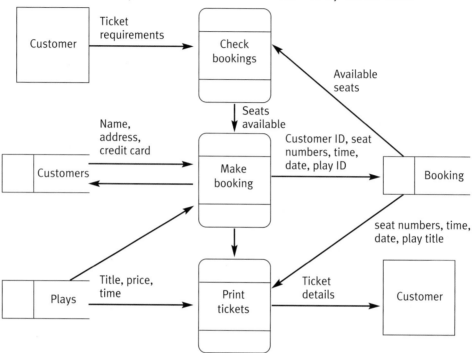

Figure 29.3: Data flow diagram of a theatre booking system

In the next chapter, the remaining stages of the system life cycle including design, implementation, testing, maintenance and evaluation will be considered.

Exercises

1 A feasibility study will often be carried out at an early stage of system development. As well as finding out if the proposal is technically possible the study will also consider economic and social feasibility.

In the context of a feasibility study describe **one** cost, **one** benefit and **three** possible social effects that would be considered. (5)

AEB AS Computing Qu 7 1996

2 State **three** different methods of fact finding available during the systems analysis stage of the systems life cycle, and for each of these three methods, give **one** reason for its use. (6)

AEB Computing Paper 1 Qu 11 1996

3 A proposed computerised information system will be used in a number of separate departments within a large organisation.

(a) Suggest and justify **two** criteria which the systems analyst might use when selecting the personnel to be interviewed. (4)

(b) State **two** disadvantages of interviewing as a fact finding method. (2)

CCEA Module 3 Qu 1 May 1999

4 During system development a *data flow diagram* may be used to represent all or part of the system. Below is an outline of a data flow diagram for a system to produce gas bills where the meter readings, having been recorded using a hand held device, are processed against the customer master file to produce the printed gas bills for the customers and a printed error report.

Give an appropriate label to **each** of the numbered elements A to E. (5)

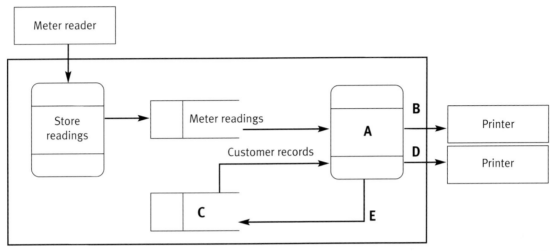

AEB Paper 2 Qu 7 1998

The following question is from the 2003 practical exercise (UKAB Re-marks)

5 This question relates to the ANALYSIS process.

  (a) Candidate, Centre and Subject are three entities in this system. Draw the Entity Relationship diagrams between
    (i)   Candidate and Centre
    (ii) Candidate and Subject
    (iii) Centre and Subject (3)

  (b) The analysis of this problem has already been carried out. How might the systems analyst have found out **each** of the following and from what data source? (Your two methods and two sources should be different.)
    (i)   The reports which were required from the system, and how frequently they need to be produced?
    (ii) The volume of data the system would have to deal with? (4)

AQA CPT3 Qu 5 May 2003

The following question is from the 2002 practical exercise (Hospital Equipment Loan System)

6 This question relates to the ANALYSIS process.
   When analysing the manual system, the analyst needed to gather information from a variety of sources. Suggest **two** different sources in the hospital and for each, suggest one method the analyst would use. Explain why that method would be appropriate to that source. Your two methods and your explanations must be different. (6)

AQA CPT3 Qu 8 May 2002

Note: The practical exercises may be downloaded from the AQA website **www.aqa.org.uk.**

Chapter 30 – From Design to Evaluation

System design

The design specifies the following aspects of a system:

- The hardware platform – which type of computer, network capabilities, input, storage and output devices.
- The software – programming language, package or database.
- The outputs – report layouts and screen designs.
- The inputs – documents, screen layouts and validation procedures.
- The user interface – how users will interact with the computer system.
- The modular design of each program in the application.
- The test strategy, test plan and test data.
- Conversion plan – how the new system is to be implemented.
- Documentation including systems and operations documentation. Later, a user manual will be produced.

System specification

The systems specification must describe how the new system will work. Screen layouts and report formats must be designed, file contents and organisation specified, and each program in the system must be described by means of program specifications, structure charts, pseudocode or flowcharts.

The programmers must then code, test and debug all the programs in the system. In smaller organisations the roles of programmer and analyst may overlap, and in some cases the 'analyst/programmer' may design, code and test the programs.

Program design methods

The use of structure charts and pseudocode for describing algorithms has been described in Chapter 7. An **algorithm** is a sequence of instructions to solve a given problem. **Pseudocode** is an intermediate stage between plain English and the programming language in which the solution will eventually be coded – it enables the writer to concentrate on the steps in the solution without worrying about the syntax rules of a particular language.

Prototyping

As in any other context, prototyping means building a working model of a new system in order to evaluate it, test it or have it approved before building the final product. When applied to computer systems, this could involve, for example, using special software to quickly design input screens and run a program (supplied as part of the prototyping package) to input and validate data using the screen format just created. This gives the user a chance to experience the 'look and feel' of the input process and to suggest alterations before going any further.

The prototype may then be discarded and the system built using the same or different software. This is termed **throw-away** prototyping.

Some organisations will use prototyping in the analysis stage, others in the design phase. Others may use it almost exclusively, going directly from preliminary investigation, via the prototype, to an implemented system. The analysts or programmers will simply keep refining the prototype until the user says it is acceptable. This is called **evolutionary** prototyping.

Q1: What are the advantages and disadvantages of using prototyping as a tool of systems analysis and design?

Choosing a software solution

Many different solutions to a particular problem will have been looked at before a particular solution is chosen. The criteria on which the final choice is based will include:

- **Usability** – will the users find the system easy to use, will it save them time, cut out tedious repetitive tasks, give them quick access to information they need, or help them in some way? Or will it just give them extra work with no obvious benefits, or produce mountains of paperwork from which it is hard to extract useful information?
- **Performance** – will the system function in the way that was intended? Or will it suffer from 'bugs', slow access times when retrieving data from a database, screens that take minutes to change or redraw after a command is typed, hardware that is unreliable?
- **Suitability** – does the system really provide a solution to the problem, or was it considered because for example it was the 'cheapest' solution? Will it integrate with existing software, can current manual methods be adapted for the new system?
- **Maintainability** – will it be easy to upgrade the system, add new functionality, make modifications when required?

Testing strategies

When a new system is developed, it has to undergo rigorous testing before it is released. Typically, it may undergo several phases of testing including:

- **Dry run testing:** the programmer follows through the code manually using test data to check that an algorithm is correct. This technique is useful for locating run-time errors – it would normally be carried out on a part of a program rather than the whole program. A **trace table** (see Chapter 7) is useful for checking the values of variables while following through the logic.
- **Unit testing:** this refers to the testing of each individual subroutine or module in a suite of programs.
- **Integration testing:** this involves testing a complete suite of programs to ensure that they all function correctly when they are put together – for example, by being called from a menu program.

Test plan and test data

A test plan needs to be drawn up for each program in a system. This is usually in the form of a table showing each item that needs to be tested. It should cover every possible type of input including values that are too large, too small or invalid for other reasons such as an alphabetic character being entered instead of a number. The test plan needs to show for each test what the expected result is.

Technical documentation

Technical documentation helps to ensure that a system can be maintained after completion. All too often changes of staff within a company mean that no-one who was involved in the original design or programming of a system is still with the company. It is essential that proper documentation is kept to enable a newcomer to make necessary corrections, alterations or enhancements.

Contents of a documented system

- an accurate and up-to-date systems specification;
- Data Flow Diagrams showing the inputs to the system, files required, processes to be carried out, and output from the system;
- a description of the purpose of each program within the system;
- a structure diagram, flowchart or pseudocode for each program in the system;
- organisation, contents and layout of each file used;
- layout and contents of all output prints and displays;
- current version of each program listing;
- test data and expected results.

Implementation

This phase includes both the coding and testing of the system, the acquisition of hardware and the installation of the new system or conversion of the old system to the new one.

The installation phase can include:

- installing the new hardware, which may involve extensive recabling and changes in office layouts;
- training the users on the new system;
- conversion of master files to the new system, or creation of new master files.

Evaluation

When a new software system is complete, it is very important to evaluate it to ensure that it meets the user's original specifications and is satisfactory in all respects.

Minor programming errors may have to be corrected, clerical procedures amended, or modifications made to the design of reports or screen layouts.

The solution will be evaluated in terms of

- Effectiveness: does it do what it is supposed to do?
- Usability: is it easy to use?
- Maintainability: will it be easy to maintain?

Often it is only when people start to use a new system that they realise its shortcomings! In some cases they may realise that it would be possible to get even more useful information from the system than they realised, and more programs may be requested. The process of system maintenance, in fact, has already begun, and the life cycle is complete.

3-30

System maintenance

All software systems require maintenance, and in fact the vast majority of programmers are employed to maintain existing programs rather than to write new ones. There are differing reasons for this, and different types of maintenance.

- Perfective maintenance. This implies that while the system runs satisfactorily, there is still room for improvement. For example, extra management information may be needed so that new report programs have to be written. Database queries may be very slow, and a change in a program may be able to improve response time.

- Adaptive maintenance. All systems will need to adapt to changing needs within a company. As a business expands, for example, there may be a requirement to convert a standalone system to a multi-user system. New and better hardware may become available, and changes to the software may be necessary to take advantage of this. New government legislation may mean that different methods of calculating tax, for example, are required. Competition from other firms may mean that systems have to be upgraded in order to maintain a competitive edge.

- Corrective maintenance. Problems frequently surface after a system has been in use for a short time, however thoroughly it was tested. Some part of the system may not function as expected, or a report might be wrong in some way; totals missing at the bottom, incorrect sequence of data, wrong headings, etc. Frequently errors will be hard to trace, if for example a file appears to have been wrongly updated.

3-30

Exercises

1 Software developers use prototyping for different reasons in different situations.
   (a) What is prototyping? (1)
   (b) Briefly explain two reasons for using prototypes. (2)

   AEB Paper 2 Qu 4 1998

2 Describe two methods of testing which will be used during the development of a new software system. (4)

   AEB Paper 2 Qu 5 1997

3 A typical software system will require both corrective and adaptive maintenance.
   (a) Describe the main difference between corrective maintenance and adaptive maintenance. (4)
   (b) Explain how a software system should be developed in order to
        (i) Decrease the amount of corrective maintenance required.
        (ii) Ensure adaptive maintenance is as straightforward as possible. (6)

   CCEA Module 3 Qu 4 1999

4 (a) Explain why an error in the system specification is usually more expensive to correct if it is discovered during the maintenance phase than if it is discovered during the design phase. (4)
   (b) Distinguish between evolutionary prototyping and throw-away prototyping. (4)

   CCEA Module 3 Qu 2 1999

The following questions are from the 2001 practical exercise (PostQuick Parcels)★

5   This question relates to the LEGAL implications of the use of computers.

   (a) (i) Explain what legal responsibility PostQuick have for their customer data.   (3)

       (ii) Describe **one** technique that should be used to meet this responsibility.   (2)

   (b) Describe **one** further technique you would recommend to PostQuick for the security of the data against accidental or deliberate damage.   (2)

                              AQA CPT3 Qu 6 May 2001

6   This question relates to MAINTENANCE.

When you hand over your software to PostQuick, you include in your system documentation items that could be used for subsequent maintenance and up-dating of your solution. Name and describe **two** items which should be included for this purpose.   (4)

                              AQA CPT3 Qu 9 May 2001

The following question is from the 2002 practical exercise (Hospital Equipment Loan System)★

7   This question relates to the OUTPUTS.

If a piece of equipment is due for return or renewal, the patient has to be contacted. It is stated in the brief that 'there is a standard letter for this'. The hospital could use a *mail merge* process for this.

   (a) List the steps that would be required to use mail merge to produce contact letters, (even if your solution does not support this).   (4)

   (b) Explain **two** advantages of using mail merge in this situation over typing individual letters.   (2)

                              AQA CPT3 Qu 7 May 2002

The following question is from the 2003 practical exercise (UKAB re-marks)★

8   This question relates to the INTEGRITY and SECURITY of data in your solution.

   (a) Clearly it is essential for your data to be accurate. Describe **one** technique which might be followed to improve accuracy on data entry.   (2)

   (b) It is also essential to keep your data secure against unauthorised access. The data files could be password protected with strictly defined access rights. Describe **two** other techniques which might be followed to improve data security.   (4)

                              AQA CPT3 Qu 6 May 2003

9   This question relates to the EVALUATION and MAINTENANCE of your new system.

   (a) After your system has been running for a short time, it should be evaluated. Give **three** factors which could be looked at in this evaluation.   (3)

   (b) (i) Suggest **one** reason why your system may need maintenance in the future.   (1)

       (ii) Give **three** items of documentation which would be necessary for effective maintenance of your system. These may be items you have not included in your documentation for this practical exercise.   (3)

                              AQA CPT3 Qu 7 May 2003

★ *Note: The practical exercises may be downloaded from the AQA website* **www.aqa.org.uk.**

Chapter 31 – Human Computer Interface

Introduction

The '**human computer interface**' is a term used to describe the interaction between a user and a computer; in other words, the method by which the user tells the computer what to do, and the responses that the computer makes.

It's important not to allow the word 'computer' to limit your vision to a PC sitting on an office desk. You also need to think in terms of a person getting cash from a cash machine, a pilot of a jumbo jet checking his instrument panels, the operator of a high-volume heavy duty photocopier, a scientist monitoring a chemical reaction, a musician composing a symphony using appropriate hardware and software.

> **Q1:** Name some other tasks for which computers are used, and for which special purpose interfaces are required.

The importance of good interface design

A good interface design can help to ensure that users carry out their tasks:

- **safely** (in the case of a jumbo jet pilot, for example);
- **effectively** (users don't find they have video taped two hours of Bulgarian clog dancing instead of the Cup Final);
- **efficiently** (users do not spend five minutes trying to find the correct way to insert their cash card and type in their PIN and the amount of cash they want, and then leave without remembering to extract their card);
- **enjoyably** (a primary school pupil using a program to teach multiplication tables).

Well-designed systems can improve the output of employees, improve the quality of life and make the world a safer and more enjoyable place to live in.

> **Q2:** In the early days of cash machines, it was found that users sometimes forgot to remove their cards after withdrawing their cash. What simple change was made to eliminate this fault?

Designing usable systems

In order to design a usable interface, the designer has to take into consideration:

- **who** will use the system. For example, will the users be computer professionals or members of the general public who may be wary of computers? For an educational program, will the users be young, for example primary school children, or teenagers on an A Level course? Will the system have to cater for both beginners and experienced users?
- **what tasks** the computer is performing. Is the task very repetitive, does the task require skill and knowledge? Do tasks vary greatly from one occasion to the next? A travel agent who spends most of the day making holiday bookings will require a different interface from an office worker who needs to be able to switch between word processing, accounts and accessing the company database.
- **the environment** in which the computer is used. Will the environment be hazardous (in a lifeboat setting out to rescue a stricken vessel), noisy (in a factory full of machinery), or calm and quiet (some offices)?
- **what is technologically feasible** (is it possible to simply dictate a letter to a word processor instead of typing it in?)

Interface styles

There are a number of common interface styles including:

- command line interface;
- menus;
- natural language;
- forms and dialogue boxes;
- graphical user interface (GUI).

Command-line interface

The command-line interface was the first interactive dialogue style and is still widely used in spite of the availability of menu-driven interfaces. It provides a means of expressing instructions to the computer directly using single characters, whole word commands or abbreviations.

With this type of interface very little help is given to the user, who has to type a command such as, for example, **Format a:** to format a disk. Commands enable a user to quickly and concisely instruct the computer what to do, but they do require the user to have a knowledge of the commands available and the syntax for using them.

> **Q3:** Identify TWO situations in which a command-driven interface would be appropriate.

3-31

Menus

There are several different types of menu interface, outlined below.

1 **Full screen menu.** This type of menu is often used as the 'front end' of an application. It stays on screen until the user makes a choice.

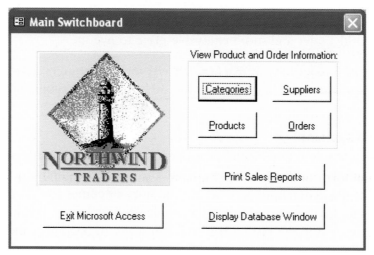

Figure 31.1: Full screen menu

2 **Pull-down menu.** This type of menu is displayed along the top of the screen, and when the user clicks on an item, a submenu appears. The menu is always present whatever screen the user is looking at in the application.

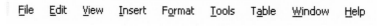

Figure 31.2: Pull-down menu

3   **Pop-up menu**. The menu pops up in response to, say, a click of the right mouse button on a particular area of the screen.

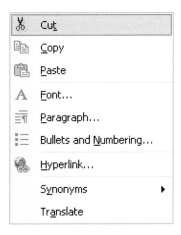

Figure 31.3: Pop-up menu

Natural language

It is a very attractive idea to have a computer that can understand natural language – 'plain English' in other words. *'How do I create an A5 folded leaflet in Word?'* is understandable to most people but does not elicit a sensible answer from the Office Assistant. (You can't, basically.) Unfortunately, the ambiguity of natural language makes it very difficult for a machine to understand. Language is ambiguous in a number of different ways. Firstly, the syntax, or structure of a sentence may not be clear – for example consider the sentences

James and Henrietta are married.

A salesman visited every house in the area.

The man hit the dog with the stick.

Are James and Henrietta married to each other? Was there only one salesman involved in the house-to-house sales operation? Who had the stick?

Secondly, many English words have more than one meaning. How many ways can the word 'match' be interpreted?

Advantages and disadvantages of natural language dialogue

Advantages:
- most natural form of dialogue for humans – no need for training in a specialised command language;
- extremely flexible and powerful;
- the user is free to construct their own commands, frame their own questions, etc.

Disadvantages:
- people find it difficult to stick to grammatically correct English;
- a well designed 'artificial language' can often say the same thing more concisely than 'natural language';
- a smooth, natural language can easily mislead the naive user into believing the computer is 'intelligent'.

Forms and dialogue boxes

When a user is required to enter data such as, for example, sales invoices or customer names and addresses, it is common to have a 'form' displayed on the screen for the user to fill in. The following points should be noted when designing forms of this type:

• the form should be given a title to identify it;

• the form should not be too cluttered – spaces and blanks are important;

• it should give some indication of how many characters can be entered in each field of data;

• the user should be given a chance to go back and correct any field before the data is accepted;

• items should appear in a logical sequence to assist the user;

• default values should wherever possible be prewritten onto the form so that a minimum of data entry is required;

• full exit and 'help' facilities should be provided – for example, users could enter '?' in a field if they require more information;

• lower case in a display is neater and easier to read than all upper-case;

• colours should be carefully chosen to be legible and easy on the eyes;

• 'attention-getting' devices such as blinking cursors, high-intensity, reverse video, underlining etc should not be over-used.

Dialogue boxes are a special type of form often associated with the Windows environment; an example shown below is the dialogue box which appears when the instruction to *Print* is given in Word 2002.

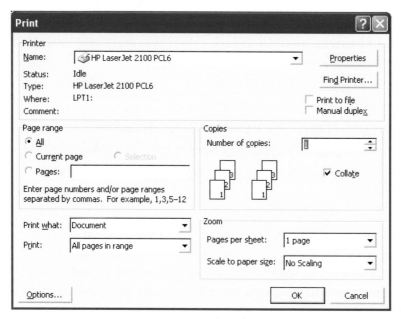

Figure 31.4: Dialogue box

186

The WIMP interface

WIMP stands for Windows, Icons, Mouse and Pull-down menus.

A **window** is an area on the screen through which a particular piece of software or a data file may be viewed. The window may occupy the whole screen, or the user can choose to have several windows on the screen with a different application running in each one. Windows can be moved, sized, stacked one on top of the other, opened and closed A Windows environment mimics a desktop on which a worker may have several books or pieces of paper spread out for reference.

An icon is a small picture representing an item such as a piece of software, a file, storage medium (such as disk or tape) or command. By pointing with a mouse at a particular icon and clicking the mouse button the user can select it.

Microsoft Windows enables the user to run several different software packages such as MS Word (a word processor), MS Excel (a spreadsheet), MS Paint (a graphics package) simultaneously and to move data and graphics from one package to another. Software packages written by other manufacturers, such as Aldus PageMaker, have been written to run under Windows because of the convenience to the user of this easy-to-use environment.

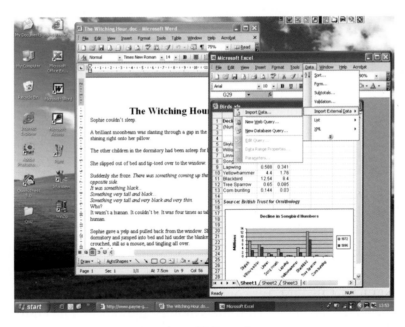

Figure 31.5: WIMP interface

Advantages of a common user interface

All the software packages mentioned above use a consistent interface and have a similar 'look and feel' so that a user familiar with one package can quickly learn a second. For example, in each package a single click of the mouse button selects an item, and a double click activates the item. In each package, the methods for opening, closing, sizing and moving windows is identical. The advantages can be summarised as:

• increased speed of learning;

• ease of use;

• confidence building for novice users;

• increased range of tasks solvable by experienced users;

• a greater range of software accessible to the average user.

Speech input (voice recognition)

The ultimate in user-friendly interfaces would probably be one in which you could simply tell your computer what to do in ordinary speech. Two distinct types of voice recognition system are emerging; small vocabulary command and control systems and large vocabulary dictation systems.

- **Command and control systems** can be relatively small and cheap because they need only a small, tightly defined vocabulary of technical terms. Such systems are coming rapidly into use as automatic call-handling systems for applications such as bank account enquiries. In PC systems, voice command can be used to bring up files, control printing and so on, effectively replacing the mouse. In some systems the computer is 'trained' by an individual user pronouncing a given vocabulary of words; it then stores a recording of the user's speech pattern for each word or syllable.

- **Large vocabulary dictation systems** can handle whole sentences and extensive vocabularies but need much greater processing power and memory space. These systems use elaborate probability distributions to estimate which word the acoustic pattern it has picked up is most likely to be, partly by looking at other words in the developing sentence and predicting what sort of word (noun or verb, for example) is likely to be used. Various voice recognition packages after suitable 'training' will take dictation at 70 words per minute and get about 97% of them correct. Voice recognition is however still an expensive technology and widespread use is some way off.

Q4: Name some other situations in which voice input would be appropriate.

Speech/sound output

A speech synthesis system works as follows:

Individual words and sounds are spoken into a microphone by a human being and recorded by the system, thereby training it to speak. Output that would normally be printed can then be spoken, so long as the word is contained in its vocabulary. A second, more flexible method uses phonemes – the individual sounds from which all words are constructed in any particular language.

Such a system has limited use but could for example be used by a bank computer connected by telephone line to customers' homes and offices. The customer could key in his account number using the telephone keypad, and the computer could then access his account and speak out the customer's account balance.

Exercises

1   You are asked to design a delivery note for registered letters delivered by courier.
    Give **two** design requirements you need to consider.   (2)

    Draw your design and show how you satisfied these requirements.   (2)

                                                                          New Question

2   You are asked to design a standard letter for the school library to send to pupils who
    have overdue books. Give **three** criteria that you need to consider for the design of
    this document.   (3)

    Draw your design and show how you satisfied these criteria.   (3)

                                                                          New Question

3   During the analysis stage of a school Book Loan, the librarian has stated that a single
    input screen should be able to accept loans and returns from pupils and staff. Initially
    the book, pupil and staff identification numbers will have to be entered manually until
    barcode readers are purchased.

    The input screen should be user friendly and should make inputting data easy and
    minimise errors. State **three** criteria you would consider in the design of this screen
    and explain how each would be relevant to good user interface design.   (6)

    Draw your design and show how you satisfied these criteria.   (3)

                                                                          New Question

4   A company is designing a software package for use by pupils in infants' schools.

    Briefly describe and justify two appropriate features of the package's human-computer
    interface.   (4)

                                                                    NEAB CP01 Qu 3 1998

5   A college uses a range of software packages from different suppliers. Each package has
    a different user interface. The college is considering changing its software to one
    supplier and to a common user interface.

    (a) Give **four** advantages of having a common user interface.   (4)

    (b) Describe four specific features of a user interface which would benefit from
         being common between packages.   (4)

    (c) Discuss the issues involved, apart from user interfaces, in the college changing
         or upgrading software packages.   (8)

                                                                    NEAB IT02 Qu 8 1997

3-31

Module 4

PROCESSING AND PROGRAMMING TECHNIQUES

In this section:

4-32

Chapter 32 – Number Bases and Representation

The denary number system

Our number system is called the denary system and uses the 10 digits 0 to 9. In this system, as we move from right to left each digit is worth 10 times as much as its right-hand neighbour. Thus for example the number 583 represents

$$5 \times \mathbf{100} + 8 \times \mathbf{10} + 3 \times \mathbf{1} = 583$$

The **number base** specifies how many digits are used and how much each digit is multiplied by as we move from right to left. The denary system is a **base 10** system.

The binary and hexadecimal number systems

The binary number system is a **base 2** system using only the two digits 0 and 1. Each digit is worth twice as much as the one to its right. Thus the binary number 10011 represents

$$1 \times \mathbf{16} + 0 \times \mathbf{8} + 0 \times \mathbf{4} + 1 \times \mathbf{2} + 1 \times \mathbf{1} = 19$$

Binary numbers are ideal for representing numbers inside a computer because the digits 0 and 1 can be represented by 'off' and 'on' in electrical circuits. However, they are very inconvenient for humans to read as even a relatively small number such as 256 requires 9 binary digits to represent it.

In order to ease the task of examining the contents of memory or a computer file, binary numbers are commonly put into groups of 4 bits and displayed in the form of **hexadecimal** numbers.

Hexadecimal: used as a shorthand notation for binary number patterns

These are numbers to **base 16**, and use the digits 0-9 and letters A to F. The table below shows the numbers 1 to 16 in denary, binary and hexadecimal.

Denary	Binary	Hexadecimal
1	1	1
2	10	2
3	11	3
4	100	4
5	101	5
6	110	6
7	111	7
8	1000	8
9	1001	9
10	1010	A
11	1011	B
12	1100	C
13	1101	D
14	1110	E
15	1111	F
16	10000	10

Table 32.1: Numbers 1-16 in denary, binary and hexadecimal

Denary to binary and hexadecimal

Suppose you are asked to translate the number 179 to binary. To translate from a denary number to binary, write down headings 1, 2, 4, 8 etc from right to left as follows:

128	64	32	16	8	4	2	1

128 is the largest of the above numbers to go into 179, so put a 1 under 128 and subtract 128 from 179 leaving 51. 32 is the largest number to go into 51, so put a 1 under 32 and subtract it from 51 leaving 19. You can repeat the process, or take a shortcut by observing that 19 = 16 + 2 + 1. Either way you end up with the following, after filling in blank spaces with 0s.

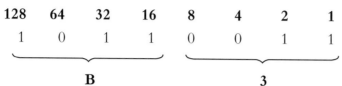

128	64	32	16	8	4	2	1
1	0	1	1	0	0	1	1

B   3

To translate the number 179 into hexadecimal, the easiest way is to first translate it into binary, and then translate each group of 4 digits into hexadecimal. Thus, 179 = B3 in hexadecimal.

> **Tip:** It is useful to remember that 1010 in binary is 10 in denary and A in hexadecimal. Also remember that 1111 is 15 in binary and F in hexadecimal. You can work the other numbers out as required.

4-32

Q1: Translate the denary number 124 into   (a) binary   (b) hexadecimal

Translating back to denary

To translate a binary number to denary, do exactly the same in reverse. Write the binary digits down under the headings 1, 2, 4, 8 etc and add up all the headings which have a 1 under them. For example, to translate the binary number 1001 0010 to denary, write down

128	64	32	16	8	4	2	1
1	0	0	1	0	0	1	0

This equals 128 + 16 + 2 = 146.

To translate the binary number above into hexadecimal, divide it into 2 groups of 4 binary digits (starting from the right). Then translate each group into its equivalent hexadecimal digit. The number above is therefore 92 in hexadecimal. (Notice that this is the same as **9 x 16 + 2**. Each digit in a hexadecimal number is worth 16 times as much as the one on its right.)

Q2: Translate the binary number   0110 1110   into   (a) denary   (b) hexadecimal

Q3: The ASCII code for the letter N is   0100 1110. Show how this would be represented in   (a) denary   (b) hexadecimal

Representation of negative numbers using two's complement

Negative numbers are commonly represented using a system called **two's complement**. To understand how this works, imagine the mileometer of a car, set at 00000 miles. If the car goes forward one mile the reading becomes 00001. If the meter was turned **back** one mile the reading would be 99999 miles. This could be interpreted as '-1' mile.

Two's complement works in the same way:

11111101	=	-3
11111110	=	-2
11111111	=	-1
00000000	=	0
00000001	=	1
00000010	=	2
00000011	=	3

Notice that if the number starts with a 1, it represents a negative number.

Adding together the binary equivalents for 3 and –3, we obtain

```
        11111101
   +    00000011
       _____
(1)     00000000    The 'carry' of 1 is ignored.
```

Converting a negative denary number to binary

The rules for converting a negative denary number to binary can be stated as follows:

• Find the binary value of the equivalent positive decimal number
• Change all the 0s to 1s and all the 1s to 0s.
• Add 1 to the result.

An even simpler way of changing the sign of a binary number can be stated as:

• Starting from the right, leave all the digits alone up to and including the first '1'.
• Change all the other digits from 0 to 1 or from 1 to 0.

Example: 00110100 = 11001100

Q4: Convert the following numbers to binary: (i) – 5   (ii) – 10   (iii) – 20

Q5: What is the largest negative number that can be held in 8 bits, assuming the leftmost bit is a sign bit?

Converting a two's complement number into denary

You can either flip the bits, add 1 and then work out the positive equivalent, or use the place values. Write the binary digits down under the headings 1, 2, 4, 8 etc, noting that the leftmost bit has a negative place value. Add up all the headings which have a 1 under them. For example, to translate the two's complement number 1001 0110 to denary, write down

-128	64	32	16	8	4	2	1
1	0	0	1	0	1	1	0

This equals -128 + 16 + 4 + 2 = -106.

Binary subtraction

The easiest way of performing binary subtraction is to first convert the number to be subtracted to a negative number, and then add it. Thus, to subtract 12 from 15, using 1 byte for each number,

12	=	00001100	in binary
− 12	=	11110100	
15	=	00001111	
add		11110100	
		00000011	

Q6: Subtract 23 from 123 in binary.

Hints

A positive number always has 0 as the MSB (most significant bit).

A negative number always has 1 as the MSB.

An even number always has 0 as the LSB (least significant bit).

An odd number always has 1 as the LSB.

-1 is always represented by a 1 in every bit, whatever the word size.

4-32

Exercises

1   The hexadecimal codes for the characters C, A, T are 43, 41 and 54. What are the equivalent binary codes? Why are ASCII codes often represented in hexadecimal rather than binary in printouts of the contents of sections of memory?   (4)

New Question

2   Translate the numbers 101 and -73 into binary using two's complement. Show in binary the result of adding these two binary numbers.   (4)

New Question

3   Using 8 bits to represent an integer in two's complement form,

(a)   Show how the decimal numbers +63 and −65 will be represented.   (2)

(b)   Show the result obtained when +63 is added to +65 using this representation. Comment on your answer.   (2)

New Question

4   (a)   Convert the decimal number 1026 into binary storing the result in a 16-bit word.   (2)

(b)   Write down the hexadecimal equivalent of your binary number from (a) above.   (2)

(c)   The hexadecimal character code for the digit 1 is 31. State how 1026 would be represented using this coding system.   (2)

New Question

Chapter 33 – Floating Point Numbers

So far we have only been able to represent whole numbers. Calculations often have fractional results, so we need to be able to store real numbers. There are an infinite number of fractions, but only a finite number of bits available to represent fractions. Trying to map an infinite number of values onto a finite number of bit patterns results in loss of precision.

Fixed point binary numbers

So far we have considered only **integers** – that is, whole numbers. The system can easily be extended to include fractions, as shown by the following example:

100	10	1		$1/10$		$1/100$
1	3	6	.	7		5

The number 136.75 represents 1 hundred, 3 tens, 6 units, 7 tenths and 5 hundredths.

In binary, the equivalent column headings are

128	64	32	16	8	4	2	1	.	$1/2$	$1/4$	$1/8$	$1/16$

The number 136.75 can be expressed as $136 + 1/2 + 1/4$, and using the column headings above converts to

128	64	32	16	8	4	2	1	.	$1/2$	$1/4$	$1/8$	$1/16$
1	0	0	0	1	0	0	0	.	1	1	0	0

Notice that the first digit after the point (called the 'binary point') is worth one half, whereas in the decimal system the equivalent digit is only worth one tenth. This means that with the same number of digits after the point, the binary system is less accurate. For example, if we write down an amount in pounds to 2 decimal places, the amount is accurate to the nearest penny. If we converted the amount to binary and only allowed two digits after the binary point, we can only hold .00 (0 pence), .01 (25 pence), .10 (50 pence) or .11 (75 pence) as the fractional part, so the amount is only accurate to the nearest 25 pence.

Fixed point notation assumes a binary point in a set position as there is no third symbol available to store it explicitly.

The following table shows some decimal fractions and their binary equivalent:

Binary fraction	Fraction	Decimal fraction	Binary fraction	Fraction	Decimal fraction
0.1	$1/2$	0.5	0.000001	$1/64$	0.015625
0.01	$1/4$	0.25	0.0000001	$1/128$	0.0078125
0.001	$1/8$	0.125	0.00000001	$1/1256$	0.00390625
0.0001	$1/16$	0.0625	0.000000001	$1/512$	0.001953125
0.00001	$1/32$	0.03125	0.0000000001	$1/1024$	0.0009765625

The advantage of fixed point notation is simple arithmetic (same as integer arithmetic) and therefore faster processing. However, a disadvantage is the limited range, as increasing the number of bits after the binary point for precision decreases the range and vice versa.

Q1: Using 1 byte to hold each number, with an imaginary binary point fixed after the fourth digit, convert the following decimal numbers to binary:
(i) 4.25   (ii) 7.1875   (iii) 3.5625   (iv) 3.5627

Q2: Convert the following numbers to decimal, assuming 4 bits after the point:
(i) 0000000001101000   (ii) 0000000000110010

Q3: What is   (i) the largest number   (ii) the smallest positive number that can be held in two bytes, assuming 4 bits after the point?

Floating point binary

Fixed point representation allows the computer to hold fractions, but the range of numbers is still limited. Even using 4 bytes (32 bits) to hold each number, with 8 bits for the fractional part after the point, the largest number that can be held is just over 8 million. Another format is needed for holding very large numbers.

In decimal, we can show very large numbers in scientific notation. For example

$$1,200,000,000,000 \qquad \text{can be written as} \qquad 0.12 \times 10^{13}$$

Here, 0.12 is called the **mantissa** (or coefficient) and 13 is called the **exponent**. The mantissa holds the digits and the exponent defines where to place the decimal point. In the example above, the point is moved 13 places to the right.

The same technique can be used for binary numbers. For example, two bytes (16 bits) might be divided into 10 bits for the mantissa and 6 for the exponent.

mantissa	exponent		
0 110100000	000011	=	0.1101×2^3

The sign bit (0) tells us that the number is positive. The mantissa represents 0.1101 and the exponent tells us to move the point 3 places right, so the number becomes 110.1, which converted to decimal is 6.5.

Note: that the point starts off between the sign bit and the first bit of the mantissa.

Q4: Convert the following binary numbers to denary:
(i) 0 101010000 000010   (ii) 0 110110000 000100

If the *exponent* is negative (indicated by a 1 in its leftmost bit), the binary point is moved left instead of right. So, for example,

mantissa	exponent
0 100000000	111110

represents a mantissa of 0.1 and an exponent of 111110 (-2), so the whole number represents 0.001, that is, one eighth or 0.125.

The rules for converting a positive binary floating point number to decimal can be summarised as follows:

- place the point between the sign bit and the first digit of the mantissa
- convert the exponent to its equivalent decimal form (positive or negative)
- move the point right if the exponent is positive, or left if the exponent is negative, the appropriate number of places
- convert the resulting binary number to denary.

Converting a negative binary floating point number to decimal is similar. However, you need to remember that, after moving the binary point, with a positive exponent the left-most bit will have a negative place value.

mantissa	exponent
1 110100000	000011

The sign bit (1) tells us that the number is negative. The mantissa represents 1.1101 and the exponent tells us to move the point 3 places right, so the number becomes 1110.1, which converted to decimal is

$$-8 + 4 + 2 + 0.5 = -1.5$$

Note: that the left-most bit has a negative place value.

If the *exponent* is negative (indicated by a 1 in its leftmost bit), the binary point is moved left instead of right. You need to fill in with extra 1's as you shift the binary point to the left. So, for example,

mantissa	exponent
1 100000000	111110

represents a mantissa of 1.1 and an exponent of 111110 (-2), so the whole number represents 1.111, which converted to decimal is

$$-1 + 0.5 + 0.25 + 0.125 = -0.125$$

4-33

Q5: Convert the following binary numbers to decimal:

(i)   0 101000000 111111   (ii) 0 001101000 000110

(iii) 1 101000000 111111   (iv) 1 001101000 000110

Normalisation

The **precision** of the floating point representation described above depends on the number of digits stored in the mantissa. Looking once again at the more familiar decimal system:

the number 34,568,000 can be expressed as $.34568 \times 10^8$, allowing 5 digits for the mantissa,

or as $.3457 \times 10^8$, allowing only 4 places for the mantissa.

Some accuracy has been sacrificed here.

The number could also be written as $.034568 \times 10^9$, but then we need 6 places in the mantissa to achieve the same accuracy. In order to achieve the most accurate representation possible for a given size of mantissa, the number should be written with no leading zeros to the left of the most significant bit.

In binary, the same principle is used. Thus using a mantissa of 9 bits plus a sign bit, the number 0.000001001 would be represented in the mantissa as 0.100100000 , with an exponent of 111011 (-5).

This is known as **normalised form**, and in the case of a positive number, is the form in which the first bit of the mantissa, not counting the sign bit, is 1.

Note: that the mantissa of a positive number in normalised form always lies between $^1/2$ and 1.

Example:

Normalise the floating point binary number: 0 000110101 000010

Step 1: Put in the assumed binary point, and convert the exponent to decimal, giving

0.000110101   Exponent = 2.

Step 2: Shift the number left 3 places so that the binary point immediately precedes the first 1, and subtract 3 from the exponent.

0.110101000   Exponent = 2 - 3 = -1.

Answer: 0.110101000 111111

Q6: Normalise the following numbers, which are held with a 10-bit mantissa and a 6-bit exponent.

(i) 0 000000110 000111   (ii) 0 000010111 000110

With negative numbers, the normalised form is the one in which the first bit of the mantissa, not counting the sign bit, is 0. To normalise a negative number, therefore, shift the number left until the first bit (not counting the sign bit) is 0, and adjust the exponent accordingly.

Note that the mantissa of a negative number in normalised form always lies between -1/2 and -1.

Example:

Normalise the following number: 1 111100100 000011

Step 1: Insert the assumed binary point to the right of the sign bit, and convert the exponent to decimal, giving

1.111100100   Exponent = 3.

Step 2: Shift the number left 4 times so that the first bit of the mantissa is 0, and subtract 4 from the exponent, giving

1.001000000   Exponent = 3 - 4 = -1.

Answer: 1 001000000 111111

Q7: Normalise the following numbers:

(i) 1 111110111 000000   (ii) 1 111111010 000011

Advantages of normalised numbers

- maximum precision for a given number of bits
- only one representation for each number

Hint
A normalised number always starts with 2 bits that are different, e.g. 01 or 10.

Exercises

1 A two byte register holds numbers in floating point form with a 10 bit mantissa and a 6 bit exponent.

   (a) Explain the terms:

      (i) mantissa;

      (ii) exponent. (2)

   (b) Each of these holds data in two's complement form. At one moment, this register holds the following bits

              0110101100000011

      (i) Label the mantissa in this data. (1)

      (ii) How can you tell if the number is positive or negative? (2)

   (c) Explain, or show, how you would subtract 3 from 5 using two's complement. (2)

   (d) Give **one** advantage of floating point notation over fixed point notation for storing real numbers. (1)

AQA CPT4 Qu 8 January 2002

4-33

Chapter 34 – Structure and Role of the Processor

Inside the CPU

We have seen that a computer consists of the processor, main memory, input and output units. The processor itself consists of three main components:

- the arithmetic-logic unit (ALU) in which all arithmetic and logic operations are carried out;
- the control unit, which coordinates the activities taking place in the CPU, memory and peripherals, by sending control signals to the various devices;
- The system clock, which generates a continuous sequence of clock pulses to step the control unit through its operation.

In addition, the CPU contains circuitry controlling the interpretation and execution of instructions. Special storage locations called **registers** are included in this circuitry to hold information temporarily while it is being decoded or manipulated. Some of these special purpose registers are shown in the block diagram and explained below.

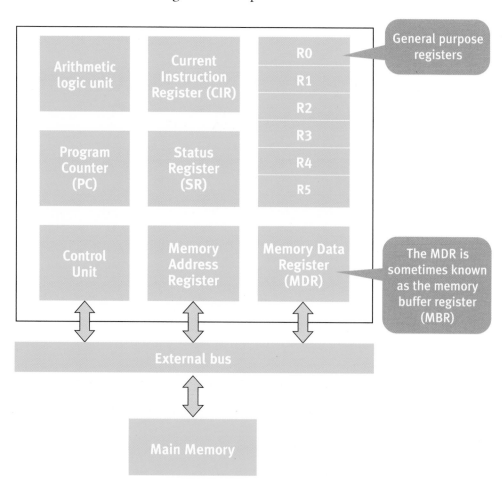

Figure 34.1: Registers inside the CPU

Register: an extremely fast piece of on-chip memory, usually 32 or 64 bits in size for temporary storage of a binary value.

The registers shown in the block diagram (Fig. 34.1), which represents a 'typical' computer, each have a specific purpose, which is described below:

- the **program counter (PC)** holds the address of the next instruction to be executed. It is also known as the **sequence control register (SCR)** or the **sequence register**.

When a sequence of instructions is being executed, the program counter is automatically incremented to point to the next instruction – that is, it holds the address of the next instruction to be executed. Depending on the length of the current instruction, this may mean that 1, 2 or 3 has to be added to its current contents. If the current instruction is a branch or jump instruction, then the address to branch to is copied from the current instruction to the program counter.

- The **general purpose registers** are used for performing arithmetic functions. In some computers, there is only one general purpose register, usually called an **accumulator**, which acts as a working area. Other computers have up to 16 general purpose registers.

For example, an instruction to add the contents of memory locations 1000 and 1001 and store the result in location 1002 might be broken down into the instructions:

```
Load contents of 1000 into the accumulator
Add contents of 1001 to the accumulator
Store contents of accumulator in 1002
```

- The **current instruction register** (**CIR** also known as **IR**) contains both the **operator** and the **operand** of the current instruction. For example, a machine language instruction to load the contents of location 1000 into the accumulator might be written

```
LDA    1000
```

where LDA is the **operator**, and 1000 is the **operand**.

- The **memory address register** (**MAR**) holds the address of the memory location from which data will be read or to which data will be written. Remember that both instructions and data are held in memory, so that sometimes the MAR will hold the address of an instruction to be fetched, and sometimes it will hold the address of data to be used in an instruction. Thus when an instruction is to be fetched, the contents of the program counter are copied to this register so that the CPU will know where in memory to get the next instruction from.

- The **memory data register** (**MDR**, also known as Memory Buffer Register **MBR**) is used to temporarily store data read from or written to memory. The instruction (for example, LDA 1000) is placed here en route to the CIR where it will be decoded. When the instruction has been decoded, the operand, 1000, will be placed in the MAR and the contents of location 1000 will then be copied to the MDR.

All transfers from memory to the CPU go via the memory data register. Both the memory data register and the memory address register serve as 'buffer' registers to compensate for the difference in speed between the CPU and memory.

- The **status register** (**SR**) contains bits that are set or cleared based on the result of an instruction. For example, one particular bit will be set if overflow occurs, and another bit set if the result of the last instruction was negative. Based on this information the CPU could make a decision on whether to branch out of a given sequence.

Status registers (also known as **program status words** or **PSW**s) also contain information about interrupts, which are discussed later in this chapter.

4-34

The steps in the fetch-execute cycle

The sequence of operations involved in executing an instruction can be subdivided into two phases – the fetch cycle and the execution cycle. In addition to executing instructions, the CPU has to supervise other operations such as data transfers between input/output devices and main memory. When an I/O device needs to transfer data, it generates an interrupt and the CPU suspends execution of the program and transfers to an appropriate interrupt handling program. A test for the presence of interrupts is carried out at the end of each instruction cycle.

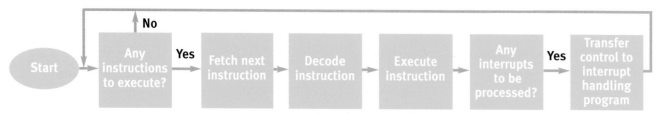

Figure 34.2: The fetch-execute cycle

How the CPU registers are used

The fetch-execute cycle may be broken down into a series of steps as follows:

(Fetch phase)

1 The address of the next instruction is copied from the PC to the MAR.

2 The instruction held at that address is copied to the MDR. Simultaneously, the content of the PC is incremented so that it holds the address of the next instruction.

3 The contents of the MDR are copied to the CIR.

(Execute phase)

1 The instruction held in the CIR is decoded.

2 The instruction is executed.

The Fetch-Execute Cycle in Register Transfer Notation

Note: ← *means 'the value on the right is transferred into the register on the left'*

[ ] means 'the contents of…'

MAR ← [PC]

MDR ← [MemoryLocation]

PC ← [PC] + 1

IR ← [MDR]

Q1: Describe the sequence of events carried out during the fetch-execute cycle when obeying the first of the instructions below, showing the contents of each of the following registers during the cycle:

program counter (PC), memory address register (MAR), memory data register (MDR), current instruction register (CIR), accumulator (ACC)

```
Address Contents    Type          Comment
500    LDA  1000    instruction   load contents of location 1000 into ACC
503    ADD  1001    instruction   add contents of location 1001 into ACC
506    STO  1002    instruction   store contents of ACC in location 1002

1000        3       data
1001        5       data
1002        0       data
```

The stack pointer

In addition to the registers mentioned above, most computers use a special register called a stack pointer which points to the top of a set of memory locations known as a stack. (A stack is a data structure which can only be accessed at the 'top', like a pile of plates). When execution of a program is interrupted for any reason the status of the interrupted program and the current contents of all the registers are saved on the stack, and the stack pointer updated.

Stacks may also be used instead of general purpose registers to store the intermediate results of arithmetic operations and to hold return addresses and parameter information when subroutines are called. Whenever a subroutine is called in the program, the contents of the program counter, which contains the address of the next instruction after the CALL, is saved on the stack. A RETURN instruction fetches this value off the stack and loads it into the program counter so that execution continues from the correct instruction.

Recap: the accumulator and general purpose registers

It is important to understand that all operations take place in the accumulator or a general purpose register. Thus for example to execute the high level instruction

        P := Q - R

the following operations are needed:

        Load Q into the accumulator
        Subtract R from the accumulator
        Store the contents of the accumulator in P

4-34

> **Q2:** What operations would be needed to execute (i) P := 100; (ii) NUM1 := NUM2;

Interrupts

In Figure 34.2 you will see that at the end of each fetch/execute cycle the processor may be required to deal with an interrupt.

Interrupt: a signal from some device or source seeking the attention of the processor. The interrupt signal is sent along a control line to the processor, and the currently executing program is suspended while control is passed to an interrupt service routine.

Types of interrupt

The following different types of interrupt may occur:

- **interrupts generated by the running process**. The process might need to perform I/O, obtain more storage or communicate with the operator.
- **I/O interrupts**. These are initiated by the I/O hardware and signal to the CPU that the status of a channel or device has changed. An I/O interrupt will occur when an I/O operation is complete, when an error occurs, or when a device is made ready.
- **Timer interrupts**. These are generated by a timer within the processor, and allow the operating system to perform certain functions at regular intervals. For example, each user in a multi-user system may be allocated a certain amount of processor time before a timer interrupt is generated and control of the processor passes to the next user in turn.
- **Program check interrupts**. These are caused by various types of error such as division by zero.
- **Machine check interrupts**. These are caused by malfunctioning hardware.

Interrupt priorities

There is a special register in the CPU called the **interrupt register**. At the beginning of each fetch-execute cycle, the interrupt register is checked. Each bit of the register represents a different type of interrupt, and if a bit is set, the state of the current process is saved and the operating system routes control to the appropriate interrupt handler.

Some interrupts, such as those generated by hardware failure, may need to be dealt with immediately, whereas others such as an I/O device signaling that it is ready for I/O, can be temporarily ignored. Interrupts are therefore assigned **priorities** so that when two interrupts are received simultaneously, the one with the highest priority is dealt with first. Only an interrupt with a higher priority is allowed to interrupt the servicing of another.

Examples of interrupt priorities are given below; one is highest priority, four is lowest.

Class of interrupt	Source of interrupt	Priority
Hardware failure:	Power failure – initiated when a decline in the internal voltages is detected, giving the OS a few milliseconds to close down as gracefully as possible.	1
	Memory parity error	1
Program:	Arithmetic overflow	2
	Division by zero	2
	Attempt to execute an illegal machine instruction	2
	Reference outside a user's allowed memory space	2
Timer	Generated by an internal clock within the processor	3
I/O	I/O device signals normal completion or the occurrence of an error condition	4

The interrupt handler

What happens when, for example, a key on the keyboard is pressed, thus generating an interrupt? A small program called an **interrupt service routine (ISR)** or **interrupt handler** is executed to transfer the character value of the key pressed into main memory. *A different ISR is provided for each different source of interrupt.* A typical sequence of actions when an interrupt occurs would be:

1   The current fetch-execute cycle is completed.

2   The contents of the program counter, which points to the next instruction of the user program to be executed, must be stored away safely so it can be restored after servicing the interrupt.

3   The contents of other registers used by the user program are stored away safely for later restoration.

4   The source of the interrupt is identified.

5   Interrupts of a lower priority are disabled.

6   The program counter is loaded with the start address of the relevant interrupt service routine.

7   The interrupt service routine is executed.

8   The saved values belonging to the user program for registers other than the program counter are restored to the processor's registers.

9   Interrupts are re-enabled.

10 The program counter is restored to point to the next instruction to be fetched and executed in user program.

The vectored interrupt mechanism

Step 6 above requires the PC to be loaded with the start address of the relevant ISR. One method of locating the correct ISR is known as the **vectored interrupt mechanism**. The complete list of interrupts and associated starting addresses of interrupt handlers is stored in a table called the **interrupt vector table**. The interrupting device supplies a vector number (an offset) which is added to a fixed number (the base address). This base address plus offset is the address of a pointer to the start address of the ISR. When the processor responds to an interrupt it copies the starting address of the relevant interrupt handler from the interrupt vector table into the program counter.

The advantage of this method is that new ISRs can be placed at any appropriate memory location and it is only necessary for the interrupting device to supply the correct offset for the vector to be located.

Processor performance

In the traditional computer (sometimes referred to as the **von Neumann machine**) instructions are fetched and executed one at a time in a serial manner. Data, instructions and addresses are transmitted between memory and the processor along **data and address buses**. A third type of bus called the control bus is used to send control and timing signals between the various components of the CPU and between the CPU and main memory (see Chapter 11, Figure 11.3).

The main features which distinguish one processor from another and which determine the performance of each are:

- Clock speed
- Word size
- Bus width
- Architecture

4-34

Clock speed

In order to synchronise the various steps carried out during the fetch-execute cycle, all processors have an internal clock which generates regularly timed pulses. All processor activities, such as fetching an instruction, reading data into the memory data register etc. must begin on a clock pulse, although some activities may take more than one clock pulse to complete. Typically, the clock pulse rate in 2004 is around 2.5 Gigahertz (2500 million cycles per second). The clock speed, therefore, is one of the factors which will influence the speed at which instructions are executed; a 2GHz processor will in general operate faster than a 1.8GHz processor.

Word length

The word size of a computer is the number of bits that the CPU can process simultaneously. Bits may be grouped into 8-, 16-, 32-, 64- or 128-bit 'words', and processed as a unit during input and output, arithmetic and logic instructions. A processor with a 32-bit word size will operate faster than a processor with a 16-bit word size. Word size is a major factor in determining the speed of a processor. In the most familiar architectures of the past few decades, a word has been 32 bits. Both IBM's mainframe processors and Intel's processors, used in standard PCs, have used a 32-bit word. Recent processor architectures from Intel and others provide for a 64-bit word.

Bus width

Both the addresses of data and instructions, and the data and instructions, are transmitted along buses. The width of the address bus determines the maximum address that can be directly referenced. For example, if the width of the address bus is 8 bits, the maximum address that can be transmitted is 11111111 in binary which is 2^8-1 or 255. In all 256 addresses, from 0 to 255, can be referenced.

The width of the data bus determines how many bits can be transferred simultaneously. This is usually but not always the same as the word size of the computer. Not all processors with a 32-bit word for example have a 32-bit **data bus**, and so the data may have to be fetched in two groups of 16 bits.

Q3: Distinguish between the **data bus** and the **address bus**.

Q4: What is the maximum address that can be directly addressed in a processor with a 16-bit address bus?

Q5: What is the lowest address?

Q6: Express the maximum number of directly addressable locations in kilobytes.

4-34

Exercises

1 (a) In the context of a computer processor, define the term *Clock Speed*. (1)

   (b) Explain how the clock speed affects the speed at which instructions can be executed. (1)

AQA CPT4 Qu 2 January 2002

2 (a) What is a *register* in a computing context? (1)

   (b) Give **one** reason for using general purpose registers rather than main memory. (1)

   (c) Some registers are used in the processor for a specific purpose. Name **three** such registers and explain the purpose of each one. (3)

AQA CPT4 Qu 3 June 2002

Chapter 35 – Assembly Language Instructions

The instruction set

Instructions in machine language are in the form of binary codes, with each different processor using different codes for the instruction set supported by its hardware. The instruction set of a typical computer includes the following types of instructions:

- **data transfer** such as MOVE, LOAD, STORE
- **arithmetic operations** such as ADD, SUBTRACT, MULTIPLY, DIVIDE, SHIFT
- **logical operations** such as AND, OR, NOT, exclusive-OR
- **test and branch instructions**; unconditional, conditional, subroutine calls and returns.

Instruction set: the set of bit patterns that represent all the possible operations for a given processor.

As it is very tedious for the programmer to use the binary representation of machine instructions, in assembly language operation codes and addresses are represented symbolically by abbreviations called **mnemonics**. Typically, two-, three- or four-character mnemonics are used for all machine code instructions. The **assembler** translates a program written in mnemonics into machine code.

Data transfer instructions

Examples of data transfer instructions include moving data from memory to a register, or from register to register; moving data from a register to memory or to an output unit; moving data from an output unit to a register:

```
MOVE R1,R2    Move contents of register R2 to R1
LDA #32       Load the number 32 into the accumulator
STA X         Store contents of the accumulator in memory location X
```

Arithmetic instructions

Some microprocessors offer only addition and subtraction as the basic arithmetic operations. Others offer a more comprehensive set such as:

ADC	addition	MPY	multiplication
SBC	subtraction	DIV	division
INC	increment	NEG	sign change
DEC	decrement	ABS	absolute value

After an arithmetic operation has been carried out, it is often useful to be able to test the result to see whether it was, say, zero or negative, or whether 'carry' or overflow occurred. The status register in some processors includes 4 bits referred to as N, Z, V and C, which are set to 1 or 0 depending on the result of the previous operation, as follows:

If result is negative, $N = 1$

If result is zero, $Z = 1$

If overflow occurred, $V = 1$

If carry occurred, $C = 1$

These bits are called **status bits** or **condition codes**. Conditional branch instructions such as BEQ (Branch if zero) check the status of the relevant status bit (often called a 'flag') and branch accordingly.

4-35

Carry and overflow

In a microprocessor using 8-bit registers, the range of integers that can be held in one register is from –128 to 127, and if the result of an arithmetic operation falls outside that range, the overflow bit will be set to 1, otherwise it will be set to 0.

Example:

$$
\begin{array}{r}
0100\ 0000\ (64) \\
+\quad 0100\ 0001\ (65) \\
\hline
1000\ 0001\ (-127)
\end{array}
$$

N Z V C
1 0 1 0

The sign bit has changed to 1, and the result is negative. This situation can be detected by examining the overflow bit, which will have been set by this operation.

The carry bit will not have been set, because there is no external carry – that is, all the binary digits still fit into the 8-bit register.

Adding two large negative numbers will cause both the overflow bit and the carry bit to be set, as shown below:

Example:

$$
\begin{array}{r}
1100\ 0000\ (-64) \\
+\quad 1011\ 1111\ (-65) \\
\hline
(1)\ 0111\ 1111\ (+127)
\end{array}
$$

N Z V C
0 0 1 1

In some situations the carry bit will be set and the overflow bit will not be set.

Example:

$$
\begin{array}{r}
1111\ 1111\ (-1) \\
+\quad 1111\ 1111\ (-1) \\
\hline
(1)\ 1111\ 1110\ (-2)
\end{array}
$$

N Z V C
1 0 0 1

Here, –2 is the correct answer and the carry bit can be ignored.

The overflow bit, then, warns that the sign of the result has been accidentally changed and action must be taken. The carry bit indicates that a ninth bit has been set and action may or may not be needed, as we shall see when performing double precision arithmetic.

Q1: Complete the following additions, showing the status of the carry and overflow bits, and stating whether or not the answers are correct.

(i)
$$
\begin{array}{l}
0000\ 0111\ \ (7) \\
+\ 1111\ 1100\ \ (-4) \\
\hline
\\
\hline
\end{array}
$$
V =   C =   Correct?

(ii)
$$
\begin{array}{l}
1111\ 1100\ (-4) \\
+\ 1111\ 1000\ (-8) \\
\hline
\\
\hline
\end{array}
$$
V =   C =   Correct?

(iii)
$$
\begin{array}{l}
0010\ 1100 \\
+\ 0100\ 1110 \\
\hline
\\
\hline
\end{array}
$$
V =   C =   Correct?

(iv)
$$
\begin{array}{l}
0111\ 1000\ (120) \\
+\ 0110\ 0001\ (97) \\
\hline
\\
\hline
\end{array}
$$
V =   C =   Correct?

(v)
$$
\begin{array}{l}
1110\ 0001\ (-31) \\
+\ 1000\ 0001\ (-127) \\
\hline
\\
\hline
\end{array}
$$
V =   C =   Correct?

Logical instructions

The instructions OR, NOT, AND and EOR (exclusive OR) have the following effects:

		OR	NOT	AND	EOR
Inputs	A	1010	1010	1010	1010
	B	1100		1100	1100
Result		1110	0101	1000	0110

The **NOT** function can be used to find the two's complement of a number:

A	0110 0111
NOT A	1001 1000
add 1	1
2's complement	1001 1001

The assembly language instructions to carry out this operation would be similar to those shown below:

```
LDA     #01100111B    ;load binary number into accumulator
NOTA                  ;complement the number in the accumulator
ADC     #1            ;add 1 to the accumulator
```

Q2: Use an EOR function to find the 2's complement of a number held in NUM. Store it in NEGNUM.

The **OR** function can be used to set certain bits to 1 without affecting the other bits in the binary code. For example, a system has eight lights that can be turned on (output 1) or off (output 0), controlled by an 8-bit binary code. At present, lights 1 to 4 are on. We now wish to turn on lights 5 and 7 as well.

Light numbers	1 2 3 4 5 6 7 8
Present output	1 1 1 1 0 0 0 0
OR with	0 0 0 0 1 0 1 0
Result	1 1 1 1 1 0 1 0

The assembly language code for this operation could be

```
LDA     LIGHT     ;load contents of LIGHT into accumulator
ORA     #1010B    ;OR operation with binary 1010
STA     LIGHT     ;store result back in LIGHT
```

The **AND** function can be used for masking out certain bits of a number. For example, if we input the ASCII character 3 at the keyboard, the ASCII pattern 00110011 is input. In order to change this to a pure binary number, we need to mask out the first 4 bits.

Q3: Use an AND operation to convert an ASCII digit to a pure binary number.

Q4: Devise an OR operation that will convert a pure binary digit to its equivalent ASCII code.

The EOR function can be used to check if two words are identical:

```
EOR #99    ;  is the contents of the accumulator equal to 99?
BZR label1 ;  branch to label1 if equal
```

4-35

Test and Conditional branches

These instructions may test the flags in the status register; typical instructions and their mnemonic codes (6502) are 'Branch if the last result was zero' – BEQ, 'Branch if carry flag set' – BCS, ' Branch on result not zero' – BNE, 'Branch on result positive' – BPL, 'branch on overflow set' - BVS.

Compare instructions may be used to compare the contents of of a memory location with the contents of a register. If the contents of the memory location and the register are equal, the zero flag in the status register is set to 1 and may be tested.

Example: Write assembly code instructions to branch to LBL1 if the contents of the accumulator is equal to zero.

Solution:
```
CMP  #0      ;compare contents of Accumulator with zero
BEQ  LBL1    ;branch if they are equal to LBL1
```

Unconditional branches

An instruction such as JMP 1000 causes an unconditional branch (this means the jump instruction is executed regardless of any previous results) to an instruction held in location 1000. The contents of the program counter (PC) will be changed to hold the address 1000. In the case of a subroutine call (JSR 2000), the return address has to be stored so that control can be returned to the next instruction after the CALL. This is usually done by pushing the address of the next instruction onto the **stack**, and updating the stack pointer. When the RETURN instruction (RTS) from the subroutine is encountered, the address is popped from the stack and loaded into the PC.

Shift instructions

There are generally 2 or 3 different shift operations available: **logical**, **arithmetic** and **rotate**.

A **logical** shift right (LSR) causes the least significant bit (lsb) to be shifted into the carry bit, and a zero moves in to occupy the vacated space.

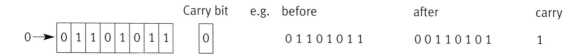

It is useful for examining the least significant bit of a number. After the operation, the carry bit can be tested and a conditional branch instruction executed.

Q5: Shift the binary pattern 0100 0111 right once and then left once, showing the contents of the carry bit after each shift.

An **arithmetic** shift is similar but it takes into account the value of the sign bit, which always remains the same. Shifting right has the effect of dividing by 2, and shifting left multiplies by 2. In a right shift, if the sign bit is 1, 1 is moved in from the left instead of 0.

Q6: Convert the number 12 to binary, and then multiply it by 4 using arithmetic shifts. Convert the result back to decimal.

Q7: Convert the number –16 to binary, and divide by 8 using arithmetic shifts.

A **rotate** or **circular** shift preserves all of the bits operated upon. In a circular right shift (ROR), the value in the carry bit is moved into the vacated position and the carry bit is moved into the most significant bit. One possible use of a cyclic shift is to test individual bits by bringing each bit successively into the carry bit position. After the operation, the carry bit can be tested and a conditional branch instruction executed.

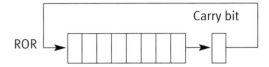

Q8: Show the result of a circular shift on the bit pattern 0100 1100, assuming the carry bit was set to 1 before the operation.

Exercises

1   Write the assembly language equivalent of the following high level language instructions, explaining each assembly language instruction used.

```
A ← 0;
Repeat
    A ← A + 1;
Until A = 99;
```
                                                                                    (6)
New Question

2   Write the assembly language equivalent of the following high level language instructions, explaining each assembly language instruction used.

```
If X = 99
    Then X ← 1
    Else X ← X + 1
EndIf
```
                                                                                    (5)
New Question

3   Write the assembly language equivalent of the following high level language instructions, explaining each assembly language instruction used.

```
For I ← 1 To 10 Do
    A ← A + 1;
```
                                                                                    (5)
New Question

4   What would be the result of performing each of the following logical operations?

(a)   NOT   0101 0100   (1)

(b)   0011 0101
      AND   0000 1111   (1)

(c)   0000 0110
      OR   1001 0000   (1)

(d)   0001 0011
      EOR   0001 0011   (1)
New Question

Chapter 36 – Instruction Formats and Addressing Modes

Instruction format for an 8-bit microprocessor

Machine code instructions, just like numbers, letters and other symbols, are stored as an arrangement of bits in a binary code. In an 8-bit microprocessor, some instructions may occupy just one byte, while others will occupy two or three bytes. The first byte will always contain the 'op code' – the code for that particular operation or instruction.

Op code: operation code that specifies which operation is to be performed.

Operand: specifies the data upon which the operation is to be performed.

Q1: How many different instructions are possible if 8 bits are used for the op code?

Zero address instructions

Instructions which occupy one byte do not involve an explicit address – they are instructions such as

```
CLC      ; clear the carry flag
RTS      ; return from subroutine
ASL      ; shift the contents of the accumulator left one bit
```

Often the address of the operand is implied, such as ASL, the accumulator holds the datum.

One address instructions

One address instructions occupy two bytes. Examples of such instructions are

```
ADC  X   ; add the contents of X to the accumulator
LDA  #23 ; load the number 23 into the accumulator
BMI  L1  ; branch to label L1 if contents of accumulator are negative
```

PC ⬚ op code

PC + 1 ⬚ operand

Two address instructions

Two address instructions occupy three bytes, either because the instruction involves two operands, or because the address of the operand is too large to fit into one byte. Examples of such instructions are

```
LDA MEM2    ; load contents of MEM2 (eg location 0DFF hex) into acc.
EOR A, MASK ; exclusive OR contents of A with MASK
```

PC ⬚ op code

PC + 1 ⬚ low address or operand 1

PC + 2 ⬚ high address or operand 2

In the first example above, FF will be stored in PC+1, and 0D in PC+2. The processor will determine from the op code how to interpret all the bytes making up the instruction.

A 16-bit instruction format

Machines which use 16-bit words also make use of 0-address, 1-address and 2-address formats, taking up one, two or three words. However, with 16 bits obviously more information can be stored in each word, and a typical instruction format is shown below.

1-word instruction

0 1 2 3	4 5	6 7 8 9 10 11 12 13 14 15
Function code	Mode	Operand address

The first 4 bits are used for the op code, and bits 4 and 5 are used to indicate the **addressing mode** being used (see below).

Microprocessors may have more than one instruction format for the one-word instructions, depending on the type of instruction being used. Instruction formats indicate not only what operation is to be performed but also how many locations are being used to hold the actual instruction, so that the PC (program counter) can be correctly incremented. The number of memory locations used for the address will depend partly on the mode of addressing being used.

> **Q2:** Does the number of words occupied by an instruction have any bearing on how fast the instruction will execute? Explain your answer.

4-36

Addressing modes

There are several different ways in which the computer can calculate the addresses holding the source and/or destination of the data being processed in a particular instruction. These are called **addressing modes**, and are described below, starting with immediate addressing.

Immediate addressing

In some instructions, the data to be operated on is held as part of the instruction format. In a 2-byte instruction format, the operand is therefore not an address at all, but a value (indicated by #). Typical instructions using immediate addressing are:

```
LDA  #&35    ;   load the hexadecimal value 35 into the accumulator
MOVE #8,  R1 ;   move the value 8 into register R1
```

This type of addressing could be used, for example, to initialise a counter to a particular value.

Direct addressing

In this mode, the operand gives the address of the data to be used in the operation. For example:

```
LDA  MEM     ;   load contents of location MEM into the accumulator
```

The number of locations which can be addressed using direct addressing is limited because only say, 10 out of 16 bits are available to hold the address, and often more than one word is used for holding the address.

This type of instruction is slow, for locating the data involves three or maybe four memory operations; three to load the 3-byte instruction, and then another to go and get the data to be operated on.

> **Q3:** If 16 bits are allowed for an address, what is the maximum memory address that can be referenced using direct addressing?

Indirect addressing

With this type of addressing, the address of the data in memory is held in another memory location, and the operand of the instruction holds the address of this memory location.

```
LDA (100)   ;   load the contents of the memory location
                whose address is stored at address 100.
```

> **Q4:** The store locations 100 and 120 contain the values 120 and 200 respectively. What value would be loaded into the accumulator by **each** of the following instructions?
> (i)   LDA #100   ; LOAD immediate 100
> (ii) LDA 100   ; LOAD direct 100
> (iii) LDA (100)   ; LOAD indirect 100

Indexed addressing

This is a variation on indirect addressing, where the operand address is calculated by adding to a base address the value held in an index register. Using this mode of addressing, the address of the operand can be modified by operating on the contents of the index register.

For example, suppose we wish to set to zero the contents of TABLE to TABLE + 99. Using an index register X, the following instructions can be used:

```
      LDA #0        ;   load 0 into the accumulator
      LDX #0        ;   load 0 into the index register
LOOP  STA TABLE,X   ;   store contents of accumulator in TABLE + X
      INX           ;   increment the index register
      CPX #99       ;   compare X with 99
      BNE LOOP      ;   branch if not equal to LOOP
```

Base register addressing

This is similar to indexed addressing, but this time the base address is held in the register, and the address field contains a displacement or offset. The following example alters a value held in a memory location &F027 (& means the number following is a hexadecimal number). Assume B, the base register, contains &F000.

```
LDA   &27,B   ;   loads accumulator with contents of address formed
                  by adding contents of B (the base register) and
                  hex 27
ADC   #5      ;   add 5 to contents of accumulator
STA   &27,B   ;   store contents of accumulator at address &F027
```

Relative addressing

This type of addressing is often used in branch instructions to specify where the next instruction is located relative to the instruction whose address is held in the PC. An example is:

```
JMP +10       ;   branch to the instruction 10 bytes on.
```

A 'jump relative' with a one-byte operand can only jump forwards or backwards 127 bytes.

Base register addressing and relative addressing allow the code to be **relocatable** anywhere in memory. This means the program can be located in different parts of main memory at different times. All modern computers run relocatable code.

Exercises

1 (a) Describe each of the following addressing modes.

    (i) Immediate addressing   (1)

    (ii) Direct addressing   (2)

    (iii) Indexed addressing   (2)

  (b) Storage locations 120 onwards hold the values as shown below.

120	1
121	2
122	3
123	4
124	5
125	6

The following instructions are part of a program. If the accumulator and register X both initially hold the value zero, what value would each hold after **each** instruction in the program is executed?

Instruction		Acc	Reg X
	At start	0	0
(i) LDX #5	; load immediate 5 into register X	_____	_____
(ii) LDA #120	; load immediate 120 into Accumulator	_____	_____
(iii) ADD 120	; add direct 120 into Accumulator	_____	_____
(iv) ADD X (120)	; add indexed 120 into Accumulator	_____	_____ (4)

AQA CPT4 Qu 8 January 2003

2 A computer design company has produced a design for an elementary computer. It is to be used to teach students about machine architecture, machine operations and the design of an *instruction set*.

The current instruction register has a length of 16 bits.

The accumulator has a length of 16 bits.

The size of each memory location is 16 bits.

The current instruction register is designed to hold one instruction at a time.

A machine instruction is 16 bits in length.

The most significant eight bits of a machine instruction denote the machine operation. The least significant bits denote an operand or the address of an operand.

Main memory stores both instructions and data.

continues over

4-36

The structure of a machine instruction is as follows.

(a) Define the term instruction set. (1)

(b) With 6 bits of the operation code reserved to denote basic machine operations, how many basic machine operations may be coded? (1)

(c) With reference to the operand field of a machine instruction, describe the following addressing modes:

(i) Immediate (1)

(ii) Direct (1)

(iii) Indirect (2)

(d) The following machine operations have their operation codes expressed in hexadecimal.

Mochine operation	Addressing Mode	Operation Code (hex)	Description
LDA	Immediate	A1	Load accumulator
	Direct	A2	
	Indirect	A3	
STA	Direct	B2	Store accumulator
	Indirect	B3	
ADD	Immediate	61	Add operand to contents of accumulator, storing result in accumulator
	Direct	62	
	Indirect	63	

(i) Convert the operation code for the operation STA for indirect addressing from hexadecimal to binary. (1)

(ii) It is required to add the hexadecimal number 6 to the contents of a main memory location whose address in hexadecimal is C1, with the result being stored in another memory location at hexadecimal address AB.

Complete the sequence of instructions, in hexadecimal, to perform this task on the machine above.

A1 06

_____

_____

(4)

(e) For the given machine:

(i) What is the highest memory address that can be addressed by an instruction using direct addressing? (1)

(ii) What is the highest address that can be addressed by an instruction using indirect addressing? (2)

AQA CPT4 Qu 9 June 2003

Chapter 37 – High Level Languages

High and low level languages

Computer languages may be classified as being either **low level**, (such as assembly language) or **high level** (such as Pascal, BASIC, PROLOG or 'C').

The characteristics of a **low level language** are:

• they are machine oriented; an assembly language program written for one machine will not work on any other type of machine (unless it happens to use the same processor chip);

• each assembly language statement (apart from macros) generally translates into one machine code instruction. Hence, programming is a lengthy and time-consuming business.

Assembly language is generally used when there is a requirement to access machine registers or exact memory addresses directly, write code that executes as fast as possible, or write code that occupies as little memory as possible. An example of an application with all three of these requirements is a **device driver**; that is, a program which allows the computer to interface with an external device such as a printer. When you buy a printer to use with a PC, for example, it will come with an appropriate printer driver supplied on a floppy disk or CD and the driver has to be installed on the hard disk before the printer can be used.

The characteristics of a **high level language** are:

• They are not machine oriented; in theory they are portable which means that a program written for one machine will run (with minor modifications) on any other machine for which the appropriate compiler or interpreter is available.

• They are problem oriented; each high level language has structures and facilities appropriate to a particular use or type of problem. For example FORTRAN was developed for use in solving mathematical problems, whereas COBOL was written especially for data processing applications. Some languages such as Pascal were developed as general purpose languages.

• Statements in a high level language generally resemble English sentences or mathematical expressions and these languages tend to be easier to learn and understand than assembly language. Each statement in a high level language will be translated into several machine code instructions.

Typical high level language facilities

High level languages have many facilities not found in low level languages; for example:

• selection structures such as **if .. then .. else, case**;

• iteration structures such as **while .. endwhile, repeat .. until** and **for .. endfor**. Instead of selection and iteration statements, assembly language programmers must use conditional branch statements such as **branch if equal, branch if non-zero**, etc.

• built-in routines to simplify input and output (e.g. **readln, writeln** in Pascal);

• built-in functions such as **sqr, log, chr**;

• data structures such as **string, array, record**.

Procedural (imperative) languages

High-level languages such as Pascal, C, COBOL and BASIC are classified as **procedural** or **imperative** languages. The program consists of a sequence of instructions which the computer will execute in the order specified by the programmer. There are dozens of procedural languages in use today, including:

- **Pascal**, which was developed in the 1970s to teach structured programming.

- **FORTRAN (FORmula TRANslation)** developed for use in scientific and engineering applications in the 1950s and still used. The features which make it suitable for mathematical applications include the following:

  - it has a large library of inbuilt mathematical functions such as log, sqrt, sin, arctan etc.;

  - comprehensive libraries of statistical, scientific and engineering routines are readily available, well-documented and easy to incorporate into the user's program;

  - double-precision arithmetic (using, say, 64 bits instead of 32 bits to represent a real number) means that calculations can be performed with great accuracy;

  - good array-handling capabilities mean that it is suitable for solving, for example, large sets of simultaneous equations.

- **COBOL (COmmon Business Oriented Language)**, developed in the 1950's (see Chapter 6). A new version of COBOL called COBOL97 was issued in 1997 so in spite of predictions that it would be dead and buried before the end of the century, it looks set to continue for some time yet! It has many facilities which make it suitable for data processing applications, including:

  - good validation facilities;

  - a **sort** verb to allow files to be sorted into any sequence;

  - excellent file-handling capabilities;

  - good report-formatting facilities;

  - facility to access databases from within a COBOL program.

  - new versions now incorporate object-oriented and web-based features

- **C**, developed by Dennis Richie at Bell Laboratories in the USA around 1972. It was originally developed for systems programming for the operating system UNIX. It is a relatively low-level language which has many of the advantages of Assembly language (facilitating very efficient programs for operating systems, text processing and compilers) and at the same time has the advantages of a high level language in that it is easy to learn, portable and hides the details of the computer's architecture from the user.

Object-oriented languages

Languages such as Java, C++ and Delphi are called **object-oriented** languages. In this type of language, the programmer uses objects, which are data items with all the processing possible on the data item attached to it. Object-oriented programming is discussed in more detail in the next chapter.

Declarative languages

There is another class of programming language called **declarative** languages which consist of a series of facts and rules about a particular subject, rather than a sequence of instructions. Prolog is an example of a declarative language, and is discussed in more depth in Chapter 39.

4-37

Languages for real-time embedded systems

As computers have become smaller, faster and more reliable, their range of applications has widened. One of the fastest expanding areas of computer applications is embedded systems, in which the computer is just one component within a larger engineering system. Such systems include:

- a microprocessor-controlled washing machine or video recorder;
- a modern jet aircraft;
- a system for controlling traffic lights;
- a process control system for controlling the flow of water along a pipe by means of a valve;
- a robot used in a car assembly plant.

Some of these systems may be extremely large and complex; for example the US Air Force C-17 transport aircraft has 19 different embedded computers incorporating over 80 microprocessors on board which utilise about 1.35 million lines of software code.

Languages for programming real-time systems need the following facilities:

- **real-time control facilities**. The programmer needs to be able to specify times at which actions are to be performed or completed, or take readings at regular time intervals, say every 5 seconds. For example an electric power station needs to increase supply at 5pm on Monday to Friday to cope with the surge in demand caused by families returning home, switching on lights, cooking dinner and so on. Traffic lights at an intersection may change every 30 seconds or less if an oncoming car is detected coming from a particular direction.

  An embedded system also needs to be able to recognise and act upon the **non-occurrence** of some external event. For example, a temperature sensor in a nuclear reactor may be required to log a new reading every second, with the failure to give a reading within 10 seconds being defined as a fault. The programmer has to be able to code a **timeout**; that is, what action to take after the 10 seconds are up.

- **interaction with hardware interfaces**. The language must contain statements to monitor sensors and control actuators (which make something happen). It also needs to be able to identify and handle interrupts from devices such as the sensor detecting oncoming traffic.

- **ability to support concurrent programming**. More than one action may need to be carried out simultaneously.

The languages C, Ada, Modula-2 and Occam all contain these facilities.

Criteria for selecting a programming language

A programming task can be made considerably easier, faster to complete, and more maintainable when a suitable language for the task is chosen. Criteria for making this choice will include:

- the nature of the application;
- the availability of facilities within the language for implementing the software design;
- the availability of a suitable compiler/interpreter for the hardware;
- the expertise of the programmers.

Exercises

1   It has been decided to re-write an existing system. What factors should be considered when deciding on the programming language to use? Give **three** factors, and explain why each is important.

(6)

AQA CPT4 Qu 1 June 2002

Chapter 38 – Object-Oriented Programming

History of Object-Oriented Programming

The structured programming approach involves decomposing a large problem into smaller problems until the smaller problems become solvable. These smaller problems are usually coded as procedures or functions and data is passed to these using parameters (procedural-oriented programming). Data and procedures remain separate.

The object-oriented programming approach models the real world more closely by using objects that store both data and the code for the operations that may be applied to that data.

Some more recent versions of procedural programming languages such as Pascal have object-oriented features built-in (Object Pascal). C++ was developed from C by adding object-oriented programming capability. Other languages such as Java are truly object-oriented.

Any object-oriented programming environment must support at least the following basic concepts:

• encapsulation

• inheritance

• polymorphism

Objects and classes

Objects represent 'things' from the real world, such as my car or Joe Blogg's car. Classes represent all objects of a kind, such as car. An object has attributes: the colour of my car is red and its make is a VW. These values are stored in fields. The class defines what fields an object has (owner, colour, make, mileage), but each object stores its own set of values (the **state** of the object). Objects have operations (methods) that can be used, such as *update mileage*. These describe the object's **behaviour**. Each class has source code associated with it that defines its details (**fields** and **methods**).

> **Q1:** 'Book' is a real-world classification. Name several attributes and activities associated with this class. Identify several instances of the class.

> **Q2:** Think of some other classes, and list the attributes and activities associated with each class. Identify instances of each class.

A class is an Abstract Data Type (ADT). A class declaration is a kind of type declaration. It describes the fields and methods of the class. A class has one or more sections for different access levels (private, protected, public, published).

Class: a set of objects which share a common data structure and a common behaviour.

Pascal Examples

The following programs show the difference between procedural programming and object-oriented programming using a very simple example of a clock with integer values for hours and minutes.

If you have Delphi or ObjectPascal available, you may wish to try these programs to fully understand the differences.

The following programs were written using a console application in Delphi.

```
program ProceduralExample;
{$APPTYPE CONSOLE}
uses  SysUtils;

var Hours, Minutes : Integer;

procedure ShowTime;
  begin
    writeln('The time is ', hours,':',minutes);
  end;

  procedure SetTime;
  begin
    write('Type in the number of hours: ');
    readln(Hours);
    write('Type in the number of minutes: ');
    readln(Minutes);
  end;

//********* main program body ***************
begin
  SetTime;
  ShowTime;
  Hours := Hours + 1;
  ShowTime;
  Readln;
end.
```

Program 1:
This program was written using procedural techniques.

The main program body calls procedures that access global variables.

The global variables Hours and Minutes represent the clock settings.

These global variables can be altered from anywhere within the main program body without calling the procedure SetTime.

```
program RecordExample;
{$APPTYPE CONSOLE}
uses SysUtils;

type TClock = record
                  Hours: Integer;
                  Minutes: Integer;
               end;

var Clock: TClock;

procedure ShowTime;
  begin
    writeln('The time is ',Clock.Hours,':',Clock.Minutes);
  end;

  procedure SetTime;
  begin
    write('Type in the number of hours: ');
    readln(Clock.Hours);
    write('Type in the number of minutes: ');
    readln(Clock.Minutes);
  end;

//********* main program body ***************

begin
  SetTime;
  ShowTime;
  Clock.Hours := Clock.Hours + 1;
  ShowTime;
  Readln;
end.
```

Program 2:
This program was also written using procedural techniques.

However the data has been grouped into a record, representing the clock settings. This makes the code more transparent.

The clock settings can still be altered without calling SetTime.

4-38

```
unit Unit1;
interface
type TClock = record
                Hours: Integer;
                Minutes: Integer;
            end;

implementation
end.
```

```
program TypeInSeparateUnitExample;
{$APPTYPE CONSOLE}
uses SysUtils, Unit1 in 'Unit1.pas';

var Clock: TClock;

procedure ShowTime;
  begin
    writeln('The time is ',Clock.Hours,':',Clock.Minutes);
  end;

  procedure SetTime;
  begin
    write('Type in the number of hours: ');
    readln(Clock.Hours);
    write('Type in the number of minutes: ');
    readln(Clock.Minutes);
  end;

begin
  SetTime;
  ShowTime;
  Clock.Hours := Clock.Hours + 1;
  ShowTime;
  Readln;
end.
```

Program 3:
Program 2 is split into main program and a unit (Unit1) that stores the type declaration.

Clock is a record of type TClock.
Note that the record fields are still accessible anywhere in the program.

4-38

```
program ObjectExample1;
{$APPTYPE CONSOLE}
uses SysUtils, Unit1 in 'Unit1.pas';

var Clock: TClock;

begin
  Clock := TClock.Create;
  Clock.SetTime;
  Clock.ShowTime;
  Clock.Hours := Clock.Hours + 1;
  Clock.ShowTime;
  Clock.Free;
  Readln;
end.
```

```
unit Unit1;
interface
type TClock = class
                Hours: Integer;
                Minutes: Integer;
                procedure ShowTime;
                procedure SetTime;
            end;
```

Program 4:
This program uses an object Clock of class TClock, declared in Unit1 below.

It also uses the clock's methods SetTime and ShowTime, also declared in Unit1.

Note that the clock fields are still accessible from anywhere in the program.

This is Unit1, which contains the class definition and ....

| ```pascal
implementation
procedure TClock.ShowTime;
  begin
    writeln('The time is ', Hours,':', Minutes);
  end;


  procedure TCLock.SetTime;
  begin
    write('Type in the number of hours: '); readln(Hours);
    write('Type in the number of minutes: ');
    readln(Minutes);
  end;

end.
``` | the code for the class methods.

(procedural encapsulation) |
| ```pascal
unit Unit1;

interface
type TClock = class
                Private
                   Hours: Integer;
                   Minutes: Integer;
                Public
                   procedure ShowTime;
                   procedure SetTime;
                end;

implementation
{methods code as above for Program 4}
``` | **Program 5:**
This is Unit1 from the above program, modified to make the clock's fields inaccessible (data encapsulation) from the program except through TClock's public methods. |

4-38

Encapsulation

Data encapsulation means restricting access to the data (fields).

Procedural encapsulation means that we do not need to know how the behaviour happens, i.e. how the methods are implemented.

Encapsulation: the technique that combines operations (methods) and data (fields) into one unit.

Class Definition using Object Pascal	Class Definition using Java
| ```pascal
type TClock = class
                Private
                   Hours: Integer;
                   Minutes: Integer;
                Public
                   procedure ShowTime;
                   procedure SetTime;
                end;
implementation
{methods code goes here}
``` | ```java
public class TClock
{
    private int hours;
    private int minutes;

    public TClock()
    {
        // constructor code goes here
    }
    public void setTime(int h,int m)
    {
        // constructor code goes here
    }
    public void showTime()
    {
    // method code goes here
    }
}
``` |

Inheritance

Many objects are related to other objects in some way. For example, a sports car and a lorry are both types of vehicle. Humans, tigers and whales are all members of the MAMMAL class. You can often define a new type of object by amending the definition of some other object. In object-oriented programming, this has the advantage of allowing the reuse of existing code, and is known as inheritance.

Inheritance: a relationship among classes where a sub-class shares all the fields and methods of a parent class (base class).

The class that you start with is called the **base class**. From the base class you can derive other classes which inherit all the properties and methods of the base class. In addition the new classes can have new fields and new methods or re-defined methods of their own. The relationships between classes may be shown in an **Inheritance diagram**. Notice which way the arrows point – this is the standard way of drawing such a diagram.

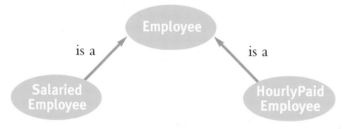

Figure 38.1: An Inheritance diagram

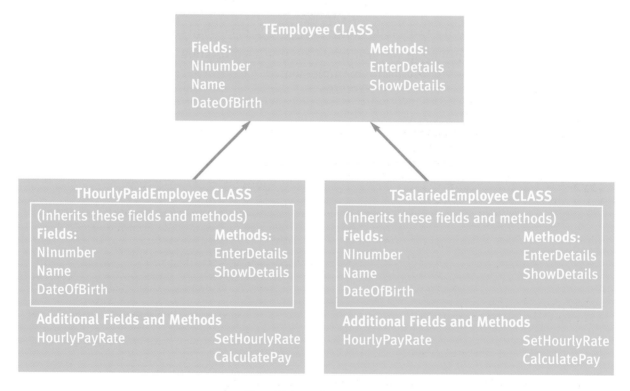

Figure 38.2: A Class Diagram

Example of Object Pascal Class Definitions using Inheritance

```
unit Unit1;

interface

uses SysUtils;

type TEmployee = class
                    private
                       NINumber: String[9];
                       Name: String[30];
                       DoB: TDateTime;
                    public
                       procedure EnterDetails;
                       procedure ShowDetails;
                 end;

type THourlyPaidEmployee = class (TEmployee)
                              private
                                 HourlyPayRate : Currency;
                              public
                                 procedure SetHourlyRate;
                                 procedure CalculatePay;
                           end;

type TSalariedEmployee = class (TEmployee)
                            private
                               AnnualSalary: Currency;
                            public
                               procedure SetAnnualSalary;
                               procedure CalculatePay;
                         end;

implementation

procedure TEmployee.EnterDetails;
var DoBString: String;
begin
  Write('National Insurance Number: '); Readln(NINumber);
  Write('Name: '); Readln(Name);
  Write('Date of Birth: '); Readln(DoBString);
  DoB := StrToDateTime(DoBString);
end;

procedure TEmployee.ShowDetails;
var DoBString: String;
begin
  Writeln('National Insurance Number: ',NINumber);
  Writeln('Name: ',Name);
  DoBString := DateTimeToStr(DoB);
  Writeln('Date of Birth: ',DoBString);
end;

procedure THourlyPaidEmployee.SetHourlyRate;
begin
  Write('Hourly Rate: '); Readln(HourlyPayRate);
end;

procedure THourlyPaidEmployee.CalculatePay;
var HoursWorked: Integer; MonthlyPay : Currency;
```

Base class
TEmployee

Sub class
THourlyPaidEmployee
inheriting from
TEmployee

Sub class
TSalariedEmployee
inheriting from
TEmployee

4-38

```
begin
  write('Enter number of hours worked this month: ');
  readln(HoursWorked);
  MonthlyPay := HoursWorked * HourlyPayRate;
  Writeln('Pay this month: ', MonthlyPay:5:2);
end;

procedure TSalariedEmployee.SetAnnualSalary;
begin
  Write('Annual Salary: '); Readln(AnnualSalary);
end;

procedure TSalariedEmployee.CalculatePay;
var MonthlyPay: Currency;
begin
  MonthlyPay := AnnualSalary/12;
  Writeln('Pay this month: ', MonthlyPay:5:2);
end;

end.
```

Q3: Use the above class definitions in a program with an object of each of the given classes and use the methods to check they are working correctly.

Polymorphism

A derived class can implement inherited methods differently if necessary. When new classes are derived from a base class they may redefine some of the base methods. Polymorphism allows for objects of different classes to recognise and process the same messages, using either the same or different methods.

Polymorphism: the same name is used in the class hierarchy for a method but each class may implement this method differently.

```
unit Unit1;

interface

uses
  Windows, Messages, SysUtils, Variants, Classes, Graphics, Controls, Forms,
  Dialogs, StdCtrls;

type
  TForm1 = class(TForm)
    btnRun: TButton;
    procedure btnRunClick(Sender: TObject);
  private
    { Private declarations }
  public
    { Public declarations }
  end;

type
  TShape = class
    procedure Display; virtual;
  end;

type
  TRectangle = class (TShape)
    procedure Display; override;
  end;
```

> Base class TShape.
> It only has one method Display, which will be redefined by the subclasses

> Sub class TRectangle.
> It inherits the method Display from TShape, but this method will be redefined for TRectangle

```
type
  TEllipse = class (TShape)
    procedure Display; override;
  end;
var
  Form1: TForm1;

implementation

procedure TShape.Display;
begin
  Form1.Canvas.LineTo(100,200);
end;

procedure TRectangle.Display;
begin
  Form1.Canvas.Rectangle(150,20,250,200);
end;

procedure TEllipse.Display;
begin
  Form1.Canvas.Ellipse(300,100,500,200);
end;

var  Shape : TShape;
{$R *.dfm}


procedure TForm1.btnRunClick(Sender: TObject);
begin
  Shape := TShape.Create;
  Shape.Display;
  Shape.Free;
  Shape := TRectangle.Create;
  Shape.Display;
  Shape.Free;
  Shape := TEllipse.Create;
  Shape.Display;
  Shape.Free;
end;

end.
```

> Sub class TEllipse.
> It inherits the method Display from TShape, but this method will be redefined for TEllipse.

> Object Shape of class TShape is created. Its method Display is invoked, which will draw a straight line.

> Object Shape of class TRectangle is created. Its method Display is invoked, which will draw a rectangle.

> Object Shape of class TEllipse is created. Its method Display is invoked, which will draw an ellipse.

Figure 38.3: Example program (Delphi) demonstrating polymorphism

Q4: If you have Delphi available, you can try this program out for yourself, to check that the methods *Display* really behave differently, depending on which object invokes it.

Containment

In an object-oriented system, many objects of different classes may be sending messages to each other as the program runs. For this to work, we have to provide links between objects which allow them to communicate. These links are known as associations. Associations can be described as aggregation, composition or containment. Objects can contain (are composed of) other objects. For example, the GUI program above defines a class *Tform1* that contains a button *btnRun*. Usually a GUI program will have many objects contained on a form. During design stage a containment diagram may be drawn. Note the diamond-shaped end 'pointing' to the container object. The number shows how many of each type of object are used.

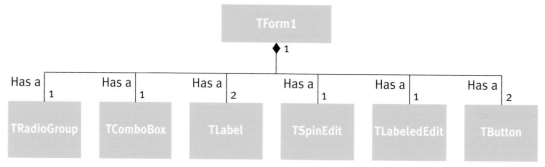

Figure 38.4: Containment diagram for the Delphi GUI form below

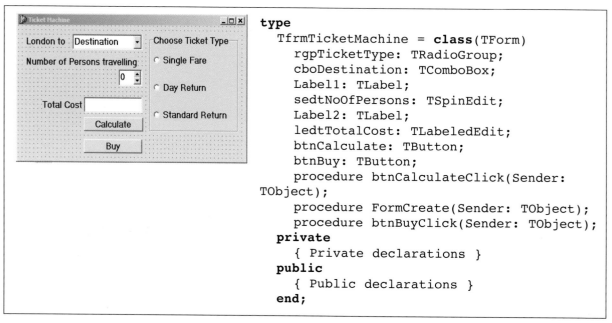

Figure 38.5: Delphi Form and code defining the TfrmTicketMachine class and the objects contained in it

Event-driven programming

Unlike traditional programs event-driven programs do not have a predefined pathway in the execution of the code. Most modern applications are said to be event-driven, because they are designed to respond to events. In a program, the programmer has no way of predicting the exact sequence of actions a user will perform next. They may choose a menu item or click a button. You can write code to handle the events you're interested in, rather than writing code that always executes in the same restricted order. Event-driven programs typically consist of a number of small programs called event handlers, which are to be called in response to external events, and a dispatcher, which calls the event handlers, often using an event queue to hold unprocessed events.

Event-driven program: user actions (external events) determine the sequence of code executions.

Graphical user interface programs are typically programmed in an event-driven style. Visual Basic and Delphi are examples of event-driven programming languages.

Figure 38.6: GUI program with a button the user can click

Figure 38.7: GUI program after the user clicked the button

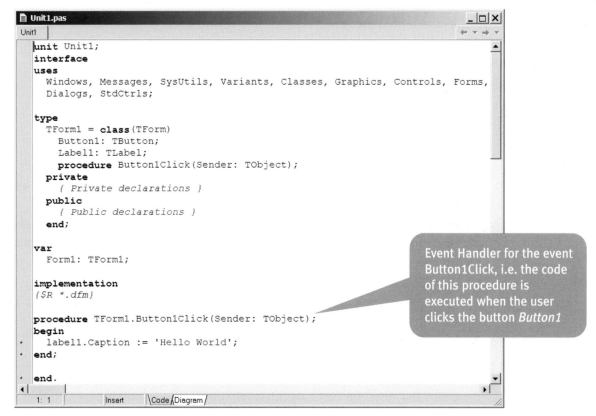

Figure 38.8: Code of GUI program written in Delphi

Benefits of Object-Oriented Programming

Data is protected and only accessible in well-defined ways. Storage structures of an object or the implementation of an object may be altered without affecting the programs that make use of the object.

Rather than starting from scratch with each new application, a programmer can re-use existing components (class definitions) from a component library. The programmer can create sub-classes from classes found in the component library and add new fields and methods as required.

This approach has the following benefits:

- Reliability: Components built by specialists are more likely to be designed correctly and reliably. They are likely to have been extensively tested.
- Time Saving: Re-using existing components means less code to write and test.
- Decreased maintenance: the maintenance of the re-used component is the responsibility of the component supplier. This means the programmers have less code to maintain themselves.
- Consistency: the library is the basis of a standard that will make the design process coherent and consistent.

Exercises

1   A supermarket has a section labelled 'Bottled Water'. Bottled water comes as 'still bottled water' or 'carbonated bottled water'.

In an object-oriented program, 'bottled water', 'still bottled water' and 'carbonated bottled water' are three defined *classes*. The classes 'still bottled water' and 'carbonated bottled water' are related, by single *inheritance*, to 'bottled water'.

(a)   What is meant here by:
    (i)   class;
    (ii) inheritance? (2)

(b)   Draw an inheritance diagram for the given classes. (3)

AQA CPT4 Qu 7 June 2002

2   (a)   State **two** advantages of the object-oriented approach to program design over the structured approach to program design. (2)

(b)   A sailing club has both junior and senior members. Each member has a unique membership number, a name and an address recorded. Three classes have been identified:

Member
JuniorMember
SeniorMember

The classes JuniorMember and SeniorMember are related, by single inheritance, to the class Member.

Draw an inheritance diagram for the given classes. (2)

(c)   Programs that use objects of the class Member need to add a new member's details, amend a member's details, and show a member's details. No other form of access is to be allowed. Write a class definition for this class.

Member = **Class**

End; (4)

AQA CPT4 Qu 10 January 2003

4-38

Chapter 39 – Prolog Programming

Procedural and declarative languages

Human beings possess two different kinds of knowledge:

- **declarative** knowledge – facts about people, objects and events and how they relate to each other;
- **procedural** knowledge – how to do things, how to use their declarative knowledge, and how to work things out.

Computers may also be programmed with these two different kinds of knowledge.

High level languages such as Pascal, COBOL or FORTRAN are all examples of **procedural** languages, where the program consists of a sequence of instructions telling the machine what to do. The programmer has to show exactly what steps must be executed in order to solve the problem, and in what order, for any given set of data. As instructions are executed, program variables are modified using assignment statements.

Declarative languages such as **Prolog** work in a different way.

Prolog

Prolog (which stands for PROgramming in LOGic) is a particular type of declarative language known as a **logic** programming language. It has the following characteristics:

- Instead of defining **how** a problem is solved, the programmer states the facts and rules associated with the problem. A **fact** is something that is always unconditionally true, and a **rule** is true depending on a given condition.
- The **order** in which the rules and facts are stated is not important, unlike the statements in an imperative (i.e. procedural) language. It is therefore easy to add new rules, delete rules or change existing rules.
- Executing a Prolog program involves stating a goal to be achieved and allowing Prolog to determine whether the goal can be achieved with the given facts and rules.
- The route through the program does not have to be explicitly stated by the programmer. Like Theseus with his ball of string in the Minotaur's maze, who could select a route at a junction and always find his way back if it proved to be a dead end, Prolog will select a possible route through a program and if that fails, it will **backtrack** to that point and try another route until either the goal is achieved or there are no further routes to try.

Prolog is especially well suited to programming **expert systems**, which embody the facts and rules about a particular field of knowledge such as oil prospecting, social security regulations or medical diagnosis. In an expert system, facts and rules are described in the program to form the 'expert knowledge', and a user can then query the program to obtain answers to problems, given that certain facts or conditions are true.

It is also suited to the **processing of natural language** (trying to get a computer to understand ordinary English, Chinese or Urdu) because each of these languages has its own syntax rules which can be stated in the program to help the computer decide whether a group of words make a sentence, and what it means.

The example of a Prolog program which follows can be used to determine relationships between members of a family – useful perhaps in one of those 500-page family sagas when you can never remember who is related to whom...

The 'knowledge' that has to be programmed is a representation of the family tree below, and rules about relationships.

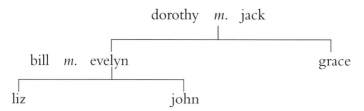

A Prolog program

```
/* Family tree program written by Sylvia Langfield 30 March 2004 */

/* facts */
    male(jack).
    male(bill).
    male(john).
    female(dorothy).
    female(evelyn).
    female(grace).
    female(liz).
    parent(dorothy, evelyn).
    parent(jack, evelyn).
    parent(dorothy, grace).
    parent(jack, grace).
    parent(bill, liz).
    parent(evelyn, liz).
    parent(bill, john).
    parent(evelyn, john).

/* rules */
    mother(M,X):-           /* M is the mother of X if    */
        parent(M,X),        /* M is a parent of X and     */
        female(M).          /* M is female                */

    father(F,X):-           /* F is the father of X if    */
        parent(F,X),        /* F is a parent of X and     */
        male(F).            /* F is male                  */

    grandparent(G,X):-      /* G is a grandparent of X if */
        parent(G,P),        /* G is a parent of P and     */
        parent(P,X).        /* P is a parent of X         */

    brother(X,Y):-          /* X is a brother of Y if     */
        parent(Z,X),        /* Z is a parent of X and     */
        parent(Z,Y),        /* Z is a parent of Y and     */
        male(X),            /* X is male and              */
        not(X=Y).           /* X is not his own brother   */
```

Queries can now be made to find out relationships; for example if the user wants to know "Does Liz have a brother?" the query is typed in at the **?** prompt as follows:

	`?- brother(X,liz).`	and the program will respond
	`X=john`	

To ask "Who is the mother of Evelyn?" type

	`?- mother (X,evelyn).`	and the program will respond
	`X=dorothy`	
Type	`?- father(Who,john).`	and the program will respond
	`Who=bill`	
Type	`?- brother(Who,john).`	and the program will respond
	`no`	(because john has no brother)

Practical Prolog

It will be very helpful to have some practical experience of programming in Prolog. Many different versions of Prolog are available for downloading free from various sites on the Internet. The examples used below use a version called SWI-Prolog, which can be downloaded from the site

http://www.swi-prolog.org/download.html

When you install this version of Prolog, it will install a shortcut into the Start menu. To run Prolog, choose **Programs**, **SWI-Prolog**, **Prolog** from the **Start** menu.

Using facts in Prolog

A Prolog program consists not of instructions but of a collection of facts and rules. Prolog can be seen as a database where some data items are stored directly as facts and other data items can be deduced by applying rules. These facts and rules are then acted on by the Prolog interpreter in response to goals that you give it.

A fact consists of a predicate and zero, one or more arguments.

e.g.   carnivore(lion).

isa(table, furniture).

animal(reptile, large, crocodile).

Predicate names must be **atoms** (see below), but arguments can consist of a variety of data types. Prolog recognises data types without you having to declare them at the top of the program. The most common data types are:

Integers	consist entirely of digits.
Reals	consist of digits and a decimal point.
Atoms	start with a lower case letter. They can contain numbers, letters and the underscore.
Strings	any characters enclosed in single quotes.
Variables	start with an uppercase letter.

Look at the sample program on the previous page. Note that each line (clause) has to end in a full-stop, and that the names *jack*, *dorothy* etc. have to be written with lower case letters because they are atoms, not variables.

Predicates such as *carnivore* above are programmer-defined predicates. Prolog also has built-in predicates such as *not* (to reverse anything given as its argument) and *listing* (to write out the whole of the current database).

Note the meaning of the following symbols:

:-	IF
,	logical AND
;	logical OR
=	tests whether two things are identically the same
_	anonymous variable (see p. 237)

Entering items in a Prolog database

You can enter facts and rules while Prolog is running, but they will all be deleted as soon as you close Prolog, so this is a not a very practical way of programming! Nevertheless it is a quick way to get started on your first Prolog program, and you can try it now.

• Start Prolog.

• You will see the prompt **?-** Type the text shown below, remembering to type a full-stop at the end of each line. Prolog answers **Yes** and inserts the prompt ?- after each line.

```
assert(carnivore(lion)).
assert(carnivore(tiger).
assert(herbivore(cow).
assert(herbivore(deer)).
```

assert is a predicate in Prolog's built-in database, and succeeds by 'asserting' its argument, for example **carnivore(lion)**, which is why Prolog answers **Yes** after each line is entered.

Note that if you make a mistake, Prolog may display several lines of error messages followed by the prompt

```
Action?
```

You can type **a** for 'Abort' to get back to the prompt. If you have missed out a fullstop on the previous line, Prolog will not display a prompt. Type the fullstop, and you will get the prompt.

You can now ask Prolog to answer simple questions from the database of facts.
For example, at the prompt type

```
carnivore(lion).
```

Prolog finds this fact in the database and replies **Yes**.

To find all the carnivores in the database, type

```
carnivore(X).
```

Prolog will respond X=**lion**. To get Prolog to continue searching, type a semi-colon. Prolog responds X=**tiger**. Type another semi-colon and Prolog responds **No**, since there are no more carnivores in the database.

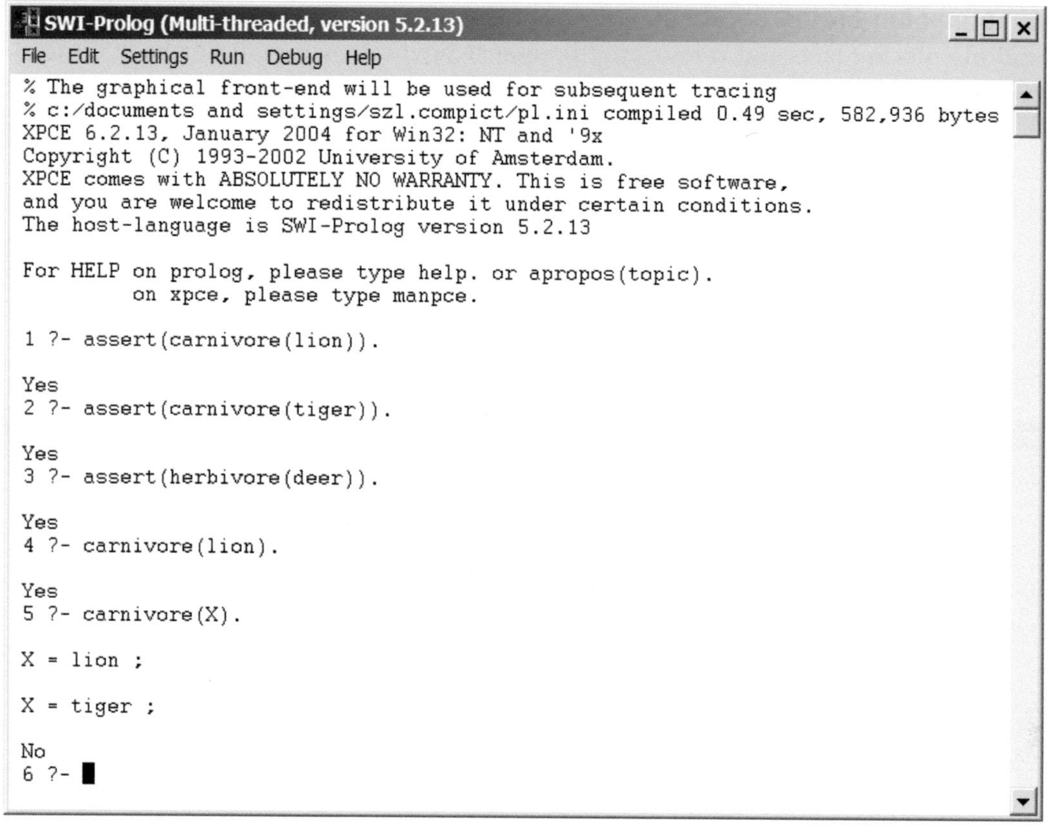

```
SWI-Prolog (Multi-threaded, version 5.2.13)                    _ □ ×

File  Edit  Settings  Run  Debug  Help

% The graphical front-end will be used for subsequent tracing
% c:/documents and settings/szl.compict/pl.ini compiled 0.49 sec, 582,936 bytes
XPCE 6.2.13, January 2004 for Win32: NT and '9x
Copyright (C) 1993-2002 University of Amsterdam.
XPCE comes with ABSOLUTELY NO WARRANTY. This is free software,
and you are welcome to redistribute it under certain conditions.
The host-language is SWI-Prolog version 5.2.13

For HELP on prolog, please type help. or apropos(topic).
        on xpce, please type manpce.

1 ?- assert(carnivore(lion)).

Yes
2 ?- assert(carnivore(tiger)).

Yes
3 ?- assert(herbivore(deer)).

Yes
4 ?- carnivore(lion).

Yes
5 ?- carnivore(X).

X = lion ;

X = tiger ;

No
6 ?- █
```

Figure 39.1: Inserting facts and making queries in Prolog

Entering rules

We can add a rule to say that X eats meat if X is a carnivore. Similarly Y eats grass if Y is a herbivore. (You could use the same variable X in both statements since the scope of a variable is only the rule it occurs in.) Type the following:

```
assert(eats(X,meat):-carnivore(X)).
assert(eats(Y,grass):-herbivore(Y)).
```

(Press Enter if you get a strange message such as X = _G369)

Now you can pose the question: *Which animals eat meat?* Type

```
eats(X,meat).
```

Prolog will reply

```
X = lion
```

Type a semi-colon, and Prolog continues

```
X = tiger
```

Type a semi-colon, and Prolog says

```
No
```

because it cannot find any more meat-eaters.

Exit from Prolog by typing **halt**. This will clear all the entries from the database.

Creating a permanent Prolog database

Instead of entering facts and rules using the **assert** predicate, you will normally create a Prolog database using an editor such as Notepad (in Windows Accessories) or SWI-Prolog's built-in editor (choose New from SWI-Prolog's File menu). The file should be saved with an extension of **.pl** (that is PL, not p-one!). You can then load and run your program by doubling-clicking this file name.

The advantage of using the built-in editor is that you get colour formatting, which makes your program easier to read and understand.

As with all program code writing, ensure a clear layout: indent and use empty lines and comments.

```
test1.pl                                                    _ □ ×
File   Edit   Browse   Compile   Prolog   Pce   Help
/* Family tree program written by Sylvia Langfield 30 March 2004 */

/* facts */
    male(jack).
    male(bill).
    male(john).
    female(dorothy).
    female(evelyn).
    female(grace).
    female(liz).
    parent(dorothy, evelyn).
    parent(jack, evelyn).
    parent(dorothy, grace).
    parent(jack, grace).
    parent(bill, liz).
    parent(evelyn, liz).
    parent(bill, john).
    parent(evelyn, john).

/* rules */
    mother(M,X):-           /* M is the mother of X if    */
       parent(M,X),         /* M is a parent of X and     */
       female(M).           /* M is female                */

    father(F,X):-           /* F is the father of X if    */
       parent(F,X),         /* F is a parent of X and     */
       male(F).             /* F is male                  */

    grandparent(G,X):-      /* G is a grandparent of X if */
       parent(G,P),         /* G is a parent of P and     */
       parent(P,X).         /* P is a parent of X         */

                                                      Line: 31
```

Figure 39.2: using SWI-Prolog's built-in editor to write a program

Q1: Enter the sample program shown in figure 39.2. (You will need this database again later.)

(a) What queries will you type to ask the following questions:

(i) Who is Grace's mother?

(ii) Who are Jack's grandchildren?

(iii) Who are John's grandparents?

(b) Write the rule to say that S is the sister of X.

Test your answers out in Prolog.

Producing a user-friendly interface

The built-in predicates **read** and **write** are used to read from the keyboard and write to the screen respectively. **nl** will generate a new line on the screen. Note that input from the keyboard must always end with a full-stop and each word must begin with a lower-case letter as otherwise Prolog will treat it as a variable.

Add the following clause to your family tree program from earlier:

```
findMother:- write('Whose mother do you wish to find? '),
             read(Name),
             mother(X,Name),
             write('The mother of '), write(Name), write(' is '),
write(X), nl.
```

Now test this by typing at the prompt:

```
findMother.
```

Your program should respond as follows:

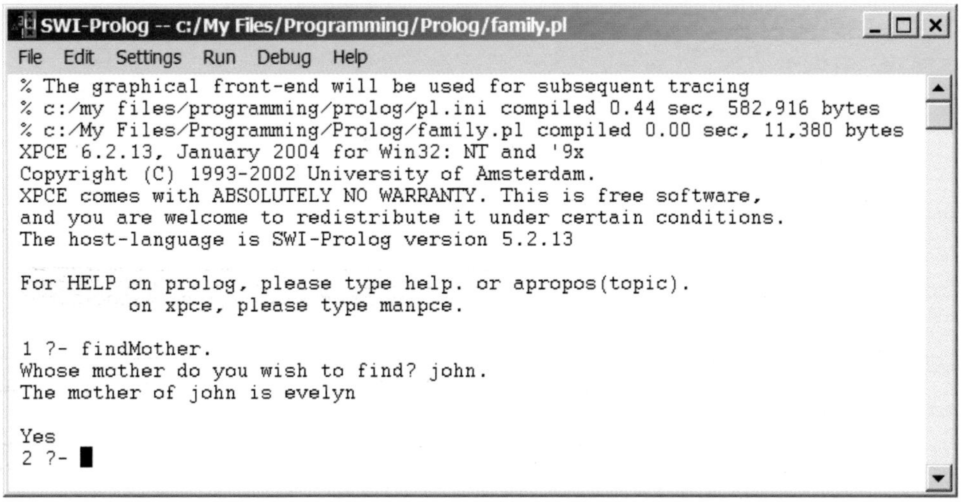

```
SWI-Prolog -- c:/My Files/Programming/Prolog/family.pl
File  Edit  Settings  Run  Debug  Help

% The graphical front-end will be used for subsequent tracing
% c:/my files/programming/prolog/pl.ini compiled 0.44 sec, 582,916 bytes
% c:/My Files/Programming/Prolog/family.pl compiled 0.00 sec, 11,380 bytes
XPCE 6.2.13, January 2004 for Win32: NT and '9x
Copyright (C) 1993-2002 University of Amsterdam.
XPCE comes with ABSOLUTELY NO WARRANTY. This is free software,
and you are welcome to redistribute it under certain conditions.
The host-language is SWI-Prolog version 5.2.13

For HELP on prolog, please type help. or apropos(topic).
        on xpce, please type manpce.

1 ?- findMother.
Whose mother do you wish to find? john.
The mother of john is evelyn

Yes
2 ?- █
```

Figure 39.3: demonstrating a user-friendly interface with a Prolog program

The anonymous variable

If you want to list all those people who are mothers in the family tree program above, without wanting to list whose mother they are, type at the prompt:

```
mother(Who, _).
```

When we are searching for information, the anonymous variable (the underscore symbol) is used frequently to blank out arguments we are not interested in.

Changing facts at run-time

Enter the following program and save it as weather v1.pl:

```
/* today's weather facts */
    temp(warm).
    windspeed(low).
    sky(sunny).

/* rules for the weather */

weather(good):-
    temp(warm),
    windspeed(low),
    sky(sunny).

weather(bad):-
    windspeed(high);
    temp(cold);
    sky(cloudy).
```

You can run this program by typing weather(Today).

However, if you want to use different weather conditions for another day, you would need to edit your Prolog program. We can improve the program by not storing any weather conditions but getting the user to enter them when prompted and then add them to the database with **assert**.

Enter the following program and save it as weather v2.pl:

```
/* weather rules */

weather(good):-
  temp(warm),
  windspeed(low),
  sky(sunny).

weather(bad):-
  windspeed(high);
  temp(cold);
  sky(cloudy).

/* interface */

todaysWeather:-
  write('Is the temperature warm or cold? '),
  read(Temp),nl,
  write('Is the sky sunny or cloudy? '),
  read(Sky),nl,
  write('Is the windspeed low or high? '),
  read(Wind),nl,
  /* 'assert' is used to put these facts into a database */
  assert(temp(Temp)),
  assert(sky(Sky)),
  assert(windspeed(Wind)),
  weather(Weather),
  write('The weather is '), write(Weather),
  /* 'retractall' is used to remove the weather conditions from the   */
  /* database, so the program can be run again with different weather */
  /* conditions   */
  retractall(temp(_)),
  retractall(sky(_)),
  retractall(windspeed(_)).
```

To run this program, type at the prompt:

```
todaysWeather.
```

Listing a Prolog program

You can get a listing of the current program by typing **listing**.

Tracing Prolog executions

You need to be able to trace through Prolog executions and show what facts and rules have been used in finding the answer to a question.

Type in the following Prolog program and save it as office.pl:

```
adminWorker(black).
adminWorker(white).

officeJunior(green).

manager(brown).
manager(grey).

supervises(X,Y) :- manager(X), adminWorker(Y).
supervises(X,Y) :- adminWorker(X), officeJunior(Y).
supervises(X,Y) :- manager(X), officeJunior(Y).
```

Switch on the trace facility in Prolog by typing at the prompt:

```
trace.
```

Now enter at the prompt the query that is going to find out who supervises Green:

```
supervises(Supervisor,green).
```

You can step through the actions of Prolog by pressing the Spacebar. The following figures show what you should see. Carefully read the explanations to understand what exactly is happening.

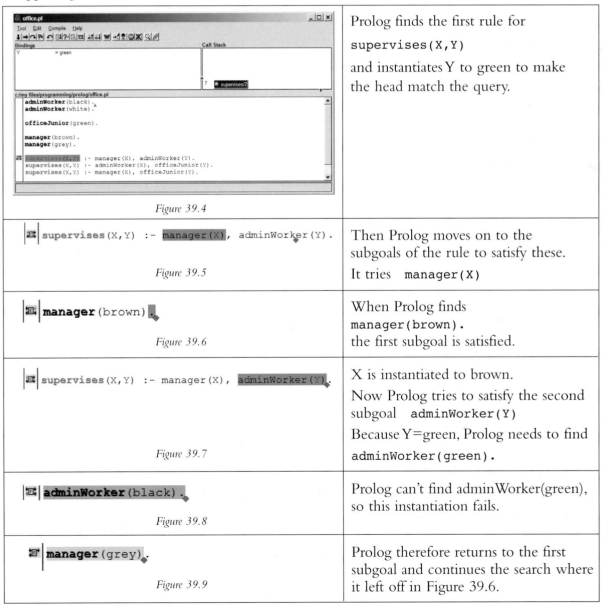

Figure 39.4	Prolog finds the first rule for `supervises(X,Y)` and instantiates Y to green to make the head match the query.
Figure 39.5	Then Prolog moves on to the subgoals of the rule to satisfy these. It tries `manager(X)`
Figure 39.6	When Prolog finds `manager(brown).` the first subgoal is satisfied.
Figure 39.7	X is instantiated to brown. Now Prolog tries to satisfy the second subgoal `adminWorker(Y)` Because Y=green, Prolog needs to find `adminWorker(green).`
Figure 39.8	Prolog can't find adminWorker(green), so this instantiation fails.
Figure 39.9	Prolog therefore returns to the first subgoal and continues the search where it left off in Figure 39.6.

manager(grey). *Figure 39.10*	It finds `manager(grey).` The first subgoal is satisfied.
supervises(X,Y) :- manager(X), adminWorker(Y). *Figure 39.11*	Now Prolog tries to find `adminWorker(green).`
adminWorker(black). *Figure 39.12*	This subgoal fails again. There are no more manager predicates.
supervises(X,Y) :- adminWorker(X), officeJunior(Y). *Figure 39.13*	Prolog moves to the next supervises(X,Y) rule. It instantiates Y to green.
supervises(X,Y) :- adminWorker(X), officeJunior(Y). *Figure 39.14*	It finds the first subgoal `adminWorker(X)` and tries to satisfy this.
adminWorker(black). *Figure 39.15*	`adminWorker(black).` satisfies this subgoal.
supervises(X,Y) :- adminWorker(X), officeJunior(Y). *Figure 39.16*	Now Prolog tries to satisfy the second subgoal `officeJunior(green).`
officeJunior(green). *Figure 39.17*	It finds `officeJunior(green).` so the second subgoal is also satified.
supervises(X,Y) :- adminWorker(X), officeJunior(Y). *Figure 39.18*	This satisfies the rule and Prolog outputs `Supervisor = black`

If you type a ; (semicolon) to find further solutions, the trace will continue where it left off. So it will look for further solutions to adminWorker(X) and eventually will output

`Supervisor = white`

If you type further semicolons, the search continues from the third supervises(X,Y) rule and in due course will output

`Supervisor = brown;`
`Supervisor = grey;`

If you do not get the GUI version of the trace as above, you may get the following output:

```
Call: (7) supervises(_G507, green) ? creep
Call: (8) manager(_G507) ? creep
Exit: (8) manager(brown) ? creep
Call: (8) adminWorker(green) ? creep
Fail: (8) adminWorker(green) ? creep
Redo: (8) manager(_G507) ? creep
Exit: (8) manager(grey) ? creep
Call: (8) adminWorker(green) ? creep
Fail: (8) adminWorker(green) ? creep
Redo: (7) supervises(_G507, green) ? creep
```

You need to press the Spacebar after Prolog outputs a '?'

Note: _G507 is a local variable Prolog uses instead of our X

```
      Call: (8) adminWorker(_G507) ? creep
      Exit: (8) adminWorker(black) ? creep
      Call: (8) officeJunior(green) ? creep
      Exit: (8) officeJunior(green) ? creep
      Exit: (7) supervises(black, green) ? creep
Supervisor = black ;
      Redo: (8) adminWorker(_G507) ? creep
      Exit: (8) adminWorker(white) ? creep
      Call: (8) officeJunior(green) ? creep
      Exit: (8) officeJunior(green) ? creep
      Exit: (7) supervises(white, green) ? creep
Supervisor = white ;
      Redo: (7) supervises(_G507, green) ? creep
      Call: (8) manager(_G507) ? creep
      Exit: (8) manager(brown) ? creep
      Call: (8) officeJunior(green) ? creep
      Exit: (8) officeJunior(green) ? creep
      Exit: (7) supervises(brown, green) ? creep
Supervisor = brown ;
      Redo: (8) manager(_G507) ? creep
      Exit: (8) manager(grey) ? creep
      Call: (8) officeJunior(green) ? creep
      Exit: (8) officeJunior(green) ? creep
      Exit: (7) supervises(grey, green) ? creep
Supervisor = grey ;
No
```

> Type a semicolon (;) after Prolog outputs the first solution and Prolog will continue the trace.

4-39

Exercises

1   A simple logic processing language is used to represent, as a set of facts and rules, the valid constructions of numbers for a particular task. The set of facts and rules are shown below in clauses labelled i to vi.

i   digit (1|2|3|4|5|6|7|8|9|0)

ii   sign (+|−)

iii integer IF digit

iv   integer IF digit AND integer

v   number IF integer

vi   number IF sign AND integer

Clause i has the meaning "1, 2, 3, ...0 are all digits"

Clause iv has the meaning "something is an integer if it is a digit followed by an integer"

(a)   State whether or not the following numbers are valid and list the clauses used to justify your answer.

(i) 79   (3)

(ii) 148.5   (2)

(iii) −2003598   (3)

(b)   One of these numbers is invalid according to the above facts and rules.
Write the clause(s) that would make this number valid.   (2)

AQA CPT4 Qu 7 January 2002

2   A simple logic processing language is used to represent, as a set of facts and rules, the valid construction of sentences. The set of facts and rules is shown below in clauses labelled 1 to 13.

1   determiner(the).

2   adjective(big).

3   adjective(little).

4   verb(is).

5   verb(climbs).

6   noun(thomas).

7   noun(hill).

8   noun_phrase(X) IF noun(X).

9   noun_phrase(X,Y) IF determiner(X) AND noun(Y).

10 noun_phrase(X,Y,Z) IF determiner(X) AND adjective(Y) AND noun(Z).

11 sentence(A,B,C) IF noun_phrase(A) AND verb(B) AND noun_phrase(C).

12 sentence(A,B,C,D,E) IF noun_phrase(A) AND verb(B) AND noun_phrase(C,D,E).

13 sentence(A,B,C,D,E) IF noun_phrase(A,B,C) AND verb(D) AND noun_phrase(E).

Clause 1 has the meaning "the is a determiner"

Clause 9 has the meaning "X followed by Y is a noun phrase if X is a determiner and Y is a noun".

(a)   Using the given set of facts and rules (1–13) above, give one example of

   (i) a fact;

   (ii) a rule.   (2)

(b)   Using the given set of facts and rules (1–13) above, state whether or not the following sentences are valid.

   (i) thomas climbs the little hill.

   (ii) the little hill climbs thomas.   (2)

(c)   The sentence "little thomas climbs the hill" is not valid according to the facts and rules (1–13) above. Write a further rule or set of rules which would make it valid.   (6)

AQA CPT4 Qu 10 June 2003

3 (a)   Write and test a Prolog program with a database of English-French word pairs, such as

                    meaning(hello, bonjour).

   (b)   Now add a rule *toFrench* that reads in an English word and displays the French equivalent in a user-friendly manner, for example:

                    Enter your English word: dog.
                    The French is: chien.

New Question

Chapter 40 – Recursion

Recursion is an important technique in many different types of programming language, including imperative languages such as Pascal and declarative languages such as Prolog. The data structure called a **stack** is of crucial importance in understanding how recursion works.

Using stacks to store return addresses

Stacks are used to store the return address when a subroutine is called. The principle is shown below:

Instruction Address	Instruction
1	**subroutine** suba
2	....
3	....
4	**return**
5	**begin** { *** MAIN PROGRAM *** EXECUTION STARTS HERE}
6	**call** suba
7	....
8	**end**

4-40

The return address (7) will be placed on a stack when SUBA is called and popped when the RETURN statement is encountered.

Q1: Show the contents of the stack as addresses are pushed and popped during the execution of the following simplified program outline.

```
Instruction     Instruction
  Address
    1           subroutine suba
    2           .......
    3           return

    4           subroutine subb
    5           .......
    6           return

    7           subroutine sub1
    8           .......
    9           call suba
   10           call subb
   11           return

   12           subroutine sub2
   13           .......
   14           call suba
   15           .......
   16           return

   17           begin{*** MAIN PROGRAM ***  EXECUTION STARTS HERE}
   18                   call sub1
   19                   call sub2
   20           end
```

A subroutine is recursive if it is defined in terms of itself, and the process is called recursion.

The short program below calls the recursive procedure **PrintList**.

```
program Recurs;
var abc:integer;

      procedure PrintList(num:integer);
      begin
            num := num-1;
            if num > 1 then PrintList(num);
            writeln(num)                    {LINE A}
      end; {procedure PrintList}

{***** main program*****}

begin
      abc := 4;
      PrintList(abc);
      writeln(abc)                          {LINE B}
end.
```

What happens when this program is run? The diagram of the stack in the margin shows the return address and the value of the parameter which will be displayed when a writeln statement is executed.

- First, the procedure PrintList is called with the parameter abc set to 4.

- The address of the instruction marked {LINE B} is stored on the return address stack, and execution will proceed from that line when the end statement in the procedure is reached.

  Line B 4

- Now execution of PrintList begins; num is decremented by 1 and becomes 3. The procedure calls itself, and the address of the instruction marked {LINE A} is stored on the procedure stack, together with the information that num=3. When this line is eventually executed, the number 3 will be displayed.

  Line A 3
  Line B 4

- PrintList now begins again, with the value of the actual parameter num set to 3. It is decremented to 2, the procedure is called again, the return address stored.

  Line A 2
  Line A 3
  Line B 4

- PrintList begins again, num becomes 1 and the procedure call is not executed. At this point LINE A is executed for the first time and the number 1 is displayed.
  Output   1

  Line A 2
  Line A 3
  Line B 4

- The end of the procedure has been reached, so the first return address is taken off the stack; this is also LINE A, with a parameter of 2, so the number 2 is displayed.
  Output   2

  Line A 3
  Line B 4

- The end of the procedure is reached again, so the next return address is taken off the stack; LINE A again, this time with a parameter of 3.
  Output   3

  Line B 4

- Finally the end of the procedure is reached again and the address of the next instruction is LINE B, so the number 4 is written.
  Output   4

The above example illustrates three essential ingredients that must be present in any recursive process.

1 A stopping condition must be included which when met means that the routine will not call itself and will start to 'unwind'.

2 For input values other than the stopping condition, the routine must call itself.

3 The stopping condition must be reached after a finite number of calls.

Another example of recursion

Recursion is a useful technique for the programmer when the algorithm itself is essentially recursive. An example of this is the calculation of a factorial, where **n!** (read as **factorial n**) is defined as follows:

If n = 1 then n! = 1

otherwise n! = n x (n-1) x (n-2) x .... x 3 x 2 x 1

Thus for example 4! = 4 x 3 x 2 x 1, and 0! = 1 (by definition).

This can be defined recursively as

If n = 1 then n! = 1

otherwise n! = n x (n-1)!   (For example 4! = 4 x 3!)

The pseudocode for a recursive function to calculate n! is as follows:

```
function factorial(n)
begin
  if n = 1
    then factorial = 1
    else  factorial = n*factorial(n-1)
  endif
end
```

Q2: Dry run the above function when it is called with the statement answer = factorial(4).

Q3: What happens if the function is called with answer = factorial(-3)?

Q4: Which of the 3 'essential ingredients' of a recursive function is not present?

Advantages and disadvantages of recursion

In general, a non-recursive solution is more efficient in terms of both computer time and space. This is because when using a recursive solution, the computer has to make multiple procedure or function calls, each time storing return addresses and copies of local or temporary variables, all of which takes time and space. Another point to consider is that if the recursion continues too long, the stack containing return addresses may overflow and the program will crash. If for example you try to calculate factorial 2000 using a recursive routine, 2000 return addresses have to be stored before the routine begins to unwind, and the computer may run out of memory while doing this.

For some problems, however, a recursive solution is more natural and easier for the programmer to write. (You will encounter a good example of this later when studying tree traversals).

Generally speaking, if the recursive solution is not much shorter than the non-recursive one, use the non-recursive one. Going by this rule, it would be better to use iteration rather than recursion to work out a factorial; it serves as a neat example of recursion but would be more efficiently and just as simply written iteratively, using a For..Next loop, for example. This is left as an exercise for the reader!

4-40

Recursion in Prolog

A rule is recursive if it is defined in terms of itself. A recursive rule uses itself as a subgoal.

For example,

```
loop :- write('Hello World'), nl, loop.
```

will repeatedly display 'Hello World' on separate lines. It will never end. If you try it in SWI Prolog, use **Ctrl+c** and then **a** to terminate the loop.

To end a recursive loop, we need to supply a stopping condition in a separate rule:

```
loop(end).
loop(_) :- write('Type end to finish: '),read(Reply), loop(Reply).
```

Enter the above code and test it by typing:

```
loop(hello).
```

The first predicate fails, so Prolog will try the second predicate and loop is called again with the word typed in at the prompt 'Type end to finish: '. If the word entered is 'end' then the first predicate will succeed and the second rule will not be entered. So this is a recursive rule with the stopping condition that the user has to enter 'end'.

Here is an example of a recursive rule that will stop when the supplied number has counted down to 0:

```
loop(0).
loop(N) :- write(N), nl, M is N-1, loop(M).
```

Test it by typing:

```
loop(5).
```

The first predicate fails, so Prolog enters the second predicate and outputs the number and a new line. Then M is set to N-1 and loop is called again with this new value. Eventually the value supplied will be zero, then the first predicate will succeed and the second one will not be attempted. Thus the loop will terminate. Note that for an assignment you need to use **is** in Prolog (M is N-1).

The calculation of factorial can also be coded in Prolog:

```
factorial(1,1).                  /* stopping condition: 1! = 1     */
factorial(N,Result) :-           /* Result = N!                    */
M is N-1,                        /* Let M = N-1                    */
factorial(M,PartResult),         /* PartResult = (N-1)!            */
Result is PartResult * N.        /* Result = N * (N-1)!            */
```

Exercises

1   (a)   Distinguish between **iteration** and **recursion**, giving an example of each.   (4)

    (b)   Give **two** advantages of using recursive routines and **two** disadvantages.   (4)

New Question

2   The following is a *recursively defined* function which calculates the result of multiplying together all the positive integers between n and 1, inclusively. For example, the factorial of 3 is the result of evaluating 3 x 2 x 1, i.e. 6.

```
Define Factorial(n)
if n = 1
    then Factorial := 1
    else Factorial := n * Factorial(n - 1)
EndDefine
```

    (a)   What is meant by *recursively defined*?   (1)

    (b)   Trace the execution of this function for n = 4 showing carefully, for each re-entry into the factorial function, the value passed to the function and the results returned.   (6)

    (c)   Why should this function not be used when n = 0?   (1)

    (d)   (i)   Describe the data structure known as a *stack*.   (1)

          (ii) Carefully explain the role of the stack in the execution of the factorial function.

    (e)   Write a pseudocode non-recursive version of the factorial function.   (6)

    (f)   (i)   Give **one** reason why a non-recursive factorial function may be preferred to a recursive one.   (1)

          (ii) Give **one** reason why a recursive factorial function may be preferred to a non-recursive one.   (1)

AEB Paper 2 1995

4-40

Chapter 41 – Lists

Definition of a list in Prolog

In Prolog, a list is a collection of data items stored in some sequence, with the following properties:

- data items may be inserted or deleted at any point in the list;
- data items may be repeated in the list;
- lists may contain any type of object;
- a particular list may contain different object types.

The elements of a list are enclosed in square brackets and separated by commas. For example a list named Colours containing 6 items may be represented as follows:

Colours = [red,orange,yellow,green,indigo,violet]

A more complex list may contain items of different types, including a list:

Class = [2.15,14,12,[maths,physics,computing],jones]

Manipulating lists

Lists are manipulated by separating the head from the tail. The separator used is a vertical line, |.

e.g. List = [Head|Tail]

Note that the tail of a list is itself a list.

e.g. [focus|[fiesta,escort,mondeo]]

    [a|[b,c]]

    [a|[b]]

Note that [a|b] is not a valid list because the tail is an atom, not a list.

> **Q1:** Write the following as a list, with elements separated by commas.
> anna bob claire damon emma

> **Q2:** Write the above list in Head|Tail form.

> **Q3:** Are the following valid lists?
> (i)   [a|b,c]
> (ii) [x]
> (iii) [a|[c|[d,e]]]
> (iv) a
> (v) [a,b,c]

Writing out a list

Operations on lists are carried out by working through the list, successively removing the head from the tail.

A Prolog procedure to write out a list follows:

```
writelist([]).
writelist([Head|Tail]):-write(Head),nl,writelist(Tail).
```

Enter these statements into a Prolog program, either directly using the **assert** verb or by entering them into a text file. (**nl** stands for new line and makes the output move to the next line.)

You can then ask Prolog to write out the list [apple,banana,pear] by typing:

```
?- writelist([apple,banana,pear]).
```

- The interpreter searches for writelist, passes over writelist([ ])since the list is not empty, and comes to the second rule.

- The list is split up into head and tail form as follows:
writelist(apple | [banana,pear]):-write(apple),nl,writelist([banana,pear]).

- **apple** is written and the rule calls itself.
writelist(banana | [pear]):-write(banana),nl,writelist([pear]).

- **banana** is written out and the rule calls itself again:
writelist(pear | [ ]):-write(pear),nl,writelist([ ]).

- **pear** is written out and writelist is searched for again. This time the first writelist([ ]) rule succeeds and stops the recursion.

Operations on a list

Lists can also be processed in a procedural language.

Several functions may be defined which take a list as their single argument and return a result that is either an element of a list, another list or a Boolean value.

Head(List)   returns the element at the head of the list if the list is non-empty, otherwise reports an error.

         e.g. Head[red,orange,yellow,green,indigo,violet] = red

Tail(List)   returns a new list containing all but the first element of the original list.

         e.g. Tail[red,orange,yellow,green,indigo,violet] = [orange,yellow,green,indigo,violet]

Empty(List)   returns TRUE if the list is empty or FALSE otherwise. The empty list is denoted by [ ].

Example:

What is the result returned by the following functions applied to the list Colours = [red,orange,yellow,green,indigo,violet]?

(a)   Head(Tail(Colours))   Answer: orange

(b)   Empty(Colours)   Answer: FALSE

(c)   Tail(Tail(Tail(Tail(Colours))))   Answer: [indigo,violet]

(d)   Tail(Tail(Tail(Tail(Tail(Colours)))))   Answer: [violet]

4-41

A recursive procedure to print a list

Pseudocode for a recursive procedure to print a list is shown below:

```
Procedure T(List)
   If not Empty(List)
   Then
      T(Tail(List));
      Print(Head(List));
   Endif;
EndProc
```

The procedure keeps on recursively calling the procedure T(List), not executing the Print statement until the list is empty and the procedure runs to completion, when it begins to 'unwind'. It thus prints the list in reverse order.

Implementation of a list using an array

The elements of a list may be held in an array. The array needs to be large enough to hold the maximum number of elements that are likely to occur, and two additional variables are needed to hold the current size of the list and the size of the array. An example of a list is a display on a railway station that gives the arrival times of trains in order of arrival times, shown below with the two extra variables **size** and **max**.

e.g.

size	5

max	20

item		time	starting_point
	1	1450	Norwich
	2	1458	Colchester
	3	1520	Stowmarket
	4	1545	Cambridge
	5	1555	Liverpool Street

The sequence may be **initialized** simply by setting **size** to 0.

Two other procedures can be performed on a linear list; **insertion** and **deletion**.

Inserting an item

Suppose we wish to insert an arrival, the 1455 from Liverpool Street. The best way of inserting an item into a list is to:

(a) include an extra item at the beginning of the list, with an index of 0 which is used to hold the item to be inserted, and

(b) search backwards instead of forwards through the list for the correct position of the new item.

The steps are given below:

```
Put the new item in item[0]
If the list is full, display a message 'list is full'.
Otherwise, start at the end of the list and examine each item.
While time of the current item is greater than time of the new item,
     move current item down one place.
Insert the new item.
```

Example:

Show how the list of arrival times and starting points of trains can be held in a **table** (an array of records) in memory.

Write pseudocode for an algorithm to insert a new element in the list.

Answer:

The table to hold the list can be declared as follows:

```
type
   item-_type = record
      time             : integer;
      starting_point : string;
   end;
var
   item                 : array[0..20] of item_type;
```

Pseudocode for inserting a new element in the list is as follows:

```
Procedure Insert_Item
begin
   get new item
   item[0] = new item
   p = size
   if size = max then write 'list full'
   else
      while item[p].time > item[0].time
            item[p+1] = item[p]
            p = p-1
      endwhile
      size = size + 1
      item[p+1] = item[0]
   endif
end procedure
```

Retrieving and deleting an item from a list

To retrieve an item from a list, we again put the given item in item[0] and search backwards from the end of the list, for a time less than or equal to the time of the given item.

The pseudocode for a procedure to find an item is shown below. If the item is in the list, a flag called **found** will be set to **true**, and **p** will indicate its position, otherwise **found** will be set to **false**.

```
procedure Find_Item
begin
   item[0].time = given_time
   p = size                         ( set pointer to end of list )
   found = false
   while item[p].time > given_time
       p = p - 1                    (  continue searching  )
   endwhile
   (if p = 0 on exit from the loop, then given_time is not in the list.
   If p is not = 0 then given_time may be present in the list)
   if p <> 0 then
       if item[p].time = given_time
          then found = true
       endif
   endif
end procedure
```

Example:

Write an algorithm to delete an item from the list. (Use the above procedure Find_Item).

```
procedure Delete_Item
begin
  get item to delete
  call Find_Item to see if item is in the list
  if found = false then write error message   (ie item is not in list)
  else                       (p gives the position of the item)
    while p < size      (if it's the last item, no need to move anything)
      item[p] = item[p+1]
      p = p + 1
    endwhile
    size = size - 1
  endif
end procedure
```

Exercises

1   The list Ports contains the following names:

[Southampton, Barcelona, Athens, Alexandria, Tunis, Lisbon].

The table below shows some functions which take a list as their single argument and return a result which is either an element of a list, another list or a boolean value.

Head(list) – If the list is non-empty, it returns the element at the head of the list (e.g. Head(Ports) → Southampton) otherwise it reports an error.
Tail(list) – If the list is non-empty it returns a new list containing all but the first element of the original list otherwise it reports an error.
Empty(list) – If the list is the empty list it returns True otherwise it returns False. The empty list is denoted by [ ].

(a)   What result is returned when the following function calls are made?

   (i)   Tail(Ports)   (1)

   (ii) Head(Tail(Tail(Ports)))   (2)

   (iii) Empty(Tail(Tail(Tail(Tail(Tail(Tail(Ports)))))))   (2)

A *recursively-defined* procedure P, which takes a list as its single parameter, is defined below.

```
Define Procedure P(list)
  If Not Empty(list)
    Then
        P(Tail(list))
        Print Head(list)
    EndIf
EndDefine
```

(b)   What is meant by recursively defined?   (1)

(c)   Explain why a stack is needed to execute procedure P recursively.   (2)

(d)   For the procedure call P(Ports), give the PRINTed output in the order in which it is produced.   (4)

continues on next page

(e) Complete the table to show the list Ports as a linked list so that the ports can be accessed in alphabetical order.

1	Southampton	
2	Barcelona	
3	Athens	
4	Alexandria	
5	Tunis	
6	Lisbon	

Head Pointer

(2)

AQA CPT4 Qu 10 January 2002

Note: Linked Lists for exercise 1(e) above are covered in the next chapter.

4-41

Chapter 42 – Linked Lists

Definition

A linked list is a dynamic data structure used to hold a sequence, as described below:

- The items which form the sequence are not necessarily held in contiguous data locations, or in the order in which they occur in the sequence.

- Each item in the list is called a **node** and contains a **data** field and a **next address** field called a **link** or **pointer** field. (The data field may consist of several subfields.)

- The data field holds the actual data associated with the list item, and the link field contains the address of the next item in the sequence.

- The link field in the last item indicates in some way that there are no further items by the use of a null pointer (e.g. has a value of 0).

- Associated with the list is a **pointer variable** which points to (i.e. contains the address of) the first node in the list.

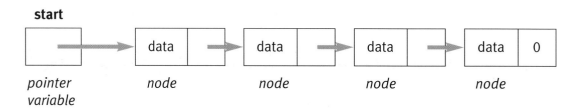

4-42

Operations on linked lists

In the examples which follow we will assume that the linked list is held in a table in memory, and that each node consists of a person's name (the data field) and a pointer to the next item in the list. We will explore how to set up or initialise an empty list, insert new data in the correct place in the list, delete an unwanted item and print out all items in the list. We will also look at the problem of managing the free space in the list.

Imagine that the table holding the list has room for 6 entries, and 4 names have already been inserted into it in such a way that they can be retrieved in alphabetical order, so that it is currently in the following state.

Address	Name	Pointer
1	Browning	4
2	Turner	0
3	Johnson	2
4	Cray	3
5		
6		

start = 1

nextfree = 5

Figure 42.1

Notice that

- a pointer **start** points to the first item in the list;
- **nextfree** is a pointer to the next free location in the table;
- by following the links, names can be retrieved in alphabetical order.

To insert a new name, for example Mortimer, into the list, pointers will have to be changed so that it is linked into the correct place. At this stage we have not really decided how to manage the free space in the list, so we will simply add 1 to **nextfree**.

The table will now appear as in Figure 42.2.

Address	Name	Pointer
1	Browning	4
2	Turner	0
3	Johnson	5
4	Cray	3
5	Mortimer	2
6		

start = 1

nextfree = 6

Figure 42.2

Q1: Show the state of the table and pointers after insertion of the name Allen. Write down the steps involved in inserting a new name to the list, so that alphabetical sequence is maintained.

Now we will delete a name. Return to the table as shown above in Figure 42.2 (before inserting Allen), and delete the name Johnson. After adjusting the pointers, the table looks like this:

Address	Name	Pointer
1	Browning	4
2	Turner	0
3	Johnson	5
4	Cray	5
5	Mortimer	2
6		

start = 1

nextfree = 6

Figure 42.3

Note that

- Johnson is still physically in the table, but not part of the list any more;
- **nextfree** hasn't altered, and we have come up against a problem; there is no way to reclaim the vacancy left by Johnson. If the table is not to become full of unwanted records with no room left in it to add new records, we will have to address this problem. (Note, however, that the so-called 'management of free space' adds a degree of complexity to algorithms which is not always required in answers to exam questions unless specifically asked for.)

Management of free space

The solution is to keep **two** linked lists; one for the actual data, and one for the free space. When a new item is added, a node is grabbed from the free space list, and when a node is deleted, it is linked into the free space list.

When the table is first initialised prior to entering any names, it will consist of just one linked list of free space:

Address	Name	Pointer
1		2
2		3
3		4
4		5
5		6
6		0

start = 0

nextfree = 1

Figure 42.4

After the names Browning, Turner, Johnson and Cray have been added (don't worry about how they were inserted, we're coming to that) the table will look like this:

Address	Name	Pointer
1	Browning	4
2	Turner	0
3	Johnson	2
4	Cray	3
5		6
6		0

start = 1

nextfree = 5

Figure 42.5

Notice that we now have two linked lists going. The list linking the nodes containing names and the list linking the free nodes. We'll now work out an algorithm for inserting a name into the list. As an example, we'll insert Mortimer between Johnson and Turner.

Inserting an item

Here are the steps:

```
store the new name Mortimer in the node pointed to by nextfree
determine, by following the links, where the new item should be linked in
change nextfree to point to next free location
change Mortimer's pointer to point to Turner
change Johnson's pointer to point to Mortimer
```

Some extra steps would need to be inserted to cope with various special cases such as inserting a name at the very front of the list (e.g. Allen), or inserting the first name into an empty list, but we'll ignore these cases for now.

Diagrammatically, this is what we have done:

Before insertion:

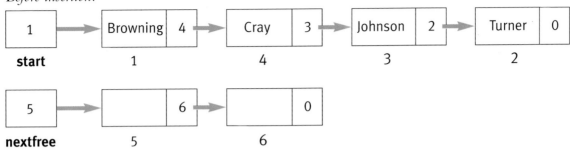

After insertion:

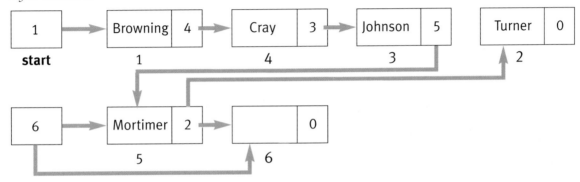

Figure 42.6

Before we go further and express this algorithm in more formal pseudocode, you need to make sure you clearly understand the notation used.

node[p].name holds the name in the node pointed to by p

node[p].pointer holds the value of the pointer in the node pointed to by p

Q2: Looking at Figure 43.6, node[3].name = Johnson, and node[3].pointer = 2.
What is the value of   (i)   node[start].pointer?

(ii)   node[4].name?

(iii) node[node[3].pointer].pointer?

(iv) node[node[start].pointer].name?

Notice how we can 'peek ahead' using the pointers to see what name is in the next node, or even the node after that one, and so on. Here's a first attempt at the pseudocode for the algorithm to add a new name to the list.

```
begin procedure
    node[nextfree].name = new name        (store the new name in next free node)
    p = start
    follow pointers until node[p].pointer points to a name > new name
    temp = nextfree                       (put 5 in temp)
    nextfree = node[nextfree].pointer        (put 6 in nextfree)
    node [temp].pointer = node[p].pointer  (put 2 in Mortimer's pointer field)
    node[p].pointer = temp                 (put 5 in Johnson's pointer)
end procedure
```

This algorithm is in enough detail to get you through most questions on how to insert a node into a linked list. However, to deal with the special cases (checking for a full list and inserting at the head of the list) and to specify how to follow the pointers until you reach the correct insertion point, you need the following:

```
begin procedure
    if nextfree = 0
        then write ('List is full') and exit procedure.
    node [nextfree].name = new name   (store the new name in next free node)
    if start = 0
        then                                        (insert into empty list)
            temp = node[nextfree] .pointer
            node [nextfree].pointer = 0
            start = nextfree
            nextfree = temp
        else
            p = start     (check for special case inserting in front of list)
    endif
    if new name < node[p].name
        then node[nextfree].pointer = start
            start = nextfree
        else                                        (start general case)
            placefound = false
            while node[p].pointer<>0 and not placefound
                if newname >= node[node[p].pointer].name    (peek ahead)
                    then p = node[p].pointer
                    else placefound = true
                endif
            endwhile
            temp = nextfree
            nextfree = node[nextfree].pointer
            node[temp].pointer = node[p].pointer
            node[p].pointer = temp
    endif (general case)
end procedure
```

Deleting an item

Returning to the table as in Figure 43.1, we will delete Johnson. The steps are as follows:

```
follow the pointers until Johnson is found
change Cray's pointer to point to Turner
change Johnson's pointer to nextfree
change nextfree to point to Johnson
```

This is shown diagramatically on the next page.

Before deletion:

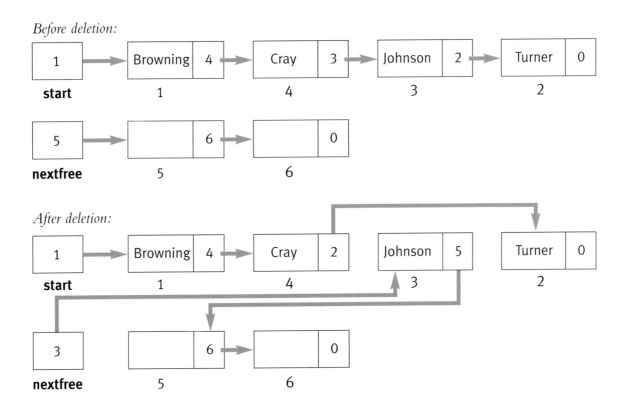

Figure 42.7

In pseudocode:

```
begin procedure
    p = start
    follow pointers until node[p].pointer points to the name to delete
    temp = node[p].pointer                    (put 3 in temp)
    node[p].pointer = node[temp].pointer (put 2 in Cray's pointer field)
    node[temp].pointer = nextfree        (put 5 in Johnson's pointer field)
    nextfree = temp                       (put 3 in nextfree)
end procedure
```

This is enough level of detail to show the concept of deleting from a linked list and you may wish to skip the next couple of paragraphs. However, for those who wish to go deeper, a fuller discussion follows.

Once again, deleting the first node in the list is a special case because **start** has to be altered. In the general case, following the pointers until node[p].pointer points to the name to delete again involves 'peeking ahead' to see what is in the next node, because once we are at a node we can't get back to change the previous pointer. So we want to stop following pointers not when node[p].name = name to delete, but at the node before that; i.e. when node[node[p].pointer].name = name to delete.

Note that deleting the last node (or inserting onto the end of the list, in the case of insertion) causes no special problems; try it and you will see this is true.

The full pseudocode is given on the next page.

Pseudocode for deleting an item from a linked list

```
begin procedure
   if start = 0
      then write ('List is empty') and exit procedure.
      p = start
   if deletename = node[start].name
      then                              (special case for first node)
         temp = node[start].pointer
         node[start].pointer = nextfree
         nextfree = start
         start = temp
      else                             (general case)
         while deletename <> node[node[p].pointer].pointer
            p = node[p].pointer          (advance the pointer)
         endwhile
         (node[p] now points to the node to be deleted; adjust the pointers)
         temp = node[p].pointer
         node[p].pointer = node[temp].pointer
         node[temp].pointer = nextfree
         nextfree = temp
   endif                               (general case)
end procedure
```

Printing out all the names in a linked list

To print all the names in the list, follow the pointers, printing each name in turn.

```
begin procedure
   p = start
   while p <> 0
      current = node[p]
      print current.name
      p = current.pointer
   endwhile
end procedure
```

Use of free memory, heap and pointers

So far, we have been using arrays to implement a linked list. Because the size of the array data structure has to be declared and is fixed prior to its application, it is **static**. Main memory is wasted if too many locations are reserved in advance. On the other hand, errors result if too few are reserved and an attempt is made to access locations outside the declared range.

Static data structure: a data structure of a size declared before the program is run.

Files are **dynamic structures**, in that the size of a file does not have to be declared in advance and is restricted only by how much data can be held on the storage medium, e.g. disk. A linked list is also a dynamic data structure but by implementing it using arrays this property is effectively lost. **Pointer data types** allow the creation of dynamic data structures in memory, using locations only when needed.

Dynamic data structure: the memory space taken up by the data structure varies at run time.

No memory locations have to be reserved before they are referenced. When a location is needed, it is pulled from a pool of all the available locations in main memory called the **heap**. When it is no longer required, the locations can be returned to the heap for use by other applications.

Heap: an area of memory used for dynamic memory allocation where blocks of memory are allocated.

Array and pointer variables differ in the manner in which they reference a main memory location. The name given to an array element represents the location in which a data item is stored.

The name given to a pointer represents the location that contains the address of the location you are using – you never know the address of the location being referenced; the pointer finds it for you from the heap.

Pointer variables

A pointer variable is one that is used for the sole purpose of pointing to another address in memory. The data type of a pointer depends on what it is pointing to.

Pointer: a variable used to point to a memory address.

In Pascal, for example, you can use the following statements to define a pointer data type:

```
type
     pointertype = ^integer;
var
     p : pointertype;
```

start and **nextfree** may be defined as pointer variables in the linked list examples. In this case, the pointer points to a node in the linked list, and each node can be defined as a record data type. Thus:

```
type
     pointertype = ^nodetype;

     nodetype = record
          name        : string;
          pointer     : pointertype;
     end;
var
     p           : pointertype;
     start       : pointertype;
     current     : nodetype;
```

In this notation, if **start** is a pointer variable, **start^** is the variable to which **start** points.

Thus, looking at Figure 42.1, start^.name = Browning, and start^.pointer = 4

Using this notation, the pseudocode algorithm for printing out the names in the list becomes

```
begin procedure
   p=start
   while p <> 0
      current = p^
      print current.name
      p = current.pointer
   endwhile
end procedure
```

Getting and returning memory locations dynamically

When a new item is added to a linked list, a new location has to be taken from the heap. The **New** procedure in Pascal takes an available location and assigns a pointer variable to it.

e.g.   `New(p)`

To return a variable to the heap, the procedure **Dispose** is used.

e.g.   `Dispose(p)`

You will not be expected to write procedures using **New** and **Dispose**. Knowledge of the general principles is sufficient. You may be asked to trace through a given algorithm or write a simple procedure using pointer notation.

4-42

Exercises

1 (a) (i) The birds Pheasant, Teal, Widgeon, Partridge, Woodpigeon are entered, in the order given, into a linked list so that they may be processed alphabetically. Draw this linked list.   (2)

(ii) Redraw the list after two additional items, Grouse and Snipe, are added.   (2)

(b) This linked list is said to be a *dynamic structure*. What is meant by the term dynamic structure?   (2)

(c) Explain how memory was allocated for the two additional data items.   (2)

AQA CPT4 Qu 1 January 2003

Chapter 43 – Stacks

Definition of a Stack

A stack is an Abstract Data Structure (ADT). Items can be added (pushed) on to the stack or removed (popped or pulled) from the stack. Items are added or removed from one end only, the top of the stack. It is a dynamic data structure since the size of the stack varies according to the number of elements currently in the stack.

Stack: a Last In, First Out data structure (LIFO).

A stack may be implemented using an array and two additional variables, *MaxStackSize* holding the size of the array (i.e. the maximum size of the stack) and *Top* holding a pointer to the top of the stack. To initialise the stack the pointer *(Top)* will be set to zero, representing an empty stack.

The diagram below shows an array that can hold a maximum of 6 elements with 3 items currently in the stack.

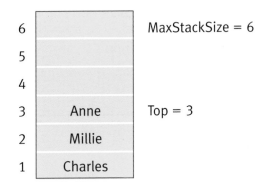

The following pseudocode procedure may be used to add ('push') an element onto a stack:

```
Procedure Push
    If Top = MaxStackSize
        Then Write 'Stack is full'
        Else
            Add 1 to Top
            Stack[Top] := NewItem
    EndIf
EndProc
```

To remove ('pop') an element from a stack:

```
Procedure Pop
    If Top = 0
        Then Write 'Stack is empty'
        Else
            PoppedItem := Stack[Top]
            Subtract 1 from Top
    EndIf
EndProc
```

Q1: Write a program, using a high level language of your choice, to implement a stack. You will need to code the procedures *push* and *pop* above. You will also need to initialize an empty stack and some means of displaying what is currently in the stack, so you can check that your code works correctly.

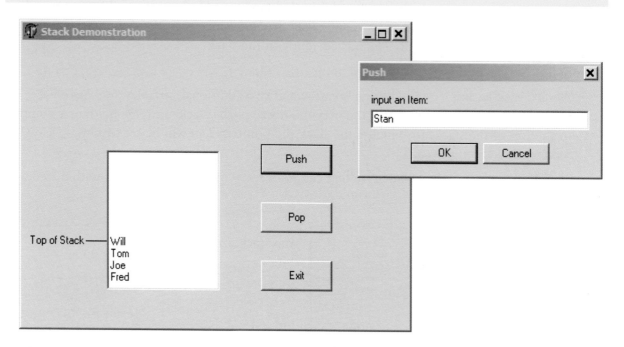

Figure 43.1: Demo program showing the operation of a stack

Uses of Stacks

Stacks are used in many different situations in computing, for example:

• To store return addresses, parameters and register contents when subroutines are called. When the subroutine ends, the address at the top of the stack is popped and the computer continues execution from that address.

• In evaluating mathematical expressions held in reverse Polish notation, i.e. a form of notation used by compilers as an intermediate step in translating expressions such as A:= (B★C) + D/E.

Exercises

1 (a) Describe the data structure known as a stack.   (3)

   (b) Describe how values are

        (i) added to a stack,   (4)

        (ii) removed from a stack.   (4)

   (c) Why is a stack used when a high level language program calls procedures?   (3)

UCLES Paper 2 Qu 6 May 1998

Chapter 44 – Queues

Definition of a queue

A queue is an Abstract Data Structure (ADT). New elements are added to the rear of the queue, and elements leave from the front of the queue.

Queue: a First In First Out data structure (FIFO).

A queue can be implemented as an array with a pointer to the front of the queue and a pointer to the rear of the queue. An integer holding the size of the array (the maximum size of the queue) is needed, and it is useful to have an extra variable giving the number of items currently in the queue.

John	Catherine	Rob			

Front = 1   Rear = 3

MaxSize = 6   NumberInQueue = 3

After 2 people have left the queue and 3 more have joined, the queue will look like this:

		Rob	Max	Lisa	Anna

Front = 3   Rear = 6

MaxSize = 6   NumberInQueue = 4

Now what? Only 4 people are in the queue but the end of the array has been reached. To overcome this problem, the elements could be shuffled along, so the front of the queue is always in location 1. This is known as a **linear queue**. However, busy queues would spend rather a lot of time shuffling elements. Another method to overcome the problem is to implement the queue as a **circular queue**, so that when the next person joins they enter at the front of the array:

Ben		Rob	Max	Lisa	Anna

Rear = 1   Front = 3

MaxSize = 6   NumberInQueue = 5

Procedures to implement a circular queue

The above queue may be implemented by declaring variables as follows:

```
Q                 : array [1..6] of string;
Front             : integer;
Rear              : integer;
NumberInQueue     : integer;
```

To initialise the queue:

```
Procedure Initialise
     Front := 1
     Rear  := 6       {or Rear = 0}
     NumberInQueue := 0
EndProc
```

To add an element to the queue:

```
Procedure EnQueue
    If   NumberInQueue = 6
      Then Write ('Queue overflow')
      Else
        If   Rear = 6
          Then Rear := 1                    or Rear := (Rear Mod 6) + 1
          Else Add 1 to Rear
        EndIf
        Q[Rear] := NewItem
        Add 1 to NumberInQueue
    EndIf
  EndProc
```

To remove an element from the queue:

```
Procedure DeQueue
    If   NumberInQueue = 0
      Then Write ('Queue empty')
      Else
        NewItem :=  Q[Front]
        Subtract 1 from NumberInQueue
        If   Front = 6
          Then Front := 1                   or Front := (Front Mod 6) + 1
          Else Add 1 to Front
        EndIf
    EndIf
  EndProc
```

Implementing a queue as a linked list

A queue may be implemented as a special kind of linked list, with each element in the queue pointing to the next item. An external pointer points to the front of the queue, and items may only be removed from the front of the list and added to the end of the list.

front

The front of the queue is accessed through the pointer **front**. To add an element to the queue, the pointers have to be followed until the node containing a pointer of 0 is reached, signifying the end of the queue, and this pointer is then changed to point to the new node. (In some implementations two pointers are kept; one to the front and one to the rear. This saves having to traverse the whole queue when a new element is to be added.)

Uses of Queues

Queues are used in a variety of applications such as:

• holding jobs waiting to be run by the computer;

• a keyboard buffer, to allow a whole line to be typed and edited while the processor is busy doing something else;

• spooling output onto a disk to await printing.

Exercises

1 The following data is input to a program, in alphabetical order, and it stored.

Anne

Bob

Claire

Dean

(a) Draw a diagram to show how this data is stored for:

(i) a stack;

(ii) a queue (4)

(b) One item is retrieved from these data structures for processing, and Eden is input. Draw the diagrams of this new situation for:

(i) the stack;

(ii) the queue. (3)

(c) Why are queues in computer systems usually implemented as circular queues? (2)

AQA CPT4 Qu 5 June 2002

2 Keystrokes at a computer keyboard generate character codes which are temporarily stored in the order in which they are generated in a data storage area known as the *keyboard buffer*. A program which requires keyboard input accesses this buffer and removes one character code at a time. The code which is removed each time is the one which has been in the buffer the longest. New characters arriving may wrap around to the beginning of the buffer.

(a) What name best describes the structure of the keyboard buffer? (2)

(b) The keyboard buffer is designed to hold up to 100 character codes at any one time but during the execution of the program several thousand character codes will enter and leave the keyboard buffer. Describe how the buffer can be best structured to make this possible. Use diagrams to illustrate your answer, clearly showing the full structure for:

(i) an empty buffer;

(ii) a full buffer before any characters have been removed;

(iii) a full buffer after less than 100 character codes have been removed and some new characters have arrived. (5)

(c) Using pseudo code describe algorithms which:

(i) initialise the buffer;

(ii) add a character code to the buffer;

(iii) remove a character code from the buffer.

The algorithm should handle the error conditions generated when an attempt is made to add an item to an already full buffer and when an attempt is made to remove an item from an empty buffer. (13)

AEB Paper 2 Qu 17 1993

Chapter 45 – Trees

Definition

A tree is a dynamic data structure which has zero or more nodes organised in a hierarchical way such that:

- except when the tree is empty, there is one node called the **root** at the beginning of the tree structure;
- lines connecting the nodes are called **branches** and every node except the root is joined to just one node at the next higher level (its parent);
- nodes that have no children are called **leaf nodes** or **terminal** nodes.

Binary tree: an Abstract Data Type (ADT) consisting of nodes arranged in hierarchical fashion, starting with a root node. Each node is the parent of at most two other nodes.

Note that every tree has only one root, but each node in the tree can be regarded as the root of a **subtree** of the tree. Thus a tree consists of a root and one or more subtrees, each of which is a tree. (This is an example of a **recursive** definition).

You first met trees in Chapter 10 and it would be a good idea to revise this chapter before proceeding.

In that chapter, the following names were entered into a binary tree so that they could be retrieved in alphabetical order:

Long, Charlesworth, Illman, Hawthorne, Todd, Youngman, Jones, Ravage.

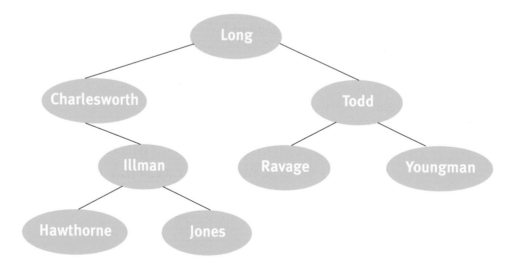

Figure 45.1: A binary tree

Q1: Insert the following items into a binary tree for subsequent retrieval in alphabetical sequence: goldfinch, dove, robin, chaffinch, blackbird, wren, jay, sparrow, partridge.

Traversal of a Binary Tree

To output all the nodes of a binary tree in a particular order we need to traverse the tree. There are three different methods commonly used:

- Pre-order traversal
- In-order traversal
- Post-order traversal

Pre-order traversal

Draw an outline around the tree structure, as shown below, starting to the left of the root. As you pass to the left of a node (where the red dot is marked), output the data in that node:

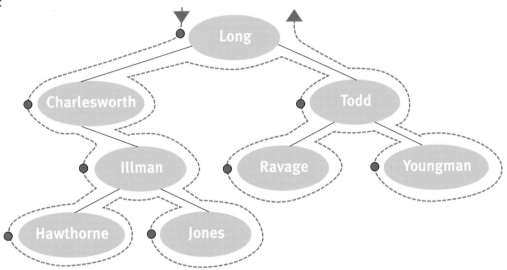

Figure 45.2: Pre-order traversal

This will produce the following output:

Long, Charlesworth, Illman, Hawthorne, Jones, Todd, Ravage, Youngman.

In-order traversal

Draw an outline around the tree structure, as shown below, starting to the left of the root. As you pass underneath a node (where the blue dot is marked), output the data in that node:

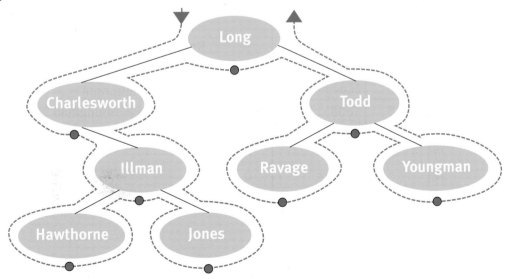

Figure 45.3: In-order traversal

This will produce the following output:

Charlesworth, Hawthorne, Illman, Jones, Long, Ravage, Todd, Youngman.

Post-order traversal

Draw an outline around the tree structure, as shown below, starting to the left of the root. As you pass to the right of a node (where the green dot is marked), output the data in that node:

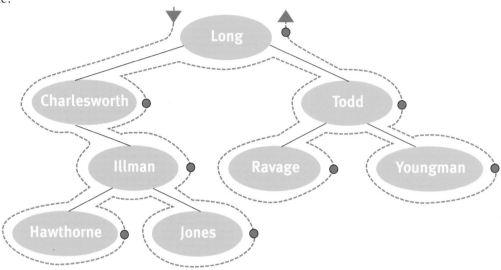

Figure 45.4: Post-order traversal

This will produce the following output:

Hawthorne, Jones, Illman, Charlesworth, Ravage, Youngman, Todd, Long.

Implementation of trees using arrays

Binary trees can be implemented using left and right pointers at each node. A node will consist of:

- a left pointer
- data item
- a right pointer.

	left	data	right
tree[1]	2	Long	5
[2]	0	Charlesworth	3
[3]	4	Illman	7
[4]	0	Hawthorne	0
[5]	8	Todd	6
[6]	0	Youngman	0
[7]	0	Jones	0
[8]	0	Ravage	0
[9]			
[10]			

A pointer value of 0 indicates a 'nil' pointer

Note that, for example:

tree[1].left = 2

tree[tree[1].left].right = 3

tree[6].data = 'Youngman'

Figure 45.5

Q2: Show how the binary tree structure created in Q1 may be stored in an array similar to the one above.

Algorithm to construct a binary tree

Place first item into root node

for subsequent items start at root node

repeat

    if new item > this node item

        then follow right pointer

        else follow left pointer

until pointer = 0

place item at this node

Algorithm to search a binary tree

Start at the root node

repeat

    if wanted item = this item

      then found := true

      else

        if wanted item > this item

          then follow right pointer

          else follow left pointer

until found or null pointer encountered

A recursive algorithm for an inorder tree traversal

The algorithm for an inorder traversal is:

1 Traverse the left subtree

2 Visit the root node

3 Traverse the right subtree.

This can be implemented in pseudocode as a recursive algorithm as follows:

```
Procedure traverse_from(p);
  if tree[p].left <> 0 then traverse_from(left);
  endif
  writeln (data);
  if tree[p].right <> 0 then traverse_from(right);
  endif
endproc
```

The procedure, when called with the statement **traverse_from(1)** will print out the contents of the tree in figure 45.5 in alphabetical sequence.

Q3: What is a 'recursive algorithm'?

Preorder tree traversal

The algorithm for a preorder traversal is:

1 Visit the root node

2 Traverse the left subtree

3 Traverse the right subtree.

This can be implemented in Pascal as follows:

```
Procedure traverse_from(p);
   writeln (data);
   if tree[p].left <> 0 then traverse_from(left);
   endif
   if tree[p].right <> 0 then traverse_from(right);
   endif
endproc
```

The procedure, when called with the statement **traverse_from(1)** will print out the contents of the tree in Figure 45.5 in the sequence Long, Charlesworth, Illman, Hawthorne, Jones, Todd, Ravage, Youngman.

Postorder tree traversal

The algorithm for a postorder traversal is:

1 Traverse the left subtree

2 Traverse the right subtree.

3 Visit the root node

This can be implemented in Pascal as follows:

```
Procedure traverse_from(p:integer);
   if tree[p].left <> 0 then traverse_from(left);
   endif
   if tree[p].right <> 0 then traverse_from(right);
   endif
   writeln (data);
endproc
```

The procedure, when called with the statement **traverse_from(1)** will print out the contents of the tree in Figure 45.5 in the sequence Hawthorne, Jones, Illman, Charlesworth, Ravage, Youngman, Todd, Long

Recursion

The routine above illustrates just how useful recursion can be to the programmer. The code mirrors the high-level solution arrived at in thinking about the problem, and is far shorter and less complex than a non-recursive solution, which would involve having to store the addresses of nodes that had been visited in order to work back up each subtree.

Summary

A binary tree is an appropriate data structure when a large number of items need to be held in such a way that any item may be quickly accessed, or sequenced lists need to be produced. Additions are easily handled since they require only the adjustment of a single pointer. Different ways of traversing a tree mean that items can be stored in one sequence and retrieved in a different sequence.

Exercises

1 An algebraic expression is represented in a binary tree as follows.

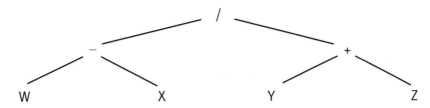

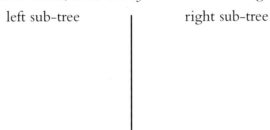

(a) On the above diagram, circle and label the *root* of this tree, a *branch* and a *leaf node*. (3)

(b) In the spaces below, draw the *left sub-tree* and the *right sub-tree* of this tree.

left sub-tree | right sub-tree

(2)

(c) What is the result if this tree is printed using in-order traversal? (3)

AQA CPT4 Qu 8 June 2003

2 An algebraic expression is represented by the following binary tree.

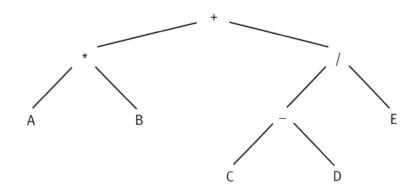

Show the output produced if the tree is traversed using

(a) pre-order traversal (4)

(b) in-order traversal (4)

(c) post-order traversal (4)

New Question

Chapter 46 – Searching and Sorting

Linear search

Sometimes it is necessary to search for items in a file, a table or an array in memory. If the items are not in any particular sequence, the data items have to be searched one by one until the required one is found or the end of the list is reached. This is called a **linear search**.

Algorithm for linear search:

```
Start at beginning of list
Repeat
   test next item for a match
until item found or end of list reached
```

Binary search

A binary search is used for searching an ordered array, and is much faster than a linear search for arrays of more than a few items.

The ordered array is divided into three parts; a middle item, the lower part of the array and the upper part. The middle item is examined to see if it is equal to the sought item. If it is not, then if it is greater than the sought item, the upper half of the array is of no further interest. The number of items being searched is therefore halved and the process repeated until the last item is examined, with either the upper half or lower half of the items searched being eliminated at each pass.

The basic concept of the binary search is in fact recursive. Two pseudocode procedures, one iterative and one recursive, for a binary search on an array of *n* items in an array A are given below.

ItemFound, SearchFailed are boolean variables, Top, Bottom and Midpoint are integer variables and A is an array of *n* items (could be any type). ItemSought is a variable of the same type as the items in the array A.

Iterative solution:

```
Procedure BinarySearch
   ItemFound := False;   SearchFailed := False
   Top := N;             Bottom := 1
   Repeat
     Midpoint := Integer part of ((Top + Bottom)/2)
     If A[Midpoint] = ItemSought
       Then Found := True
       Else
         If Bottom > Top
           Then   SearchFailed := True
           Else
             If A[Midpoint] < ItemSought
               Then Bottom := Midpoint + 1
               Else Top := Midpoint - 1
            EndIf
         EndIf
     EndIf
   Until ItemFound or SearchFailed
EndProc
```

The maximum number of comparisons that has to be made in a binary search of 2^n items is $n + 1$. Thus any item in a list of 1024 (2^{10}) items can be found in a maximum of 11 comparisons. Try it! By comparison, it will take an average 512 comparisons to find an item using a linear search.

Recursive solution:

```
Procedure BinarySearch (Bottom, Top, ItemSought)
  ItemFound := False;    SearchFailed := False
 Midpoint := Integer part of ((Top + Bottom)/2)
 If A[Midpoint] = ItemSought
   Then Found := True
   Else
     If Bottom > Top
       Then   SearchFailed := True
       Else
        If A[Midpoint] < ItemSought
          Then BinarySearch(Midpoint+1, Top, ItemSought)
          Else BinarySearch(Bottom, Midpoint-1, ItemSought)
        EndIf
      EndIf
   EndIf
EndProc
```

Sorting

There are several methods of sorting items held in an array in memory into ascending (or descending) sequence. Both alphabetic and numeric items can be sorted in an identical manner; the sort algorithm is the same whether you are sorting integers or strings.

Bubble sort

This is a slow method but simple to understand and useful when there is a small number of items to be sorted. To sort an array of n items, a maximum of $n-1$ 'passes' is made through the array, with each item being compared with the adjacent item and swapped if necessary. A 'flag' can be initialised at the beginning of each pass and set to a particular value (e.g. True) if a swap is made; at the end of the pass it is checked and if it has not been set, the values are already in sequence and no further passes need to be made.

The following pseudocode algorithm sorts an array of n items into ascending sequence.

Flag is a Boolean variable, Count is an integer variable and A is an array of N items (could be any type). Temp is a variable of the same type as the items in the array A.

```
Procedure BubbleSort
    Repeat
        Flag := False
        For Count := 1 To N - 1
            If A[Count] > A[Count + 1]
                Then
                        Temp := A[Count]
                        A[Count] := A[Count + 1]
                        A[Count + 1] := Temp
                        Flag := True
            EndIf
        EndFor
        Subtract 1 from N
    Until Flag = False Or N = 1
EndProc
```

A bubble sort is not a suitable algorithm to use when there are more than say, 50-100 items to be sorted. There are other much faster sort algorithms, which may be used when there is a large number of items to be sorted. The Insertion Sort and Quicksort below are not part of the AQA 'A' Level specification.

Quicksort

The quicksort is a very fast sort invented by C.Hoare, based on the general principle that exchanges should be made between items which are a large distance apart in the array holding them. It works by splitting the array into two sublists, and then quicksorting each sublist by splitting them into two sublists and .... remember **recursion**? The quicksort uses a complex recursive algorithm which starts by comparing the first and last elements in the array. For large arrays, it can be hundreds of times faster than the simple bubble sort.

Insertion sort

Items from the input array are copied one at a time to the output array. Each new item is inserted into the right place so that the output array is always in order.

The insertion sort is considerably faster than the bubble sort, but not nearly as fast as the quicksort, which with a given processor would take, say, about 3 seconds to sort an array of 2000 items, a minute using an insertion sort and 5 or 6 minutes using a bubble sort.

Exercises

1   A procedure to process an array of numbers is defined as follows.

```
Procedure P(Number)
  Repeat
    X ← StartofArray
    Flag ← False
    Repeat
      If Number(X) > Number (X+1)
        Then
          Begin
            Temp ← Number(X)
            Number (X) ← Number (X+1)
            Number(X+1) ← Temp
            Flag ← True
          End
        X ← X+1
    Until EndofArray
  Until Flag = False
Endproc
```

The array number, containing 17, 11, 21, 9, 23, 15, is to be processed by this procedure.

(a)   List the array after the outer Repeat loop has been executed once.   (2)

(b)   What algorithm does the procedure P describe?   (1)

(c)   What is the purpose of Flag in this procedure?   (1)

AQA CPT4 Qu 4 June 2002

2   An array A[1] .. A[n] contains a list of random numbers.

(a)   Produce a structured algorithm which will reverse the order of the values in the array.   (6)

(b)   Briefly describe **one** method of sorting the array and comment on its efficiency if it is used when the elements of the array are already sorted.   (4)

CCEA Module 2 Qu 5 May 1999

3   A *binary* search and a *linear* search are two different methods of searching a list.

A given list contains 137 items.

(a) (i) What is the maximum number of items accessed when searching for a particular item from the given list using a binary search?

(ii) Explain your answer.

(b) (i) What is the maximum number of items accessed when searching for a particular item from the given list using a linear search?

(ii) Explain your answer.   (4)

AQA CPT4 Qu 3 January 2003

4   The following section of pseudo-code processes a one-dimensional integer array called *List*. The numbers in *List* are stored in ascending order, and *x*, *Low*, *High*, *Middle* are all integer variables. (The function Int returns the whole number part of its parameter.)

```
Proc Process(Low, High, x)
    Found ← False
    Repeat
       Middle ← Int((Low + High)/2)
       If List(Middle) = x
       Then Found ← True
       Else If List(Middle) > x
          Then High ← Middle − 1
          Else Low ← Middle +1          {List(Middle) < x}
    Until Found = True
```

(a) Complete the following dry-run table for Process (1, 10, 19), given that the integers in the list are:

$$2, 4, 6, 7, 11, 13, 19, 21, 27, 29$$

Low	High	Middle	Found
1	10		

(7)

(b) What type of routine does this pseudo-code define?   (1)

AEB Paper 2 Qu 14 1999

Chapter 47 – Operating System Classification

The operating system

An operating system is a program or set of programs that manages the operation of the computer. The most frequently used instructions in the operating system must be stored in main memory and remain there whilst other programs such as application programs are being executed. This portion of the operating system is called by many different names such as **kernel**, **control program**, **nucleus**, **monitor**, **supervisor** or **executive**.

Figure 47.1

Operating System: program that controls the execution of all other programs (applications) and acts as an intermediary between users and computer.

Loading an operating system

On all large computers and most micros, the operating system is held on disk and has to be loaded into main memory once the computer has been switched on, before any other programs can be run. The process of loading the operating system is called **booting** the system.

On a microcomputer system, the operating system is usually held on the hard disk. A small program held in ROM (the 'loader') will tell the computer where to look for the operating system, and give instructions for loading at least part of it into memory. Once part of the operating system has been loaded, more instructions can be executed to load the rest of the kernel. This method of 'pulling itself up by its own bootstraps' is where the expression 'booting' comes from.

In smaller hand-held computers the control program is permanently held in ROM.

Modes of operation

Operating systems vary considerably in their capabilities, from relatively simple single-user microcomputer systems, to sophisticated mainframe computers. Various modes of operation are described below.

Batch

In a batch operating system, a job runs from beginning to end without intervention from the user. The running of batch jobs is normally controlled by a program written in Job Control Language (JCL), which specifies for example the job priority, maximum memory, print lines and execution time required. JCL is discussed in more detail in the next chapter.

Interactive

With this type of system the user interacts directly with the system to supply commands and data as the application program executes and the user receives the results of processing immediately. The user and computer are in direct two-way communication.

Real-Time

Real-time operating systems can be of different types; process control, information storage and retrieval, and transaction processing. In any of these systems, the data input to the computer must be processed immediately, though in an information storage and retrieval system, or a transaction processing system, a delay of a few seconds is acceptable. Not so in the on-board computer controlling the 10.30 flight to Moscow! Real-time systems need to produce correct results and meet predefined deadlines.

Some systems are safety-critical meaning they must be **fault-tolerant** and guarantee a response within a specified time interval. Such systems have built-in redundancy – the processor may not be used at its full capacity for a large part of the time so that it can respond instantly when required. In addition many components may be duplicated. On airlines, three computers running programs developed by different programmers, but performing identical tasks, run concurrently to ensure that software or hardware errors will not result in disaster.

Any real-time system has to be able to respond to events happening at unpredictable times and which may happen in parallel.

Examples of real-time operating systems are:

• Nuclear reactor safety system. The response time must be less than one thousandth of a second.

• Booking systems for theatres, flights etc. The response time must be not more than a few seconds.

Single-user single-process

The operating system supervises the loading and running of one program at a time, and the input and output of data to and from peripheral devices.

Multi-programming

A multi-programming operating system enables two or more programs to be held in memory at the same time, with each program being given a small amount of processor time before moving on to the next. This system makes efficient use of valuable processor time because when one program is held up waiting for input or output, the processor can be allocated to another program. It is the job of the operating system to maximise throughput while ensuring that all jobs are completed in a reasonable time.

Multi-programming: the concurrent (apparent simultaneous) execution of two or more programs.

Multi-programming systems were developed when all computers operated in batch mode. Thus several batch jobs may be running simultaneously in a multi-programming batch environment.

Multi-user

By applying the concept of multi-programming to interactive processing it is possible to develop a multi-user operating system. A **multi-user** (multi-access) operating system is defined as one that **allows two or more users to communicate with the computer at any one time**, with each user interacting with the computer via a terminal (which must have, at the minimum, a keyboard and VDU). As with multi-programming, each program (or in this case, user) in turn is given a small amount of processor time. While some users are typing at the keyboard or using a disk or printer, the processor is working on other users' programs. So long as there are not too many users on the system, each user has the impression that they have sole use of the computer.

Multi-user and batch

Some operating systems provide for both multi-user and batch processing. In such systems batch processing jobs are run at times of low interactive demand, e.g., during the night when few users are active on the system. In this way expensive mainframe computers are kept productive twenty four hours a day.

Multi-tasking

Multi-tasking is usually taken to mean multi-programming on a single-user machine such as a PC running Windows XP, which is termed a 'multi-tasking operating system'. The user can switch between one program and another, for example running a query on a database in one window while using a word processor in another window. As with multi-programming, only one program is actually being executed at any one moment, with the user switching freely between tasks or applications.

Multi-tasking: the concurrent execution of two or more related tasks between which communication is possible.

Network operating systems

For computers to communicate with other computers, they must be linked physically into a network and run software (a network operation system) to enable communication. Networks can be run either as peer-to-peer networks (see chapter 59) or as client-server systems.

4-47

Client-server system

Most network operating systems operate a client-server system. Client-server computing splits processing between "clients" and "servers". Both are on the network, with the server machine usually being a more powerful machine holding the application programs and files. The clients are each loaded with an operating system which allows work to be carried out at the client computer, e.g., Windows XP, but in addition they contain an extension which intercepts requests to run application programs or to access files or other services which can only be met by the server.

Client-server system: a network organisation in which work stations make use of resources available at one or more servers (printer server, file server, database server, application server, web server......).

The client-server approach is also used when printing work from an application running on a client computer. A **printer server** allows all the networked machines to have access to a variety of different printers. Printing jobs sent to the server from client computers are held in a queue on a disk (known as 'spooling') and sent to the printer when it is free.

Distributed systems

With the development of the personal computer (PC), the need arose for stand-alone PCs to be able to share expensive peripheral devices such as printers. This led, in the early 1980s, to PCs being organised in local-area networks (LANs) using interconnection technologies such as Ethernet. Allowing PCs access to the file system of another PC located somewhere else on the network became a requirement as well, especially as the cost of hard disk drives was still relatively high.

The file server and print server networks are examples of distributed computer systems.

Distributed system: a system in which resources, e.g. processors, disk storage, printers exist in separate nodes of a network with transparent access to these resources by users being possible.

For example, computer A can run a program on computer B, using a file located elsewhere on the network without the user being aware of where execution is taking place or where the files are physically located.

Exercises

1   A *multi-user, multi-tasking* operating system is installed in a microcomputer system. The operating system supports multi-programming. The microcomputer is used for both *batch* and *interactive* work.

Explain the differences between:

(i)   multi-programming, multi-access and multitasking;

(ii) interactive and batch programs.   (5)

New Question

2   Computer controlled greenhouses and computer controlled nuclear power stations would both be run using *real-time* operating systems.

(a)   Outline and explain one important difference in the requirements of these two examples of real-time systems.   (2)

(b)   Suggest a suitable operating system for producing gas bills. State **two** characteristics of this operating system and **two** characteristics of the real-time control operating system, which distinguishes each from the other.   (4)

AEB Paper 1 Qu 10 1995

4-47

Chapter 48 – Operating System Concepts

Overview of an operating system

The operating system is a large and complex program, and in this chapter we will be looking in more detail at some basic terms and concepts, and how the operating system works to make the most efficient use of processor time in a multi-programming environment. First of all the different types of user interface used by different operating systems are described.

User Interface

The user interface is the way in which a human user and the computer communicate. User interfaces may be classified as

• command-line;

• job-control language (JCL);

• graphical user interface or GUI.

Command line interface

In a command-line user interface, an interactive terminal allows the system to prompt and the user to type a command to initiate program execution or to perform housekeeping tasks, e.g.

C:\>Copy Project.* a:

will cause all files named *Project* (with any extension) in the current folder to be copied to the current folder on the A drive. The command prompt is the > character and the **C:** is the pathname for the current folder. The user interface module contains a **command-line interpreter (CLI)**, which performs the actual task of identifying and executing the command.

MS-DOS uses an interface of this type.

Job control language

In a job control language interface a user has no direct interaction with the computer system. Instead a user prepares a series of instructions off-line using a JCL to describe to the system the requirements of his/her task. Eventually, when a user's job is executed the execution is guided by the JCL-prepared description and the results made available at a later time via some off-line medium, e.g., line printer paper.

Typically, Job Control statements will specify:

• who owns the job;

• job priority;

• the maximum processor time to allow the job;

• the maximum lines to be printed;

• the names of data files used;

• what action to take if one of the programs in the job fails to execute correctly.

A sample JCL program to compile and execute a COBOL program might look something like the following:

```
$JOB USER123  G.MARRIOTT
$PRIORITY 2
$COBOL
$INPUT PROG1 (DISK 1)
$LIST LP
$IF ERROR THEN END
$RUN
$MEMORY 250K
$TIME 5
$FILES 'PAYFILE'
$IF ERROR THEN DUMP
$END
```

Q1: What is the purpose of each of the statements in the above JCL program?

Graphical user interface

A graphical user interface (GUI) allows the user to interact with the system using windows, icons, menus and a pointer to control the operating system. Icons represent programs, groups of programs, folders, devices and files. Figure 48.1 illustrates a typical GUI. Instead of typing a command or file name, selection is achieved by moving a pointer with a mouse and clicking a mouse button.

Figure 48.1: Windows XP Graphical User Interface

GUIs are easier for the novice to use because they are more intuitive. The screen is arranged as a metaphor of a desktop with graphical symbols to represent familiar objects. Only valid options are available and there is a consistency of layout and command representation in applications which can be launched into execution through operation of the GUI. Comprehensive on-line help is available.

Disadvantages of a GUI over a command-line interface are:

- they use more main memory and hard disk space;
- they require a more powerful processor and a better graphics display;
- they are slower when executing a command because much more interpretation takes place;
- they can be irritating to use for simple tasks because a greater number of operations is required.

Operating system functions

The OS has four main functions:

- process management;
- memory management;
- I/O control;
- file management.

We will look at the first of these for the rest of this chapter.

The 'process' concept

From a user's point of view, the operating system is there to execute programs. In batch systems these are referred to as jobs. In interactive systems these are referred to as processes. A program is not the same as a process. A program is static while a **process** is dynamic. The concept of a process is important in multi-programming operating systems. For example, the same program, say a Pascal compiler, may be being executed by several people simultaneously. There will only be one copy in memory with different parts of it being executed as several people compile their programs, effectively sharing the same code. Each instance of the program running is a process, with separate data areas maintained for each 'execution'. A program working in this way is said to be **re-entrant**.

Process: a program in execution.

Process states

A process may be in any one of three states:

- a process is **running** or **current** if it is actually using the CPU;
- a process is **runnable** or **ready** when it *could* make use of the CPU if it was available;
- a process is **suspended** or **blocked** when it is waiting for I/O and could not use the CPU even if it were free.

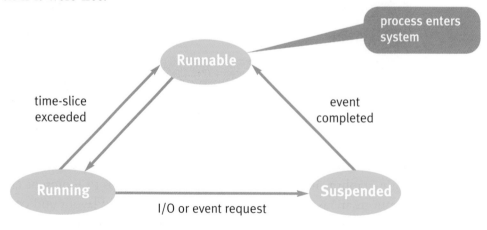

Figure 48.2: Running, Runnable and Suspended Processes

The relationship between the three states for a particular process is shown above. For example, if a currently running process requests I/O, it relinquishes the processor and goes into the *suspended* state. If it uses up its time slice before completing then it is placed in a *runnable* state while some other process gains the use of the processor.

The process control block (PCB)

When a process gives up the processor, it is necessary to save the details of where the process was in its execution when it was interrupted so that it can resume from exactly the same place later on. In order to be able to do this, the operating system maintains information about every process within the system in a data structure called a **process control block**. This contains the following information:

• process ID (unique process identifier)

• current process state (runnable, running, suspended)

• job priority or other scheduling information

• Program Counter

• register save area, where the current contents of all registers are saved before they are taken over by the next process

• a pointer to the processor's allocated memory area

• pointers to other allocated resources (open files, disk, printer etc)

• CPU time used so far

• estimated time to completion

• links to other PCBs

Threads

A process can have one or more threads. Each thread has a scheduling state (runnable, running, suspended). All threads in a process share most of their environment. They have the same virtual address space for instructions and global variables, but they have their own local variables, program counter, registers and stack pointer. Each thread has its own thread control block (TCB). The PCB holds references to one or more TCBs. This means less main memory is used and it requires less work to create or delete threads than separate processes because threads share virtual address space.

A thread is a path of execution within a process (a lightweight sub-process).

Operating systems that support multi-threading enable programmers to design programs whose threaded parts can execute concurrently. This is used particularly when writing client-server applications. The programmer must design the program in such a way that all threads can run concurrently without interfering with each other.

Allocating job priorities

In a multi-programming environment, users can allocate priorities to their jobs so that jobs with a high priority will gain processor time ahead of those with a low priority. Short program compilations, for example, may be given a higher priority than less urgent batch jobs.

The operating system also allocates priorities to jobs. Deciding which process to run next is the job of the **scheduler**, and will be done in accordance with a **scheduling policy**. This cannot be too complex or the computer will spend more time deciding whose turn it is than getting on with the job! It is not unknown for an operating system to occupy about 90% of the CPU's time, leaving 10% to be shared out among the users. Some compromise has to be reached.

Scheduling objectives

A scheduling policy should try to

- maximise throughput – try to process as many jobs as possible in as little time as possible;

- maximise the number of interactive users receiving acceptable response times (i.e. at most a few seconds);

- balance resource use – if for example a printer is idle, a high priority could be given to a job that uses the printer;

- avoid pushing the low priority jobs to the back of the queue indefinitely. This can be achieved by giving jobs a higher priority based on how long they have been in the queue;

- enforce priorities – in environments where users can assign priorities to jobs, the scheduler must favour the high priority jobs;

- achieve a balance between response time and utilisation of resources;

Some of these objectives may conflict with each other, making scheduling a complex process!

The scheduler will use a number of criteria such as:

- how much I/O a process needs;

- how much CPU time a process needs;

- whether the process is batch or interactive;

- the urgency of a fast response;

- process priority – high priority processes should be favoured;

- accumulated waiting time;

- how much more time the process needs to complete, though this is often not known.

Scheduling algorithms

There are a number of possible strategies that the scheduler could use in deciding which process to run next. The main ones are:

- Shortest job first

- Shortest remaining time first

- Round Robin

Round robin scheduling

In round robin scheduling processes are dispatched on a first in first out (FIFO) basis, with each process in turn being given a limited amount of CPU time called a **time slice** or **quantum**. If it does not complete before its time expires (usually a few milliseconds) the dispatcher gives the CPU to the next process.

In order to do this, the OS sets an interrupting clock or interval timer to generate interrupts at specific times. This method of scheduling helps to guarantee a reasonable response time to interactive users. In some systems users who have requested a high priority for their jobs may have more than one consecutive time slice each time their turn comes round.

Deadlock

Deadlock occurs when two processes each have a resource which the other needs in order to execute. Since both processes do not have all the resources they need to execute, neither can continue. The scheduler is responsible for detecting deadlock and resolving it.

Exercises

1

```
P:\TL01>cd May 2001
P:\TL01\May 2001>dir
    Volume in drive P has no label.
    Volume Serial Number is E04F-F00A

Directory of P:\May 2001

.               <DIR>                    28/05/01   11.37a
..              <DIR>                    28/05/01   11.37a
Seniors         <DIR>                    30/05/01   04.16p
Juniors         <DIR>                    30/05/01   04.15p
Summer                      92,160       31/05/01   10.37a
            5 File(s)   92,160 bytes
```

(a) What type of operating system interface is shown above? (1)

(b) What program receives the instructions entered via this interface and analyses them? (1)

(c) Give **two** advantages of this type of interface over alternative types of operating interface. (2)

(d) Give **one** disadvantage of this type of interface over alternative types of operating system interface. (1)

AQA CPT4 Qu 4 January 2003

2 Job Control Language is used to control how jobs that are to be run in a batch processing system.

(a) List **two** pieces of information which might be specified in the Job Control Language script for a particular job.

(2)

(b) Some Job Control Languages allow statements which specify to the Operating System the amount of Input and Output expected relative to the amount of processor time required. How would a Batch multi-programming operating system use this information? (3)

AQA CPT4 Qu 4 January 2002

3 (a) Describe the vectored interrupt mechanism. (3)

(b) How does this mechanism make the use of interrupts more flexible? (1)

AQA CPT4 Qu 2 June 2003

4-48

4   On a single processor machine the scheduler program for a particular multi-programming, multi-user operating system which supports both *interactive* and *batch processing*, maintains a *list of currently active jobs* and a *list of inactive jobs*.

The *inactive list* consists solely of *batch jobs* whereas the *active list* contains a mixture of *interactive* and *batch*. New *batch jobs* are added to the *inactive list*. The scheduler transfers *batch jobs* from the *inactive list* to the *active list* when appropriate.

A job on the *active list* may be running, runnable or suspended; if it is running it will be at the front of the list. When a job is completed it is removed from the *active list*.

(a)   Distinguish between *interactive* and *batch processing*.   (2)

(b)   State **three** items of control that will need to be specified by a job control language for **each** batch job.   (3)

(c)   Describe **two** situations that would lead to a job in the *active list* being suspended.   (2)

(d)   With the aid of a diagram/s describe appropriate data structure/s for storing the list of active jobs.   (2)

(e)   The operating system groups all information that it needs about a particular active job into a data structure called a process descriptor. Describe **three** distinct items of information of an active job that will need to be stored in this structure.   (3)

(f)   Give **three** factors on which the transition from the *inactive list* to the *active list* depends.   (3)

(g)   Describe **two** different events that lead to the scheduler being called upon.   (2)

(h)   With reference to the *active list*, briefly explain the method of round robin scheduling.   (3)

AEB Paper 2 Qu 11 Specimen Paper for 2000

Chapter 49 – Memory, File and I/O Management

Memory management

The memory manager is primarily concerned with the allocation of the physical main memory to processes. No process may exist until a certain amount of main memory is allocated to it.

The objectives of memory management are:

• to allocate memory space to enable several processes to be executed concurrently;

• to protect processes from each other when executing concurrently;

• to enable sharing of memory space between processes when required;

• to provide a satisfactory level of performance;

• to make the addressing of memory space as transparent as possible to the programmer.

A process to be executed is loaded into main memory by a program called a **loader**, which may be one of two basic types:

• an **absolute loader**, which loads the program into a single fixed area of main memory. All address references in the program are fixed at translation time (when the program is assembled or compiled) and it will only work properly when loaded into one specific position in main memory.

• a **relocating loader** which can load the program anywhere in main memory because the program has been translated in such a way that all addresses are relative to the start of the program. The start address of the program can be held in a special register called the **base register**.

For an object program to be relocatable it must have been prepared with a translator which has been designed for the purpose.

There are two basic forms in which a relocatable object program can be prepared. For the first form, **static relocation**, once the object program has been loaded into main memory relocatability is lost and the process cannot be moved again. For the second form, **dynamic relocation**, relocatability is retained and a process may be moved to a different memory area during its execution (essential in a multi-programming set-up where programs are constantly being swapped in and out of main memory). This is made possible by not replacing any logical address references with physical addresses. The logical to physical mapping is done at run time by the hardware Memory Management Unit (MMU) using **base register addressing**.

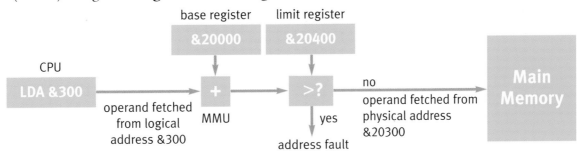

Figure 49.1: Logical vs Physical addresses

Another register called the **limit register** holds the highest addressable location of the process, and this enables the memory manager to protect other programs' memory space from being accidentally addressed by program error.

Virtual memory and paging

Virtual memory: memory on hard disk where pages of program and data of currently running processes are stored temporarily.

In early multiprogramming systems, the whole of an executing program had to be loaded into main memory. The amount of available main memory limited the number of programs that could be run concurrently. Virtual memory management is a technique for making a computer appear to have more main memory than it actually has. Main memory (physical memory) is divided into fixed size blocks (typically 4K), called **frames**. Each process (logical memory) is divided into blocks of the same size, called **pages**. Pages of processes are stored in a special area on disk (the virtual memory). When a process is to be executed, only the pages that are immediately required are loaded into main memory. If necessary, pages of another process are 'swapped' out onto disk to make room for the new pages. Program pages are loaded when in demand and unloaded when not.

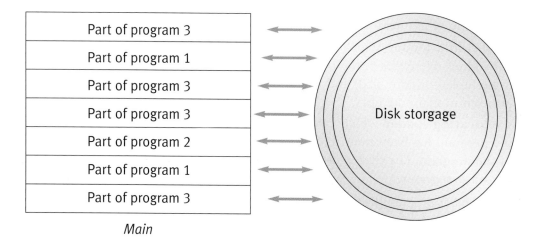

Figure 49.2: Virtual memory

Each process has a corresponding **page management table (PMT)** which indicates whether a particular page of the process is loaded or not, and which page-frame it is occupying in memory.

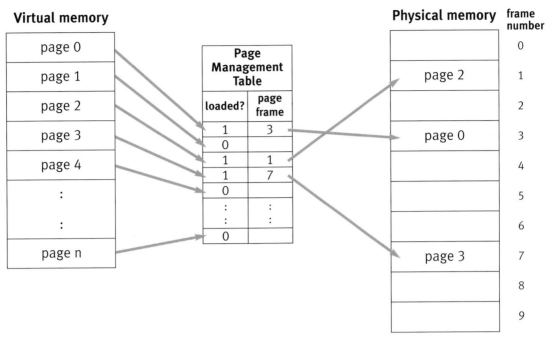

Figure 49.3: Paged Virtual Memory

An address of a location in a program takes the form (p,d)

where   p is the number of the page containing the location and

                 d is the displacement or offset of the location from the start of the page.

This allows processes to be **relocatable**; the displacement from the start of a page remains the same wherever the page is. The MMU uses p as an index into the page-management table to obtain the page-frame address.

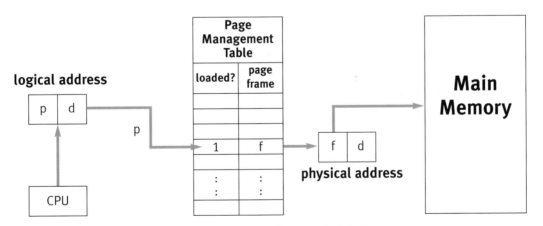

Figure 49.4: MMU changes logical address into physical address

As more processes enter the system, the number of frames allocated to each process can get very small. At some point one process needs more frames, so takes them from other processes. These processes need those pages, so load them back in again. This rapid up-loading and down-loading of pages is known as **thrashing**. You can recognize this by a very high rate of disk access.

Dynamically linked libraries

A library is a collection of subprograms used to develop software. Libraries are distinguished from executables in that they are not independent programs. Library linking means including one or more of these software libraries into a new program. This can be done at compile time (static linking) or at load or run time (dynamic linking). Virtually all programs depend on libraries to execute. Using dynamically linked libraries means the library can be updated and all programs using that library will use the new version. In most cases multiple applications can use the same copy of the library at the same time and there is no need for the operating system to load multiple instances of the library into memory concurrently.

For example, all the Microsoft Office programs require the Print function, and use it in the same way. It would be wasteful to include the code for printing in all the programs in the Office suite separately. Instead, this code is included in a DLL file, which can be called by any program requiring access to the printer.

Another advantage of the use of DLLs is that the code for printing does not need to be loaded into the computer memory when the main program is loaded. Instead, it can be loaded whilst the printing function is being executed and unloaded subsequently. This makes the operation of the program more efficient, as more of the resources are available for active processes more of the time.

4-49

Dynamic link library (DLL): a pre-compiled and linked executable file, which is stored separately on the computer's hard disk. It is loaded only when needed by an application (at run time, not compile time).

Parameters may be required to be passed to or by the DLL according to the required function definition. If a call to a DLL is made incorrectly, for example by passing the wrong number of parameters, then a General Protection Fault (GPF) will occur.

File management

The file management part of an operating system has four basic functions:

- To allocate space on the storage device to hold each file stored, and to deallocate space when a file is deleted. Space is usually divided into fixed size *allocation units* (**addressable blocks**) of say 512 or 1024 bytes.

- To keep track of the allocation units occupied by each file. Files may be split over several allocation units, not necessarily contiguous (i.e. together). A file may initially occupy one unit of 512 bytes, and then when updated by a user, need extra space which may have to be found somewhere else on the disk.

- To control file access rights and permissions (see Chapter 24).

- To map logical file addresses to physical disk addresses. For example, a physical disk may be split into several logical drives C, D, E, F, G.

A disk is divided into partitions or logical drives (known as volumes in NTFS). In the FAT file system each partition is divided into clusters (4 Kbytes), each of which can be one or more sectors. Each cluster is either allocated to a file or directory or it is free. A directory lists the name, size and starting cluster of each file or subdirectory it contains. At the start of the partition is a table called the **File Allocation Table** (FAT), which details the contents and status of each addressable block on the disk. The FAT is also stored on disk. The first few clusters after the FAT contain the root directory.

Blocks and buffers

Data is always transferred to and from disk in units of the physical block size of the disk – say 512 bytes. If the first 100 bytes of a file are requested by a program, the operating system reads the whole block of 512 bytes into a file buffer in memory and the 100 bytes requested are extracted from the buffer. Similarly, when data is written, it is assembled in the file buffer and written when a complete block is ready or when the file is closed. This process minimizes the number of disk transfers at the expense of a small amount of memory space and some extra processing complexity.

Input/Output management

The computer communicates with I/O devices by means of an I/O bus system. Each I/O device has an associated hardware controller unit attached to this bus system which can transmit data to, or receive data from, main memory. Each device attached to the bus has its own address which is used to identify it. A system of interrupts is used to enable each I/O device to transfer data independently of the processor. The device sends an interrupt signal to the processor when it has completed its task, and the processor then initiates a further data transfer if required.

The device controller provides a hardware interface between the computer and the I/O device. The controller connects to the computer bus and is designed for a particular computer system but conforms in interface terms with the requirements of the I/O device. If it were not for the controller, different I/O devices would be required for each different type of computer.

Device drivers

A device driver is a software module which manages the communication with a specific I/O device. The driver converts an I/O request from the user into specific commands to the device. For example, a request from the user to 'save a file' onto a disk will be translated by the device driver into a series of actions such as checking for the presence of the disk, locating the space for the file, positioning the read-write heads etc. Each different type of device needs a corresponding device driver.

Interrupt handling

All of the state changes described above are *interrupt-driven*. An **interrupt** is a signal generated by an event which requires the attention of the processor. When the operating system is ready to service the interrupt, the operating system saves the state of the interrupted process and passes control to the appropriate routine.

An interrupt may be initiated by the currently running process (perhaps it has some data to output, for example), or it may be caused by some event which may or may not be related to the currently running process.

Types of interrupt

The following different types of interrupt may occur:

- **interrupts generated by the running process**. The process might need to perform I/O, obtain more storage or communicate with the operator.

- **I/O interrupts**. These are initiated by the I/O hardware and signal to the CPU that the status of a channel or device has changed. An I/O interrupt will occur when an I/O operation is complete, when an error occurs, or when a device is made ready.

- **Timer interrupts**. These are generated by a timer within the processor, and allow the operating system to perform certain functions at regular intervals. For example, each user in a multi-user system may be allocated a certain amount of processor time before a timer interrupt is generated and control of the processor passes to the next user in turn.

- **Program check interrupts**. These are caused by various types of error such as division by zero.

- **Machine check interrupts**. These are caused by malfunctioning hardware.

How the interrupt mechanism works

There is a special register in the CPU called the interrupt register. At the beginning of each fetch-execute cycle, the interrupt register is checked. Each bit of the register represents a different type of interrupt, and if a bit is set, the state of the current process is saved and the OS routes control to the appropriate interrupt handler.

Since more than one device may request an interrupt simultaneously, each device is assigned a priority. Slow-speed devices such as terminals and printers are given a high priority, since they are more liable to get behind with what they are doing, and so should be allowed to start as soon as possible so that they do not eventually hold up processing.

In some cases if an interrupt occurs during data transfer, some data could be lost, and so the OS will **disable** other interrupts until it completes its task.

In a large multi-user system there is a constant stream of interrupts directed at the processor, and it must respond as quickly as possible to these in order to provide an acceptable response time. Once an interrupt is received, the OS disables interrupts while it deals with the current interrupt. Since this could mean that interrupts are disabled for a large proportion of the time, the nucleus (i.e. the part of the OS that is always in main memory) on large systems simply determines the cause of the interrupt and then passes the problem over to the specific interrupt handler, leaving itself free to deal with the next interrupt.

A special register called the PSW (program status word) indicates the types of interrupts currently **enabled** and those currently **disabled**. The CPU allows enabled interrupts to occur; disabled interrupts remain pending, or in some cases are ignored.

In smaller systems, the OS handles all interrupts itself, which means that the interrupts are disabled for a larger proportion of time.

Example:

Program A is the currently running process. It needs to retrieve some data from disk, so an interrupt is generated. The interrupt handler changes the status of A to 'blocked', makes a request to the disk drive for data, and invokes a program called the **dispatcher** which selects Job B to run next. After a while, the disk drive has filled the buffer area and generates an interrupt to say it is ready. The interrupt handler is invoked, and changes the status of program A from 'blocked' to 'runnable', but B is left running. One millisecond later B's time up is called by the interrupting clock and the dispatcher hands the CPU back to A, leaving B's status as 'runnable'.

Exercises

1 (a) A process is a program whose execution has started but not yet finished. Give two reasons why a process might not execute continuously in a multi-programming environment. (2)

 (b) Distinguish between *processes* and *threads* in a multi-programming environment. (2)

AQA CPT4 Qu 5 June 2003

Module 5

Advanced Systems Development

In this section:

5

Chapter 50 – Database Concepts

Traditional file approach

Most organisations began information processing on a small scale, buying a computer for perhaps one or two individual applications, and then computerising other departments one by one. Applications were developed independently, and files of information relevant to one particular department were created and processed by dozens or even hundreds of separate programs. This situation led to several problems.

- **Data redundancy.** The same data was duplicated in many different files. For example, details of a salesperson's name, address and pay rate might be held on a payroll file for calculating the payroll. The same data may be held on a file in the Personnel department along with a lot of other personal data, and in the Sales Department which has a program to keep track of each salesman's record and performance.

- **Data inconsistency.** When the same items of data are held in several different files, the data has to be updated in each separate file when it changes. The Payroll Department, for example, may change the commission rates paid to sales staff but the Sales Department file may fail to update its files and so be producing reports calculated with out-of-date figures.

- **Program-data dependence.** Every computer program in each department has to specify exactly what data fields constitute a record in the file being processed. Any change to the format of the data fields – for example, adding a new field or changing the length of a field – means that every program which uses that file has to be changed, since the file format is specified within each program.

- **Lack of flexibility.** In such a system, when information of a non-routine nature is needed, it can take weeks to assemble the data from the various files and write new programs to produce the required reports.

- **Data was not shareable.** If one department had data that was required by another department, it was awkward to obtain it. A second copy of the file could be made, but this would obviously soon lead to problems of inconsistency. If the same file was used, it would almost certainly be necessary to add extra fields for the new application, and that would mean the original programs would have to be changed to reflect the new file structure.

The database approach

In an attempt to solve these problems, the concept of a database was born.

Database: a collection of non-redundant data shareable between different applications.

All the data belonging to the entire organisation would be centralised in a common pool of data, accessible by all applications. This solved the problems of redundancy and inconsistency, but two major problems remained to be addressed.

- **Unproductive maintenance.** Programs were still dependent on the structure of the data, so that when one department needed to add a new field to a particular file, all other programs accessing that file had to be changed.

- **Lack of security.** All the data in the database, even confidential or commercially sensitive data, was accessible by all applications.

Database Management Systems (DBMSs) are used to improve security and eliminate unproductive maintenance, as explained below.

The Database Management System (DBMS)

DBMS: software used to control access to the data.

Two essential features of the DBMS are:

- Program-data independence, whereby the storage structure of the data is hidden from each application/user;
- Restricted user access to the data – each user is given a limited view of the data according to need.

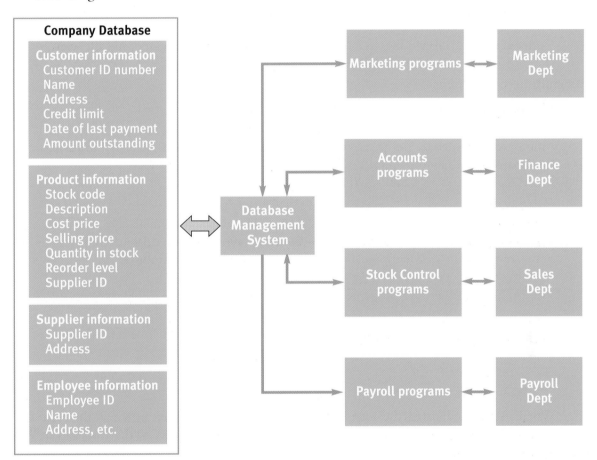

Figure 50.1: The DBMS acts as an interface between application programs and data

The three-level architecture of a DBMS

A database may be considered from several different levels or 'views' known as **schema.** The three levels of schema are:

1 **External** or **user schema.** This is the individual's view of the database – in a multi-user database, there will generally be several different external schema representing each user's view according to their needs and access rights.

2 **Conceptual** or **logical schema.** The overall view of the entire database, including entities, attributes and relationships, as designed by the database designer.

3 **Internal** or **storage schema.** This describes how the data will be stored and is concerned with file organisation and access methods. It is generally transparent to the user.

The DBMS provides an interface between the operating system and the user in order to make access to the data as simple as possible. It has several other functions as well, and these are described below.

1 **Data storage, retrieval and update.** The DBMS must allow users to store, retrieve and update information as easily as possible, without having to be aware of the internal structure of the database.

2 **Creation and maintenance of the data dictionary.**

3 **Managing the facilities for sharing the database.** The DBMS has to ensure that problems do not arise when two people simultaneously access a record and try to update it.

4 **Backup and recovery.** The DBMS must provide the ability to recover the database in the event of system failure.

5 **Security.** The DBMS must handle password allocation and checking, and the 'view' of the database that a given user is allowed.

The multi-access database

Many organisations have database software installed on a shared drive (file server) on a local area network. This means that:

• more than one person can use the actual **program (such as MS Access, Paradox, FoxPro etc)** at the same time;

• users can work with **databases (customised applications)** which are stored on the shared drive, as well as with tables stored on their local workstation hard drives.

If the database is appropriately configured, more than one person will be able to open it at the same time, and be able to view and update the same tables and other database objects **concurrently.** This is what is meant by the term **multi-access database.**

> **Q1:** Can you foresee any potential problems that may arise with a multi-access database?

Ensuring the integrity of a shared database

'Ensuring the integrity' means making sure that no data is accidentally lost or corrupted. For example, allowing multiple users to simultaneously update a database table may cause one of the updates to be lost unless measures are taken to prevent this.

When an item is updated, the entire record (indeed the whole **block** in which the record is physically held) will be copied into the user's own local memory area at the workstation. When the record is saved, the block is rewritten to the file server. Imagine the following situation:

> User A accesses a customer record, thereby causing it to be copied into the memory at his/her workstation, and starts to type in a new address for the customer.
>
> User B accesses the same customer record, and alters the credit limit and then saves the record and calls up the next record that needs updating.
>
> User A completes the address change, and saves the record.

> **Q2:** What state will the record be in? (i.e. which address and credit limit will it hold?)

Locking

All multi-user database programs offer several ways of avoiding the type of conflict described above.

1 **Open the entire database in exclusive mode,** which prohibits all simultaneous access. This option is impractical when several users need to access the database, but it will give the fastest performance, because the software does not have to check for potential conflicts.

It could be used, for example, on an overnight run to perform a time-consuming analysis and report, locking out the occasional stressed-out worker who has come in after hours to catch up on some work.

2 **Lock all records in the table being modified.** Once the first user opens the table, the software will prevent any other user from opening the same table in any view that would allow updating (but still allow it to be opened in read-only mode). This is usually unnecessarily restrictive and may prevent other users from getting on with routine tasks.

3 **Lock the record currently being edited.** The moment the first user begins typing changes, the record will be automatically locked by the database software so that no one else may update it. A user who attempts to do so will be presented with a warning message on screen.

4 **The user specifies no locks.** It is then up to the software to ensure that the users are aware of the situation when a record is being simultaneously updated from two or more workstations, and it is up to the users to resolve the conflict.

5 **Open a table in Read Only mode.** If you do not need to update a table, but simply need to look up a record or print a report, you can avoid conflict by opening the table in Read Only mode.

Deadlock... or 'Deadly embrace'

If two users are attempting to update two related records in the same table, a situation can arise in which neither can proceed.

User1	User2
locks record1	locks record2
tries to access record2	tries to access record1
waits ..	waits ..

DEADLOCK!

The DBMS must recognise when this situation has occurred and take action. One of the two user's tasks must be aborted to allow the other to proceed. Another strategy would be to ensure that in a situation where two records are modified, the records are always updated in the same sequence so that no user calls up record 2 before record 1.

Software protection techniques

There are several ways in which a DBMS can control who has access to particular information. A typical security system will allow the Database Administrator to allocate individual users to named groups of one or more, and assign each group a set of **permissions** or **privileges.** The permissions determine whether a given user can view, modify, execute or update a particular object in a database.

Each user will be identified by a name (e.g. **K.Smith**, or **Accounts Group**), assigned by the Database Administrator. Each individual user will then have a password which he or she can and should change regularly. Using passwords, users are allowed access to the entire database or subsets of the database, called subschemas. For example, an employee database can contain all the data about an individual employee, but one group of users may be authorised to view only payroll data, while others are allowed access to only view employment history and contact details.

If an individual forgets their password, the Database Administrator can reset it. If the Administrator forgets **his/her** password, he/she will never again gain access to the database.

The database may be encrypted, for example in MS Access by selecting the **Encrypt** option from the File menu. All information regarding user groups and passwords is automatically encrypted and stored on a separate database to prevent anyone gaining information about user IDs or passwords.

Open systems and ODBC (Open Database Connectivity)

Open systems provide a standard to which applications may be written to allow portability to multiple systems. *Portability is the key*. Portability enables data to be transferred from one system to another. ODBC is a standard for accessing different database systems.

An ODBC interface provides a means of accessing data held in one type of database (such as Access, Oracle or SQL Server) from say, a Visual Basic or Delphi program or from another database or spreadsheet. The data source may be any file for which an ODBC driver is available – the ODBC driver translates ODBC requests into the correct format for a particular data source. The underlying principle is to provide a layer of software that reconciles the differences between the client and the server such that a client program written using ODBC will be able to communicate unchanged with any ODBC-compliant server.

This facility is extremely useful in many circumstances. For example, an Examination Board may use an Oracle database to store grades for all subjects taken by all students. Individual centres (schools or colleges) may not have the facility to access an Oracle database but using ODBC, the Exam Board can store the results for any centre in, say, an Excel spreadsheet which can then be electronically transmitted to the centre. The school or college administration can then manipulate this data in any way to produce a variety of reports and statistics relevant to their centre.

ADO components in Delphi allow us to connect to a MS Access Database using the ODBC standard. This means we can write programs that use an Access database to store data and the end user running the compiled Delphi program does not need to have Access installed on their machine to access this data.

Client-server database

Many modern database management systems provide an option for **client–server** operation. Using a client-server DBMS, **DBMS server software** runs on the network server, and **DBMS client software** runs on individual workstations. The server software processes requests for data searches, sorts and reports that originate from individual workstations running DBMS client software. For example, a car dealer might want to search the manufacturer's database to find out whether there are any cars of a particular specification available. The DBMS client refers this request to the DBMS server, which searches for the information and sends it back to the client workstation. Once the information is at the workstation, the dealer can sort the list and produce a customised report. If the DBMS did not have client-server capability, the entire database would be copied to the workstation and software held on the workstation would search for the requested data – involving a large amount of time being spent on transmitting irrelevant data and probably a longer search using a less powerful machine.

The advantages of a client-server database are, therefore:

- an expensive resource (powerful computer and large database) can be made available to a large number of users;
- client stations can, if authorised, update the database rather than just view the data;
- the consistency of the database is maintained because only one copy of the data is held (on the server) rather than a copy at each workstation;
- the database processing is normally carried out by the server, with the query being sent by a client station to the server and the results assembled by the server and returned to the client station;
- communication time between client and server is minimised because only the results of a query, not the entire database, is transmitted between the server and client;
- relevant programs and report formats can be held on client workstations and customised for a particular department.

Sage Accounting software, for example, has a client-server version. The Server Network Installation procedure installs the software and data files on the server. The Client version of the software is then installed at each workstation. Report formats for Stock, Invoices, Customers etc. can be stored locally on the relevant client workstations where they can be customised and altered. Each client workstation is allocated access rights to particular files on the database; it may be possible for example to view stock levels, but not alter them from one workstation ('read-only access'), to make stock adjustments from another workstation ('read-write access'), or have no access at all to Customer account records from, say, a workstation in the warehouse.

Object-oriented databases

Conventional DBMSs were designed for homogeneous data that can be easily structured into predefined data fields and records. Many applications today, however, require databases that can store and retrieve not only structured numbers and characters but also drawings, images, photographs, voice and full-motion video. For example a patient database might need to store not only information on name, address, test results and diagnosis but also X-ray images. Conventional DBMSs are not well-suited to handling graphics-based or multimedia applications. An object-oriented database stores the data and methods as objects that can be automatically retrieved and shared.

Object-oriented Database: offers DBMS facilities with object-oriented programming. Data stored as objects can only be interpreted using the methods specified by its class.

5-50

Exercises

1   Distinguish between a database and a database management system (DBMS).   (2)

    What is meant by unproductive maintenance in the contect of a database?   (1)

    What is meant by program-data independence in the context of a DBMS?   (2)

                                                                     New Question

2   (i)   What is meant by ODBC (Open Database Connectivity)?   (2)

    (ii) Describe one situation in which ODBC might be used.   (2)

                                                                     New Question

3   What are Object-Oriented Databases and why are they needed?   (3)

                                                                     New Question

4   A mail order company has a multi-user centralised database to allow its employees to process orders and deal with customer enquiries as they come in to the customer service department.

    (a)   (i) Explain why different staff will have passwords allowing them different levels of access to the data stored.   (2)

          (ii) Give two other reasons why passwords would be used for this type of system.   (2)

    (b)   A record within the main stock file is locked whenever one person is making changes to it.

          (i) Briefly explain what is meant by the term locked.   (1)

          (ii) Why is it necessary in this case to lock records?   (2)

                                                                     NEAB CP05 Qu 10 1998

Chapter 51 – Database Design and Normalisation

Entity-relationship modelling

Refer back to Chapter 22 for a discussion of entity-relationship modelling. This lays the foundation for the normalisation techniques covered in this chapter. You should also revise Chapter 23 (Database Concepts) before going on!

What is a relational database?

There are several different types of Database Management System available. The most common type of DBMS is the **relational database**, widely used on all systems from micros to mainframes. In a relational database, data is held in tables (also called relations) and the tables are linked by means of common attributes.

Relational Database: a collection of tables in which relationships are modelled by shared attributes.

Linking database tables

Tables may be linked through the use of a common attribute. This attribute must be the primary key of one of the tables, and is known as a **foreign key** in the second table. An example best illustrates this.

In a library database, two entities named **Book** and **Borrower** have been identified. An entity-relationship diagram may be used to describe the relationship between these two entities.

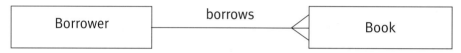

Figure 51.1: One-to-many relationship between Borrower and Book

The **Borrower** and **Book** tables can be described using standard notation as follows:

Borrower (<u>BorrowerID</u>, Name, Address)

Book (<u>AccessionNumber</u>, DeweyCode, Title, Author, DatePublished, *BorrowerID*, DateDue)

In practice, since only a very small proportion of books are on loan at any one time, it would be sensible to have a third table holding data about books on loan, who had borrowed them and when they were due back. The three tables would then look like this:

Borrower (<u>BorrowerID</u>, Name, Address)

Book (<u>AccessionNumber</u>, DeweyCode, Title, Author, DatePublished)

Loan (<u>AccessionNumber</u>, *BorrowerID*, DateDue)

The entity-relationship diagram would then look like this:

Figure 51.2: Entity-relationship diagram for a library database

Q1: The model above assumes that the Loan record will be deleted when a book is returned. If this is not going to be done, what adjustments will have to be made to the entity-relationship diagram and Loan table?

Normalisation

Normalisation is a process used to come up with the best possible design for a relational database. Tables should be organised in such a way that:

• no data is unnecessarily duplicated (i.e. the same data item held in more than one table);

• data is consistent throughout the database (e.g. Mr Bradley's address is not recorded as The White House, Sproughton on one table and as 32 Star Lane in another. Consistency should be an automatic consequence of not holding any duplicated data.);

• the structure of each table is flexible enough to allow you to enter as many or as few items (for example, books borrowed by a particular person) as required;

• the structure should enable a user to make all kinds of complex queries relating data from different tables.

• We will look at three stages of normalisation known as first, second and third normal form.

First normal form

A table is in first normal form (1NF) if it contains no repeating attribute or groups of attributes.

Let's look at a simple example of two entities Student and Course. A student can take several courses, and each course has several students attending. The relationship can be represented by the entity–relationship diagram shown below:

Figure 51.3: The many-to-many relationship between entities Student and Course

Sample data to be held in the database is shown in the table below:

Student

Student Number	Student Name	DateOf Birth	Gender	Course Number	Course Name	Lecturer Number	Lecturer Name
12345	Heathcote,R	20-08-83	M	EC6654	A-Level Computing	T345267	Glover,T
22433	Head,J	13-02-83	F	EC6654	A-Level Computing	T345267	Glover,T
				HM7756	A-Level Music	T773351	Reader,B
				AD1121	Pottery	T876541	Day,S
66688	Hargrave,R	13-09-54	M	BM3390	HNC Business	T666758	Newman,P
				HM7756	A-Level Music	T773351	Reader,B

5-51

The two tables **Student** and **Course** will be represented in standard notation as

Student (<u>StudentNumber</u>, StudentName, DateOfBirth, Gender)

Course (<u>CourseNumber</u>, CourseName, LecturerNumber, LecturerName)

The question now is, how can the relationship between these two tables be shown? How can we hold the information about which students are doing which courses?

The two tables need to be linked by means of a common attribute, but the problem is that because this is a many-to-many relationship, whichever table we put the link attribute into, there needs to be *more than one* attribute.

e.g.**Student** (<u>StudentNumber</u>, StudentName, DateOfBirth, Gender, CourseNumber)

is no good because the student is doing several courses, so which one would be mentioned?

Similarly,

Course (<u>CourseNumber</u>, CourseName, LecturerNumber,LecturerName,StudentNumber)

is no good either because each course has a number of students taking it.

One obvious solution (and unfortunately a bad one) springs to mind. How about allowing space for 3 courses on each student record?

Student (<u>StudentNumber</u>, StudentName, DateOfBirth, Gender, Course1, Course2, Course3)

Q2: Why is this not a good idea?

What we have engineered is a repeating attribute – anathema in 1st normal form. In other words, the attribute CourseNumber is repeated 3 times. The table is therefore NOT in first normal form.

It would be represented in standard notation with a line over the repeating attribute:

Student (<u>StudentNumber</u>, StudentName, DateOfBirth, Gender, $\overline{\text{CourseNumber}}$)

To put the data into first normal form, the repeating attribute must be removed. In its place, the attribute CourseNumber becomes part of the primary key in the student table. The tables are now as follows:

Student (<u>StudentNumber</u>, StudentName, DateOfBirth, Gender, <u>CourseNumber</u>)

Course (<u>CourseNumber</u>, CourseName, LecturerNumber, LecturerName)

Q3: What is a primary key? Why does course number have to be part of the primary key?

The two tables **Student** and **Course**, now in first normal form, look like this:

Student

Student Number	Student Name	DateOf Birth	Gender	Course Number
12345	Heathcote,R	20-08-83	M	EC6654
22433	Head,J	13-02-83	F	EC6654
22433	Head,J	13-02-83	F	HM7756
22433	Head,J	13-02-83	F	AD1121
66688	Hargave,R	13-09-54	M	BM3390
66688	Hargave,R	13-09-54	M	HM7756

Course

Course Number	Course Name	Lecturer Number	Lecturer Name
EC6654	A-Level Computing	T345267	Glover,T
HM7756	A-Level Music	T773351	Reader,B
AD1121	Pottery	T876541	Day,S
BM3390	HNC Business	T666758	Newman,P

Q4: Why is this a better way of holding the data than having one table with the following structure?

Student (<u>StudentNumber</u>, StudentName, DateOfBirth, Sex, Course1, Course2, Course3)

Q5: If student Head, J decides to take up A-Level Art, what changes need to be made to the table structure in Q4?

Q6: How will we find the names of all students doing A-Level Computing?

Q7: What are the weaknesses of the two-table structure illustrated above, with tables **Student** and **Course**?

Second normal form - Partial key dependence test

A table is in second normal form (2NF) if it is in first normal form and contains no partial dependencies.

This means that any non-primary key attribute that depends only on part of the primary key is moved to a separate table.

The tables above are not in second normal form. For example, StudentName is dependent only on StudentNumber and not on CourseNumber. To put the tables into second normal form, we need to introduce a third table that acts as a link between the entities Student and Course.

The tables are now as follows:

Student (<u>StudentNumber</u>, StudentName, DateOfBirth, Gender)

StudentTakes(<u>StudentNumber</u>, <u>CourseNumber</u>)

Course (<u>CourseNumber</u>, CourseName, LecturerNumber, LecturerName)

Dealing with a Many-to-Many relationship

As you get more practice in database design, you will notice that whenever two entities have a many-to-many relationship, you will *always* need a link table 'in the middle'. Thus

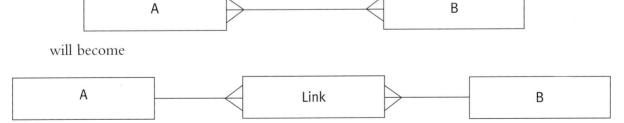

will become

Figure 51.4: A 'link' table is needed in a many-to-many relationship

Third normal form - Non-key dependence test

A table is in third normal form (3NF) if it is in second normal form and contains no 'non-key dependencies'.

Looking at the **Course** table, the lecturer name is dependent on the lecturer number, not on the course number. It therefore needs to be removed from this relation and a new relation created:

Lecturer (<u>LecturerNumber</u>, LecturerName)

The database, now in third normal form, consists of the following tables:

Student (<u>StudentNumber</u>, StudentName, DateOfBirth, Gender)

StudentTakes (<u>StudentNumber</u>, <u>CourseNumber</u>)

Course (<u>CourseNumber</u>, CourseName, LecturerNumber)

Lecturer (<u>LecturerNumber</u>, LecturerName)

Boyce-Codd Normal Form (BCNF)

A table is in BCNF if and only if every determinant in the relation is a candidate key.

A **determinant** is an attribute on which some other attribute is fully functionally dependent.

A **candidate key** is an attribute or combination of attributes that have the property of uniqueness and minimality. Such a key distinguishes one row of a table from another.

A relation may have more than one candidate key. One is chosen as the **primary key** and the others are **alternate keys.**

Informally, this can be worded as:

When a table is in BCNF, every attribute which is not part of the primary key, is a fact about the key, the whole key and nothing but the key ("so help me Codd").

For a relation with only one candidate key 3NF and BCNF are equivalent.

Foreign keys

Foreign keys are created in the process of creating a join between two tables. A foreign key is an attribute that is common to both tables; in one table it is the primary key and in the other it is the foreign key. It is usually shown in italics. If a table has two foreign keys, it is joined to two other tables.

Foreign key: an attribute in one table that is a primary key in another table.

In the tables above, **StudentTakes** has two foreign keys, StudentNumber (the primary key of **Student**) and CourseNumber (the primary key of **Course**). It may be written thus:

StudentTakes (*<u>StudentNumber</u>*, *<u>CourseNumber</u>*)

Q8: Which other table has a foreign key? What is it?

Exercises

1 The data requirements for a league of cross-country running clubs are defined as follows.

The league consists of a number of participating clubs whose runners race against each other in a series of races held throughout the season. The league secretary is responsible for recording data about clubs, races, race entries, race results and club league points.

Each race has a race identification number, date, start time, distance covered and venue recorded. Runners from different clubs compete in each race. Each club has its name (unique) and the name, address and telephone number of its results secretary recorded. On receipt of a race entry form from a club, the league secretary assigns each listed runner a competitor identification number in the range one to one hundred and their name and club name are recorded. This competitor identification number applies to that particular race only. A competitor's race time and position are recorded after each race. The points a club scores for each race are computed from the positions of its runners and recorded.

(a) Four entities for the league are Club, Race, ClubRacePoints and RaceCompetitor. Draw an entity-relationship diagram which shows four relationships involving the entities Club, Race, ClubRacePoints and RaceCompetitor that can be inferred from the given data requirements. (4)

(b) A relational database is to be used. Using the following format

TableName(<u>Attribute1</u>, Attribute2, Attribute3, etc)

describe tables, stating all attributes, for the following entities underlining the primary key in each case. **These are the only tables that are used**.

(i) Race (2)

(ii) Club (2)

(iii) RaceCompetitor (4)

(iv) ClubRacePoints (3)

(c) It is required to print out in race position order the results for a given race. The results are to consist of the competitor's name, club name, race position and race time. Using a query language, show how the required data may be extracted from the relevant table(s) in (b). (5)

AEB Paper 3 Qu 10 1998

Chapter 52 – Querying a Database

SQL

Although it is possible to extract a great deal of information from a database such as Access using Query by Example, there are occasions when complex queries cannot be formulated using this technique. This is when you need SQL, or Structured Query Language – pronounced either as S-Q-L or Sequel. SQL is a declarative language concerned with 'what' rather than 'how'. The major use of SQL is concerned with querying, but it is also possible to use SQL to perform other operations such as creating tables. SQL is the industry standard supported by all significant relational databases.

The part of the language concerned with asking questions of a database comprises the Data Manipulation Language (DML) statements of SQL. DML statements are conventionally written in UPPERCASE.

The tables shown below will be used to demonstrate some SQL statements. The tables are part of a database used by a software company to keep track of customers who have bought various software packages that it produces. Each software package sold is uniquely identified by a software licence number. There is a one-to-many relationship between customers and software packages sold.

tblCustomer

CustomerID	CompanyName	Contact	Telephone
SEYMOUR	Seymour Glass	James Bolan	01354-543666
REDCABS	Red Cabs Ltd	Fred Gordon	0181-879965
SUPAG	Supa-Goods	Mavis Hunt	01202-888557
RENTA	Rent-A-Tool	Mark Wong	01473-212777
PRADESH	Pradesh & Co Ltd	Karl Pradesh	01763-396018

tblSoftware

LicenceNo	CustomerID	Package	Version	Price	ServiceAgreement	DateOfPurchase
1000	RENTA	Payroll	4.0	£550	Y	18/02/1999
1123	SEYMOUR	Accounts	6.1	£475	N	01/07/1999
2111	RENTA	Stock	2.0	£700	Y	13/07/1999
3456	SEYMOUR	Stock	2.0	£770	Y	06/11/1999
4870	REDCABS	Payroll	5.0	£620	Y	05/12/1999
5268	SUPAG	Stock	6.2	£900	N	14/02/2000
5381	REDCABS	Accounts	6.2	£520	Y	14/02/2000
6001	PRADESH	Payroll	5.0	£620	Y	
7114	RENTA	Accounts	6.2	£500	Y	17/03/2000

5-52

SELECT .. FROM .. WHERE

The SELECT statement is used to extract a collection of fields from a given table.

```
SELECT LicenceNo, CustomerID, Package, DateOfPurchase
FROM tblSoftware;
```

will produce the following Answer table:

LicenceNo	CustomerID	Package	DateOfPurchase
1000	RENTA	Payroll	18/02/1999
1123	SEYMOUR	Accounts	01/07/1999
2111	RENTA	Stock	13/07/1999
3456	SEYMOUR	Stock	06/11/1999
4870	REDCABS	Payroll	05/12/1999
5268	SUPAG	Stock	14/02/2000
5381	REDCABS	Accounts	14/02/2000
6001	PRADESH	Payroll	
7114	RENTA	Accounts	17/03/2000

SQL does not eliminate duplicates by default, so for example

```
SELECT CustomerID, ServiceAgreement
FROM tblSoftware;
```

will produce:

CustomerID	ServiceAgreement
RENTA	Y
SEYMOUR	N
RENTA	Y
SEYMOUR	Y
REDCABS	Y
SUPAG	N
REDCABS	Y
PRADESH	Y
RENTA	Y

You can force SQL to remove the duplicates by using the statement DISTINCT, which only displays distinct rows. Thus

```
SELECT DISTINCT CustomerID, ServiceAgreement
FROM tblSoftware;
```

will produce:

CustomerID	ServiceAgreement
RENTA	Y
SEYMOUR	N
SEYMOUR	Y
REDCABS	Y
SUPAG	N
PRADESH	Y

5-52

You can impose conditions on which records are found using the WHERE statement. Thus

```
SELECT LicenceNo, CustomerID, Package, ServiceAgreement
FROM tblSoftware
WHERE ServiceAgreement = "N";
```

will produce:

LicenceNo	CustomerID	Package	ServiceAgreement
1123	SEYMOUR	Accounts	N
5268	SUPAG	Stock	N

Conditions

Conditions in SQL are constructed from the following operators:

Symbol	Meaning	Example	Notes
=	Equal to	LicenceNo=1123	
>	Greater than	DateOfPurchase > #01/01/2000#	MS Access requires that the date is enclosed in # symbols.
<	Less than	DateOfPurchase < #01/01/2000#	
<>	Not equal to	Package <> "Payroll"	
>=	Greater than or equal to	DateOfPurchase >= #02/02/2000#	
<=	Less than or equal to	DateOfPurchase <= #31/12/1999#	
IN	Equal to a value within a set of values	Package IN ("Payroll", "Accounts")	
LIKE	Similar to	CustomerID LIKE "S*"	Finds SEYMOUR, SUPAG
BETWEEN...AND	Within a range, including the two values which define the limits	DateOfPurchase BETWEEN #01/01/2000# AND #31/12/2000#	
IS NULL	Field does not contain a value	DateOfPurchase IS NULL	
AND	Both expressions must be true for the entire expression to be judged true	Package = "Accounts" AND Version = 6.1	
OR	If either or both of the expressions are true, the entire expression is judged true	Package = "Accounts" OR Package = "Payroll"	Equivalent to Package IN ("Payroll", "Accounts")
NOT	Inverts truth	Package NOT IN ("Payroll", "Accounts")	

Q1: SQL statements are written in the format

```
SELECT *
FROM tblSoftware
WHERE condition
```

Which records will be found from tblSoftware using each of the condition examples given above? (Note that the * means 'Display all fields in the record'.)

Specifying a sort order

ORDER BY gives you control over the order in which records appear in the Answer table. If for example you want the records in the Answer table to be displayed in ascending order of CustomerID and within that, ascending order of Package, you would write, for example:

```
SELECT *
FROM tblSoftware
WHERE DateOfPurchase  BETWEEN  #01/01/1999# AND #28/02/2000#
ORDER BY CustomerID, Package;
```

This would produce the following Answer table:

Licence No	Customer ID	Package	Version	Price	ServiceAgreement	DateOfPurchase
5381	REDCABS	Accounts	6.2	£520	Y	14/02/2000
4870	REDCABS	Payroll	5.0	£620	Y	05/12/1999
1000	RENTA	Payroll	4.0	£550	Y	18/02/1999
2111	RENTA	Stock	2.0	£700	Y	13/07/1999
1123	SEYMOUR	Accounts	6.1	£475	N	01/07/1999
3456	SEYMOUR	Stock	2.0	£770	Y	06/11/1999
5268	SUPAG	Stock	6.2	£900	N	14/02/2000

Ascending sequence is the default sort order. If you wanted Package to be displayed in descending order rather than ascending order, you would write:

```
SELECT *
FROM tblSoftware
WHERE DateOfPurchase  BETWEEN  #01/01/1999# AND #28/02/2000#
ORDER BY CustomerID, Package DESC;
```

This would produce:

Licence No	Customer ID	Package	Version	Price	Service Agreement	Date Of Purchase
4870	REDCABS	Payroll	5.0	£620	Y	05/12/1999
5381	REDCABS	Accounts	6.2	£520	Y	14/02/2000
2111	RENTA	Stock	2.0	£700	Y	13/07/1999
1000	RENTA	Payroll	4.0	£550	Y	18/02/1999
3456	SEYMOUR	Stock	2.0	£770	Y	06/11/1999
1123	SEYMOUR	Accounts	6.1	£475	N	01/07/1999
5268	SUPAG	Stock	6.2	£900	N	14/02/2000

GROUP BY

The GROUP BY command is useful for finding sums and averages of values for one particular customer. For example, consider first the statement

```
SELECT SUM (Price) AS SumOfPrice
FROM tblSoftware
WHERE CustomerID = "REDCABS";
```

This would give the following table:

Sum Of Price
£1140

5-52

If you want to find the total amount spent by each customer, you can use the GROUP BY statement.

```
SELECT CustomerID, SUM(Price) AS SumOfPrice
FROM tblSoftware
Group by CustomerID;
```

This will give the following result:

CustomerID	SumOfPrice
PRADESH	£620
REDCABS	£1140
RENTA	£1750
SEYMOUR	£1245
SUPAG	£900

Extracting data from several tables

So far we have only taken data from one table. Using SQL you can easily combine data from two or more tables, by specifying which table the data is held in. For example, suppose you wanted to list the company name and contact, the licence number, name and date of purchase of each software package. You would write:

```
SELECT tblCustomer.CompanyName, tblCustomer.Contact,
    tblSoftware.LicenceNo,
    tblSoftware.Package, tblSoftware.DateOfPurchase
FROM tblCustomer, tblSoftware
WHERE tblCustomer.CustomerID = tblSoftware.CustomerID;
```

This will produce the following Answer table:

CompanyName	Contact	LicenceNo	Package	DateOfPurchase
Pradesh & Co Ltd	Karl Pradesh	6001	Payroll	
Red Cabs Ltd	Fred Gordon	4870	Payroll	05/12/1999
Red Cabs Ltd	Fred Gordon	5381	Accounts	14/02/2000
Rent-A-Tool	Mark Wong	1000	Payroll	18/02/1999
Rent-A-Tool	Mark Wong	2111	Stock	13/07/1999
Rent-A-Tool	Mark Wong	7114	Accounts	17/03/2000
Seymour Glass	James Bolan	1123	Accounts	01/07/1999
Seymour Glass	James Bolan	3456	Stock	06/11/1999
Supa-Goods	Mavis Hunt	5268	Stock	14/02/2000

Exercises

1 Customers placing orders with ABC Ltd for ABC's products have their orders recorded by ABC in a database.

The data requirements for the database system are defined as follows:

- Each product is assigned a unique product code, ProductId and has a product description.

- The quantity in stock of a particular product is recorded.

- Each customer is assigned a unique customer code, CustomerId and has their name, address and telephone number recorded.

- An order placed by a customer will be for one or more products.

- ABC Ltd assigns a unique code to each customer order, ABCOrderNo.
- A customer placing an order must supply a code, CustomerOrderNo, which the customer uses to identify the particular order.
- A customer may place one or more orders.
- Each new order from a particular customer will have a different customer order code but two different customers may use, independently, the same values of customer order code.
- Whether an order has been despatched or not will be recorded.
- A particular order will contain one or more lines.
- Each line is numbered, the first is one, the second is two, and so on.
- Each line will reference a specific product and specify the quantity ordered.
- A specific product reference will appear only once in any particular order placed with ABC Ltd.

After normalisation the database contains four tables based on the entities:

Customer, Product, Order, OrderLine

(a) **Figure 1** below is a partially complete entity-relationship diagram. Show the degree of **three** more relationships which exist between the given entities.

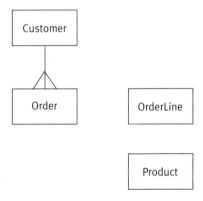

Figure 1   (3)

(b) Using the following format:
TableName(Primary Key, Non-key Attribute1, Non-key Attribute2, etc)
describe tables, stating all attributes, for the following entities underlining the primary key in each case.

    (i)   Product   (2)

    (ii) Customer   (2)

    (iii) Order   (3)

    (iv) OrderLine   (4)

(c) Using the SQL commands SELECT, FROM, WHERE, ORDER BY, write an SQL statement to query the database tables for all customer names where the orders have been despatched. The result of the query is to be ordered in ascending order of ABCOrderNo.   (6)

AQA CPT5 Qu 8 June 2002

Chapter 53 – Data Definition and Data Manipulation

Data Definition Language (DDL)

The database schema, including aspects such as 'who has access to which data', may be modelled by the Database Administrator (i.e. the person in charge of the database design and maintenance) using a special programming language called a **Data Definition Language (DDL)**. Using this language the logical structure and the files within the database may be defined. Attributes such as record layouts, fields, key fields and validations can all be described using a DDL. This provides an alternative to the way in which tables, forms, reports etc are normally created in a database such as Access.

DDL: a language to define the structure and instances of a database.

You can try the following examples by using the SQL view in MS Access to create queries which you can then run to test the DDL statements work.

Example:

A table named Employee, with four fields: EmpID (a compulsory int field which is the primary key), Name (a compulsory character field of length 10), HiredDate (an optional date field) and Salary (an optional currency field) can be created with the DDL statement:

```
CREATE TABLE Employee
(EmpID      INT NOT NULL PRIMARY KEY,
Name        VARCHAR(10) NOT NULL,
HiredDate   DATE,
Salary      CURRENCY)
```

You can add another field to an existing table with the DDL statement:

```
ALTER TABLE Employee
ADD Department VARCHAR(10)
```

You can create an index for a table using the statement:

```
CREATE INDEX NameIndex ON Employee(EmpID);
```

If you set up several tables, you can link tables by creating foreign keys:

```
CREATE TABLE Training
(EmpID INT NOT NULL,
CourseTitle VARCHAR(30) NOT NULL,
CourseDate Date NOT NULL,
PRIMARY KEY (EmpID, CourseDate),
FOREIGN KEY (EmpID) REFERENCES Employee(EmpID))
```

If you use Borland Interbase (free with Delphi) you can even create a database from scratch with the following DDL statement:

```
CREATE DATABASE 'Personnel.Gdb'  USER 'SZL' PASSWORD 'password'
```

Subschema can be set by the creator (owner) of the database to allow other users to have insert/update/delete access. The statement

```
GRANT <privileges> ON <table> TO <users>
```

sets such privileges.

For example:

```
GRANT DELETE, UPDATE(Salary) ON Employee TO PayrollOfficer
```

will allow the usergroup PayrollOfficer to delete records in the Employee table and update the salary field in the Employee table.

Data Manipulation Language (DML)

The DML provides a comprehensive set of commands to allow modification of the data within a database. Some facilities of the language (such as SQL statements) enable users to execute queries (see Chapter 52). Other facilities of a DML allow advanced users to write programs to carry out sophisticated processing of the database.

DML: a language for the manipulation of data in a database.

Example:

get a list of Employee names

```
SELECT Name FROM Employee
```

Example:

add a record for employee number 1122, Bloggs, who was hired on 1/1/2001 for the technical department at a salary of £18000.

```
INSERT INTO Employee (EmpID, Name, HireDate, Salary, Department)
VALUES ('1122', 'Bloggs', '1/1/2001', '18000', 'Technical')
```

Example:

increase all salaries of members of the Technical department by 10%

```
UPDATE Employee
SET Salary = Salary*1.1
WHERE Department = 'Technical'
```

Example:

delete the record for employee named Bloggs

```
DELETE FROM Employee
WHERE Name ='Bloggs'
```

Exercises

1 (a) (i) Explain the role of a Data Definition Language (DDL) in the context of a DBMS   (3)

(ii) Give two DDL commands that could be used in the formation of the structure of a database, including how to specify the data items to which each user has access.   (2)

(b) (i) Explain the role of a Data Manipulation Language (DML) in the context of a DBMS including how a DML is used to insert a record to an existing table.(3)

(ii) Explain why a programmer might choose to use an ODBC (Open Database Connectivity) compliant database.   (1)

New Question

5-53

Chapter 54 – Analysing a System

Systems investigation

The first stage in the Systems Life Cycle is the Problem Definition, followed by a feasibility study to determine whether a proposed solution is feasible, or achievable, given the organisation's resources and constraints.

Once the decision has been made to go ahead, a much more detailed investigation can take place. One of the most difficult tasks of the analyst is to define the specific information requirements that must be met by the new system. The aim is to gain a complete understanding of the existing system, and how it will change in the future. It will cover:

- the data – its origin, uses, volumes and characteristics;
- the procedures – what is done, where, when and how, and how errors and exceptions are handled;
- the future – development plans and expected growth rates;
- management reports – requirements for new reports and their contents and frequency;
- problems with the existing system.

Methods of fact finding

There are a number of ways of finding out about existing procedures and problems. These include:

- observation – spending some time in the department concerned, seeing at first hand the procedures used, workloads and bottlenecks;
- examination of paperwork - reading the documentation associated with the system;
- asking clerical staff to keep special counts during a trial period to establish where problems might lie;
- surveys/questionnaires – these can be useful when a lot of people will be affected by a new system;
- interviews – the most common and most useful way of fact finding. Interviews must be well planned and consideration given to such factors as:
  - whom to interview;
  - when to interview;
  - what to ask;
  - where to hold the interview.

Reporting techniques

The analyst may use different diagrammatic ways of reporting on the findings of the analysis. Data flow diagrams (DFDs) are a useful tool for showing:

- where the data originates;
- what processing is performed on it and by whom;
- who uses the data;
- what data is stored and where;
- what output is received and who uses it.

Data Flow Diagrams

The symbols used in DFDs are shown below:

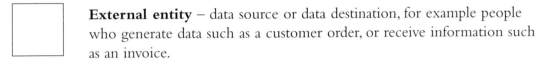

External entity – data source or data destination, for example people who generate data such as a customer order, or receive information such as an invoice.

Process – an operation performed on the data. The two lines are optional; the top section of the box can be used to label the process, the middle to give a brief explanation, the bottom to say where the process takes place. Make the first word an active verb – e.g. **validate** data, **adjust** stock level.

Data store – such as a file held on disk or tape.

Data flow – the arrow represents movement between entities, processes or data stores. The arrow should be labelled to describe what data is involved

Levelled DFDs

It is often impossible to represent a complete business system in a single diagram, so two or three levels of data flow diagrams may be used, each showing more detail.

Example 1:

The payroll system in a certain company may be described as follows:

At the end of each week, time sheets are collected and sent to the computer centre. There, the payroll data is entered via a key-to-disk system, verified and validated, producing a new file of valid transactions on disk and an error report. This file is used to update the employee master file, payslips are printed and funds are electronically transferred to employees' bank accounts.

Draw two levels of Data Flow Diagram, the top level showing a single process, and the second level showing the detailed system as described above.

Solution:

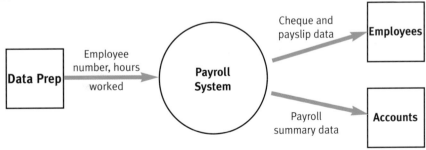

Figure 54.1: Context Diagram (Level zero DFD)

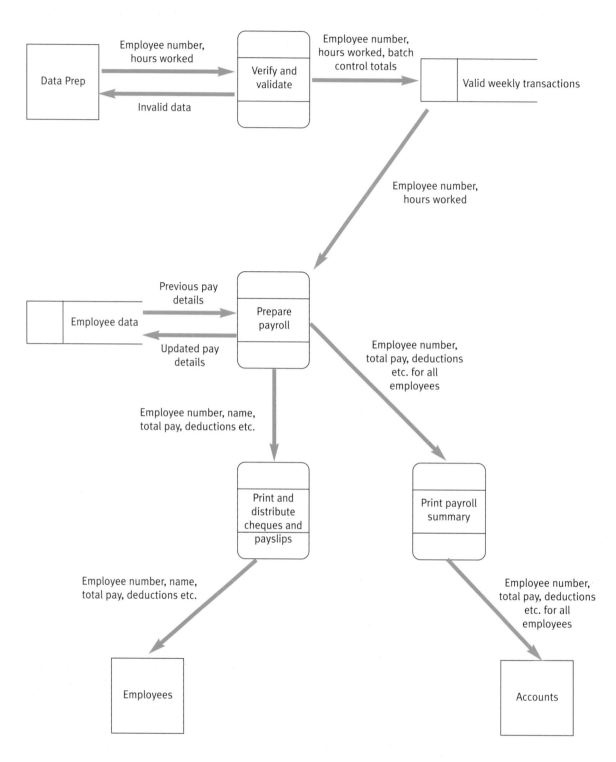

Figure 54.2: A level one data flow diagram

Example 2:

A student can register by mail for a college course by submitting a registration form with their name, ID number and the numbers of the courses they wish to take. The system verifies that the course is not full and enrolls the student on each course for which a place is still free. The course file and student master files are updated and a confirmation letter is sent to the student to notify them of their acceptance or rejection for each requested course.

Solution:

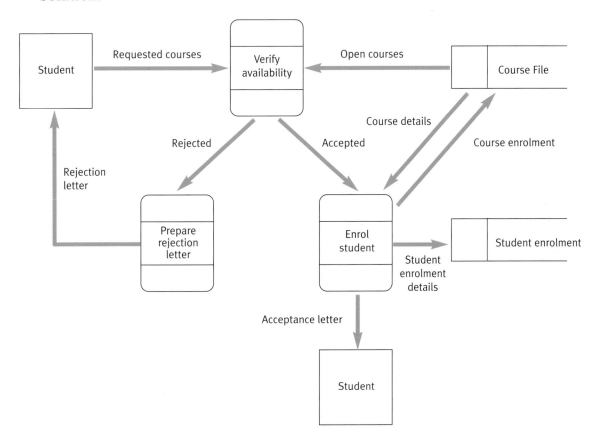

Figure 54.3: Data flow diagram for student registration

Entity Attribute Modelling

The system designer may produce a conceptual design identifying the various entities and attributes, and showing how these entities are related. This may then be documented in an Entity-Relationship diagram. These diagrams are covered in Chapter 22.

Data dictionary

The data dictionary is a table that stores data about data (meta data). It stores names of data items (fields or variables), data types, length, validation criteria and other characteristics such as usage, physical representation, ownership, authorisation and security. It will also show which programs or modules read or write the data.

Example of a data dictionary

Name	Data Type	Length	Validation	Example Data	Comment
SubjectRefCode	String	5 chars	5 digits, must exist	54821	Unique to each subject
CentreNo	Integer	4 bytes	10000 to 80000	12345	Unique to each centre
CandidateNo	String	4 chars	4 digits	2345	unique to each candidate **within** a centre
CandidateName	String	25 chars		BLOGGS, Joe Fred	Full name, Surname in capitals, other names after comma
OrigMark	Byte	1 byte	0 to 100	76	mark when script first marked
ReMark	Byte	1 byte	0 to 100	80	mark after re-mark
OrigGrade	String	1 char	A to E	C	looked up from grade boundary table, by SubjectRefCode
ReGrade	String	1 char	A to E	C	looked up from grade boundary table, by SubjectRefCode
ScriptReturn	Boolean	1 byte		True	Centre may request script to be returned
DateRequest	Date			06/03/03	Today's date when request is entered into system
DateRemark	Date			31/03/03	Today's date when ReMark is entered into system

Object-oriented Analysis Diagrams

When designing a system that is going to be programmed in an object-oriented programming language, the analysis must include which classes make up the system and what methods act on these classes. The results of this analysis are shown in a class diagram. (see Chapter 38).

Volumetrics

This refers to the volume of data to be processed and the characteristics of the users. The system will have to take into account, for example:

- the number of input documents or on-line requests to the system each day;
- the number of users and whether on-line or batch processing is required.

Exercises

1   State two techniques that a systems analyst, employed to investigate computerising a small business, might use to identify the business's data processing requirements.   (2)

AEB Paper 2 Qu 2 1997

2   A college library system identifies each book in its stock by a unique BookID. The BookID is encoded in a barcode attached to the book. When a borrower returns a book it is scanned and any fine that is due is calculated by extracting from the library database the date that the book was due back. Draw a Data Flow Diagram that models the library loans system.   (7)

New Question

Chapter 55 – Systems Design, Development and Testing

Systems design

The systems designer will consider

- output: content, format, sequence, frequency, medium (e.g. screen or hard copy) etc;
- input: volume, frequency, documents used, input methods;
- user interface: screens and dialogues, menus, special-purpose requirements;
- type of system: batch, on-line, real-time;
- files: contents, record layout, organisation and access methods;
- processing: the programs and procedures needed and their detailed design;
- security: how the data is to be kept secure from accidental corruption or deliberate tampering or hacking;
- testing strategies: how the system is to be thoroughly tested before going 'live';
- hardware: selection of an appropriate configuration.

Prototyping

Prototyping is a useful design tool. It involves building a working model of a system in order to evaluate it, test it or have it approved before building the final product. When applied to computer systems, this could involve, for example, using special software to quickly design input screens and running a program to input data. The user can then experience the 'look and feel' of the input process and suggest alterations before going any further.

Sometimes prototypes are simply discarded before the real system is started ('throwaway' prototyping), and in other cases the prototype may be developed into a working system ('evolutionary' prototyping).

The prototyping approach is supported by a different life cycle model which spirals towards a final solution, and hence is known as the **spiral** model, contrasting with the traditional **waterfall** model (see Chapter 29).

Systems flowcharts

When a systems analyst is developing a new computer system, his or her ideas need to be written down. Frequently a pictorial representation of how the system will work is easier to understand and take in than a lengthy text. A **systems flowchart** is a diagram showing an overview of a complete system. It will show:

- the tasks to be carried out in the new system, whether manual or by the computer;
- the devices (disk drives, tape drives, terminals etc.) that are to be used in the system;
- the media used for input, storage and output;
- the files used by the system.

You should be familiar with the standard symbols used in systems flowcharts.

Systems flowchart symbols

The NCC (National Computing Centre) suggest using the following symbols in systems flowcharts:

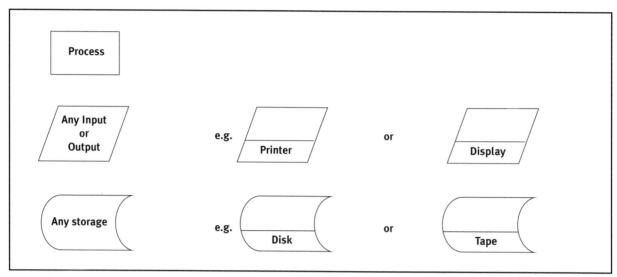

Figure 55.1: Systems Flowchart Symbols

5-55

Example:

A customer file is held on tape. Receipts are held on a transaction file (also on tape) and are sorted and then used to update the master file, creating a new master file. Draw a systems flowchart to illustrate this process.

Notes:

The system flowchart should show the files being used and the processes being carried out. The direction of the arrows on the flow lines indicates whether a file is being used for input, output or both.

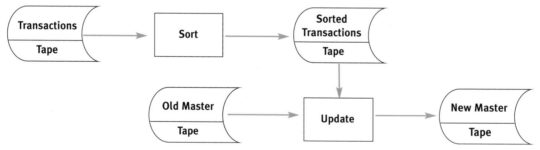

Example:

A transaction file is used to update an indexed sequential master file held on disk.

Notes:

This differs from the first example in that no new file is created; on an indexed-sequential file the updates will be done 'in situ'. Also, be careful to show the master file on disk, not tape, since it must be a direct access file if it is indexed.

Example:

A stock master file stored in sequence order of a numeric key is updated by a transaction file using sequential file access. Transaction records, which represent additions and deletions to the stock levels, are collected in batches over a period of time and validated before being sorted into key order. Invalid data is corrected and entered into the next batch of transactions. The ordered transactions are used to update the master file. The update process produces a new master file and a file of all changes to records for audit purposes.

Draw a systems flowchart of the system described above.

(Note: Read the whole text through carefully first in order to work out what happens first; in this case, the second sentence is really the starting point of the whole process.)

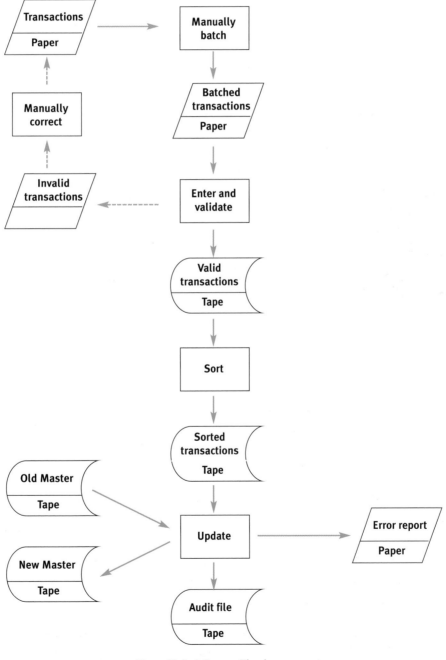

Figure 55.2: A Systems Flowchart

User Interface

A good user interface design is an important aspect of a successful system. The design must take into consideration:

- **who** is going to use the system – members of the public, experienced computer users, young children, etc.;
- **what tasks** the computer is performing; repetitive tasks, life-critical tasks such as flying a plane or dispensing radioactive doses to cancer patients, or variable tasks such as switching between a word processor, spreadsheet and database;
- the **environment** in which the computer is used: hazardous, noisy, or comparatively calm and quiet:
- what is **technologically feasible**.

In particular, careful **screen design** can make a huge difference to the usability of a system. When designing an input screen, the following points should be borne in mind:

- the display should be given a title to identify it;
- it should not be too cluttered. Spaces and blanks are important;
- it should indicate the size and format of data entry in each field; i.e. don't just put

Date: _____

- items should be put into a logical sequence to assist the user;
- colour should be carefully used;
- default values should be written in where possible;
- help facilities should be provided where necessary;
- user should be able to go back and correct entries before they are accepted;
- dialogues should be relevant, simple and clear;
- helpful error messages and other feedback should be provided;
- some users may prefer keyboard shortcuts;
- exits should be clearly marked.

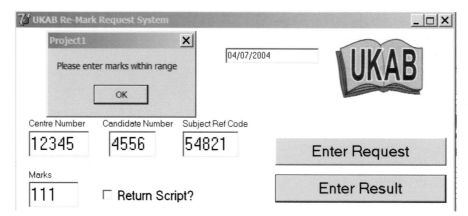

Figure 55.3: An input screen

Q1: Look at the above screen design. What is good about it? What could be improved?

Program design

This involves drawing hierarchy charts and structure charts (see Chapter 7) and writing detailed program specifications. This is followed by algorithm design and pseudocode before the program is coded in the chosen programming language.

Test Data

During the design stage, test data needs to be selected. This should include typical data, extreme data and erroneous data. For example (referring back to the data dictionary in chapter 54) typical data for OrigMark might be 76 or 80. Extreme data would be 0 or 100 and erroneous data 112 or −23.

Development

Development in this context refers to the coding and testing of the programs which make up the system, and the testing of the system as a whole. If a software package is being used it will probably involve tailoring the package, implementing screen designs and reports, writing macros etc.

Testing strategies

Obviously a system must be thoroughly tested before being installed to make sure that all errors are discovered and corrected before going 'live'. It is part of the designer's job to come up with a test strategy which will ensure that all parts of the system are properly tested.

Program testing

There are several possible strategies:

Bottom-up testing

1 Each individual module is tested as soon as it is written using pre-prepared test data. The data must include:
   - normal data which the procedure is designed to handle;
   - extreme values which test the behaviour of the module at the upper and lower limits of acceptability;
   - exceptional or invalid data which the procedure should reject rather than attempting to process it.

2 Each complete program in the system is tested. Data should be chosen which:
   - ensures that every route through the program is tested;
   - ensures that every statement in the program is executed at least once;
   - verifies the accuracy of the processing ;
   - verifies that the program operates according to the original specifications.

Top-down testing

The skeleton of the complete system is tested, with individual modules being replaced by 'stubs' which may, for example, display a message to say that a certain procedure has been executed. As individual modules are completed they are included in subsequent tests.

Testing each part of the system is sometimes referred to as **unit testing**.

Black box testing (functional testing)

Black box testing is carried out independently of the code used in the program. It involves looking at the program specification and creating a set of test data that covers all the inputs and outputs and program functions.

White box testing (structural testing)

White box testing is dependent on the code logic, and derives from the program structure rather than its function. The program code is studied and tests are devised which test each possible path at least once. The weakness of white box testing is that it will not detect missing functions – you cannot test what isn't there!

All software has to undergo a rigorous testing process before it can be released. When a new system is developed, the testing process may typically consist of five stages:

1 **Unit testing.** Each individual component (such as a subroutine or code for a particular function) of the new system is tested.

2 **Module testing.** A module is defined in this context as a collection of dependent components or subroutines.

3 **Subsystem testing.** This phase involves testing collections of modules which have been integrated into subsystems. (For example, the Purchase Order function may be one of the subsystems of an Accounting system.) Subsystems are often independently designed and programmed and problems can arise owing to interface mismatches. Therefore, these interfaces need to be thoroughly tested.

4 **System / Integration testing.** The subsystems are integrated to make up the entire system. The testing may reveal errors resulting from the interaction between different subsystems. This stage of testing is also concerned with ensuring that the system meets all the requirements of the original specification.

5 **Acceptance testing.** This is the final stage in the testing process before the system is accepted for operational use. It involves testing the system with data supplied by the system purchaser rather than with simulated data developed specially for testing purposes. It has the following objectives:
   • to confirm that the system delivered meets the original customer specifications;
   • to find out whether any major changes in operating procedures will be needed;
   • to test the system in the environment in which it will run, with realistic volumes of data.

   The customer signs off the system as accepted at this stage.

Testing is an iterative process, with each stage in the test process being repeated when modifications have to be made owing to errors coming to light at a subsequent stage.

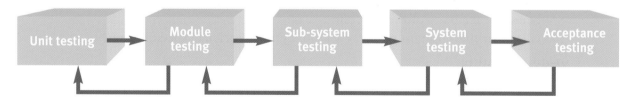

Figure 55.4: Stages in testing new software

Alpha testing

Alpha testing is carried out by the software developer's in-house testing team. It is essential because it often reveals both errors and omissions in the system requirements definition. The user may discover that the system does not in fact have the required functionality because the requirements were not specified carefully enough, or because the developer has overlooked or misunderstood something in the specification.

Beta testing

When a new package is being developed for release as a software package, **beta testing** is often used. This involves giving the package to a number of potential users who agree to use the system and report any problems to the developers. Microsoft, for example, delivers beta versions of its products to hundreds of sites for testing. This exposes the product to real use and detects problems and errors that may not have been anticipated by the developers. The product can then be modified and sent out for further beta testing until the developer is confident enough in the product to put it on the market.

Exercises

1   Customer payments are processed by a computer system that stores customer accounts on magnetic disk in a database, **Customer Accounts**. The amount paid by a customer is encoded on a **payment stub**. A process, **Process Payments**, is then applied to batches of **payment stubs** and the database **Customer Accounts** updated. A **progress report** is sent to a **VDU**. The system is controlled by **commands** from a **keyboard**.

5-55

   (a)   Complete the diagram shown in **Figure 1**.

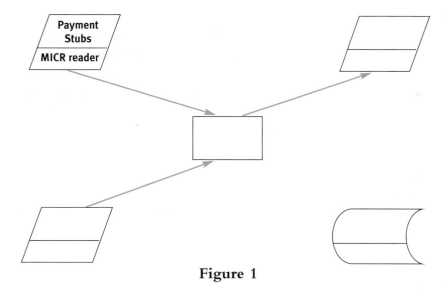

Figure 1

(5)

   (b)   Name this type of diagram.   (1)

   (c)   What encoding method is used for the payment stubs?   (1)

AQA CPT5 Qu 3 June 2003

Chapter 56 – Implementation, Evaluation and Maintenance

Implementation

This is the stage in the systems life cycle when people actually begin to use a new system. There are several tasks to be faced before the changeover is complete.

Installing the hardware

Before a new system can be put into operation, any new hardware will have to be installed. Even if it is only a matter of bringing in a couple of new PCs, this may mean changing office layouts, rewiring, acquiring new office furniture and moving personnel. In the case of a new mainframe, it will probably involve putting in a false floor in a specially designed computer room, laying cables and installing air-conditioning.

Installing the software

All the programs making up the new system need to be installed. Users need to be given appropriate access rights to the programs they need to use.

Creation of master files

Data for all master files will have to be entered before the new system can be used. This usually takes place in two phases: the 'standing data' can be typed in over a few days or weeks, and the rest of the data immediately before the changeover takes place.

> **Q1:** In a new stock control system, what data could be entered in advance on the stock master file?

> **Q2:** What data will need to be entered immediately before the system goes live?

Methods of conversion

There are several choices when converting from an old system to a new one:

Direct changeover. The user stops using the old system one day and starts using the new system the next – usually over a weekend or during a slack period. The advantage of this system is that it is fast and efficient, with minimum duplication of work involved. The disadvantage is that normal operations could be seriously disrupted if the new system has errors in it or does not work quite as expected.

Parallel conversion. The old system continues alongside the new system for a few weeks or months. The advantage is that results from the new system can be checked against known results, and if any difficulties occur, operations can continue under the old system while the errors or omissions are sorted out. The disadvantage of parallel running is the duplication of effort required to keep both systems running, which may put a strain on personnel.

Phased conversion. This is used with larger systems that can be broken down into individual modules that can be implemented separately at different times. It could also be used where for example only a few customer accounts are processed using the new system, while the rest remain for a time on the old system. Phased conversion may be direct or parallel.

Pilot conversion. This means that the new system will be used first by only a portion of the organisation, for example at one branch or factory.

Q3: For each of the following examples, state with reasons what type of conversion method would be suitable.

(a) A bakery is introducing a system to input orders from each salesperson and use this data to calculate how much of each product to bake each day, and also to calculate the sales commission.

(b) A chain store is introducing EPOS terminals connected to a mainframe computer, which holds details of stock levels and prices.

(c) A public library is introducing a computerised system for the lending and return of books.

(d) A large hospital is introducing a computerised system for keeping patient records and appointments.

(e) A college is introducing a computerised timetabling and room allocation system.

(f) A company manufacturing electronic components is introducing an integrated system for production control, stock control and order processing.

(g) A Local Authority is introducing a computerised system for the collection of a new type of tax.

5-56

Training for users

Moving from an old system to a new one requires that end-users be trained to use the new system. They will need to have hands-on practice with realistic test data before the system goes live. Detailed documentation showing how the system works from both a technical and end-user standpoint is finalised during conversion time for use in training and everyday operations.

Training staff in the use of new technology is crucial to the success of any computer system. Unless staff at all levels of an organisation know how to use the new technology effectively, investment in a computer system can be a waste of money.

Users at different levels of the company may require different levels of training. At the lowest level, for example, a clerical worker may need to know how to enter the daily or weekly sales figures and print a report. A member of the sales staff in an electrical retailer's may need to know how to enter a customer's details to check their credit rating, and put through a sale.

Managers will also need to be trained to use the new computer system. They need to feel confident that they can show their staff how to perform certain tasks, and they need to be able to use the system effectively to extract information for decision-making.

Technical staff will need to be trained in correct backup procedures, customisation for specific user needs, trouble-shooting when things go wrong.

Training may be provided in a number of different ways, including:
• a training manual which includes a step-by-step guide on using the system;
• an on-line tutorial supplied with the software;
• a video training course;
• formal, instructor-led training courses.

Installation manual

The installation manual will cover the following aspects:

- hardware requirements;

- operating system requirements, e.g. Windows 2003;

- details of how to install the software, folders used, etc.;

- how to customise the system by setting default values, etc.;

- special instructions for multi-user or networked versions;

- how to create new data files, set parameters for the first time,

- software registration instructions;

- upgrade instructions if upgrading from a previous version.

Operations manual

This document will be used by anyone concerned with the day-to-day operation of the computer system, including scheduled events such as generating summary reports for management and backups of the database and/or files. The operations manual will specify when and how these jobs are done. It may include:

- details of the procedure for starting the program;

- details of disks or tapes required;

- special stationery to be used;

- the number of copies of each report, and who is to receive them;

- backup procedures to be followed;

- recovery procedures in the event of hardware failure.

User manual

The user manual will be aimed at the various levels of end-user who will be using the system. End-users may include:

- senior managers who will be using the system to extract strategic information which they will be using for decision-making;

- middle managers who may want to produce extra reports or look up information on the latest sales figures, stock levels etc.

- clerical workers who are using the system for the daily input of data, and for answering queries such as 'When was the order despatched to Cardinal Newman College?'

The manual will therefore contain detailed instructions showing:

- the menu structure of the system;

- how to navigate around the package;

- how to enter data;

- the format of reports and how to print them;

- how to undo actions when an error has been made;

- how to get on-line help;

- a user support telephone number;

- possibly also a tutorial (training manual) taking the user through the various facilities available.

Post implementation review (evaluation)

The post-implementation review is a critical examination of the system three to six months after it has been put into operation. This waiting period allows users and technical staff to learn how to use the system, get used to new ways of working and understand the new procedures required. It allows management a chance to evaluate the usefulness of the reports and on-line queries that they can make, and go through several 'month-end' periods when various routine reports will be produced. Shortcomings of the system, if there are any, will be becoming apparent at all levels of the organisation, and users will want a chance to air their views and discuss improvements. The solution should be evaluated on the basis of effectiveness, usability and maintainability.

- The post-implementation review will focus on the following:
- a comparison of the system's actual performance with the anticipated performance objectives;
- an assessment of each aspect of the system against preset criteria;
- errors which were made during system development;
- unexpected benefits and problems.

Software maintenance

It is impossible to produce software which does not need to be maintained. Over the lifetime of any software system or package, maintenance will be required for a number of reasons:

- errors may be discovered in the software;
- the original requirements are modified to reflect changing needs;
- hardware developments may give scope for advances in software;
- new legislation may be introduced which impacts upon software systems (e.g. the introduction of a new tax).

Maintenance falls into three categories.

- **Perfective maintenance**. The system can be made better in some way without changing its functionality. For example it could be made to run faster or produce reports in a clearer format.
- **Adaptive maintenance**. Changing needs in a company may mean systems need to be adapted – for example, a single-user system may be adapted to a multi-user system. A new operating system or new hardware may also necessitate adaptive maintenance.
- **Corrective maintenance**. This involves the correction of previously undetected errors. Systems may appear to work correctly for some time before errors are discovered. Many commercial software programs such as Windows, Word or Access have bugs in them and maintenance releases are regularly brought out.

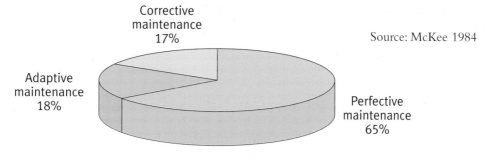

Source: McKee 1984

Figure 56.2: Maintenance effort distribution

Factors affecting maintainability

The maintenance process is generally triggered by requests for changes from system users or by management.

A study by Lehman and Belady carried out in 1985 resulted in a set of 'laws' of software maintenance.

1 The law of continuing change

A program that is used in a real-world environment necessarily must change or become progressively less useful in that environment.

2 The law of increasing complexity

As an evolving program changes, its structure tends to become more complex. Extra resources must be devoted to preserving and simplifying the structure.

3 The law of large program evolution

Program evolution is a self-regulating process. System attributes such as size, time between releases and the number of reported errors are approximately invariant for each system release.

4 The law of organisational stability

Over a program's lifetime, its rate of development is approximately constant and independent of the resources devoted to system development.

5 The law of conservation of familiarity

Over the lifetime of a system, the incremental change in each release is approximately constant.

The third law above suggests that large systems have a dynamic of their own. Maintenance teams cannot simply make any changes they want to, because of structural and organisational factors. As changes are made to a system, new errors are introduced which then necessitate more changes. Major changes tend to be inhibited because these changes would be expensive and may result in a less reliable system. The number of changes which may be implemented at any one time is limited.

Maintenance is very expensive, being by far the greatest cost incurred in the overall systems life cycle. It is therefore cost-effective to put time and effort into developing systems which are as easy as possible to maintain. Factors affecting maintainability include:

• good program design;

• well-structured programs written in a modular fashion and following standards of best practice (comprehensible variable names, comments etc.);

• use of an appropriate high-level language such as an object-oriented language;

• using tried and tested library routines and components;

• good system and program documentation;

• the availability of a record of all maintenance work carried out, when, why and by whom.

Maintenance documentation

The programmers who wrote the system are not usually the ones to maintain the system. This means it is important that suitable systems documentation is available to maintenance programmers, so they can make the necessary changes. Typically maintenance documentation should include the following:

- requirement specification;
- hardware and software specification;
- design diagrams such as Data Flow diagrams, System flowcharts, E-R diagrams, Class diagrams;
- overall system design showing the component parts and data structures;
- data dictionary;
- algorithms;
- clearly annotated program listings;
- configuration settings.

Exercises

1. (a) Give **three** different methods a systems analyst might use to gather information during the analysis of a large system. (3)

   (b) Describe **three** ways in which this system might be evaluated after installation and testing have been completed. (3)

   (c) Give **three** reasons why maintenance may be required after the system has been fully implemented. (3)

   (d) Why is maintenance documentation so important? (2)

   New Question

2. A medium sized bookshop wishes to replace its existing data processing system with a more up-to-date system.

   (a) Which method of conversion, parallel, direct or phased, would be appropriate? Justify your choice. (2)

   (b) The bookshop management wishes to assess how maintainable the new system will be. Give **two** questions for the management to put to the software developers of the new system to help in their assessment. (2)

   New Question

3. With a new computerised system, documentation needs to be provided. Name **two** types of documentation, other than the user manual, that would be included, and describe what each should contain. (6)

   New Question

4. Describe briefly **three** different ways in which training may be provided to the users of a recently installed computer system. (6)

   New Question

Chapter 57 – Input and Output Methods

Hardware devices

Hardware devices have been described in Chapter 25 and it would be a good idea to revise this chapter. In this chapter the principle of operation of some of the most common devices such as a scanner, touch screen and analogue input device will be briefly described.

How a scanner works

The scanner shines a bright light onto the image being scanned while the scan head moves from the top of the document to the bottom at a constant rate. As it moves over each 'line' of the image, the scan head collects data by measuring the intensity of the light that is reflected back from the document. Each scanned line therefore results in a stream of data which the scanner converts into digital information, with a certain number of bits representing each tiny area in the scanned picture. For line drawings or text which are only black and white, only 1 bit will be required; for 256 shades of grey, 8 bits will be required. This information is then stored in the computer's memory, and can be saved on disk.

The **resolution** of the scanner is measured in dots per inch (dpi) along the x and y axes, and this can be varied on more sophisticated scanners. The higher the resolution, the sharper the image, but the scanned image will take up more memory.

Three passes of the scan head, one each with a filter for red, green and blue, are required for colour scanning. Each filter eliminates all colours except the one that matches the filter, and the three resulting images are then combined into one complete full colour image.

Figure 57.1: A UMAX scanner

Touch screens

A touch screen allows a user to touch an area of the screen in order to enter data, rather than having to type the data on a keyboard. They are widely used in industrial environments such as manufacturing, warehousing and security systems, and also in avionics and medicine. They are very suitable in situations where the operator is moving about and can quickly and easily enter commands by touching the screen. They are less suitable for everyday work in an office, because it is tiring to have to continually reach out to touch a screen.

Touch screens are now available in hand-held portable models and are used, for example, by airlines to record receipts for bar sales, by hospitals to collect information on maternity patients and by local authorities for door-to-door collection of taxes.

There are many different sensor technologies available for different applications. Some respond to pressure, and some use capacitive overlay screens which must be touched by the naked finger. These consist of two primary elements, a glass substrate covered with a tight fitting plastic sheet. Conductive coatings are applied to the inner surface of both elements. Separating the cover sheet from the glass substrate are separator

Figure 57.2: A touch screen

dots, evenly distributed across the active area. Light finger pressure causes internal electrical contact at the point of touch, supplying the controller with the analogue voltage needed for digitisation.

Q1: Describe briefly some applications of touch screens.

Analogue to digital conversion

In many cases input devices generate signals which are analogue in nature rather than digital; that is they vary continuously between two values. Temperature, pressure, sound and movement are all analogue in nature, so that for example the movement of a **mouse** generates an analogue signal.

A computer cannot process analogue signals and therefore a special interface known as **an analogue-to-digital** converter is required to convert the continuously varying analogue signal to a digital form.

The basic process is as follows:

• The input signal range is divided up into a number of discrete levels, with the number of levels determining the resolution with which the analogue signal can be accurately reproduced.

• Samples of the analogue signals are taken at frequent intervals and converted in real time to digital values.

There are two fundamental ways in which such inputs may be detected. In an interrupt-driven system, the computer receives a signal as soon as data is collected, and can then decide what action, if any, to take. The cable that controls traffic lights is a familiar example of an interrupt-driven input to a processor; when a car drives over the cable (which is buried under the road), the processor that controls the lights is activated, increments a count and decides whether to change the lights or wait for another event, such as several more cars crossing the cable.

In a polled system, the computer periodically checks the input level from a device. One example is the device used on roads that automatically switches on speed limit signs when visibility is poor; the processor automatically checks a light meter in the device at fixed intervals.

Outputs from computers in automated processes can control other machines. They may switch devices on and off, or alter the level at which they operate. Computers in aircraft control the height, direction, state of wingflaps etc. In production control systems, the system often provides some output to machines and some to screens, and receives some input from sensors and some from keyboards. In some systems, such as the control of power stations, the computers propose a course of action and humans approve them for safety. In other systems, the humans may propose a course of action which the computers assess and either carry out or override.

In fly-by-wire aircraft, for example, the computer system checks the pilot's manipulation of the aircraft. The computer constructs a range of settings that it regards as safe, and within these settings, the pilot can decide whether to go faster or slower, higher or lower, etc. If the pilot moves outside these settings, the instructions are blocked.

5-57

Choice of input method

Methods of input will depend upon both the nature and volume of the data to be input and the characteristics of the user. In high-volume applications such as cheque processing by banks, the entry of details of gas and electricity consumption by customers, marking multiple choice examinations by a large examination board, input methods are used which cut out the manual process of keying in data. MICR (Magnetic Ink Character Recognition), OCR (Optical Character Recognition) and OMR (Optical Mark Recognition) respectively are suitable for the three applications mentioned. Mail-order systems often use key-to-disk data entry which is suitable for high volume batch applications. In some situations voice recognition may be ideal, for example when the operator needs both hands free or is disabled and unable to use a keyboard.

Exercises

1 "Firemen will be able to respond faster to emergency calls thanks to a system which relays data from the control room computer to the fire engine."

Data that could be transmitted include maps or directions to give the best route to a fire and information on the hazardous chemicals that might be used at the site of the fire.

Suggest and justify an appropriate device that could be used effectively in a fire engine cab for this system for:

    (i) input   (2)

    (ii) output.   (2)

AEB Paper 2 Qu 3 1999

2 A city council wishes to reduce the number of private cars entering the city centre. A car rental scheme is proposed whereby users in the scheme (registered users) can use one of the rental cars:
- parked outside the city
- parked in the centre of the city.

The rental cars will not use conventional key locks or ignition keys. Instead, the rental car will use a computer system in the car, together with a remote computer system, to
- identify a registered user automatically before they will be allowed to enter the car and drive it away.
- charge the user's account, stored on a remote computer system, automatically for the cost of the hire.

The cost of the hire will be directly related to
- the quantity of electrical energy consumed by the car's electric battery-powered engine.

(a) Explain how the computer system in the rental car together with the remote computer system could identify a registered user.   (2)

(b) How could the accounting information for a journey be relayed to a remote computer system that handles users' rental accounts?   (2)

(c) Suggest **one** reliable way the system could supply the user with an electronic record for a journey.   (1)

AQA CPT5 Qu 3 January 2003

Chapter 58 – Networking Methods

Networks

When the devices in a network are close together, for example in the same building, they can be linked by means of cables, and this is what is meant by a Local Area Network. However, when devices are separated by more than a few hundred yards, data has to be sent over a communications link (e.g. telephone line) and extra equipment such as a modem is required.

A Wide Area Network is a collection of computers spread over a wide geographical area, possibly spanning several continents, linked via microwave, satellite link or telephone line, or a combination of these. The use of global networks (including the Internet) has increased enormously over the past few years, owing to:

- changeover of telephone networks from old-style analogue to high-speed digital technology;
- reduction in the cost of connecting to and using networks;
- improved compression techniques which allow faster transmission of text, sound and graphics.

Modes of Network Operation

- **Baseband** carries one signal at a time. A bit value of 1 or 0 is sent by the presence or absence of a voltage in the cable. The whole bandwidth is dedicated to one data channel. Baseband signals can travel very fast, but can only be sent over short distances. Over about 1000 feet special booster equipment is needed. Local Area Networks typically operate in baseband mode.

Baseband Mode of Operation: one-channel system where the whole bandwidth is dedicated to one data channel.

- **Broadband** can carry multiple signals on a fixed carrier wave, with the signals for 0 and 1 sent as variations on this wave. The bandwidth is shared by several data channels. ISDN (Integrated Services Digital Network) is a broadband digital communications technology which offers faster transmission rates than with a modem and ordinary POTS (plain old telephone system) line and enables the transmission of voice, video and computer data simultaneously (e.g. for videoconferencing). Wide Area Networks usually use broadband media because it is expensive to install and maintain long-distance communications media. Some Local Area Networks now use broadband media.

Broadband Mode of Operation: multi-channel system where several channels are combined onto one carrier signal. The bandwidth is shared by several data channels.

Synchronous data transmission

In **synchronous transmission mode**, timing signals synchronise the transmission at the sending and receiving end so there is no need for start and stop bits for each character, only at the beginning and end of the whole block. This makes it possible to achieve higher transfer rates, but there may be more errors. This mode of transmission is widely used in local area networks.

Synchronous data transmission: communication in which sender and receiver share a common clock, often provided by the sender. Timing signals synchronise the transmission at the sending and receiving end.

5-58

Time-division multiplexing (TDM)

A **multiplexor** combines more than one data stream into a single stream of data that can be transmitted over a communication channel. This increases the efficiency of communication and saves on the cost of individual channels.

At the receiving end, the multiplexor (sometimes called the demultiplexor) separates the single stream of data into its separate data streams.

In time-division multiplexing, the transmission time is split up into tiny time-slots, with a time-slot assigned to each data stream. The time-slots are transmitted continuously whether data is being sent or not. The sending and receiving devices must be synchronised to recognise the same time-slots. Because a high bandwidth is used for the line, thousands of users can have telephone conversations or transmit digital data, apparently simultaneously, down a single high-speed line. The speed of this line must be greater than the individual lines. In the example of Figure 58.1 below, the high-speed line must be three times faster.

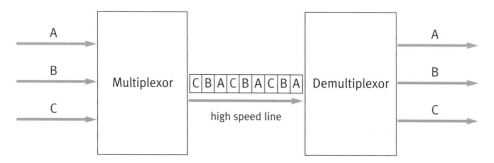

Figure 58.1: Time-division multiplexing

Time-division multiplexing: to enable many data streams to share a high-bandwidth medium, the data-carrying capacity of the medium is divided into fixed size time-slots, with a time-slot assigned to each data stream.

Circuit switching

The public telephone system is an example of a switched network using **circuit-switched** paths. When a caller dials a number, the path between the two telephones is set up by operating switches in all of the exchanges involved in the path. The circuit is set up and held for the whole duration of the call, even through periods of silence or heavy breathing. This permits the two people on the phone to hold a conversation with no waiting at either end for the message to arrive.

If two computers exchange data they can use a circuit through the network. If devices do not transmit continuously bandwidth is wasted. The two devices must transmit and receive data at the same rate, so circuit switched networks can only connect computers or devices that operate at the same data transfer rate. However, the data segments arrive in the same order in which they were sent so little processing is required to reconstruct the original message.

Because switches are used to connect and disconnect the circuits, electrical interference is produced, and although this is not a serious problem for speech, it may produce corrupt or lost data if the path is being used to transmit computer data. If this is likely to be a serious problem, a leased line may be used instead.

Circuit switching: a physical pathway is established between sender and receiver for the duration of the data transfer.

Packet switching

In a **packet switching system (PSS)** messages are divided into **packets** – fixed length blocks of data of say 128 bytes. As well as the data, each packet also carries:

- the source and destination address;
- a packet sequence number so that the whole message can be correctly reassembled;
- a checksum (longitudinal parity check) for the purposes of error checking.

Packet switching: the message to be transmitted is split into packets and these are routed via intermediary nodes.

Datagrams

In some protocols (e.g. TCP/IP, see below) a packet is known as a **datagram**.

The PSS (such as the one in Britain which is owned by British Telecom) takes the form of a computer network in which each computer (packet-switched node) redirects the packets it receives to the next node along an appropriate route to its destination. The packets from different users to different destinations may be interleaved, and all the packets making up one transmission need not necessarily travel by the same route or arrive in the right order. The PSS ensures that they are all reassembled in the correct order at their destination.

The nodes in the PSS are able to store packets until the nodes are ready to transmit, and to perform error checking and request retransmission of packets found to be in error. They are also able to perform error correction so that even if a transmission contained some errors, perhaps due to distortion on the line, it may be possible to correct these without having to retransmit.

In order to use the PSS, a user requires a network user identity, which is registered at his/her local packet switching exchange. The Internet is a prime example of a packet-switching network.

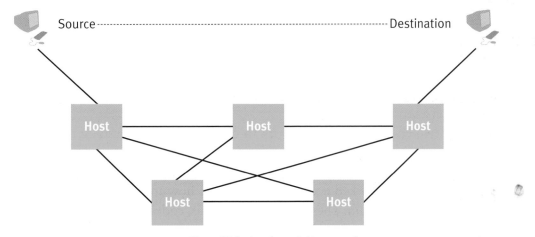

Figure 58.2: A packet-switching network

Datagrams: a packet switching service that routes each packet as it arrives with no prior route plan.

Virtual circuits

Many packet-switching networks employ virtual circuits to provide temporary 'dedicated' pathways between two points. There is no real cable between the two endpoints; rather, a virtual circuit consists of a logical sequence of connections where bandwidth is allocated for a specific transmission pathway. This pathway between sender and receiver is created once both computers agree on bandwidth requirements and request a pathway.

For example, if compuer A wants to send a message to computer B, it first sends a **Call Request** packet to the first node. This node decides which node to route the request to and the next node repeats the routing decision until the request arrives at computer B. Computer B now sends a **Call Accept** packet that retraces the route of the call request packet. Computer A can now transfer the message to computer B through this established route.

Virtual circuit: A packet switching service that establishes the route between sender and receiver before transmission of data packets starts.

Advantages of packet switching over circuit switching

- more efficient use of lines;
- cost depends only on the number of packets sent, not on distance so all data can be transmitted at local call rates;
- less likely to be affected by network failure because of the multiple routes available to transmit data packets;
- better security; data is less likely to be intercepted because the packets may be sent along different routes or be interleaved with other unrelated packets.

Asynchronous Transfer Mode (ATM)

ATM uses virtual circuits to provide multiple data channels with the data rate on each channel dynamically set on demand. It can support a wide range of different data types including computer data, voice, fax, CD-quality audio and real-time video. In the ATM system packets of data are referred to as cells: each ATM cell is 48 bytes of data plus 5 bytes of header information containing destination address and other information.

Digital lines are used to support ATM, and the resulting noise- and error-free communication enables ATM to deliver amazingly high transmission rates, typically 622Mbps.

ATM: a packet-switching service that transmits data in short, fixed-length packets referred to as cells, using a virtual circuit.

Standard protocols

Protocol: pre-agreed signals, codes and rules to be used for data and information exchange between systems

In order for two computers on a network to communicate successfully, they must share a common set of rules about how to communicate. At a minimum, such rules must include how to interpret signals, how to identify 'oneself' and other computers on a network, how to initiate and end networked communications, and how to manage information exchange across the network medium. These pre-agreed signals, codes and rules to be used for data exchange between systems are called network protocols.

A standard protocol is a protocol that conforms to a standard laid down by a standards authority to allow data exchange between any computer systems conforming to the standard.

Any computer that can access a network must have a protocol stack made up of protocol layers. Each layer has its own function. This provides the software that enables computers to communicate across a network.

The International Organisation for Standardisation provided a design framework for data communication networks known as the OSI (Open Systems Interconnection) seven-layer model.

TCP/IP Protocol Stack

The most common standard protocol is the **Transmission Control Protocol/Internet Protocol (TCP/IP)**. Although it predates the OSI model by nearly a decade, it has similar protocols and functions. The TCP/IP protocol allows different computers, from many different suppliers, running different operating systems, and located anywhere to communicate with each other. It is the protocol on which the Internet is based. More correctly it is referred to as a protocol suite because it is a collection of protocols.

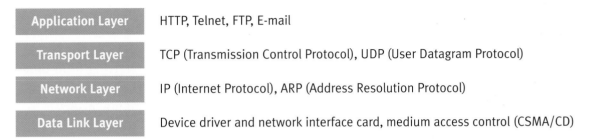

Application Layer	HTTP, Telnet, FTP, E-mail
Transport Layer	TCP (Transmission Control Protocol), UDP (User Datagram Protocol)
Network Layer	IP (Internet Protocol), ARP (Address Resolution Protocol)
Data Link Layer	Device driver and network interface card, medium access control (CSMA/CD)

The **application layer** provides application access to the communication environment. The application sends a continuous data stream.

The **transport layer** divides the data passed to it from the application layer into packets for the network layer to send. It acknowledges received packets, sets timeouts to make sure the source acknowledges packets that are sent, retransmitting packets if necessary. TCP is a reliable, connection-oriented protocol that provides error checking and flow control. It is used by FTP and SMTP (Simple Mail Transfer Protocol). UDP is an unreliable, connectionless protocol that provides data transport with lower overheads.

IP is a **network layer** protocol that provides source and destination addressing (IP addresses), sequencing and routing in the TCP/IP suite. IP is a connectionless datagram protocol that, like all connectionless protocols, is fast but unreliable. IP assumes that other protocols used by the computer ensure reliable delivery of data.

The **data link layer** handles the physical details of interfacing with the cable. It handles data flow control. It can support Ethernet, Token Ring, FDDI (Fibre Distributed Data Interface), RS232 etc.

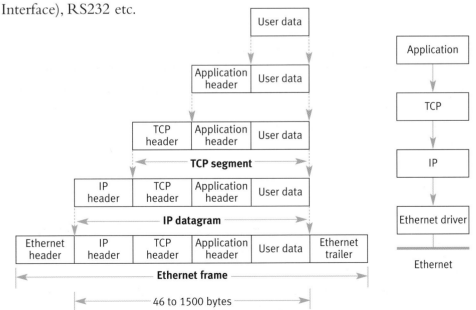

Figure 58.3 Encapsulation of user data

Sockets

A socket allows programmers to establish communication between processes running on different computers connected by a TCP/IP network. There are two types of socket. Datagram sockets allow a computer to send a single message, while a stream socket supports ongoing data exchange between participating processes. A socket address has two components: the IP address of the host and a port number to identify the process involved on that host.

Socket: the combination of IP address and port number, for example 196.102.89.124:80. This is used in a similar way to a file, giving programs the opportunity to exchange data across a network.

A web server uses ports to service multiple requests for web pages arriving from different clients by listening on a well-known port for clients' requests and then selects a new, unused port for each client request in order to free up the publicly-known socket for fresh contacts to be made.

5-58

Exercises

1 Transmission of data over a wide area network may be carried out by circuit or packet switching.

  (a) Explain the difference between circuit and packet switching. (2)

  (b) Give three advantages of packet switching compared with circuit switching. (3)

  (c) Give one example of a packet switched network. (1)

  (d) State **three** items that will be transmitted with a data packet in addition to the data itself. (3)

  New Question

2 (a) What is meant by a wide area network? (1)

  (b) Explain the term protocol in the context of data transmission over a wide area network. (2)

  (c) Why is a protocol needed for a wide area network? (1)

  (d) One widely used protocol is TCP/IP. Describe one of the four layers that make up the TCP/IP protocol stack. (2)

  New Question

3 What is a socket in the context of network applications? (2)

  New Question

Chapter 59 – Local Area Networks

Local Area Network: a set of links that connect together computers that are geographically close.

Types of Cable

Type of cabling has a major bearing on a network's speed, performance, cost and practicality (a very thick cable being much harder to lay in or along walls). **Twisted pair**, like telephone wire, is the cheapest but has slow transmission rates and suffers from electronic interference. **Coaxial cable** is high quality, well insulated cable which can transmit data much faster and more accurately than twisted pair.

- twisted pair (copper cable), used in much of the telephone network;
- baseband coaxial cable – high quality, well insulated cable that can transmit data at higher speeds;
- broadband coaxial cable – high quality, well insulated cable that can transmit data at higher speeds;
- fibre optic cable through which pulses of light, rather than electricity, are sent in digital form;

Other communication methods

- radio waves – these provide the basis for the now very popular wireless networks (WLANs);
- microwave – similar to radio waves. Microwave stations cannot be much more than 30 miles apart because of the earth's curvature as microwaves travel in straight lines. Mobile telephones use microwave radio links;
- communications satellite, using one of the hundreds of satellites now in geosynchronous orbit about 22,000 miles above the earth. (Geosynchronous orbit means that they are orbiting at the same speed as the earth, and are therefore stationary relative to earth.)

A computer is connected to a network via a network interface card (network adapter). A network interface card must match the type of network to which it is connected and the type of medium to which it is attached. Examples of network types: Ethernet, Token Ring, ATM.

Network topology

Topology: the structure of the inter-connections of components of a network.

When a network is to be implemented a decision has to be made on how best to arrange the components in a **topology**. A network's topology refers not only to the physical layout of its computers, cables and other resources but also how these components communicate with each other. A network's topology has a significant effect on its performance as well as its potential for growth.

Networks are generally based on one of three basic topologies: **star**, **bus** and **ring**. These three topologies and their advantages and disadvantages were described in Chapter 13, which you should revise before proceeding. In this chapter we will cover the operation of each of these networks.

5-59

Bus

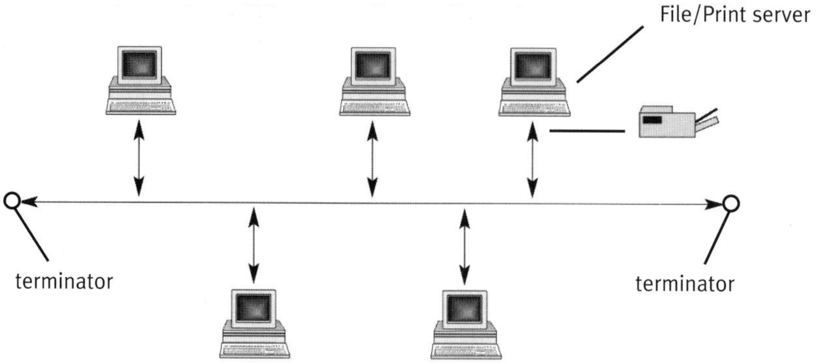

Figure 59.1: Bus network

In a bus network, all components are connected via a single cable connecting all the computers in a line. The weakness of this arrangement is that the entire network will be brought down by a single cable break. At each end of the line there is a terminator, which absorbs all the signals that reach it, thus clearing the network for new communication.

When a computer has data to send, the data is addressed, broken into packets and sent across the network as electronic signals. These signals are placed on the cable and received by all connected computers; because of the address given to the packets, however, only one computer accepts the data.

In a bus environment, only one computer can send information at a time. The problem here is that several stations may want to transmit down the same line simultaneously, and there has to be some strategy for deciding who gets the line. A popular scheme called **Ethernet** uses a collision system known as '**carrier sense multiple access with collision detection**' (CSMA-CD). Before a station begins to transmit, it checks that the channel is not busy; if it is, it has to wait before transmission can begin. Once it begins transmission, it listens for other nodes also beginning transmission. If the transmitted message collides with another, both stations abort and wait a random period of time before trying again.

This system works well if the channels are not too heavily loaded. On the other hand if sixteen students sit down at sixteen computers all at once and all try to load software from the network's hard disk, the whole system may grind to a halt!

Segments and Bridges

Segment: A segment is a run of cable to which are attached a number of workstations

In most network implementations, having a large number of computers and heavy traffic can slow down the network unacceptably. One way to ease this problem is by segmenting the network into manageable segments by inserting a **bridge** or router between each network segment. Traffic is then reduced on each segment, giving better network performance.

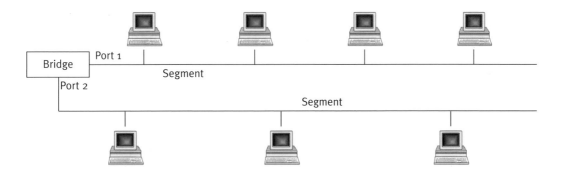

Figure 59.2: Bridge connecting network segments

Bridge: Connects two segments at MAC (Media Access Control) address level.

The bridge amplifies the signals that pass through it. The bridge 'learns' which addresses are connected to which port. It will examine the data frames and extract the source and destination MAC addresses. (MAC addresses are hard-coded into network interface cards by the manufacturer.) The bridge uses a table of MAC addresses to establish if the frame's destination is the same segment as its source or whether its destination is a device on the other segment. In that case the bridge will broadcast the frame on the other segment. So the bridge blocks frames destined for an address on the same segment from being passed to the other segment.

5-59

Ring

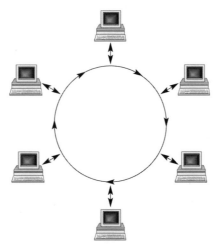

Figure 59.3: Ring network

In a ring network, signals travel in one direction only around the ring. **Token passing** is one method of sending data in a ring. A small packet, called the **token**, is passed around the ring to each computer in turn. If the computer has information to send, it modifies the token, adds address information and the data, and sends it down the ring. The information travels around the ring until it reaches the destination or returns to the sender. When a packet is received by the intended destination computer, it returns a message to the sender indicating its arrival. A new token is then created by the sender and sent down the ring.

This topology is surprisingly fast. A token can make a complete circuit of a 200-metre ring 10,000 times per second!

A disadvantage of the ring topology is that if one node fails, the whole network will go down.

Star

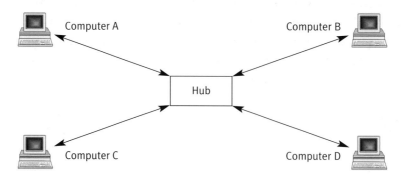

Figure 59.4: Star network

In a star topology, computers are connected by cable segments to a central **hub**. When a signal is sent from a computer, it is received by the hub and retransmitted down every other cable segment to all the other computers on the network. Again, only the computer the signal is addressed to acts upon the data.

If one computer fails in a star network, the others are unaffected, but if the hub goes down, the whole network goes down.

The hub regenerates the signals as they are received and sends them on.

Although in a hub-based network the computers are physically wired in a star configuration, the network operates as a bus-wired network. When the hub detects the presence of a data packet it broadcasts this packet onto all the other cables connected to the hub. Every node competes for a fraction of the total bandwidth.

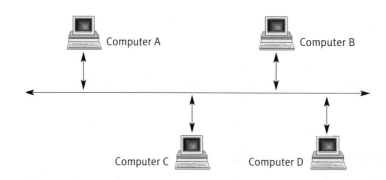

Figure 59.5 Bus network equivalent to above star network

Switched Ethernet

Ethernet is a network architecture, available in several different implementations using different types of cable (coaxial, twisted-pair or fibre-optic). Each Ethernet has limitations on the total distance the network can cover. For example in 10Base5 Thick Ethernet each cable **segment** can be a maximum of 500 metres long. Up to five cable segments can be attached using hubs/repeaters, creating a network with a total length of 2,500 metres.

Switch: an intelligent 'hub' which interconnects computers. The switch looks at the destination address of each packet it receives and delivers each packet directly to the correct destination, avoiding collisions.

If, in a hub-based network, the hub is replaced by a switch, each node attached to the switch can transmit to the switch at the same time. Switches can receive and send data simultaneously to all connections. No collisions occur in a switched network. There are two wire pairs connecting a node to a switch. One is used for transmitting and the other for receiving data (full duplex operation). When each cable is operated as an Ethernet cable, this is known as **Switched Ethernet**.

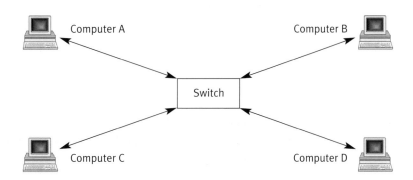

Figure 59.6: Switched Ethernet network

In the above example, switched Ethernet allows Computer A to send a packet to Computer B at the same time as Computer C sends a packet to Computer D. In a hub-based network this would cause a collision.

A backbone is a network segment used to connect other segments. It usually consists of a faster medium than the segments it is interconnecting in order to cater for the larger bandwidth demands.

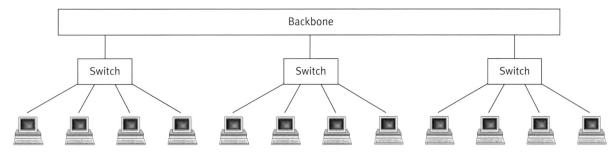

Figure 59.7: Switched segments interconnected by a bus backbone

Server-based vs peer-to-peer networks

There are two types of local area network: a **server-based** network is generally used when there are more than 3 or 4 computers on the network. A **peer-to-peer** network is suitable for a small company organisation with a few computers in different offices because data can easily be accessed from any computer, and documents can be printed on any of the printers connected to any computer, for example.

Server-based Network: a network in which resource security and administration and other functions are provided by dedicated servers.

In *client-server architecture*, different devices on the network are treated as clients or servers. The client devices send requests for service, such as printing or retrieval of data, to specific server devices that perform the requested processing. For example, the client devices might consist of twenty workstations in a room, and the server devices might be a laser printer and a computer dedicated to managing the network (the file server).

5-59

Peer-to-peer Network: A network where all computers have equal status. There are no dedicated servers.

Peer-to-peer architecture is an alternative to client-server for small computer networks. In peer-to-peer, each workstation can use resources from any other workstation and communicate directly with every other workstation on the network without going through a server. Peer-to-peer is most appropriate when the network users mostly do their own work but occasionally need to share data or communicate with each other. One disadvantage of this arrangement is that if the workstation from which a user wishes to retrieve data is switched off, the data cannot be retrieved!

The differences between the client-server and peer-to-peer networks are summarised in the table below:

Server-based networks	Peer-to-peer networks
Example: Windows 2000 Server	**Example: Microsoft Windows 2000**
A central backing store is available to all users.	Storage facilities are distributed throughout the network. It can be difficult to remember which files are held on which computer.
Software is centrally held and shared. The server distributes the programs and data to the other microcomputers in the network (the 'clients') as they request them. Some processing tasks are performed by the desktop computer; others are handled by the file server. This is **termed 'client-server'** architecture. The use of servers provides the network with more speed and power, but adds expense and complication.	Copies of software may be held on individual machines. Peer-to-peer networks provide basic network services such as software, file and print sharing, and are less expensive and less difficult to administer than those set up with servers. They are most appropriate for smaller businesses that do not need the power and speed of client-server architecture.
User IDs, passwords and access levels are controlled by the central computer. Servers may be physically located in a secure office.	Security is not centrally controlled. Users may need to remember different passwords for each resource they wish to access.
Backup facilities are centralised; data and information held centrally are backed up regularly.	Backup is the responsibility of individual computer users.
All users are reliant on the service provided by the central facility. If the central computer goes down, all users are affected.	There is no central computer. Every time a shared resource such as a printer is used, the user at the machine where the resource resides will experience a drop in performance.
Can support hundreds or even thousands of users and grow to keep pace with an organisation's growth and expansion.	Works best with under 10 users, is easy and cheap to set up and requires no special network operating system.

Figure 59.8: Comparison of client-server and peer-to-peer networks

Exercises

1 (a) Explain why performance degrades rapidly when large numbers of users log on to a bus network.   (2)

   (b) Suggest **two** ways this could be remedied.   (2)

New Question

2   Describe briefly the main features of a client-server network and a
    peer-to-peer network. Give **two** advantages and **two** disadvantages of using
    a peer-to-peer network.   (8)

New Question

3   **Figure 1** below shows the physical layout of a small local area network consisting
    of three workstations and one file server interconnected via a hub. The network
    is Ethernet-based.

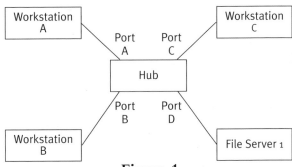

Figure 1

(a) The network in **Figure 1** behaves as a bus network. Draw a carefully labelled
     diagram of the bus equivalent of the hub-based network of **Figure 1**.   (2)

(b) (i) Three more workstations – D, E, F – and another file server – Files Server 2 –
          are added but network users complain that the performance of the network
          is now very slow. In terms of the operation of this network what is the most
          likely cause for the slowing of the network, assuming no hardware faults?   (2)

     (ii) To overcome this problem the network is split into two segments and bridged
          by a bridge with two ports, Port 1 and Port 2. Draw a carefully labelled
          diagram of the physical configuration of this new network.   (2)

(c) **Figure 2** shows another way that the computers in the local area network can
     be connected. The network uses switched Ethernet.

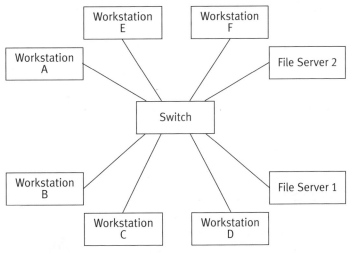

Figure 2

(i) Explain how the operation of switched Ethernet differs from that of
     hub-based Ethernet.   (2)

(ii) What is the advantage of the switch-based network in **Figure 2** compared with
     the hub-based network in **Figure 1** for the same number of computers?   (1)

AQA CPT5 Qu 9 Jan 2003

Chapter 60 – Wide Area Networks

Wide area network (WAN)

Wide Area Network: a set of links that connect together geographically remote computers.

WANs span broad geographical distances, ranging from several miles to across the world. Carriers such as BT typically determine transmission rates and interconnection between lines. The communication links may consist of a variety of cable, satellite and microwave technologies. There are two options for communication over a WAN:

• Dial-up networking. The user connects to the WAN using the standard telephone network (public lines). The dial-up line is only connected while in use.

• Dedicated or leased lines. The user's computer is permanently connected to the WAN. Therefore, no call set up and call disconnection is involved.

Dedicated lines are often set up to transmit data at higher speeds than public lines and are more appropriate for high-volume transmission. Public lines, on the other hand, are less expensive and more appropriate for low-volume applications requiring only occasional transmission.

5-60

> **Q1:** A bank has cashpoint machines in towns all over the UK, connected via a private wide area network to the bank's mainframe computer. What sort of line, public or leased, would you recommend? Why?

Value-added networks (VANs)

VAN: a privately owned wide area network that provides a specific service, not readily available on public networks.

Networks may be public, like the Internet, or privately-owned, as in the case of the bank mentioned above. An alternative to firms designing and managing their own private network is the **value-added network (VAN)**. A VAN is a private, multipath, data-only, third-party managed network that can provide economies in the cost of service and in network management because they are used by multiple organisations.

The VAN is set up by a firm that is in charge of managing the network. They then sell subscriptions to other firms wishing to use the network, and charge a subscription fee plus a charge for data transmission time. The network may use ISDN lines, satellite links or other communications channels.

The term 'value-added' refers to the extra value that subscribers get out of the arrangement by not having to invest in network equipment and software or perform their own error-checking, editing, routing and protocol conversion. Subscribers may achieve savings in line charges and transmission costs because the costs of using the network are shared among many users. A Value Added Network's customers typically purchase leased lines that connect them to the network or they use a dial-up number, given by the network owner, to gain access to the network.

Electronic data interchange (EDI)

EDI: Transmission of business data from one computer system to another computer system via a wide area network.

Electronic Electronic data interchange (EDI) is the electronic transmission of business data, such as purchase orders and invoices, from one firm's computerised information to that of another firm using standardised document forms between computer systems for business use. EDI is part of electronic commerce. Since EDI transmission is virtually instantaneous, the supplier's computer system can check for availability and respond quickly with a confirmation. As more and more companies get connected to the Internet, EDI is becoming increasingly important as an easy mechanism for companies to trade.

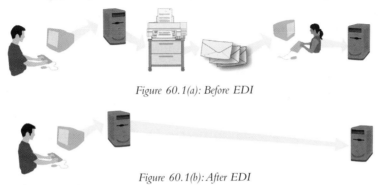

Figure 60.1(a): Before EDI

Figure 60.1(b): After EDI

Speed and reliability are major advantages of EDI. It does away with re-keying data, increases accuracy and eliminates delays. Data such as 'A' Level results are now commonly transmitted direct to schools and colleges rather than being sent by mail. Using an online service, schools and colleges are able to download results in encrypted form up to two days before their official release date; at one minute past midnight on results day, they are sent a password which allows them to decode the results. Having the results on computer also makes it far easier for the schools and colleges to collate exam results and produce the various statistics and performance indicators required by the DfEE for national league tables.

Connecting to a wide area network

Dial-up Line and Modem

The most common way to connect to a wide area network such as the Internet is to use a dial-up telephone line and a **modem**. A modem converts a digital signal received from a computer into an analogue signal that can be sent along ordinary telephone lines, and back to digital at the other end.

Figure 60.2: A modem (MOdulator/DEModulator)

Modem speed is measured in the number of bits per second (bps) that can be transmitted. A common speed in 2003 is 56Kbps. When a modem is first installed, various parameters have to be specified, including:

- the telephone number of your ISP;
- The baud rate of your modem;
- Number of data bits per block;
- Number of stop bits;
- Whether odd or even parity is used.

ISDN

When an ISDN line is used, a modem is not required as the line is itself digital. Instead, a **network termination device** and a **terminal adapter** are required. However, because most users are familiar with the term modem, the manufacturers of these devices often refer to them as **digital modems**. ISDN is offered by local telephone companies. There are different kinds of ISDN connection of varying bandwidth. The original version of ISDN employs baseband transmission. Another version, called B–ISDN, uses broadband transmission, and is able to support transmission rates of 1.5 Mbps. B–ISDN requires fibre optic cables and is not widely available.

Cable Modem

Cable Television companies' desire to compete in the world of Internet access has driven the development of **cable modems**, which employ broadband transmission across regular cable television wires. A cable modem can transfer data at 500 kbps or higher, compared with 28.8 to 56 kbps for common telephone line modems, but the actual transfer rates may be lower depending on the number of other simultaneous users on the same cable.

ADSL

Another new development is the **Asymmetric Digital Subscriber Line (ADSL)**, a technology which turns traditional copper wires into 'fat data pipes'. This means that existing telephone lines can provide broadband data transmission. ADSL offers Internet connections up to 30 times faster than the fastest dial-up modem. This makes video conferencing possible. ADSL also provides a voice channel that can be used for voice telephone calls at the same time as using the Internet. ADSL and cable represent the claims of two separate and hostile industries to be the standard-bearers of the data revolution, thus offering the promise to the consumer of rapid investment and genuine price competition. ADSL supports data rates of from 1.5 to 9 Mbps when receiving data (known as the *downstream* rate) and from 16 to 640 Kbps when sending data (known as the *upstream* rate). ADSL requires a special ADSL modem.

CODEC

CODEC: a device that encodes or decodes a signal and may compress and decompress these signals in the process.

For example, a CODEC can be used to compress video from a video camera so that it can be stored and played on a computer. Digital signals are encoded so that redundancy is reduced. CODECs can be implemented in software or hardware or a combination of hardware and software. CODEC implemented using hardware and software has the advantage of faster processing. Some popular codecs for computer video include mpeg, Indeo and Cinepak.

5-60

Exercises

1 **Figure 1** below shows part of a video editing computer system. The digital video camera records video and audio onto magnetic tape cassette using a digital format called **DV**. When the video camera is set to play mode the video and audio data are retrieved from the magnetic tape cassette at a rate of 3.6 Megabytes per second (MB/s). The storage capacity of a DV tape is 13 Gigabytes (GB).

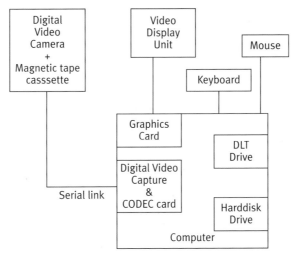

Figure 1

Table 1 below shows typical characteristics of four storage media, DLT magnetic tape, magnetic hard disk, Compact Disk-Recordable, Digital Versatile Disk-Recordable.

Medium	Data Transfer Rate Megabytes per second	Storage Capacity Gigabytes
Digital Linear Tape (DLT)	6	40
Magnetic Hard Disk	100	30
CD-R	0.176	0.635
DVD-R	1.25	4.37

Table 1

(a) Which of the four media shown in **Table 1** is most suitable for storing the video and audio data stream obtained by the computer from the video camera in real time, without compression, so that the data can be accessed for editing purposes using random access? Justify your answer. (2)

(b) A CODEC (Coder-Decoder) is often used to compress (and decompress) video and audio data.

(i) On some video-capture and editing systems the CODEC is entirely software-based whereas in others the CODEC is implemented in hardware and software on a plug-in board. Why is the hardware and software CODEC preferred to the software only CODEC? (1)

(ii) Why must a CODEC be used if a movie from the video camera is to be stored on DVD-R? (1)

(c) What purpose might the DLT drive be used for? (1)

AQA CPT5 Q6 June 2003

2 A university is considering installing an Ethernet backbone to connect various departments' Local Area Networks to their mainframe computer. They also want to connect to external networks at other universities.

   (a) When would it be necessary to use a gateway rather than a bridge to join two networks? (2)

   (b) Two methods of linking to the external networks are public dialled lines and fixed leased lines. Give one advantage and one disadvantage of each of these methods. (4)

New Question

3 (a) What is the function of a modem? (2)

   (b) Why does using an ISDN telephone line to connect a computer to a wide area network eliminate the need for a modem? (1)

   (c) What is a cable modem? (2)

New Question

4 A large international company wants to upgrade its network facilities. They are considering two options: a private network, or a value-added network. Give two advantages to the company of using a value-added network. (2)

New Question

5 (a) Explain the modes of network operation:
     (i) Baseband; (2)
     (ii) Broadband. (2)

   (b) Bus local area networks such as Ethernet operate in baseband mode. Wide area networks operate in broadband mode.

     (i) Give **two** reasons why wide area networks are operated in broadband mode. (2)

     (ii) Explain why the performance of a bus local area network such as Ethernet degrades with increase in network traffic. (2)

     (iii) Explain how switched Ethernet overcomes this problem. (2)

   (b) Figure 2 below shows an arrangement for a time-division multiplexing system. Input and output channels A, B, C, D each operate at 10 Megabit ber second.

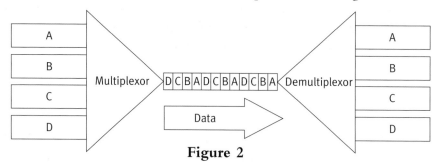

Figure 2

At what bit rate must the cable operate between the multiplexor and the demultiplexor for successful transmission? (2)

AQA CPT5 Qu 4 June 2002

Chapter 61 – Inter-networking

An inter-network is created when two or more independent networks are connected yet continue to function separately. The best known inter-network today is the Internet, which is, in essence, a large number of small networks connected to share information. The protocol suite used across the Internet to inter-connect LANs is TCP/IP.

Inter-net: a collection of networks that all use the same protocol suite.

As networks grow and become a more integral part of an organisation, it is common to supply multiple paths through a network to provide fault tolerance. A bridge cannot handle multiple paths for data; instead, a router is used.

Routers

Router: a device that forwards packets between networks using IP addresses.

A router is connected to at least two networks, commonly two LANs or WANs or a LAN and its ISP's network. Routers use headers and forwarding tables to determine the best path for forwarding the packets, and they use protocols such as TCP/IP to communicate with each other and configure the best route between any two hosts.

Routers can be used like bridges to connect multiple network segments and filter traffic. But, unlike bridges, routers can be used to form complex networks with multiple paths between network. Each network segment, also called a subnetwork (or subnet), is assigned a network address. Each node on a subnet is assigned an address as well. Using a combination of the network and node address, the router can route a packet from the source to a destination address somewhere else on the network. The router operates at the Network Layer level. It stores logical addresses (IP addresses), whereas a bridge operates at the Data Link Layer level. It stores physical addresses (MAC addresses) of devices.

Routers can route packets of the same protocol (such as TCP/IP) over networks with dissimilar architectures (such as Ethernet to token ring).

The act of traversing a router from one network to another is referred to as a hop. To connect a local area network to another on the other side of the world, a number of routers are required. Each router maintains a routing table containing the addresses of networks that it can connect to.

When a router is used to connect to the Internet, the IP address of the port connecting it to the internet must be registered with the internet registrar because this IP address must be unique over the whole Internet. (See next chapter).

Gateways

Gateway: a device used to connect networks using different protocols. It repackages the data so it can be read correctly at the receiving end.

To connect two networks with different architectures and different protocols, a **gateway** is required. For example, a gateway can be used to allow network communication between a TCP/IP LAN and an IBM mainframe system. When packets arrive at a gateway, the software strips all networking information from the packet, leaving only the raw data. The gateway then translates the data into the new format and sends it on, using the networking protocols of the destination system. A gateway is also known as a protocol converter.

5-61

TCP/IP

TCP/IP is a collection of software (a suite of protocols) used by the Internet and many LANs.

TCP (Transmission Control Protocol)

TCP performs handshake, packet sequencing, flow control and error handling (see Chapter 58).

IP (Internet Protocol)

IP allows messages to travel from one part of a network to another. In a single Ethernet segment there is no routing as all communication is via broadcasting. An intranet has at least 2 subnets and a router. Computers are connected to the network via an Ethernet card (or Network Interface Card (NIC)). These cards have predetermined MAC (Media Access Control) addresses hard-coded into the board. These are 48-bit addresses expressed as 12 hex digits such as 00-09-7C-F1-F7-85.

IP addresses get assigned to each Ethernet card.

IP Addresses

IP addresses are hierarchical addresses like telephone numbers. The first part is the network address and the second part is the node (host) address.

IP addresses are 32-bit addresses written in dotted quad notation format w.x.y.z where each of the letters stands for a number between 0-255 (representing an 8-bit pattern).

For example the IP address   11000000101010000000000011001011

broken up into 8-bit groups would read: 11000000   10101000   00000000   11001011

converting each of these groups into denary: 192   168   0   203

would be written as   192.168.0.203.

IP addresses are divided into several classes (A=Assigned by InterNIC, L=Locally administered):

	w	x	y	z	
Class A	**0XXXXXXX AAAAAAAA (0-126)**	**LLLLLLLL**	**LLLLLLLL**	**LLLLLLLL**	**Assigned to large companies (all given out) such as IBM, Xerox.**
	00001010 (value 10)	XXXXXXXX	XXXXXXXX	XXXXXXXX	non-routable addresses
	01111111 (value 127)				reserved loopback address
Class B	**10XXXXXX AAAAAAAA (128-191)**	**AAAAAAAA**	**LLLLLLLL**	**LLLLLLLL**	**assigned to medium-sized companies (all given out) such as Microsoft**
	10101100 (value 172)	0001XXXX (16-31)	XXXXXXXX	XXXXXXXX	non-routable addresses
Class C	**110XXXXX AAAAAAAA (192-223)**	**AAAAAAAA**	**AAAAAAAA**	**LLLLLLLL**	**still available for others such as your school or college or you**
	11000000 (192)	10101000 (168)	XXXXXXXX	XXXXXXXX	non-routable addresses
Class D	**1110XXXX (224-239)**				**reserved as multi-cast addresse**
Class E	**11110XXX (240-255)**				**reserved for experimental addresses**

Unusable addresses:

- 0.x.y.z means "the entire Internet"

- 127.x.y.z (127.0.0.1 is the loopback address, messages to the loopback don't go out on the network, but instead stay within a particular machine's IP software.

- w.x.y.0 means all addresses on that subnet

- w.x.y.255 is reserved as the broadcast address to the whole subnet.

- w.x.y.1 is **by convention** the default gateway (router) address

Non-routable addresses were set aside to test intranets. Anyone can use these addresses. Routers are programmed to ignore them. Organisations are choosing these addresses for security reasons because no-one can connect to them. Most use two sets of IP addresses, those used internally (on the intranet) and 'official' Internet addresses obtained and registered by an Internet Registrar. NAT routers (Network Address Translation routers) lets computers with non-routable addresses initiate conversations with computers on the public Internet but doesn't allow computers on the Internet to initiate conversations with computers on the intranet.

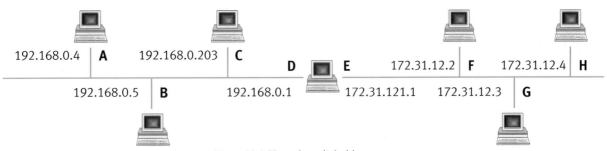

Figure 61.1: Two subnets linked by a router

Computers A, B and C (segment 1) can communicate directly with one another.

Computers F, G and H (segment 2) can communicate directly with one another.

The computer with network cards D and E can function as a router. If a computer in segment 1 wants to communicate with a computer in segment 2 it needs to send the message to D, which passes it on to E, and then the message can be broadcast on segment 2.

If A is trying to send a message to G but does not know how to get to G, it uses a 'catchall' address called a default router or **default gateway** address. The network administrator will have configured A's default router as D, so A sends the message to D. When D gets the message it resends the message from board E.

Subnet masks

Subnet masks make it possible for a host (PC) to determine whether it can send a message to another host directly or whether it must go through routers.

Subnet mask:	11111111 11111111 11111111 00000000	= 255.255.255.0
A's address:	11000000 10101000 00000000 11001011	= 192.168.0.203
B's address:	11000000 10101000 00000000 00000100	= 192.168.0.4

Look down from each of the 1s on the subnet mask and you see that A and B match at each of these positions. This means the two addresses are on the same subnet.

If you want to refer to IP addresses by name you can either use a name server such as DNS (Domain Name System) or WINS (Windows Internet Name Service) or set up a HOSTS file on each PC.

Exercises

1 **Figure 1** below shows part of the logical layout of an Ethernet-based local area network consisting of several desktop PCs connected using a bus topology. The network is split into two *segments* linked by a bridge.

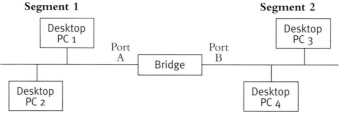

Figure 1

(a) (i) Why is is necessary sometimes to split local area networks based on a bus topology into two or more segments? (1)

(ii) Describe the involvement of the bridge in **Figure 1** in traffic management on the Ethernet segments. (2)

(iii) The network in **Figure 1** is physically realised using two hubs, a bridge and twisted-pair cabling to interconnect the desktop PCs. Draw a labelled diagram of the layout of the network that uses these components. (2)

(iv) The network in **Figure 1** is operated as a *peer-to-peer* network. Explain peer-to-peer networking. (1)

(b) **Figure 2** below shows how three desktop PCs may share via an Ethernet switch and router an ADSL line connection to the Internet.

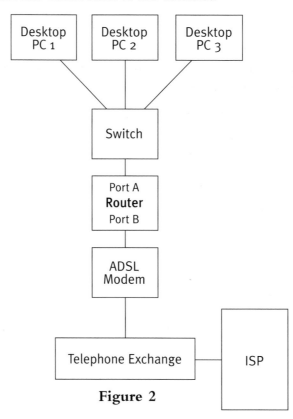

Figure 2

continues on next page

5-61

(i) What is the role of an Internet Service Provider (ISP)? (1)

(ii) Give **two** advantages of an ADSL line connection to the Internet over a dial-up line and modem. (2)

(iii) What is a router? (1)

(iv) Port A of the router in **Figure 2** is assigned the IP address 192.168.1.1. Port B is assigned the IP address 213.208.10.146. Which of these IP addresses needs to be registered with the Internet registrar and why? (2)

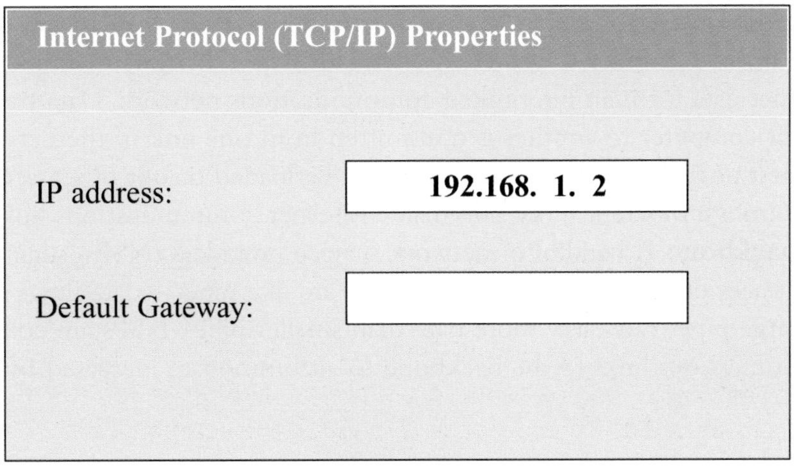

```
┌─────────────────────────────────────────────────────┐
│ Internet Protocol (TCP/IP) Properties                │
├─────────────────────────────────────────────────────┤
│                                                       │
│                                                       │
│                          ┌──────────────────────┐     │
│   IP address:            │   192.168. 1. 2      │     │
│                          └──────────────────────┘     │
│                                                       │
│                          ┌──────────────────────┐     │
│   Default Gateway:       │                      │     │
│                          └──────────────────────┘     │
│                                                       │
│                                                       │
└─────────────────────────────────────────────────────┘
```

Figure 3

(v) **Figure 3** above shows part of the TCP/IP configuration window displayed on the VDU of Desktop PC 1. What IP address should be entered for the Default Gateway? (1)

(c) In the client/server model of the Internet a web server offers an HTTP service on port 80. A web browser on a client computer such as Desktop PC 1 connects to the Internet to access a web server **www.difficultexaminations.co.uk** at IP address 198.112.57.124.

(i) What is the socket address of the web server's HTTP service? (1)

(ii) Explain how a web server is able to use ports to service multiple requests for web pages arriving from different clients. (2)

AQA CPT5 Qu 9 June 2003

Chapter 62 – The Internet

Internet: a world-wide collection of networks, gateways, servers and computers using a common set of telecommunications protocols to link them together.

Structure of the Internet

The Internet is a network of networks, connecting computers all over the globe. In 1969, the Internet started life as the ARPANET (Advanced Research Projects Agency Network) and consisted of just 4 computers. By the beginning of 1997, it included 1.7 million computers and it continues to grow exponentially. The cables, wires and satellites that carry Internet data form an interlinked communications network. Data travelling from one Internet computer to another is transmitted from one link in the network to another, along the best possible route. If some links are overloaded or out of service, the data can be routed through different links. The major Internet communications links are called the **Internet backbone**. A handful of network service providers (NSPs) such as BT each maintain a series of nationwide links. The links are like pipes – data flows through the pipes and large pipes can carry more data than smaller pipes. NSPs are continually adding new communications links to the backbone to accommodate increased Internet use.

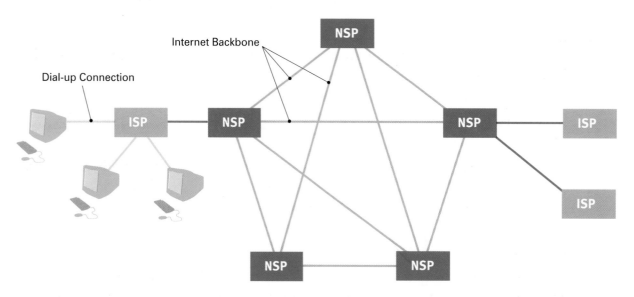

Figure 62.1: Structure of the Internet

When you connect your computer to the Internet, you do not connect directly to the backbone. Instead, you connect to an ISP (Internet Service Provider), which in turn connects to the backbone.

An ISP generally charges you a monthly fee for Internet access and provides you with communications software and a user account. You need a computer with a modem to connect your computer to a phone line, and when you log on, your computer dials the ISP and establishes a connection over the phone line. Once you are connected, the ISP routes data between your computer and the Internet backbone. A phone line provides a very narrow pipe for transmitting data, having a typical capacity of 56K bits per second. Using a phone line, the time taken to transfer the contents of a 680Mb CD-ROM would be over 26 hours! Using a dedicated line such as cable offered by providers such as NTL or ADSL will greatly improve your connection speed.

Some of the services available on the Internet:

World Wide Web
File Transfer Protocol Servers
Electronic Mail
News
Gopher (a system that was in use before the World Wide Web)
Telnet

Client-Server model of the Internet: users connecting to the Internet act as clients and there are many dedicated servers providing web pages, e-mail etc.

The World Wide Web

The World Wide Web is a special part of the Internet that allows people to view information stored on participating computers. It is an easy-to-use, graphical source of information that has opened the Internet to millions of people interested in finding out information. It consists of documents called pages that contain information on a particular topic, and links to other Web pages, which may be stored on other computers in different countries.

On-line Service Providers

To access the Internet you have a basic choice between **internet service providers** and **on-line services**.

Internet Service Provider: a company that provides access to the Internet, usually for a monthly fee. It provides the registered user with a username, password and access telephone number and usually an electronic mail box.

An on-line service provider will give you access to the net and to their own private networks of services – databases of information, on-line editions of well-known magazines and newspapers, cinema listings, travel information, shopping, user forums, live chat rooms etc.

Online Service Provider: a business that provides subscribers with an infrastructure to connect to a huge number of information providers.

The difference between an on-line service and some ISPs is, like so much else in computing, often less than clear. Virgin Net, for example, sells itself as an ISP but when you sign up with them you get access to various members-only services. AOL (America On-Line) started out as an on-line service provider but is now the biggest ISP in the world.

5-62

Figure 62.2: An on-line service provider

Usenet newsgroups

Usenet: a worldwide bulletin board system that can be accessed through the Internet or online services. It contains newsgroups on many different topics.

Usenet was created in 1979 by a group of American Computer Science graduates who wanted to share their knowledge of the bugs and quirks of the Unix operating system with others and collectively make it better. Since then Usenet has grown to over 25,000 different newsgroups, most devoted to specific areas of interest. Usenet is one of the more controversial areas of the Internet, as it contains many undesirable groups such as paedophile groups and those wishing to exchange pornography. Newsgroups have also been hit by a plague of bulk junk mail messages (known as SPAM), which makes certain newsgroups unusable. Usenet II was set up, according to its creators, 'to create a structure where the traditional Usenet model of co-operation and trust can be made to work in the 21st century.' You can read about it on their Web site **www.usenet2.org**.

Internet Relay Chat (IRC)

Unlike Usenet and e-mail, conversations on IRC are live. Whatever you say on the channel is instantly broadcast to everyone on the same channel, even if they are logged on to a server the other side of the world, and you can expect them to reply instantly.

Some channels are dedicated to particular topics, for example cricket, games or politics. To use IRC you need the right software: PC users can download mIRC from **www.mirc.co.uk**, and Mac users can download IRCLE from **www.xs4all.nl/~ircle**.

For an interview with the Finnish programmer Jarkko Oikarinen who started IRC in 1988, in which he talks about the ideas behind IRC and how he thinks it will develop in the future, log on to **www.mirc.co.uk/help/jarkko2.txt**.

You can also chat on the on-line services such as AOL, by clicking on the CHAT button on the main screen. You should never give out personal details on a chat line like your real name, address, phone number, credit card number or details of your net account and password. For general tips on netiquette try **www.albion.com**.

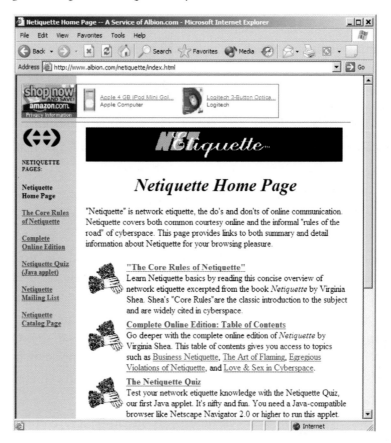

Figure 62.3: Tips for chat-line etiquette

Videoconferencing

Video Conferencing: conducting a conference between two or more participants at different sites by using computer networks to transmit audio and video data.

Each participant has a video camera (webcam), microphone and speakers attached to their computer. As the participants speak, their voices are carried over the network and played back to the other participants' speakers. The images captured by the cameras are displayed on the other participants' computer monitors.

E-mail

Writing your first e-mail to someone on the other side of the world and getting a reply within an hour or two is, no question, an exciting experience. Once you're hooked on e-mail you will probably never again use the regular mail service to post a letter to a friend. For both personal and business use, e-mail is a 'Killer App' that has significant advantages over snail mail, fax and phone.

5-62

First of all, we will look at some of the facilities of e-mail:

- send a message anywhere in the world for the price of a local call;

- attach files such as documents, photographs, maps, executable programs;

- keep an address book of people you regularly e-mail;

- send the same letter to a group of people simultaneously;

- reply to an e-mail simply by clicking on the reply button, inserting text from the original message as required;

- forward a received message with comments on to an individual or group;

- with the right software or a Web-based e-mail address such as HotMail, pick up your mail from anywhere in the world, useful for example while travelling.

- join a mailing list and get free information sent to you on a regular basis. Alternatively, you can join a two-way mailing list where you can send a message on a particular topic and it goes to everyone on the mailing list. Similarly, you receive all the messages posted by anyone else, which can lead to a lot of mail.

Advantages of e-mail

- It is cheaper than fax or telephone for messages sent over long distances.

- You can e-mail someone in Australia, for example, without having to worry about time zones – the message will be picked up at a convenient time.

- You receive an answer much more quickly than by mail, and it is preferable to leaving a message on a telephone answering machine, as you know it has been received. (If the message does not reach the address you will be automatically notified.)

- It is easy to use and encourages friendly conversations and directness – you don't have to be formal in a business e-mail, and rules about the correct way to set out a letter simply don't apply. It breaks down barriers and cuts across hierarchies, which helps effective communication.

Disadvantages of e-mail

- Perhaps because it is so direct, it can be easy to offend people without meaning to. You can add little smiley faces :-) to show you are trying to be funny, but these can have limited appeal!

- Busy people may be overloaded with e-mail; it can be a bit depressing to get your mail at 9 a.m. and find you have 53 e-mails waiting to be answered. Junk mail can also be a problem.

- Viruses can be spread in e-mail attachments. You should always virus-check attached files before opening them, even if they are sent by a friend, as viruses can be passed on unwittingly.

Registering a domain name

If you want to set up in business on the Internet, or if you would like a snappy e-mail address, you need to register your chosen domain name and a few other details. You also need an Internet Service Provider (ISP). No one 'owns' domain names. The organisation responsible for registration of ".co.uk" and ".org.uk" names is Nominet (**www.nic.co.uk**) and this is a good place to check for the availability of your chosen domain name. If it is already taken, you can find out who by. You can register your domain name here for a fee (around £80.00 for the first two years) or you can find out how to get a free domain name by logging on to **www.freename.co.uk**. Nominet is an **Internet Registrar**.

Internet Registrar: an organisation that will register a domain name and IP address.

You can use an agent such as 123-reg to register a domain name. Some agents also offer to host your web site. You can remotely maintain your web site using FTP.

Internet Registry: stores the domain names registered through internet registrars. Each major domain, such as .com, has its own registry.

Cybersquatting

Many people try and speculate in domain names ("squatting") in order to try and earn a profit by selling the names they have registered. In 2000, Volkswagen successfully fought off an attempt by cybersquatters to hold the domain name VW.net for ransom. The name had been registered by Virtual Works, which attempted to sell the domain name to Volkswagen in December 1998. Virtual Works threatened that if Volkswagen did not buy the domain name, the company would sell it to the highest bidder.

A US Court saw differently, however, and ruled that Volkswagen was entitled to the Internet domain name VW.net. The Court ruled that under the recently enacted Anticybersquatting Consumer Protection Act, "Virtual Works has attempted to profit from the trafficking of a domain name of a previously trademarked name".

Uniform Resource Locator (URL)

To access resources on the Internet, you need to use a URL. The first part of the URL shows what protocol to use and the second part is the domain name or the IP address it maps to. The last part is the path name where the resource is located on the Web server. (see also Chapter 14).

For example, the two URLs below point to two different files at the domain *pcwebopedia.com*:

ftp://www.pcwebopedia.com/stuff.exe specifies an executable file that should be fetched using the FTP protocol.

http://www.pcwebopedia.com/index.html specifies a Web page that should be fetched using the HTTP protocol.

An IP address is a 4-byte binary number (Ipv4) that contains a network identifier and a host identifier (specific computer on the network). The number of IP addresses is running out. A new scheme (Ipv6) is replacing the 32-bit number by a 128-bit number. Ipv6 fixes a number of problems in Ipv4, such as the limited number of available Ipv4 addresses. It also adds many improvements to Ipv4 in areas such as routing and network autoconfiguration. Ipv6 is expected to gradually replace Ipv4, with the two coexisting for a number of years during a transition period. For more information, go to their web site **www.ipv6.org**.

Exercises

1   Explain the difference between:

    (a) an *Internet Service Provider* and an *On-line Service Provider*.　　　　　(2)

    (b) *Usenet* and *Internet Relay Chat*　　　　　(2)

New Question

Chapter 63 – The World Wide Web

The World Wide Web

The World Wide Web is a collection of documents and other types of files that are stored on computers all over the world. These documents and files are called **pages**, and you can move from one page to another by clicking on **hypertext links** (usually shown in another colour and underlined). Links make use of URLs, the addresses used to find Web pages. You may need to look back at Chapter 14 to remind yourself of the relationship between URLs, domain names and IP addresses.

The World Wide Web consists of 4 major elements:

- HTTP – Hyper Text Transfer Protocol: specifies how a web client requests information from a web browser
- HTML – Hyper Text Mark-up Language : specifies how documents should be displayed on the client computer in a browser.
- URL - Uniform Resource Locator: specifies the location of the information requested by the client.
- Browser Software – a program that reads HTML files and displays them on the client computer.

Web browsers

Web browser : software used to view and download Web pages and various types of files such as text, graphics, sound and video.

If you know the URL of a Web page, you can view it by loading a Web browser such as Microsoft Internet Explorer or Netscape Navigator and typing in the URL (address) of the Web page.

The other facilities offered by a typical Web browser allow you to:

- show a Web page for which you have either entered the address or URL (Uniform Resource Locator) or clicked on a 'hot' link;
- browse back and forward through the most recently viewed pages;
- customise the basic options such as the opening page, content censorship, security levels and whether to download the page as text only to speed up transmission;
- 'bookmark' pages for quick reference. Once you have entered a URL, and found the site worthwhile, you can click on the **Favorites** menu option and save the address for recalling at a later date.
- keep a 'History' list of pages visited within a specified period;
- save the most recently visited pages for viewing off-line;
- show animation sequences programmed in Java script;
- play back sound, video clips and multimedia if the appropriate 'plug-in' software (usually a Visual Basic ActiveX control) is installed, e.g. Shockwave;
- download files to a local hard disk;
- fill in an on-line form and submit it by e-mail;
- give links to search engines;
- access personal e-mail;
- have pages 'pushed' at you (Netcasting) rather than having to request them.

5-63

Internet Search Engines

The Web is massive – more than 500 million pages worldwide, with millions more being added daily. If you need to find out something specific on the Net, or research a particular topic, you probably need to use a **search engine**. A search engine enables you to search the contents of millions of Web pages simultaneously, by going to the search engine's Web page and typing key words or search terms into a simple form. Examples of search engines include Yahoo, Google and AltaVista.

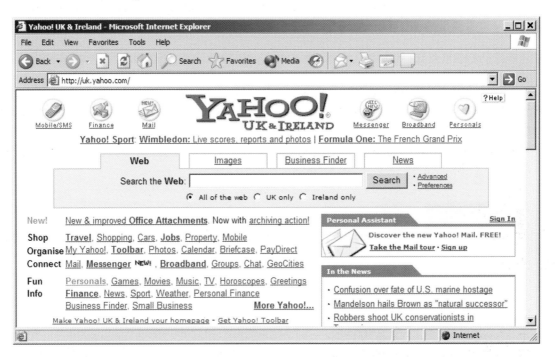

Figure 63.1: The Yahoo search engine Home Page

It is worth spending a little time learning how to use a search engine effectively otherwise it can be a very frustrating and time-wasting business. For example, if you want to look up information on the planet **Pluto**, typing the word Pluto will find you all the Web pages that include a reference to the planet but also pages to do with Walt Disney's character Pluto the dog.

Putting a + sign in front of a key word will list all pages containing the word. Putting a – sign in front will reject pages containing the word.

So typing in **Pluto +planet –dog –disney** is more likely to come up with useful information.

Typing in **Tower of London** will find all pages with the word **Tower**, and all pages with the word **London**. To get only pages containing the whole phrase, enclose it in quote marks, typing **"Tower of London"**.

E-commerce

An almost infinite variety of goods and services is available on the Internet. You can bid for a work of art at Sotheby's, swap a DVD, book your holiday, car hire, theatre tickets and restaurant meal, buy anything from groceries to a car. You can buy or sell stocks and shares on-line, do your banking, and apply for a job.

On-line banking

One of the fastest growing areas of Internet usage is on-line banking. Banks and building societies are spending millions of pounds on developing their net-related services. Smile (**www.smile.co.uk**) is a genuine on-line bank with no branch network to support customers.

Once your bank account is running, it's as easy as logging on to the Internet. By accessing your account on-line using encrypted security codes, you can pay bills, set up, amend and cancel standing orders and direct debits, and transfer money to other Smile accounts or other accounts anywhere in the world. Cheques can be paid in via a post office or bank.

Internet banking is up to four times cheaper to operate than telephone banking and 10 times cheaper than high street banking. So what are the disadvantages? When you come to plead for a loan or overdraft, there will be little personal relationship to trade on, just your records. But how many of us today have a personal relationship with the bank manager?

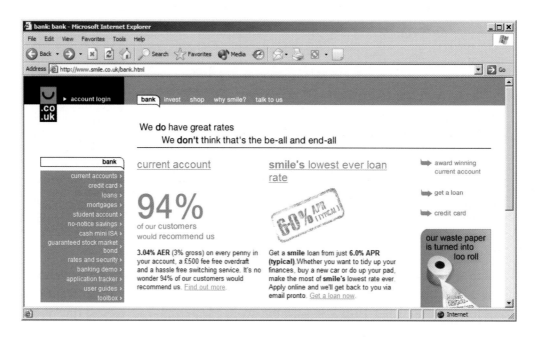

Figure 63.2: Facilities offered by Smile, the on-line bank

Shopping on the Internet

Consumers are beginning to lose their fear of buying goods and services on-line as traditional retailers move to the Internet to supplement sales from their stores. On the down side, in 1999 Consumer International (a global federation of 245 consumer organisations) ran a test of 'e-tailing' by ordering 151 items from 17 countries and found that one in ten of the items never arrived! Some e-tailers are neglecting customer service and concentrating on the front end of the business – websites and building volume. But there are many success stories.

MORI, an organisation which carries out opinion polls, sampled 2,000 people in September 1999 and found that the proportion to have shopped on-line had more than doubled in the past year. Some 40% of users had sampled buying over the Web, and 10% described themselves as regular Web shoppers. Cheap flights, books and holidays were the most popular items bought over the Web.

However, anxiety remains over the possibility of credit card fraud on the Internet, with 42% of Internet users saying they did not think it was safe to use their plastic in on-line transactions.

Doing business on the Web

Almost no business can afford to ignore the Internet. It is fast becoming an essential business tool for everyday correspondence, marketing, customer feedback and customer support. For businesses from a small country hotel to the world's largest airline, the Web can act as a shop front where customers can browse 24 hours a day, 365 days a year.

Amazon is an example of a company doing all its business over the Internet, selling books, music, videos and more. Log on by typing in the address **www.amazon.co.uk** and you will see the following screen:

Figure 63.3: The Amazon opening screen

You can browse through new releases or search for a particular product. Once you have made your selection, added it to the shopping basket and proceeded to the secure checkout, your order details will be displayed on the screen. You'll receive an e-mail confirming your order the next day, and another when your goods have been dispatched. Couldn't be simpler!

Advantages to business

For a business such as Amazon, this way of doing business has numerous advantages.

- There is a huge saving on overheads: no costly warehouse space, rent, heating or employee facilities;

- The 'virtual shop' can stock every one of the 16,000 or so CDs produced in the last year whereas a conventional store would stock only between 5-10,000;

- The shop has arrangements for 'Just In Time' delivery from its suppliers, so does not get left with books and CDs which it cannot sell;

- It is a valuable market research tool – a list of customers' names and addresses, purchases, likes, dislikes and suggestions can be built up at absolutely no cost and used to improve the service provided.

5-63

Advantages to the customers

There are advantages to the customers, too. They can:

• visit the shop without having to leave home, at any hour of the day;

• hear snatches of a song before deciding to buy;

• shop without being jostled by crowds, having to listen to music that is not to their taste.

Amazon estimate that the proportion of visitors to their site who make a purchase is much higher than for those who respond to a direct mail shot. Many of their customers return to make further purchases.

Doing the weekly shopping on-line

It is no longer necessary to fight the crowds in the supermarket on a Saturday morning. Customers can register and then do their grocery shopping from the comfort of their own home and have it delivered for a modest £5.00 charge. To make the weekly order, the customer logs on, types in their user number and password, and has the latest up-to-date list of products and prices downloaded. The customer's shopping list is saved and can be recalled to help compile next week's list, a 'recipe for the week' can be downloaded and ingredients automatically put in the shopping trolley, quantities can be edited and notes added to any product ordered, such as 'Green bananas please'.

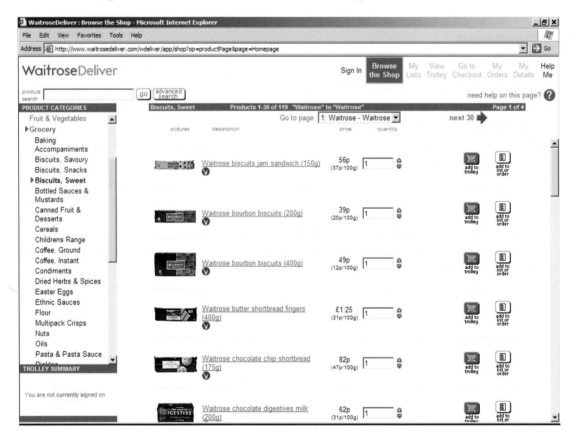

Figure 63.4: Ordering from WaitroseDeliver

Q1: What kind of people do you think are most likely to use the Internet for their grocery shopping? What do you think are the advantages and disadvantages?

Chapter 64 – HTML and ASP

HTML

HTML (Hypertext Markup Language) is the language behind each and every Web page, controlling exactly how text and graphics are displayed. HTML enables anyone, anywhere to create a page of information and make it available to anyone else.

HTML files are commonly referred to as Web pages. Web browsers read HTML files and decide how they should be displayed in a graphical manner. Browsers take the HTML code and display pages that can include text, graphics, photographs, sound and video.

It is not necessary to know HTML to create a simple Web page. HTML editors such as Microsoft FrontPage or Claris Home Page enable you to create the page as you want it to look and then convert this into HTML ready to be loaded from your computer onto the Internet.

You can even create a document in Word and view the HTML code. Better still, use Internet Explorer's editor. An easy way of getting to grips with HTML is to go to the Web site **www.webmonkey.com** which has an excellent HTML tutorial.

Another way of learning new tricks in HTML is to load a Web page that you like the look of and select **View**, **Source** from the menu to display the HTML code in Notepad.

HTML structure

HTML is inherently static. It expresses the formatting conventions of its author and has none of the features of a real programming language. It has no way of interacting with its readers. JavaScript, VBScript and DHTML (Dynamic HTML) and later versions make up for this lack of facilities.

HTML instructions or tags are enclosed in angle brackets < and >. Tags always come in pairs, there are open tags i.e. <BODY> and close tags </BODY>.

A standard page consists of two main sections – a head and a body. The head contains any scripts or codes your page may require. The head is followed by the body of the document and makes up the bulk of an HTML page.

You can type an HTML program using a text editor such as Notepad. The basic structure of an HTML file is as follows:

Figure 64.1: The basic structure of an HTML page

HTML tags

Open Tag	Close Tag	Effect
<HTML>	</HTML>	Deliminates the HTML file
<HEAD>	</HEAD>	Here the title of the page is defined (the only part of the header visible to the viewer). Meta tags used by search engines, style sheets and scripts are defined here.
<TITLE>	</TITLE>	The characters defined here are shown in the title bar
<BODY>	</BODY>	Encloses the Web page content the viewer sees. Optional: TEXT=*colour* (hex or a predefined colour) BGCOLOR="#*rrggbb*" BACKGROUND="*imagefilename*"
<Hn>	</Hn>	where n is a number between 1 and 6, depending on the level of header required. Optional: ALIGN=*direction* where *direction* can be left, center, right
<P>		New paragraph. (leaves space between paragraphs) Optional: ALIGN=*direction*
<FONT SIZE="*n*">		
<FONT FACE= "*fontname,fontstyle*">		Defines font and style
<B>	</B>	Bold
<I>	</I>	Italics
<U>	</U>	Underline
<FONT COLOR="#*rrggbb*">		Define text colour where #*rrggbb* is a hex number
<!--comment-->		Add a comment to your HTML code
 		Moves output to next line without extra space
<A HREF= "*pageURL*">	</A>	Label text goes in between opening and closing tag
<A NAME= "*anchor name*">	</A>	*anchor name* is the text used to internally identify that part of the Web page. Label text or image goes between opening and closing tag
<A HREF= "#*anchor name*">	</A>	Label text goes between opening and closing tag
<OL>	</OL>	Creates an ordered list. <LI> starts off each line in the list
<TARGET="*title*"> or <TARGET=_blank>		Allows a link to be opened in a particular window or a completely new window
<IMAGE SRC= "*imageURL*">		optional: WIDTH=*x* HEIGHT=*y*
<HR >		horizontal rule optional: SIZE=*n* WIDTH=*w* ALIGN=*direction* NOSHADE

You should be familiar with the effect of the tags in the table on the previous page. The best way is to try them out for yourself.

```
<HTML>
<HEAD>
  <TITLE> My First Test Page </TITLE>
</HEAD>
<BODY BGCOLOR = "WHITE">
<H1 ALIGN="CENTER"><FONT COLOR="RED">Centred Heading 1 in red</H1>
<H2 ALIGN="RIGHT"><FONT COLOR="GREEN">Right-aligned Heading 2 in
green</H1>
<H3 ALIGN="LEFT"><FONT COLOR="BLUE">Left-aligned Heading 3 in blue</H>
<P><FONT COLOR="BLACK"><I>This is text in italics</I></P>
<P>This is a new paragraph with one <U>underlined</U> word
<BR>This starts on a new line but is not a new paragraph
    and is followed by a horizontal rule
<HR>
<P ALIGN="LEFT"><IMG SRC="picture.jpg" width="100" height="100"></P>
<A HREF="http://www.payne-gallway.co.uk">HyperLink to Publisher</A>
</BODY>
</HTML>
```

Figure 64.2: Example HTML code

5-64

Open your file in Internet Explorer and it will be displayed as shown below:

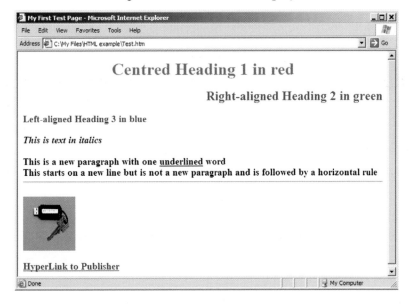

Figure 64.3: The Web page resulting from the HTML code above

FTP (File Transfer Protocol)

Using FTP you can download files from the Web. Demo versions of games and software are often available to be downloaded. FTP files have ftp as the first part of the address instead of http.

You can also use FTP to upload pages onto a Web site, for example if you have created a new Web page offline and want to load it onto the Internet. Using software such as FrontPage or SmartFTP you log onto your Web site and drag and drop the required filename from your local folder onto your Web site folder.

Forms

Forms let you communicate with the visitor to your web page. Creating a dynamic web page, requires:

- a form, i.e. the structure that consists of labels and fields that the visitor fills out and buttons the visitor clicks on;
- a processing script that takes the information from the fields and converts it into a format that you can work with.

Each element on your form will have a name (e.g. Surname) and a value (e.g. "Bloggs") associated with it. The name value pair is sent to the server and to the script (e.g. Surname="Bloggs").

The script could be written in one of many scripting languages (SGI scripts) such as Perl, VBScript or JavaScript. The script to process the data from your form is stored on the Web server. Your form then uses this script. All the processing is done on the server and any results sent back to the client.

The form starts with the form tag which includes the URL of the script (ScriptURL) that will process the form:

> <FORM METHOD="POST" ACTION= *ScriptURL*>

the form ends with the usual closing tag:

> </FORM>

Form parts

Object type	open tag	optional	close tag
Textbox	<INPUT TYPE="*text*" NAME="*name*">	VALUE="*default*" SIZE=*n* MAXLENGTH=*m*	
Password Box	<INPUT TYPE="*password*" NAME="*name*">	SIZE=*n* MAXLENGTH=*m*	
Text Area	<TEXTAREA NAME="*name*">	ROWS=*n* COLS=*m* WRAP	</TEXTAREA>
Radio Buttons	<INPUT TYPE="radio" NAME="*radioset*" VALUE="*data*">*text to identify radio button* (you need one of these statements for each radio button)	CHECKED	
Check Boxes	<INPUT TYPE="checkbox" NAME="*boxset*" VALUE="*data*">*text to identify check box* (you need one of these statements for each checkbox)	CHECKED	
Menu	<SELECT NAME="*name*"> <OPTION VALUE="*value*">option name (you need an OPTION statement for each option)	SIZE=*n* MULTIPLE	</SELECT>
Submit Button	<INPUT TYPE="submit">	VALUE="*submit message*"	
Reset form Button	<INPUT TYPE="reset">	VALUE="*reset message*"	

Active Server Pages (ASP)

ASPs can combine HTML, scripts and components to create dynamic web pages. ASP is Microsoft's solution to server-side scripting. To use ASP you must be running a Microsoft Web server. When a browser requests a file, the Web server will pre-process the file before sending it off to the client. If the file contains commands to open up a connection to a database, then a connection will be made to a named database on the Web server. If the file also contains SQL queries then the server will execute the queries and return the results of the query to the browser in a form that can be displayed by the browser.

Windows 2000 and later versions provide web server IIS (Internet Information Service) via the Windows client. This means if you activate IIS on your Windows client machine you eliminate the need to connect to an external machine for the purpose of testing your ASP.

TestForm.html	Process.asp

`<HTML>`
`<HEAD>`
   `<TITLE>Input Form Example</TITLE>`
`</HEAD>`
`<BODY>`
   `<FORM METHOD="POST"`
     `ACTION="Process.asp">`
   Please enter your username:
   `<INPUT NAME="MyName" >`
   `<INPUT TYPE="submit" VALUE=SEND>`
`</BODY>`
`</HTML>`
	`<HTML>`
	`<HEAD>`
	   `<TITLE> ASP Program Example</TITLE>`
	`</HEAD>`
	`<BODY>`
	   `<H2> The name entered into the form was:</H2>`
	   `<%`
	     `Name = Request.Form("MyName")`
	     `Response.Write Name`
	   `%>`
	`</BODY>`
	`</HTML>`

5-64

Note: Anything that should be evaluated as VBScript must be enclosed in <% and %>

Q1: Open Notepad and type the above two pages. You can test the layout of your form (TestForm.html) by viewing it in your browser. However, the script (Process.asp) can only be tested from the web server.

If you are using **IIS on your local machine** you can test the above by saving the files in C:\Inetpub\wwwroot. To view the test page, launch your browser and type **http://localhost/Test.html**

Enter your name and press 'Send'. This will display the page Process.asp after the VB script within it has been executed.

If you do not have IIS set up on your local machine, you need to **upload the files using ftp** to a remote web server.

Loading the page TestForm.html in your browser will display the following:

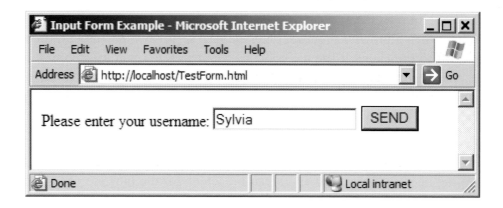

Figure 64.4: The Form page

When you have entered your name and pressed the SEND button, the server will send this page:

Figure 64.5: The Active Server Page returned

Telnet

Telnet is a terminal emulation program for TCP/IP networks such as the Internet. The telnet program runs on your computer and lets you connect to a remote computer via the Internet and then use the programs on that computer. You can access Telnet in Windows 2000/XP by opening **Run** on the **Start** menu and typing *telnet*. To start a Telnet session, you need a valid username and password. You can then enter commands through Telnet and they will be executed as though you were entering them directly on the server. Telnet is a common way to remotely control Web servers.

5-64

Exercises

1 Study **Figure 1**, Example.htm, below:

```
<HTML>
    <HEAD>
        <TITLE>Two Ways of Sending Data </TITLE>
    </HEAD>

    <BODY>
        <a HREF="Process.asp?myname=Fred">Click here</a>
        <P>
        <FORM method="POST" ACTION="Process.asp">
            Please enter your name:
            <INPUT name="myname" size=10>
            <P>
            <INPUT type="submit" value=SEND>
        </FORM>
    </BODY>
</HTML>
```

Figure 1 Example.htm

(a) With reference to **Figure 1**, draw a labelled diagram to show the appearance of the web page when viewed through a web browser. (5)

(b) A server-side script, Process.asp, processes the data posted by the web browser. Process.asp is shown in **Figure 2**.

```
<HTML>
    <HEAD>
        <TITLE>Form and Query String processing </TITLE>
    </HEAD>

    <BODY>
        <%
            Avariable = Request("myname")
            Response.Write Avariable
        %>
    </BODY>
</HTML>
```

Figure 2 Process.asp

(i) What is the value assigned to the variable **Avariable** when this script executes if the user:

(A) clicks the hyperlink in **Figure 1**? (1)

(B) clicks the SEND button after typing the name James? (1)

(ii) What value is sent to the user's browser when the user:

(A) clicks the hyperlink in **Figure 1**? (1)

(B) clicks the SEND button after typing the name James? (1)

continues over

(c) Both Example.htm and Process.asp (**Figure 1** and **Figure 2**) were created on a client computer and then uploaded to a folder D:\AQA\WWWRoot on a web server. The web server has been configured to present this folder to the World Wide Web as the web site with domain name **www.example.co.uk**.

   (i) What protocol would have been used to upload the files Example.htm and Process.asp? (1)

   (ii) What URL was used in the browser's address line for the browser to load the web page Example.htm? (3)

   (iii) What other service should the web server support to allow the owner of the web site to access the web server from a remote location in order to create a sub-folder ASPScripts in D:\AQA\WWWRoot? (1)

AQA CPT5 Qu 7 January 2003

2 A company advertises its HTML courses on the Internet. **Table 1** below shows the HTML form of a web page advertising HTML courses.

5-64

```
<HTML>
  <HEAD>
    <TITLE>
       ECS Ltd
    </TITLE>
  </HEAD>

  <BODY>
    <H1> HTML Courses</H1>
    <P> 1. Introduction to HTML
    <P> 2. Basic HTML
    <P> 3. Advanced HTML

    <A HREF=http://www.ecs.co.uk/main/page.html>more info/</A>
  </BODY>

</HTML>
```

Table 1

(a) What is the Internet? (2)

(b) With reference to the contents of **Table 1**, draw a labelled diagram to show the appearance of the web page when view through a web browser. (5)

(c) The link in **Table 1** contains the uniform resource locator (URL) of another web page. Explain the four parts of this URL. (4)

AQA CPT5 Qu 7 June 2002

Chapter 65 – Java and Applets

Java applets

The Java programming language originated from the computer company Sun Microsystems, and is an object-oriented language based on C++. Applications and applets can be programmed in Java using many pre-existing components. A Java source program has the extension .java, and its compiled equivalent is given the extension .class. Java programs are compiled into bytecode and then interpreted. Java programs executed in browsers are called **applets**. When a website that has a Java applet on it is visited by a client computer, the applet is downloaded automatically from the web servers and then executed in the client's browser. Browsers contain a piece of software called a Java Virtual Machine (JVM), which knows how to interpret bytecode. Java applets are not allowed to read, write, delete, rename or check for the existence of files on a client's machine. They cannot list or create directories. They cannot print or create a network connection to a computer other than the one from which the bytecode was loaded. This is why Java is secure (this security measure is sometimes referred to as a *sandbox*).

Applets are available to be downloaded from the Internet. For example, the site **www.thejmaker.com** has hundreds of downloadable Java applets with instructions on how to embed them into an HTML page.

5-65

Figure 65.1: Web site to look for Applets

You can write your own Java applets if you know how to program using the Java programming language.

Java applets can be called from an HTML program using the appropriate instruction. For example:

```
<APPLET CODE="Hello.class"WIDTH="200"HEIGHT="100"></APPLET>
```

The above tag causes the Java applet "Hello.class" to be loaded in an area of the page size 200 pixels wide and 100 pixels high.

```
Hello.java - Notepad
File   Edit   Format   View   Help
import java.awt.*;
import java.applet.*;
import java.awt.event.*;

public class Hello extends Applet implements ActionListener
{
  private Button helloButton;
  private Label answer;

  public void init()
  {
    setLayout(new GridLayout(5,1));
    helloButton = new Button("Press me");
    answer = new Label("");
    add(helloButton);
    add(answer);
    helloButton.addActionListener(this);
  }

  public void actionPerformed (ActionEvent a)
  {
    answer.setText("Hello World");
  }
}
```

Figure 65.2: The Java source code of a very simple applet

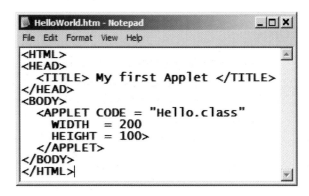

Figure 65.3: HTML code calling
the bytecode of the applet

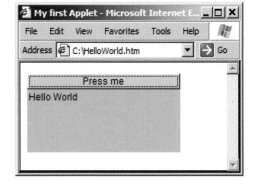

Figure 65.4: The applet being executed

Exercises

1 (a) What is a Java applet?

  (b) How can a Java applet be executed?   (4)

New Question

Chapter 66 – Internet Security

Internet-based fraud

Internet-based fraud is the fastest growing criminal activity in the UK, according to crime figures published in 2000. Although Internet purchasing makes up only 2% of credit card transactions, the banking industry's research has shown that the net generates around 50% of all credit card complaints.

In 1999 more than £2 billion was spent in the UK on the Internet, and this figure is predicted to grow rapidly. But the public does not fully trust the security of Internet transactions, and many people do not feel comfortable giving their credit card numbers over the Internet. Traders, for their part, may have no way of knowing that the person placing an order is who they say they are.

Encryption

Encryption: using an algorithm and a key to code a message written in plain text into ciphertext. Decryption is decoding the ciphertext back into plain text.

Encryption is the scrambling of data so that it becomes very difficult to unscramble and interpret. Scrambled data is called ciphertext. Unscrambled data is called plaintext. Unscrambling ciphertext back to the original plaintext is called decryption.

Data encryption is performed by the use of a cryptographic algorithm and a key. The algorithm uses the key to scramble and unscramble the data. Ideally, the algorithm should be made public (so that it can be scrutinized and analyzed by the cryptographic community), while the key remains private.

In symmetric encryption the same key is used to encrypt and decrypt the message. In asymmetric encryption, one key is used to encrypt a message and another is used to decrypt the message. This is known as public-key encryption.

Public key encryption

This is a very secure cryptographic system. Every key has two parts, a **public key** and a **private key**. They are linked and data encrypted with one key can only be decrypted with the other key. It is virtually impossible to deduce the private key from the public key. The person wanting to send an encrypted message needs to know the public key of the recipient. Since the public key is well known, it is possible that a message could be a forgery. To prevent this, a digital signature is used by the sender.

When I send a message, a **digital signature** is generated in the following manner:

A mathematical summary of the document concerned (a hash code) is generated. Since the hash code is generated from the entire document, in the right sequence, it means that the slightest difference to the document will not generate the same code. This is encrypted with my private key and appended to the document and transmitted with it. The receiver decrypts the message with their private key and recomputes the hash code from the document and decrypts the received hash code with my public key. If the two hash codes are the same, the receiver can be sure that the data has not been tampered with and that it genuinely came from me. To ensure that messages can not be copied and resent later, the original message can contain the date and time that the message was created.

Digital signature: a digital code attached to a message that uniquely identifies the sender and authenticates the message.

A digital signature thus authenticates the sender, proves that the message has not been tampered with, and prevents the sender from denying having sent it. This means, for example, that a person cannot later deny having made a purchase on a Web site, by claiming that it was made by someone else.

Digital signatures also offer some protection against viruses being downloaded in one of the thousands of Java applets or ActiveX controls that can be freely downloaded. A programmer in effect "signs" a program by attaching his or her digital signature. Theoretically, a programmer would not sign a program containing a virus, so all programs with a digital signature should be "safe". Your browser will warn you about programs that do not have a digital signature so you can decide whether or not to accept them.

Digital certificates

Digital Certificate: an electronic "credit card" issued by a certification authority that contains your name, a serial number, expiration dates, a copy of the certificate holder's public key (used for encrypting messages and digital signatures), and the digital signature of the certificate-issuing authority so that a recipient can verify that the certificate is real.

A digital certificate will verify that the sender is the person or organisation that they claim to be. An organisation or an individual can obtain a digital certificate from a Certificate Authority (CA) such as Verisign. The CA issues an encrypted digital certificate, which comes with the applicant's public key. The CA makes its own public key available through the Internet. The recipient of an encrypted message uses the CA's public key to decode the digital certificate attached to the message and then uses the enclosed public key to encode a reply. Anyone can know the public key – to enable someone to send you an encrypted message, you must send that person your public key, and the person must use the public key to encrypt the message to send to you. You can then decrypt the message using your private key, which should never be made known to anyone else. Alternatively, a person can use their private key to encrypt a message for you and you can decrypt it using their public key. Using software such as Outlook Express you can have your e-mail program automatically send your public key whenever you send an e-mail.

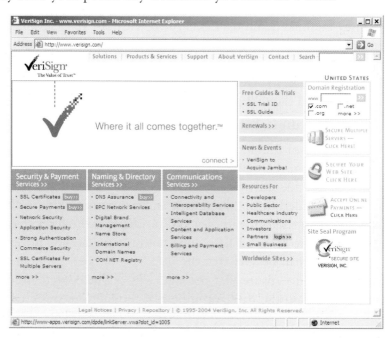

Figure 66.1: Obtaining a digital certificate

The Web site **www.itsecurity.com** has a huge amount of information on every aspect of computer security and is well worth a visit. The site **www.verisign.com** belongs to VeriSign, a Certifying Authority, where a digital certificate can be obtained.

Strong and weak encryption

The key is fundamental to the strength of the encryption. You need the one correct key before you can decrypt the ciphertext. It follows, then, that the longer the key, the greater the range of possible values it could have. The range of possible values is called the keyspace. The greater the keyspace, the more difficult it is for an unauthorized person to discover the correct key.

Encryption cannot make unauthorized decryption impossible; it can merely make it improbable. With unlimited processing capacity and unlimited time available, all cryptosystems could be broken. The purpose of encryption is to make it as unlikely as possible that a ciphertext could be broken within the period of time during which the contents should remain secret.

There is an arbitrary and subjective distinction between weak and strong encryption. Strong encryption implies that it would be practically impossible to find the key within the useful lifetime of the secret. Weak encryption implies that the key could be found with a realistic amount of processing capacity and a reasonable amount of time. The difference between weak encryption and strong encryption is thus effectively a question of processing power. As computers become more powerful and less expensive, what is now 'strong' encryption will inevitably become 'weak' encryption. At the moment, any key length above 56 bits is generally considered to be 'strong' encryption.

Many governments around the world view strong encryption with concern. The argument is that the availability of strong encryption limits their ability to monitor the messages of suspected terrorists, drug traffickers and paedophiles. Some governments would like to ban the use of strong encryption unless either a back door is made available to Law Enforcement, or a decryption key is lodged with a Trusted Third Party (Key escrow). This, needless to say, has led to considerable debate between government and government agencies on the one side, and academics, civil liberty groups and the greater part of industry on the other.

Factoring

The strength of modern encryption systems often relies on the fact that it is very difficult to factor large numbers.

If two large (say 200 digits) prime numbers are multiplied together, it would take many years of computer processing time to reverse-engineer the problem and deduce the two original prime numbers from the product. The process of doing so is known as factoring, i.e. attempting to find the two prime factors of the product.

Firewall

Firewall: a system designed to prevent unauthorised access to or from a private network.

A firewall is a mechanism for protecting a corporate network from external communications systems such as the Internet. Firewalls can be implemented in both hardware and/or software.

A firewall typically consists of a PC or Unix machine containing two network interface cards (NICs) and running a special firewall program. One network card is connected to the company's private LAN, and the other is connected to the Internet. The machine acts as a barrier through which all information passing between the two networks must travel.

5-66

The firewall software analyses each packet of information passing between the two and rejects it if it does not conform to a preconfigured rule (packet filter). A firewall may also act as a proxy server, which intercepts all messages entering and leaving a network, hiding the true network addresses.

Virus spread and detection

When you download a file from the Internet, you can use virus detection software to make sure the file is virus-free before you run it. However, some Web sites automatically send a program to your Web site and run it before you get a chance to check it for viruses. Unfortunately, it is hard to protect against this. While you are connected to the Internet, you could be unaware that a program is busy deleting your most treasured files, making your browser hang up and scanning your hard disk for your IP address, user ID and password. Beware of e-mails saying "This document is very important and you've GOT to read this". Delete them immediately without opening any attachments!

In 1999 a macro virus called Melissa, once on a system using Outlook Express, took the first 50 entries from the Address Book and then mailed itself as an attachment to the e-mail addresses. The e-mail carried the message 'Here is that document you asked for … don't show anyone else ;-)'. It rapidly spread to millions of computers worldwide, disrupting large systems by overloading servers and causing them to close down.

Security and the Law

5-66

Under the Data Protection Act (see Chapter 27), personal data must be kept secure. The reasons for this are fairly obvious.

A spate of apparently random burglaries always took place when the home owners were away. A pattern emerged, however, when the police correlated the burglaries with a customer database on a stolen PC from a local newsagent. Customers cancelled their papers when away from home. This was duly noted on the customer database, and the thieves had a nice neat list of names, and addresses of empty houses.

You can check out other legislation pertaining to computers on the Web site **www.itsecurity.com**.

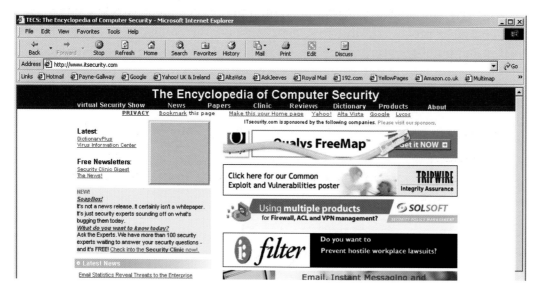

Figure 66.2: A Web site giving information about current legislation

Social and cultural issues

The Internet is used by millions and inevitably abused by a few. The net is not a totally risk-free environment and it is possible for unwanted pornographic material to find its way onto your screen via junk e-mail or a search on some perfectly innocent topic. There are racist Web sites put up by Nazi sympathisers, sites that feature information on making bombs, sites that feature accident and autopsy photographs. Stories circulate about paedophiles e-mailing schools and attempting to strike up relationships with children. To combat the dangers to children, blocking software can be installed which censors unacceptable material – among the best known are Net Nanny **www.netnanny.com** and Surf Watch **www.surfwatch.com**.

On the plus side, the ready availability of material suitable for all cultures is a real bonus. **www.blink.org.uk** is a site set up to promote good race relations from a black perspective. Sites for minority groups of all kinds – religious, ethnic or social groups, or groups brought together by a common bond of rare illness or disability – can be an invaluable source of information.

Exercises

1 Explain what is meant by strong encryption and weak encryption. Give **one** reason why strong encryption should be forbidden by law, and **one** reason why it should be allowed. (4)

New Question

2 Explain the use of digital certificates and firewalls, giving an example of when each might be used. (4)

New Question

3 E-mail may be more easily intercepted and altered than paper mail without the knowledge of either the sender or the recipient.

(a) Give one reason that supports this statement. (1)

(b) A single shared key system to encrypt and decrypt messages is not genereally used for encrypted mail sent across the Internet. Instead, a two key system is used consisting of:

- A public key, which is made publicly available.

- A private key, which is held only by its owner and should never be publicly disclosed.

(i) How is this two-key system used to encrypt and decrypt e-mails? (2)

(i) Holders of a digital certificate can digitally sign an e-mail to prove its origin and authenticity. How is this two-key public/private key system used to digitally sign an e-mail? (2)

AQA CPT5 Qu 5 January 2003

5-66

Chapter 67 – Computer Applications and Effects

Definition of artificial intelligence

Conventional data processing is concerned with inputting and processing data in the form of facts and figures in order to produce operational or management information. **Artificial intelligence**, on the other hand, is based on **knowledge**. A widely accepted definition of artificial intelligence is based on a test devised by Alan Turing in 1950:

Suppose there are two identical terminals in a room, one connected to a computer, and the other operated remotely by a person. If someone using the two terminals is unable to tell which is connected to the computer and which is operated by the person, the computer can be credited with intelligence.

Following on from this idea we could say that artificial intelligence is the science of making machines perform tasks that would require intelligence if done by people. Artificial intelligence covers such fields as expert systems, problem solving, robot control, intelligent database querying and pattern recognition. Pattern recognition includes speech comprehension and synthesis, image processing and robot vision. Getting a computer to communicate in 'natural language' is yet another field of research.

One aspect of artificially intelligent computers is that they should be capable of learning, and therefore improving their performance at a given task. Computers have been successfully "trained", for example, to recognise (with as much accuracy as a human being) a face as either male or female, and to be able to recognise an Underground train station as being "crowded" or not.

Expert systems

Expert systems are computer programs that attempt to replicate the performance of a human expert on some specialised reasoning task. Also called **knowledge-based** systems, they are able to store and manipulate knowledge so that they can help a user to solve a problem or make a decision.

The main features of an expert system are:

- it is limited to a specific domain (area of expertise);
- it is typically rule based;
- it can reason with uncertain data (the user can respond "don't know" to a question);
- it delivers advice;
- it explains its reasoning to the user.

An expert system has the following constituents:

- the 'knowledge base' that contains the facts and rules provided by a human expert;
- some means of using the knowledge (an 'inference mechanism' or 'inference engine');
- a means of communicating with the user (the 'man-machine interface' or 'human-computer interface').

The difference between a database and a knowledge base is that whilst a database contains facts, a knowledge base contains facts and rules.

Programming the knowledge base

Computer languages such as PROLOG (PROgramming LOGic) have been developed for the creation of expert systems. Using PROLOG, the facts and rules are written down using the special syntax of the language, and the user can then type in a query which the program will attempt to answer (see Chapter 39).

Expert system shells

An expert system shell is a special software program that allows a user to build an expert system without having to learn a programming language. It provides a straightforward user interface both for the expert to enter the facts and rules, and for the end-user to use the completed expert system to solve a problem.

A shell is basically an expert system without a knowledge base. It provides the developer with the inference engine, the user interface and the means of inputting the 'knowledge'. Many shells enable the developer to present examples with the correct conclusions and the system automatically builds the rules. Thus, for example, a medical team building an expert system could type in the symptoms of hundreds of patients with 'upper abdominal pain' with a known diagnosis of kidney stones, gallstones, stomach ulcers, cancer and so on for each one. The software will then calculate the significance of each symptom so that presented with a new case, it can give one or more diagnoses with an indication of the probability of each being correct.

Uses of expert systems

Expert systems are used in a wide range of applications such as:

- **medical diagnosis**;
- **fault diagnosis** of all kinds – gas boilers, computers, power stations, railway locomotives. If your gas boiler breaks down, the service engineer may well arrive with a laptop computer and type in all the symptoms to arrive at a diagnosis, and then use the system to find out the exact part numbers of any replacement parts required for your particular model of boiler;
- **geological surveys** to find oil and mineral deposits;
- **financial services** to predict stock market movement or to recommend an investment strategy;
- **social services** to calculate the benefits due to claimants;
- **industrial uses** such as quantity surveying.

And finally... applications of computers

Whole books have been devoted to the applications of computers and their effects on society and the individual. For this course, you will be expected to develop an awareness of the many different ways in which different types of computers, from an embedded computer in a washing machine, to a mainframe computer holding a giant corporate database, are used and how they affect our lives.

The best way of doing this is to look at relevant TV programmes, read relevant newspaper articles and magazines, and research some applications which interest you. Websites of publications such as **www.computerweekly.com** provide hundreds of interesting articles on current uses of computers and the issues arising from these.

5-67

The Computer Weekly website has its own search engine where you can search by keyword and also on different article types and topics. The following search criteria found 79 news articles about the new air traffic control system at Swanwick.

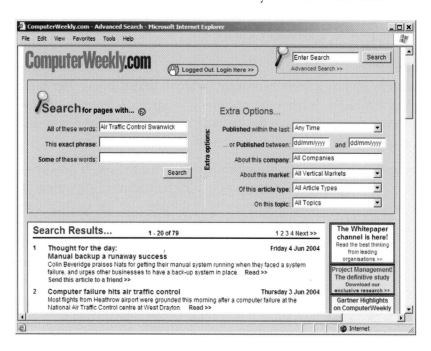

Figure 67.1: ComputerWeekly.com search engine

Read some of these articles and you will find that the contract for the new air traffic control system first went out in 1992. The system finally went live in January 2002, more than five years behind schedule. It has been in the news on numerous occasions since going live. At the time of writing this chapter all aircraft at Heathrow airport were grounded when the system crashed due to inadequate testing of a program update. Air traffic controllers had to temporarily go back to manual procedures. The site keeps articles for a number of years. Have a look at the article of Friday 4th June 2004!

The applications that you could be asked about in the examination include science, education, manufacturing industry, commercial data processing, publishing, leisure, design, communication, embedded systems, information systems, the Internet, artificial intelligence and expert systems.

Try some searches yourself to find out about different applications. You should:
• consider the purpose of the application;
• discuss the application as an information system in the context chosen;
• examine specific user-interface needs;
• examine the communication requirements of the application;
• discuss the extent to which the given system satisfies both the organisation's and user's needs;
• discuss the economic, social, legal and ethical consequences of the application;
• discuss examples of software failure such as in safety critical systems, errors in commercial transactions and errors caused by poorly specified systems;
• discuss the possible effects of failure from a social, economic and legal point of view.

Good luck and goodbye!

5-67

Exercises

1 The United Kingdom's National Health Service was created to provide health care to the nation through:

- hospitals

- health centres/GPs' (doctors') surgeries

- pharmacies (chemists).

The UK government is proposing to computerise and network the entire National Health Service (NHS) so that it will be possible to have on-line *access to the system at a level of security relevant to their status* for anyone who

- works for the NHS

- uses its services

- works at a branch of government responsible for the NHS.

Patient records will be stored in multi-user distributed relational databases managed by *Database Management Systems* (DBMS).

- Every person in the UK is assigned a unique numeric key, *the patient reference number,* and is assigned for primary health care to a doctor in a health centre or a GP's (General Practitioner's or doctor's) surgery located in a single building.

- A person's doctor may, if necessary, arrange for the person to see a specialist doctor in a hospital.

- Drugs prescribed for a person by the person's GP for the treatment of an illness are obtained from a pharmacy.

- Every computer in the service of the NHS will be interconnected in *local area networks* (LANs) and the *local area networks* will be interconnected by a *wide area network* (WAN).

(a) Which network type is most appropriate, WAN or LAN, **within** a health centre or GP's (doctor's) surgery? Justify your choice. (2)

(b) Explain **one** way in which the networked NHS can benefit each of the following. Each benefit must be different.

   (i) The patient (1)

   (ii) A health centre/GP's (doctor's) surgery (1)

   (iii) A pharmacy (1)

   (iv) The UK government (1)

(c) (i) What level of the architecture of a DBMS allows the NHS system to be designed to allow *"on-line access to the system at a level of security relevant to status for anyone who works for the NHS"*? (1)

   (ii) Explain **one** method that DBMSs use in a multi-user system to avoid losing updates to records that are accessed concurrently (at the same time). (2)

continues over

(d) For each of the following give **one** reason why large-scale software systems such as this NHS system could fail. Each reason **must** be different.

    (i) Perform as its users expect   (1)

    (ii) Work at all   (1)

    (iii) Be completed on time.   (1)

        AQA CPT5 Qu 7 June 2003

2 Some countries have introduced machine-readable passports, others are currently investigating passport-free ways of identifying an individual which rely on biometric data (any specific and uniquely identifiable human characteristic) methods.

(a) Briefly explain the operation of:

    (i) **one** technique for machine-readable passports;   (2)

    (ii) **one** technique that does **not** rely upon a passport.   (2)

(b) Give **two** advantages of a passport-free method over a machine-readable one.   (2)

(c) In addition to monitoring the flow of people into and out of a country, similar technology may be used within a country for identification purposes. One government has proposed a central database of biometric data (any specific and uniquely identifiable human characteristic) on its citizens which any legal organisation in the country can access to check the identity of a person.

    (i) Give **two** benefits to organisations and/or government of such access.   (2)

    (ii) Give **one** reason why an ordinary law-abiding citizen might not want their biometric data made widely available in this way.   (1)

        AQA CPT5 Qu 5 June 2002

3 Expert systems are suitable for many different categories of application. Give **two** different categories and, for each category, **one** typical application.   (4)

        AEB Paper 1 Qu 8 1996

4 (a) Briefly describe the three constituent parts of an expert system.   (3)

(b) Users of expert systems claim that they are 'much more useful than a very large database'. Give two reasons to justify this claim.   (2)

        AEB Paper 2 Qu 10 1998

5-67

Index

index